Northern I:
A Political L
1968–83
W. D. Flackes

W. D. FLACKES was the BBC's Northern Ireland political correspondent from 1964 to 1982 when he retired. He has been writing or broadcasting about Ulster politics for some thirty-five years. In 1981, he was awarded the OBE for his journalistic work, which has embraced the Press Association and two Belfast daily newspapers – *Belfast Telegraph* and *Newsletter*.

NORTHERN IRELAND:
A POLITICAL DIRECTORY
1968-83
W. D. FLACKES

ARIEL BOOKS
BRITISH BROADCASTING CORPORATION

First published 1980

First published in this edition in 1983 by the
British Broadcasting Corporation
35 Marylebone High Street
London WIM 4AA

© 1980, 1983 W. D. Flackes

Typeset by
Phoenix Photosetting, Chatham
Printed in England by
Mackays of Chatham Ltd

This book is set in 9/10 Ehrhardt Linotron

The map on page 6 is by John Gilkes

ISBN 0 563 20209 2

Contents

Abbreviations	7
Author's note	10
Chronology of major events, 1921–83	12
Dictionary of names and organisations	29
Election Results, 1968–83	
1968 Stormont By-Elections	258
1969 Stormont General Election	258
1969 Westminster By-Election	263
1970 Stormont By-Elections	264
1970 Westminster General Election	264
1973 District Council Elections	266
1973 Assembly Election	267
1974 (February) Westminster General Election	271
1974 (October) Westminster General Election	273
1975 Convention Election	275
1977 District Council Elections	279
1979 Westminster General Election	279
1979 European Parliament Election	281
1981 District Council Elections	284
1981 Westminster By-Elections	285
1982 Westminster By-Election	285
1982 Assembly Election	286
1983 Westminster General Election	291
Systems of Government and A List of Office Holders,	
1968–83	294
The Security System	
Changing Patterns	304
The RUC	305
The Army	309
The UDR	312
Internment without trial	312
Anti-riot tactics	315
Emergency powers	316
Security Statistics, 1968–83	
Deaths	320
Record of Violence	322
Injuries	322
Houses searched and arms finds	323
Persons Charged	323

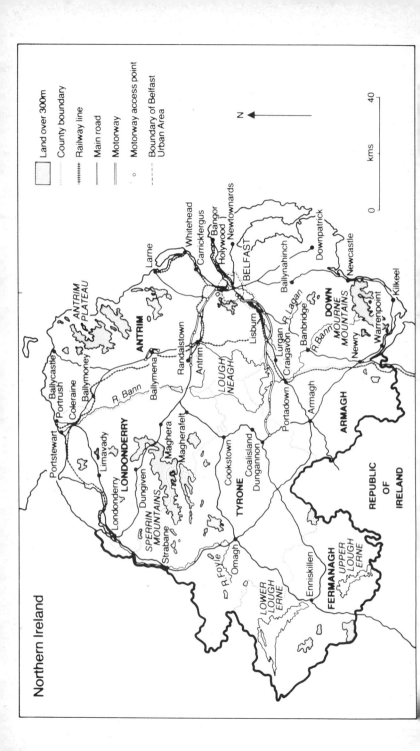

Northern Ireland

Land over 300m
County boundary
Railway line
Main road
Motorway
Motorway access point
Boundary of Belfast Urban Area

kms 0   40

N

Abbreviations

ALJ	Association for Legal Justice
All.	Alliance Party
AOH	Ancient Order of Hibernians
b.	Born
BA	Bachelor of Arts
BBC	British Broadcasting Corporation
BDS	Bachelor of Dental Surgery
B.Ed.	Bachelor of Education
B.Sc	Bachelor of Science
B.Sc.Econ.	Bachelor of Economic Science
Capt.	Captain
CCDC	Central Citizens' Defence Committee
CESA	Catholic Ex-Servicemen's Association
Comm.	Communist
DCDC	Derry Citizens' Defence Committee
D.Litt.	Doctor of Literature
DULC	Democratic Unionist Loyalist Coalition
DUP	Democratic Unionist Party
E.	East
EEC	European Economic Community
Elec.	Electorate
Gen.	General
GOC	General Officer Commanding
GB	Great Britain
HAA	Heavy Anti-Aircraft
IIP	Irish Independence Party
Ind.	Independent
Ind. Soc.	Independent Socialist
IRA	Irish Republican Army
Lab.	Labour Party
Lab. and TU	Labour and Trade Union Group
LAW	Loyalist Association of Workers
Lib.	Liberal Party
LL.B.	Bachelor of Laws
LOL	Loyal Orange Lodge
Loy.	Loyalist
Loy. Coal.	Loyalist Coalition
Lt.	Lieutenant

MA	Master of Arts
maj.	Majority
MEP	Member of European Parliament
MP	Member of Parliament
MPA	Member Parliamentary Assembly (1982)
M.Sc.	Master of Science
N.	North
NA	Not Available
Nat.	National Party
Nat. Dem.	National Democratic Party
NI	Northern Ireland
NICRA	Northern Ireland Civil Rights Association
NILP	Northern Ireland Labour Party
NIO	Northern Ireland Office
NUI	National University of Ireland
NUM	New Ulster Movement
NUU	New University of Ulster
Off. U.	Official Unionist
OIRA	Official Irish Republican Army
OUP	Official Unionist Party
PC	Privy Councillor
PD	People's Democracy
Ph.D.	Doctor of Philosophy
PIRA	Provisional Irish Republican Army
PR	Proportional Representation
PUP	Progressive Unionist Party
Prot. U.	Protestant Unionist Party
QUB	Queen's University, Belfast
Rep. C.	Republican Clubs
Rep. Lab.	Republican Labour Party
RTE	Radio Telefis Eireann
RUC	Royal Ulster Constabulary
S.	South
SDLP	Social Democratic and Labour Party
SDP	Social Democratic Party
TCD	Trinity College, Dublin
TD	Member of the Dail
U.	Unionist Party
UCD	University College, Dublin
UCDC	Ulster Constitution Defence Committee
UCG	University College, Galway
UDA	Ulster Defence Association
UDR	Ulster Defence Regiment
UFF	Ulster Freedom Fighters
UK	United Kingdom
ULCCC	Ulster Loyalist Central Co-ordinating Committee
UN	United Nations
Unoff.	Unofficial

UPNI	Unionist Party of Northern Ireland
UPUP	Ulster Popular Unionist Party
U.Pro.A.	Pro-Assembly Unionist
UPV	Ulster Protestant Volunteers
US	United States of America
USC	Ulster Special Constabulary (B Specials)
Utd. Loy.	United Loyalist
UUAC	United Unionist Action Council
UUUC	United Ulster Unionist Council (or Coalition)
UUUM	United Ulster Unionist Movement
UUUP	United Ulster Unionist Party
UWC	Ulster Workers' Council
VPP	Volunteer Political Party
VULC	Vanguard Unionist Loyalist Coalition
VUPP	Vanguard Unionist Progressive Party
W.	West
WBLC	West Belfast Loyalist Coalition
WUUC	West Ulster Unionist Council
WP	Workers' Party

Author's note

The politics of Northern Ireland have become of world interest in the fourteen years since fresh violence gave a sharp edge to age-old controversies in Ireland. The first edition of this directory was produced in response to many inquiries about the availability of a quick reference guide to the people, places, policies, parties and paramilitary organisations that make up the pattern of events, often startling in its complexity for such a small province.

Although the basic questions persist, the need for an updated version had become evident. A new British Government initiative, developments in Anglo-Irish relations, and further local elections, have given some new twists to the situation, while a new generation of politicians is beginning to grapple with the apparently intractable problems of this fringe area of the European Community.

The general format of the first edition has been preserved, since political scientists, political correspondents and even politicians, seem to have found it acceptable. And since Northern Ireland has not only a British and an Irish dimension, but provokes interest increasingly in many other countries, and particularly in the USA, Canada, and in Europe, this aspect has been reflected in the entries. While the book cannot claim to be wholly exhaustive, I have included all the political personalities who have made any significant impact on the Ulster scene. Elected status has been a key consideration, and all members of the 1982 Assembly have been included, whether or not they have chosen to take their seats.

My aim has been to produce as objective a record as possible, and the combination of the chronology, the general entries, election results, government and security sections are intended to offer a quick check on the main elements likely to figure in any major day-to-day developments. I have made some changes in response to Dennis Kennedy's perceptive review in the *Irish Times*.

The risks of error in such a publication are, of course, enormous, but I have been encouraged by the relatively small number of criticisms on this score. Those who study closely the Bernadette McAliskey entry will find, however, that it has been amended. Despite the statement by many experts that she was the youngest MP to be elected for nearly two hundred years, other and younger MPs emerged from the past. One was James Dickson, elected Liberal MP for the borough of Dungannon in 1880, who was said to be twenty-one years and two months old when elected – that is, about nine months younger than Mrs McAliskey. Another was the second Lord Rothermere, returned in 1919 when twenty-one years and 183 days old. Both these examples were spurred by an article by Anne McHardy in *The Guardian*.

I have been involved in the coverage of many of the events since 1968; nonetheless, I must record again my indebtedness to Richard Deutsch and Vivien Magowan for their Chronology (Belfast, 1968 to 1974); and also *Fortnight* magazine, for checks on dates. The annual *Who's Who* (London) and *Who's Who, What's What, and Where in Ireland* (Dublin and London, 1974), and Ian McAllister's *Convention Election, 1975* (Glasgow, 1976), have also been useful points of reference. I am also grateful to Professor Richard Rose of Strathclyde Universtity for some private comments, and for his *Governing without Consensus* (London, 1971), as well as *Ulster* (Sunday Times Insight Team – Harmondsworth, 1972), *The IRA* by Tim Pat Coogan (London, 1970), and *Point of no Return* by Robert Fisk (London, 1975).

In the elections section, I have included figures produced for the BBC by Dr Sydney Elliott and Professor Jack Smith of Queen's University, Belfast. I also much appreciate the friendly help offered by the Government information office at Stormont, and the information offices of the RUC and Army, as well as a host of political 'contacts'. But all the interpretations are my own. In the production of the book, the careful scrutiny by my editor, Victoria Huxley, of a flood of amendments has been invaluable.

In the first edition I recorded my thanks for the helpful attitude of senior BBC executives Richard Francis (managing director, BBC Radio and former Northern Ireland Controller) and Northern Ireland head of programmes, Cecil Taylor. The present BBC Controller, James Hawthorne, CBE, and Stephen Claypole, editor, news and current affairs, have been specially encouraging in respect of this edition. Finally, a belated 'thank you' to the Rockefeller Foundation in the USA, who hosted a special breakfast reception in New York on the occasion of the launching of the first edition in 1980.

W. D. Flackes
Belfast, June 1983

Chronology of major events, 1921–83

1921: *7 June* First NI parliament opened by King George V.

1922: Widespread violence, in which 232 people killed and about 1,000 wounded.

1925: Irish Free State government confirmed the border as laid down in the 1920 Act.

1931: IRA declared illegal in Irish Free State.

1932: De Valera's Fianna Fail Party secured power in Irish Free State. In Belfast, new Stormont parliament building opened by Prince of Wales.

1937: New Southern Irish constitution envisaged eventual unity.

1941: German air raids on Belfast – 949 killed and more than 2,000 injured.

1942: US troops arrived in NI on way to second front in Europe.

1943: Sir Basil Brooke (later Brookeborough) became NI Premier, amid demands for more vigorous local war effort.

1949: Southern Ireland became a full republic and British government gave new constitutional guarantee to Stormont parliament.

1956: *12 December* IRA launched border campaign which led to introduction of internment without trial both in Republic and in NI.

1962: IRA called off its campaign.

1963: Terence O'Neill became NI Premier.

1965: Sean Lemass visited Stormont for talks, the first Taoiseach of Republic to do so. The visit was attacked by many Unionists.

1966: UVF declared illegal

1967: NICRA formed.

1968: Civil rights marches began, with violence at Derry march on *5 October*. First government reforms announced but regarded as inadequate by civil rights movement. Prime Minister O'Neill sacked William Craig from cabinet.

1969: O'Neill resigned in April and was succeeded by James Chichester-Clark. In August, violence in the Bogside area of Derry led to the army being put on the streets to help the RUC. Severe rioting in Belfast, Derry and other places. Pressure from Westminster for reforms. RUC reorganised; B Specials disbanded. New electoral laws.

1970: *1 April* Ulster Defence Regiment inaugurated to replace B Specials. In June, Bernadette Devlin MP jailed for part in Bogside disturbances and the Rev. Ian Paisley elected MP for N. Antrim. SDLP formed.

1971: In March three Scottish soldiers found shot dead at Ligoniel, Belfast. Chichester-Clark resigned as Premier and was succeeded by Brian Faulkner. In July, SDLP withdrew from Stormont after refusal of inquiry into shooting by army of two men in Derry. *August* Beginning of internment without trial (*9th*) and NICRA launched civil disobedience campaign. *27–28 September* Tripartite talks at Chequers involving Edward Heath, Jack Lynch, and Brian Faulkner. Widespread violence: PIRA apparently growing in strength. *25 November* Harold Wilson put forward fifteen-year Irish unity plan. *4 December* Fifteen people died in explosion at McGurk's bar in Belfast. Victims included wife of owner, Patrick McGurk, and their fourteen-year-old daughter. (Self-confessed UVF man convicted of the explosion.)

1972: *30 January* Thirteen men shot dead by army in Derry ('Bloody Sunday'). *2 February* British Embassy in Dublin burned down. *22 February* Seven killed by bomb at Aldershot military barracks; OIRA claimed responsibility. *25 February* John Taylor, Minister of State, survived OIRA assassination attempt in Armagh. *4 March* Abercorn restaurant was bombed. *24 March* British government announced direct rule in NI after Faulkner government said they would not accept loss of law-and-order powers. *26 May* SDLP urged those who had withdrawn from public offices to return. *29 May* In situation of growing violence, OIRA called a ceasefire. *26 June* PIRA began what it called a 'bilateral truce'. *1 July* UDA set up 'no go' areas in Belfast. *7 July* William Whitelaw, Secretary of State, met PIRA leaders in secret in London. *9 July* PIRA claimed that British army had broken ceasefire in Lenadoon area of W. Belfast. *21 July* Nine people killed when twenty-two bombs exploded in Belfast ('Bloody Friday'). *31 July* Army entered W. Belfast and Bogside 'no go' areas in 'Operation Motorman'. Eight people killed by car bombs in Claudy, Co. Derry. *24 September* Darlington conference on political options. *30 October* British government published discussion paper on NI's political future, repeating guarantee of constitutional position but recognising 'Irish dimension'. *16–17 November* Edward Heath visited NI and said that UDI would lead to a 'bloodbath'. *1 December* Two people killed and 80 injured in Dublin when two bombs exploded while Dail was debating tougher anti-subversion laws. Both wings of IRA and the UDA denied responsibility.

1973: *1 January* NI, like rest of the UK, became part of the EEC. *8 March* Voting in Border Poll. In London, two car bombs exploded and one man killed and 180 injured; PIRA later claimed responsibility. *20 March* British government published White Paper, proposing an Assembly elected by PR and with Westminster retaining law-and-order powers. *28 March* Shipment of arms for PIRA found on vessel *Claudia*, off Waterford. *30 May* First elections held for the new district councils – first voting by PR in NI since 1925. *28 June* Polling for the new Assembly. *31 July* Noisy scenes at first meeting of new Assembly. *21 November* Agreement reached in Stormont talks on setting up power-sharing Executive. *6–9 December* Sunningdale conference on NI attended by British and Irish Ministers and NI power-sharing parties.

1974: *1 January* NI Executive takes office. *4 January* Ulster Unionist Council rejected the Council of Ireland proposed in the Sunningdale agreement. *7 January* Brian Faulkner (Chief Executive in power-sharing administration) resigned as Unionist Party leader. *16 January* Brian Faulkner flew to Dublin for talks with Taoiseach, Liam Cosgrave. *22 January* Loyalist disruption of Assembly proceedings led to police forcibly ejecting eighteen members, including the Rev. Ian Paisley. Harry West appointed Off. U. Party leader. *1 February* Mr. Cosgrave and seven of his Ministers flew to Hillsborough, Co. Down, for a meeting with NI Executive Ministers. *4 February* Pro-Assembly Unionist group set up to support Mr Faulkner. *28 February* In the Westminster general election, eleven seats were won by UUUC candidates and the SDLP held W. Belfast. *5 March* With Labour forming a government, Merlyn Rees became NI Secretary of State. *26 April* UUUC, after a conference in Portrush, issued a policy statement which called for a NI regional parliament in a federal UK. *14 May* The power-sharing Executive won by forty-four to twenty-eight an Assembly vote on the Sunningdale agreement. The Loyalist UWC immediately threatened power cuts in protest. *15 May* Power cuts forced the closure of several factories, and many workers, including those in Belfast shipyard, went on strike. *16 May* As the strike developed, the Secretary of State accused the organisers of intimidation, and said it was a political, not an industrial, strike. *17 May* In Dublin, twenty-two killed by car bombs which exploded without warning, and five people killed by a car bomb in Monaghan town. Two of three cars used in Dublin bombing had been hi-jacked earlier in Protestant areas of Belfast; UDA and UVF denied responsibility. (Three more people died later from injuries received in the explosions.) *25 May* Harold Wilson, in a broadcast, said the strike was being run by 'thugs and bullies'. *28 May* In face of the strike, the Unionist members of the Executive resigned, and the Executive collapsed. Direct rule was resumed. *29 May* The UWC called off its strike. *31 May* Merlyn Rees said that the rise of 'Ulster nationalism' was a major factor which the government would have to take into account. *4 July* British government announced the setting up of an elected Constitutional Convention to seek a political settlement. *1 August* Meeting between representatives of SDLP and UDA. *4 September* Brian Faulkner launched UPNI. *10 October* In the Westminster general election, UUUC candidates got ten of the twelve seats, the SDLP retaining W. Belfast and Frank Maguire, Independent, unseating Off. U. leader Harry West in Fermanagh–S. Tyrone. Enoch Powell returned in S. Down. *15 October* Republican convicted prisoners in the Maze prison set fire to a large number of huts, and troops were brought in to suppress a riot. *16 October* Secretary of State revealed that nine Maze prisoners were in hospital after disturbances, while fifteen prison officers had been injured and sixteen soldiers hurt, nine seriously. At Magilligan prison, Republican prisoners burned cookhouse, prison shop and a hut. In Armagh women's prison, the Governor and three women prison officers were held captive overnight in an attic, and were only released after they had got an assurance through clergymen that prisoners in the Maze were safe. *21 October* John Hume, deputy leader of the SDLP, said Mr Rees had lost all credibility and that they saw little point in talking to him. *22 October* UUUC MPs elected James Molyneaux as their leader. *30 October* Mr Rees said riot and burnings at Maze prison had caused £1.5m of damage, and at Magilligan, £200,000. *6 November* Thirty-three Republican prisoners escaped through a tunnel from the Maze prison; twenty-nine recaptured a few hours later and three in Andersonstown in the evening. During the escape, a twenty-four year old detainee was shot dead by a sentry. *9 November* Defence Ministry ruled that names of soldiers killed in NI not to be added to war memorials since it was not classed as war zone. *18 November* Plans announced for £30m high-security prison at Maghaberry, Co. Antrim. *21 November* Nineteen killed and 182 injured when bombs exploded in two Birmingham pubs. *22 November* PIRA denied responsibility for Birmingham bombings. *25 November* The Home Secretary, Roy Jenkins, announced that IRA was to be declared illegal in Great Britain, and tougher anti-terrorist laws would be introduced. *28 November* In Dublin, the government introduced bill to allow terrorists to be tried for offences committed outside the jurisdiction. *5 December* Parliament passed an order extending the new Prevention of Terrorism Act to NI, allowing among other things, persons to be held without charge for up to seven days. *10 December* At Feakle, Co. Clare, a group of Protestant churchmen met members of Provisional Sinn Féin and PIRA. *18 December* Churchmen met Mr Rees to report on their talks in Feakle. *20 December* PIRA announced ceasefire from midnight on 22 December to midnight on 2 January 1975. *23 December* The Prime Minister, Mr Heath, during a visit to Stormont, said he believed there was majority support in NI for power-sharing. *29 December* PIRA prisoners at Portlaoise, top security prison in the Republic, caused serious damage and held fourteen warders hostage in a bid for better conditions. The officers were freed unhurt when troops stormed the jail. *31 December* In New Year message, Mr Rees said government would not be wanting in its response if 'a genuine and sustained cessation of violence' occurred. 1975: *2 January* PIRA extended its Christmas ceasefire. *16 January* PIRA called off ceasefire. *9 February* PIRA announced new ceasefire. *12 February* Incident centres, manned by Provisional Sinn Féin, set up to monitor ceasefire in liaison with government officials. *18 February* Airey Neave MP appointed Conservative NI spokesman. *18 March* Two Price sisters, convicted for London car bombings, transferred from English prison to Armagh, following long campaign for their transfer. *25 March* Harold Wilson visited Stormont and announced 1 May as Convention election polling day. *5 April* Seven dead and seventy-five injured in two pub bombings in Belfast. *14 April* Secretary of State Merlyn Rees said Loyalist gunman had tried to murder him in 1974. *1 May* Convention polling day. *8 May* First meeting of Convention. *5 June* Common Market referendum showed narrow majority in NI for membership. *24 July* Merlyn Rees promised to release all detainees by Christmas. *31 July* Three members of Miami Showband killed and one seriously injured in

UVF gun attack. Two UVF men also died, blowing themselves up during the attack. *8 September* William Craig cast the only one vote for voluntary coalition with SDLP during UUUC meeting at Stormont. *2 October* In a series of UVF attacks, twelve people, including three women and four UVF men, killed and forty-six injured. *3 October* UVF declared illegal. *12 October* Split in VUPP after Mr Craig's support for voluntary coalition. *14 November* Conservative leader Margaret Thatcher visited Belfast. *5 December* Last detainees released. *18 December* Harold Wilson visited Londonderry, where two soldiers were killed by PIRA soon after he left. *22 December* American authorities broke up gang of IRA gun-runners.

1976: *4 January* Five Roman Catholics killed in two separate incidents near Whitecross, S. Armagh. *5 January* Ten Protestant workers shot dead at Kingsmills, S. Armagh. Republic Action Force claimed responsibility. *7 January* SAS unit moved into S. Armagh. *15 January* Prime Minister Wilson presided at first all-party security meeting on NI, held at 10 Downing Streeet. *21 January* Government said 25,000 houses damaged in violence. *3 February* Convention recalled in bid to secure agreement, and new inter-party talks started. *12 February* UUUC and SDLP inter-party talks broke down after an hour. *1 March* Persons committing terrorist-type offences no longer entitled to special category status. *3 March* Final sitting of Convention ended in uproar. *9 March* Convention formally dissolved by Westminster Order. *18 March* Merlyn Rees came out against any increase in the number of NI MPs. *30 March* NICRA called off rent and rates strike, originally started in August 1971. *5 May* Nine members of IRSP escaped from Maze prison through tunnel. *15 May* Three RUC men killed when bomb exploded under them at Belcoo, Co. Fermanagh. *22 May* UVF announced three-month ceasefire. *25 May* Loyalist vigilante group, Ulster Service Corps, announced that it was mounting patrols in view of 'deteriorating security situation'. *4 June* Ian Paisley leaked news of private talks between OUP and SDLP. *7 June* UUUC vote opposing OUP–SDLP talks. *3 August* Extensive damage caused in Portrush, Co. Antrim by six explosions for which PIRA claimed responsibility. *8 August* Gerry Fitt fought off with a gun Republican demonstrators who broke into his Belfast home. *10 August* Two young children killed in Andersonstown by a car whose driver had been shot dead by troops. *11 August* A third child died as a result of Andersonstown accident. *12 August* Women demonstrated in favour of peace in Andersonstown and sparked off the women's peace movement (later the Peace People). *18 August* Brian Faulkner announced his resignation from active politics. *21 August* Some 20,000 attended peace rally in Belfast. *1 September* Republic's government declared a state of emergency which allowed people to be held for seven days without charge. *2 September* European Commission on Human Rights decided that Britain had been guilty of torturing internees in 1971, but that internment had been justified. *9 September* Leaders of main churches supported women's peace movement. *10 September* Roy Mason succeeded Merlyn Rees as Secretary of State. *13 September* Mrs Anne Dickson became leader of UPNI. *28 October* Maire Drumm, vice-president of Provisional Sinn Féin, shot dead in Mater Hospital, Belfast, where she was a patient. *11 November* ULCCC put forward plan for NI independence with title, 'Ulster can survive unfettered'. *26 November* Roy Mason said NI in danger of being left behind by 'the tide of devolution'. *1 December* Fair Employment Act, making it an offence to discriminate in employment on religious or political grounds, became effective. *4 December* SDLP annual conference rejected by 158 to 111 a motion calling on Britain to declare its intention to withdraw from NI. *9 December* PIRA fire-bombs caused more than £1m damage to Londonderry shops. *12 December* ULCCC claimed that some Loyalist politicians, who were not named, had been involved in the past in gun-running, selecting targets for bombs, and in promising money to buy arms and explosives. *25–27 December* PIRA had Christmas ceasefire.

1977: *19 January* PIRA in S. Derry claimed it had carried out wave of booby-trap bomb attacks on members of security forces there. *23 January* Ian Paisley said he would fight European direct elections. *15 February* Rhodesia's Ian Smith thanked Portadown DUP for message of support. *21 February* Conservative leader Margaret Thatcher visited Belfast and Derry. *3 March* Lord Faulkner of Downpatrick killed in hunting accident. *6 May* SDLP leader Gerry Fitt voiced support for 'Save the Shankill' campaign. *8 March* In a Dublin court, eight SAS men who were found on the Republic side of the border were each fined £100 for carrying guns without a certificate. *11 March* Twenty-six UVF men sentenced to a total of 700 years' imprisonment. *12 March* Roy Mason denied reports that his officials were involved in 'black propaganda'. *29 March* Disclosed that Off. Unionists were boycotting UUUC. *1 April* Government backed the idea of NI as one constituency, with three seats, for European direct elections. It also supported PR. OUP and DUP attacked the plan, while SDLP and All. supported it. *17 April* Cardinal Conway died in Armagh, and there was praise of his efforts for peace and reconciliation. *23 April* UUAC said it would call a Loyalist strike in May to protest against security police and demand a return of majority government. *3 May* UUAC strike began, but many factories stayed open, although the port of Larne was closed. *4 May* As a result of the stoppage, supported by Rev. Ian Paisley and Ernest Baird, the UUUC Parliamentary Coalition was dissolved. *6 May* UUAC failed to get support of Ballylumford power station workers for strike. *9 May* Demonstrations and road blocks in many places in support of strike, and Ian Paisley joined farmers who blocked roads in Ballymena with tractors. *13 May* UUAC called off its strike, which had failed to stop industry and commerce. Critics of the strike praised the government for refusing to make concessions, but Ian Paisley claimed the stoppage had been a success. *18 May* District council elections. *23 May* Roy Mason began a new round of talks with political parties. *25 May* In a switch of policy for Labour, James Callaghan, the Prime Minister, announced that an all-party Speaker's Conference would be set up to consider the possibility of more NI MPs. *8 June* Roy Mason announced that more troops would be used on SAS-type activity and that RUC and UDR strength would be increased. UUAC claimed the move was in response to the strike, but Official Unionists, who had opposed strike, said it arose from constitutional politics. *14 June* Lord Melchett announced that the eleven-plus examination would be scrapped and that the aim of the government would be to promote comprehensive education. *16 June* In the Republic, Jack Lynch's Fianna Fail party regained power by defeating the Coalition by a record margin of twenty seats. *19 June* New Zealand Premier, Robert Muldoon, discussed with Peace People leaders in Belfast the possibility of ex-terrorists being permitted to emigrate to New Zealand. *21 June* Unemployment in NI reached 60,000, the highest June total for thirty-seven years. *5 June* In the Republic, the Lynch government formally took office. *12 July* PIRA threatened disruption during Queen's jubilee visit in August. *16 July* SDLP deputy leader John Hume appointed adviser on consumer affairs by EEC Commissioner, Richard Burke. *27 July* Four killed and eighteen injured in Belfast in feud between Official and Provisional Republicans, US naval communications base in Derry closed. *9–10 August* Queen's jubilee visit. On second day, PIRA caused some minor explosions at edge of campus of NUU, but royal programme unaffected. *30 August* President Carter of US, in a special statement, said that his administration supported a form of government in NI which would have widespread acceptance throughout both parts of the community. He also urged Americans not to support violence and said that if NI people could resolve their differences, the US would be prepared, with others, to see how additional jobs could be created for the benefit of all the people. *12 September* Roy Mason, after a year as Secretary of State, said the 'myth of British withdrawal from NI' was now dead forever. *20 September* SDLP defined its policy as 'an agreed Ireland'. *28 September* James Callaghan and Jack Lynch met in Downing Street; cross-border economic co-operation one of the main topics. *5 October* Seamus Costello, leader of IRSP, shot dead in Dublin. *7 October* Irish Independence Party launched. *10 October* Betty Williams and Mairead Corrigan, founders of the Peace People, awarded 1976 Nobel Peace Prize. *14 October* Dr Tomás O'Fiaich appointed new Roman Catholic primate. *18 October* William Craig MP, as member of Council of Europe, appointed by Council to carry out research aimed at up-dating European Convention on Human Rights. *20 October* Roy Jenkins, EEC President, on a visit to Belfast, confirmed that EEC would open NI information office in 1979. *6 November* SDLP, at its annual conference, rejected call for British withdrawal from NI. *21 November* Roy Mason suggested the setting up of a Stormont Assembly without legislative powers to run local departments. *26 November* William Craig announced that VUPP would cease to be political party. *3 December* Seamus Twomey, former PIRA chief of staff, recaptured in Dublin. *21 December* Five hotels damaged by PIRA fire-bombs. *22 December* PIRA said there would be no Christmas ceasefire.

1978: *8 January* Jack Lynch, in RTE interview, re-stated his party's support for eventual Irish unity. *9 January* OUP and DUP withdrew from talks with NI office after Mr Lynch's remarks. *11 January* A Fair Employment Agency report suggested that Catholics suffered more from unemployment than Protestants. *18 January* European Court of Human Rights in Strasbourg held that interrogation techniques used on internees in 1971 did not amount to torture, but had been 'inhuman and degrading'. *17 February* Twelve people killed and twenty-three injured when La Mon restaurant in Co. Down destroyed by PIRA fire-bombs. *25 February* Standing Committee of Irish Catholic Bishops' conference said the overwhelming majority of Irish people wanted the campaign of violence to end immediately. *6 March* Official Unionists turned down idea of talks with the Rev. Ian Paisley and Ernest Baird. *12 March* Comments by Roy Mason about the role of the Republic in terrorism brought angry retorts from government and opposition in Dublin. *26 March* Speakers at PIRA celebrations of Easter Rising said that their campaign of violence would be stepped up. *7 April* Conservative spokesman Airey Neave said that power-sharing was no longer practical politics. James Callaghan and Jack Lynch, at Copenhagen EEC summit, had talks which apparently helped to heal the breach between London and Dublin on security issues. *19 April* In the Commons, James Callaghan announced that legislation would be introduced to increase NI's representation to between sixteen and eighteen seats, in line with Speaker's Conference recommendation. *2 May* Belfast appointed its first non-Unionist Lord Mayor, David Cook (All.) *5 May* Roy Mason had talks in Dublin with Irish Ministers. *1 August* Catholic Primate, Dr O'Fiaich, after visit to Maze prison, said Republican prisoners engaged in 'no wash-no toilet' protest were living in 'inhuman' conditions. *2 August* Roy Mason announced 2,000-job sports-car factory for W. Belfast, a project hailed as a breakthrough in securing US investment. *28 August–1 September* Visit to NI by US congressmen Joshua Eilberg (Democrat) and Hamilton Fish, Jun (Republican), who later urged that the US should seek to assist in a political solution in NI, as it had done in the Middle East. They also said individual human rights were being denied every day in NI. *21 September* PIRA bomb attack on Eglinton airfield (Co. Londonderry) destroyed terminal building, two hangars and four planes. *22 September* Secretary of State Roy Mason and Conservative spokesman Airey Neave issued simultaneous statements attacking calls in GB for British withdrawal from NI. *24 September* Rev. Ian Paisley held his first religious service in Dublin, at the Mansion House. *8 October* Sixty-nine RUC men injured in Londonderry when PSF and a number of other organisations held a march to celebrate the 5 October, 1968, civil rights march, and the DUP staged a counter-demonstration. Sixty-seven of the police were injured in a clash with loyalists, and two were hurt by Republicans. *14 October* DUP march in Derry to protest against Republican march on previous Sunday. Thirty-two RUC men injured when trouble broke out near Guildhall Square, and loyalists caused much damage to property. *4 November* With only two dissenting votes, SDLP annual conference voted that British withdrawal was 'desirable and inevitable,' and called for fresh conference involving British and Irish governments and two communities in NI. *14 November* PIRA bomb attacks caused serious damage in Belfast, Armagh, Dungannon, Enniskillen, Cookstown and Castlederg. *26 November* Albert Miles, deputy governor of Belfast prison, shot dead by PIRA. *28 November* Commons passed by 350 votes to 49 the Bill to give NI five more MPs. *30 November* PIRA warned that it was 'preparing for a long war,' after admitting to setting off explosive and fire bombs in fourteen towns and villages, with the most serious damage in Armagh city.

1979: *28 March* Votes of NI MPs decisive in defeat of Labour Government by 311 votes to 310, thus precipitating a general election. Eight Unionists voted with Conservative Opposition and two Official Unionists, John Carson and Harold McCusker, voted with the Government. Gerry Fitt (SDLP) and Frank Maguire (Ind) abstained. *30 March* Conservative NI spokesman Airey Neave killed when bomb exploded in his car at House of Commons car park. INLA claimed responsibility. *17 April* Four RUC men killed by PIRA at Bessbrook, Co. Armagh, when 1,000-lb. bomb exploded in a van as they were passing in a land rover. *3 May* In Westminster general election, DUP gained two seats from OUP in Belfast. *5 May* Humphrey Atkins (Conservative) succeeded Roy Mason as NI Secretary. *7 June* In first European Election, Rev. Ian Paisley, John Hume and John Taylor elected to fill the three NI seats. *30 June* Dr Tomas O'Fiaich, Archbishop of Armagh, received his cardinal's hat at a ceremony in Rome. *2 July* INLA declared illegal throughout the UK. *17 July* Rev. Ian Paisley, at opening session of European Assembly in Strasbourg, was first MEP to speak, apart from the acting president, when he protested that the Union flag was flying the wrong way up on the Parliament Buildings. *18 July* Rev. Ian Paisley shouted down in European Parliament when he sought to interrupt Jack Lynch as European Council president. *21 July* Visit of Pope John Paul II to Ireland announced for 29 September, and Rev. Ian Paisley and Orange Order warned that NI must not be included in itinerary. *31 July* US State Department stopped private arms shipments to NI, including supplies to RUC. *11 August* Irish National Caucus deputation said in Belfast that it planned to make NI a major issue in 1980 US presidential election. *22 August* Secretary of State Humphrey Atkins rejected proposal from New York Governor Hugh Carey that he (the Governor) should preside at New York talks involving the NI Secretary and Irish Foreign Minister Michael O'Kennedy. *27 August* PIRA bombers killed eighteen soldiers near Warrenpoint, Co. Down, the biggest death toll in a single incident in ten years of violence (see separate entry). Earl Mountbatten of Burma was murdered by PIRA at Mullaghmore, Co. Sligo, when his boat was blown to pieces in a radio-triggered explosion. The Earl's fourteen-year-old grandson, Nicholas, and Paul Maxwell, aged fourteen, a crew member, also died instantly, and the Dowager Lady Brabourne died later from her injuries. *29 August* Prime Minister, Mrs Thatcher, flew to NI to discuss tightening of security. It was announced in Rome that, because of the recent violence, the Pope would not now visit Armagh in

NI. *30 August* British Cabinet decided to increase RUC by 1,000. *2 September* UFF threatened to strike back at PIRA. *5 September* Mrs Thatcher and Taoiseach Jack Lynch met in London for security talks. *29 September* The Pope, speaking in Drogheda, appealed 'on my bended knees' for an end to violence. *2 October* PIRA rejected the Pope's appeal and declared that it had widespread support, and that only force could remove the British presence. *5 October* British and Irish Governments agreed to tighten up the anti-terrorist drive, British Labour Party conference rejected a call for withdrawal from NI. *15 October* Opinion poll published by Dublin-based Economic and Social Research Institute, based on questioning in July–September, 1978, showed twenty-one per cent of people in Republic giving some degree of support to PIRA activities, with under three per cent expressing strong support. The poll was criticised by Dublin politicians and the SDLP, who said it exaggerated support for PIRA. Some Unionists said it helped to explain why the Lynch Government had not agreed to extradition. *25 October* Secretary of State announced that he was inviting four main parties – OUP, DUP, SDLP and Alliance – to a Stormont conference to discuss a possible political settlement. The OUP immediately rejected the invitation and said the Government should proceed with two-tier local government. PIRA denied that it had planned to assassinate Princess Margaret during her recent US visit. *1 November* Jack Lynch said the NI problem 'continues to be as intractable as at any stage in the last ten years'. One hundred and fifty-six guns, including a powerful M-60 machine-gun, seized at Dublin docks. They were believed to have been sent from the US for use by PIRA. *3 November* SDLP, at its annual conference, urged a joint approach by the British and Irish Governments to the NI problem. It also rejected a proposal for talks with PIRA. *22 November* SDLP leader Gerry Fitt, MP, resigned from the party because of its initial refusal to attend Atkins Conference. *28 November* John Hume, MEP, became SDLP leader. *5 December* Jack Lynch, TD, resigned as Republic's Taoiseach. *7 December* Charles Haughey, TD, appointed to succeed Lynch by 44–38 vote of Fianna Fail Parliamentary Party. *15 December* SDLP decided to attend Atkins Conference. *16 December* Five soldiers killed by PIRA landmine.

1980: *7 January* Constitutional Conference opened at Stormont. *17 January* Three people killed in terrorist train explosion at Dunmurry. *8 February* Leonard Kaitcer, Belfast antique dealer, murdered after kidnap linked with £1 million ransom demand. *11 February* Serious differences emerge within Peace People. *16 February* Charles Haughey, at Fianna Fail conference in Dublin urged joint British-Irish initiative on NI. *5 March* Cardinal O'Fiaich and Bishop Edward Daly met Secretary of State to voice concern about conditions within H-blocks. *11 March* Body of German industrialist Thomas Nedermayer found at Colin Glen Road, W. Belfast. He disappeared December, 1973. *24 March* Stormont Constitutional Conference adjourned indefinitely with no sign of agreement. *26 March* Announced that as from 1 April there would be no entitlement to special category status for terrorist offenders. *6 April*

Small bomb exploded at Milltown cemetery, Belfast, during Easter Sunday Republican parades; no casualties. *15 April* Secretary of State Atkins in Dublin for talks with Haughey Government. *30 April* Marion Price, convicted with sister Dolours for their part in London car bombing in 1973 released from Armagh prison on humanitarian grounds. *5 May* PIRA blew up pylon at Crossmaglen, part of N.–S. power link, which both Governments were seeking to re-establish. *13 May* SDLP leader John Hume met Mrs Thatcher at 10 Downing Street. *21 May* Mrs Thatcher and Mr Haughey had meeting at 10 Downing Street. Communique promised closer political co-operation and referred to 'unique relationship' between the two countries. *4 June* John Turnley, Protestant joint chairman of IIP shot dead at Carnlough home in front of his family. *5 June* Presbyterian General Assembly voted 443–322 to take Church out of World Council of Churches on the basis that the Council supported terrorist groups. *9 June* Mr Haughey appealed to Britain to accept that withdrawal was in the best interests of UK and Ireland. On BBC *Panorama* programme he also mentioned the possibility of some form of federation and separate social laws for NI. *11 June* PIRA threatened to renew attacks on prison officers, suspended since March. *12 June* Markethill town centre seriously damaged by PIRA car bomb. *19 June* European Commission of Human Rights rejected the case of protesting H-block prisoners, finding that the debasement arising from the 'dirty protest' was self-inflicted. The Commission also criticised British Government for 'inflexibility'. *25 June* US Democratic Party adopted Sen. Kennedy's policy, calling for 'an end to the divisions of the Irish people', and a solution based on the consent of all the parties to the conflict. *26 June* Dr Miriam Daly, prominent Republican member of National H-Block Committee, shot dead at her home in Andersonstown. *2 July* British Government published two-option document on NI devolution. It produced no agreement, since Unionists rejected the option with a large element of power-sharing and anti-Unionists turned down the option of majority rule. *9 July* Internment law dropped. It had not been used since 1975. *20 July* Car bomb in Lisnaskea caused extensive damage. *6 August* Extra Government spending of £48 million in NI announced after ICTU delegation had met Mrs Thatcher to protest at 14.7 per cent unemployment. *8 August* Three killed and eighteen injured in widespread violence on ninth anniversary of internment. *24 September* Cardinal O'Fiaich 'hopeful of progress' on H-Block issue. *27 October* Seven H-Block prisoners began hunger strike in support of demand for, among other things, the right to wear their own clothing. *8 December* Mrs Thatcher, accompanied by three Cabinet Ministers – Lord Carrington (Foreign Secretary), Sir Geoffrey Howe (Chancellor of Exchequer) and Humphrey Atkins – had talks in Dublin with Mr Haughey and senior colleagues. The meeting agreed to joint studies on a wide range of subjects and Mr Haughey called it 'an historic breakthrough'. *18 December* H-Block hunger strike called off with one PIRA prisoner critically ill.

1981: *16 January* Bernadette McAliskey and husband shot and seriously

CHRONOLOGY OF MAJOR EVENTS, 1921–83

wounded by gunmen at their home near Coalisland. *21 January* Two leading Unionists – Sir Norman Stronge and son James – shot dead by PIRA gunmen at their Tynan home. *6 February* British coal boat, *Nellie M*, sunk by PIRA off Moville, Co. Donegal. *9 February* Ian Paisley launched 'Ulster Declaration' against Anglo-Irish talks. *12 February* Ian Paisley suspended from Commons when he persisted in calling Humphrey Atkins a 'liar'. *19 February* James Molyneaux, Off. U. leader, described as 'ludicrous' an allegation by Ian Paisley that there was an OUP plot to kill him. *21 February* Eight stores in Belfast and three in Londonderry damaged by PIRA fire bombs. *27 February* 300-pound van bomb damaged forty premises in Limavady. *1 March* New H-Block hunger strike in support of political status began when PIRA prisoner Bobby Sands refused food. *3 March* In Commons, Humphrey Atkins said there would be no political status for prisoners, regardless of protests inside or outside the prison. *5 March* Frank Maguire, Ind. MP for Fermanagh and S. Tyrone, died. Mrs Thatcher on a visit to NI, again denied that Anglo-Irish talks threatened NI's constitutional position. *21 March* Cardinal O'Fiaich called on PIRA to end violence. *22 March* Republic's Foreign Minister, Brian Lenihan, said Anglo-Irish talks could lead to Irish unity in ten years. *28 March* Ian Paisley attracted large attendance at Stormont rally against Anglo-Irish talks. RUC estimated 30,000 audience. *1 April* DUP held three late-night rallies on hillsides near Gortin, Newry and Armagh. At Gortin, two RUC vehicles were overturned. *9 April* Hunger striker Bobby Sands won the Fermanagh and S. Tyrone by-election. *11 April* Riots in Belfast, Lurgan and Cookstown after celebrations of Sands' election. *19 April* On fifth successive night of rioting in Derry, two nineteen-year-old youths were killed when struck by Army landrover. *22 April* Dolours Price released from Armagh prison since her life was said to be in danger from anorexia nervosa; her sister Marion had been released in 1980 for the same reason. *28 April* President Reagan said US would not intervene in NI, but he was 'deeply concerned at the tragic situation'. *5 May* Bobby Sands, MP, died on 66th day of his fast. There was rioting in Belfast and Londonderry, and also in Dublin. *6 May* 600 extra troops sent to NI as sporadic violence continued. *7 May* Massive attendance at Bobby Sands' funeral in Milltown cemetery. *9 May* PIRA claimed they had planted a bomb at the Sullom Voe oil terminal in the Shetlands to explode during the Queen's visit there. *12 May* Hunger striker Francis Hughes died and blast and petrol bombs were thrown at security forces during riots in Belfast and Derry. *13 May* John Hume met Mrs Thatcher and unsuccessfully urged concessions to hunger strikers on clothing and association. *19 May* Five soldiers killed when their Saracen armoured car blown up by land-mine near Bessbrook. *20 May* Polling in council elections (see Elections Section). *21 May* Cardinal O'Fiaich criticised 'rigid stance' of Government on hunger strike. *26 May* Arms found in RUC raid on UDA HQ in Belfast. *11 June* Eight PIRA men awaiting sentence escaped from Belfast prison. Two H-Block prisoners elected to Dail in general election which resulted in return to power of Fine Gael–Labour Coalition. *2 July* Humphrey

Atkins suggested an Advisory Council of already elected representatives; the idea was later dropped because of lack of support. *4 July* H-Block hunger strikers said they would be happy that any concessions granted to them should apply to all prisoners, *14 July* Irish Government asked US to intervene with Britain over the hunger strike. *18 July* In Dublin, over 200 people were injured during a riot when an H-Block march was prevented by Gardai from passing British Embassy. *2 August* Hunger-striker Kieran Doherty, TD, died. *5 August* Concentrated PIRA car-bomb and incendiary attack in seven centres, including Belfast, Londonderry and Lisburn, caused widespread damage, but no serious injuries. *8 August* Two people died during violence in Belfast; more than 1,000 petrol bombs were thrown at security forces. *20 August* Owen Carron won Fermanagh and S. Tyrone by-election. *2 September* Ian Paisley called for 'third force' on lines of former B-Specials. *7 September* Two RUC men killed by PIRA landmine near Pomeroy. *13 September* James Prior became NI Secretary of State and Humphrey Atkins deputy Foreign Secretary. *17 September* Mr Prior visited Maze prison for three hours, with growing signs that the hunger strike was collapsing. *29 September* British Labour conference voted to 'campaign actively' for united Ireland by consent. *3 October* H-Block hunger strike, which had led to deaths of ten Republican prisoners, called off. *6 October* Secretary of State announced that all prisoners would now be allowed to wear their own clothes. *8 October* Belfast Independent councillor Lawrence Kennedy shot dead in Ardoyne, apparently by Loyalist gunman. *10 October* PIRA set off remotely controlled nail-bomb outside Chelsea Barracks in London. One woman killed and twenty-three soldiers and seventeen civilians injured. *22 October* European Court of Human Rights ruled that NI law banning male homosexuality was a breach of European Convention. *6 November* Mrs Thatcher and Irish Premier Dr Garret Fitzgerald decided in London talks to set up Inter-Governmental Council. *14 November* Rev. Robert Bradford, MP, assassinated by PIRA gunmen at Finaghy, Belfast. *16 November* Three DUP MPs suspended from Commons after protests on security. 'Third Force' march in Enniskillen. *17 November* Mr Prior faced barrage of verbal abuse at Robert Bradford funeral at Dundonald. RUC leave cancelled. *23 November* Loyalist 'Day of Action' to protest against security policy marked by rallies and stoppages of work in Protestant areas. Both OUP and DUP had separate rallies at Belfast City Hall. Some 5,000 men paraded at a DUP rally in Newtownards, addressed by Ian Paisley. *25 November* INLA bomb exploded at British army camp at Herford, W. Germany, but caused no injuries. *30 November* Several Unionist-controlled councils adjourned in protest at the security situation. *3 December* Ian Paisley claimed 'Third Force' had 15,000–20,000 members. James Prior said private armies would not be tolerated. *21 December* Revealed that US State Department had revoked Ian Paisley's visa.

1982: *29 January* A prominent East Belfast loyalist, John McKeague, shot dead in his shop, apparently by INLA. *1 February* OUP delegation met Secretary of State to tell him they were opposed to his 'rolling devolution' plan and reaffirmed support for Convention report. Labour leader Michael Foot arrived in NI for three-day visit and said more jobs was the top priority. *8 February* Five Belfast men arrested when they tried to enter US from Canada with lists of firearms. *18 February* General election in Republic returned Fianna Fail to power when the party secured the backing of Worker's Party and Independent TDs. None of the PSF's seven candidates returned. *23 February* PIRA used bombs to sink coal boat *St Bedan* in Lough Foyle. At European security conference in Madrid, Poland alleged Britain was using torture in NI. *24 February* Government said it would bring homosexual laws in NI into line with rest of UK, following European Court of Human Rights' ruling against existing laws. Catholic Bishops and DUP opposed reforms. *4 March* Rev. Martin Smyth, Off. U., returned in S. Belfast by-election. *6 March* Gerard Tuite, who escaped from prison in London, was charged in Dublin with causing explosions in London. He was the first person charged in Republic with a crime committed in GB. *14 March* SDLP leader John Hume called the new devolution plan 'unworkable.' *16 March* Eleven-year-old boy killed and thirty-four people injured, some seriously, by a bomb which exploded without warning in Banbridge. *17 March* On a St. Patrick's Day visit to the US Taoiseach Charles Haughey said US Government should bring more pressure on Britain to adopt a more positive attitude to Irish unity. President Reagan said any solution must come from NI people themselves. *25 March* Three soldiers killed in PIRA ambush in Crocus Street, W. Belfast. M60 machine-gun used. British Cabinet approved 'rolling devolution' plan. *26 March* PIRA offered 'amnesty' to informers if they retracted their evidence. *28 March* RUC Inspector Norman Duddy, forty-five, shot dead by PIRA in Londonderry. *1 April* Two plain-clothes soldiers killed in Derry in PIRA machine-gun attack. *14 April* Four leading members of UDA arrested after ammunition and some gun parts found in Belfast HQ during police raid. *16 April* Mr Prior said he had no plans to proscribe UDA. He also said Falklands crisis would not delay devolution plans (see Government Section). *17 April* A soldier who rammed 'Free Derry Wall' in a personnel carrier was taken into military custody. *19 April* James Molyneaux, MP, said the Falklands crisis had vindicated the Unionist position and his suspicion of the Foreign Office. *20 April* Two killed, twelve injured and £1 million damage caused by PIRA bomb attacks in Belfast, Derry, Armagh, Strabane, Ballymena, Bessbrook and Magherafelt. *22 April* Workers' Party in Dublin denied a claim in *Magill* magazine that Official IRA was still active and involved in murders and armed robberies. *24 April* Alliance leader Oliver Napier told his party's conference that devolution plan might be last chance for NI to solve its own problems. *25 April* Sinn Fein, the Workers' Party known in NI as Workers' Party, Republican Clubs, decided to call itself simply 'The Workers' Party'. *27 April* Queen Mother made short visit to Omagh army base. *3 May* Republic's Defence Minister Paddy Power described Britain as the 'aggressor' over the Falklands. *10 May* Charles Haughey appointed Seamus Mallon, SDLP deputy leader, and John Robb of

New Ireland Group, to Republic's Senate. *13 May* European Parliament called for ban on use of plastic bullets throughout EEC. *20 May* INLA bomb defused at home of Rev. William Beattie of DUP. *24 May* Closure of De Lorean car plant at Dunmurry announced, with loss of 1,500 jobs. *28 May* British and Irish Governments said NI would get natural gas from Republic in about two years' time. *29 May* Friends of Ireland Group in US Congress on fact-finding visit to NI. *18 June* Ex-RUC Inspector Albert White, sixty, shot dead near his home in Newry. *19 June* RUC said it was expecting information about PIRA suspects captured by Israeli forces in Lebanon. *21 June* FBI arrested four men in New York who were said to have tried to buy 'Redeye' surface-to-air missiles for PIRA. *25 June* Devolution Bill amended to ensure that both Commons and Lords must be satisfied about 'cross-community support' before transfer of powers. *30 June* In Commons, Mr Prior promised review by senior legal figure of Emergency Provisions Act. *1 July* Gardai found large cache of bombs at Castlefin, Co. Donegal. *19 July* Mr Prior left on short visit to US to explain his devolution scheme. *20 July* Eight soldiers died and fifty-one people were injured by two PIRA bombs in London – one near the Household Cavalry barracks at Knightsbridge and the other at the Regent's Park bandstand, where an army band was playing. Three people died later. *23 July* NI Assembly Bill got royal assent. *27 July* Disclosed that British Government had told Irish Ambassador in London that it was under no obligation to consult Republic about NI matters. *2 August* A parade led by Rev. Ian Paisley in Downpatrick led to a counter-demonstration. *8 August* Representatives of Noraid and PLO spoke at internment anniversary demonstration in W. Belfast. *15 August* In the US, Rev. Martin Smyth, MP, claimed that he knew who killed the Rev. Robert Bradford, and he alleged that CIA was involved in NI. *25 August* SDLP decided to contest Assembly elections, but not to take seats. *28 August* PIRA was believed to have suffered one of its biggest setbacks through seizures of arms and explosives. The RUC found about one and a half tons of gelignite hidden in a lorry near Banbridge; the Gardai seized a smaller quantity of gelignite and 10,000 rounds of ammunition at Glencree, Co. Wicklow. *1 September* Merger of departments of Commerce and Manpower took effect to create new Department of Economic Development. Belfast DUP councillor Billy Dickson wounded in INLA gun attack at his home. *16 September* INLA bomb at Divis flats in W. Belfast killed a soldier and two boys of eleven and fourteen. *20 September* INLA blew up radar station at Schull, Co. Cork. *23 September* RUC Chief Constable Sir John Hermon said PIRA and INLA 'reeling' from arrests arising from evidence of informers. *2 October* British Labour Party Conference calls for ban on use of plastic bullets throughout UK. *20 October* Polling day in Assembly election (see Elections Section). Closure of de Lorean car factory announced as John de Lorean charged in California with drug smuggling offences. *27 October* Three RUC men killed in booby-trap landmine explosion near Lurgan. *2 November* SDLP delegation told Mr Prior they would continue their boycott of the Assembly. *3 November*

Queen's speech at opening of Parliament re-affirmed Government's intention to carry on with Assembly. *9 November* RUC constable and woman leisure centre worker died in Enniskillen in booby-trapped car. *11 November* At Assembly's first session, James Kilfedder, MP, elected Speaker. Three PIRA men shot dead by RUC when they were alleged to have driven through checkpoint near Lurgan. *16 November* Two RUC Reserve constables shot dead in Markethill. Leonard Murphy, reputed to have been leader of the notorious 'Shankill butcher gang', shot dead. *25 November* In Republic's general election, Fine Gael and Labour secured overall majority, paving the way for a Coalition. *30 November* Mr Prior addressed Assembly, and announced increase in RUC strength. *6 December* seventeen people, including eleven soldiers, died in INLA bombing of the 'Droppin' Well' pub disco in Ballykelly, Co. Londonderry. *16 December* Election Petition Court in Armagh deprived SDLP deputy leader Seamus Mallon of his Assembly seat on the ground that he was a member of the Republic's Senate when returned. *23 December* Mrs Thatcher made one-day visit to NI, mainly to meet members of security forces.

1983: *5 January* INLA declared illegal in Irish Republic. *6 January* Two RUC men shot dead by PIRA in Rostrevor, Co. Down. *16 January* County court judge William Doyle shot dead by PIRA as he left Catholic church in S. Belfast. *28 January* Republic's Government announced that it would give full voting rights to 20,000 British citizens. *30 January* SDLP annual conference reaffirmed Assembly boycott and voted to fight all 17 NI seats at next Westminster election. *1 February* Irish Foreign Minister Peter Barry met Secretary of State Prior in London and expressed doubts as to whether the Assembly had a useful future. *17 February* At Westminster Labour Party decided to oppose Prevention of Terrorism Act in its present form. *23 February* European Parliament's political committee voted for an inquiry as to whether EEC could help to solve NI's economic and political problems, despite opposition by British Government and Conservative and Unionist MEPs. *26 February* GLC leader Ken Livingstone flew to Belfast for two-day visit at the invitation of Sinn Fein – a visit strongly attacked by Unionists. *27 February* Charles Haughey at Fianna Fail conference in Dublin urged British and Irish Governments to organise a constitutional conference as a prelude to final British withdrawal from NI. *2 March* NI Assembly voted unanimously for a halt to European Parliament inquiry. *7 March* Home Secretary announced new anti-terrorism Bill with 5-year life, subject to annual renewal. *11 March* Republic's Government announced it would set up all-Ireland Forum on lines suggested by SDLP. *17 March* President Reagan said those who supported terrorism were no friends of Ireland. Senator Kennedy called for Irish unity in a Senate motion. *21 March* Mrs Thatcher's meeting with Garret Fitzgerald at Brussels EEC summit was her first with an Irish Prime Minister for nearly 16 months. *24 March* OUP, DUP and Alliance Party rejected Garret Fitzgerald's invitation to take part in all-Ireland Forum. *3 April* Statements at Republican Easter Rising celebrations indicated that PIRA was dropping punishment shootings commonly known as 'kneecappings.' *8 April* Secretary of State Prior announced an inquiry into working of Emergency Provisions Act. *11 April* Fourteen UVF men jailed, two for life, on evidence of 'supergrass' Joseph Bennett, former UVF battalion commander, who had been granted immunity in respect of two murders and other terrorist offences. *21 April* Parties involved in New Ireland Forum announced it would have first meeting in Dublin Castle on 30 May. *25 April* Republic's Coalition Government suffered first Parliamentary defeat when its proposed wording for anti-abortion referendum was defeated by 22 votes. *5 May* Secretary of State James Prior in Dublin for talks with the Government. But occasion over-shadowed by Irish Government protest to London about remarks in NI by Defence Secretary Michael Heseltine that small neutral countries allowed NATO 'to carry responsibility for the whole area'. *10–11 May* NI Assembly had all-night sitting on devolution, but failed to agree on any clear-cut approach. *24 May* 1,000-lb PIRA bomb outside Andersonstown police station in W. Belfast caused £1m. damage. *30 May* Forum for a New Ireland held initial meeting in Dublin. *9 June* In Westminster election, Unionists took fifteen of the seventeen NI seats, with SDLP and PSF getting one each. *11 June* James Prior reappointed NI Secretary in Mrs Thatcher's new Cabinet. *28 June* SDLP leader John Hume in maiden Commons' speech, spoke of Britain's 'psychological withdrawal' from NI. *3 July* Unoccupied Belfast home of ex-MP Gerry Fitt (now Lord Fitt) set alight by youths from nearby New Lodge Road. *4 July* Catholic Bishops in NI warned against reintroduction of death penalty and called for ban on use of plastic bullets. *8 July* NI Assembly voted 35 to 11 for death penalty for terrorist murders. *10 July* Secretary of State James Prior said return of capital punishment would increase terrorism and lead to 'violent disorders' in NI. *13 July* Commons rejected death penalty for terrorist murders by majority of 116. Four UDR soldiers killed by PIRA landmine in Co. Tyrone – the regiment's heaviest loss in a single incident. *17 July* Former NI Secretary Merlyn Rees said a Cabinet subcommittee had considered withdrawal from NI between 1974 and 1976 but no Minister had favoured it. *21 July* Ex-MP Gerry Fitt became Life Peer; former NI Secretary Humphrey Atkins was knighted; and OUP leader James Molyneaux was appointed Privy Councillor. *26 July* Irish Foreign Minister Peter Barry told MPs at Westminster that democracy in NI was being undermined by increased PSF vote. Gerry Adams, PSF MP for W. Belfast, in London as guest of GLC leader Ken Livingstone, said Britain had erected 'Wall of misinformation' around NI. *5 August* One-hundred-and-twenty-day trial of thirty-eight people implicated in terrorism by PIRA 'supergrass' Christopher Black ended in Belfast. Mr Justice Kelly jailed twenty-two of the accused, with sentences totalling more than 4,000 years. Four were acquitted and the others got mainly suspended sentences.

Dictionary of names and organisations

A

ABERCORN, DUKE OF.
Unionist MP for Fermanagh and
S. Tyrone, 1964–70. Sat in Parliament as Marquess of Hamilton,
succeeding to Dukedom in June,
1979. b. 4 July 1934. Member,
Council of Europe, 1966–70;
European Economic and Social
Committee, 1973–8. Specially
interested in development of NI's
natural resources and cross-border economic development.

**ABERCORN RESTAURANT
BOMBING.** The explosion of a
bomb in the crowded central Belfast restaurant, the Abercorn, on 4
March 1972, was one of the most
horrific incidents of the NI violence. Two women were killed
and some 130 people injured.
There was no warning and the
casualties were mainly women and
children having a break from
Saturday afternoon shopping.
Two women died, and many suffered severe mutilation. Two sisters out shopping were among the
most seriously affected, each lost
both legs and one of them, who
was buying her wedding dress,
also lost an arm and an eye.

ACTIVE SERVICE UNIT.
See PROVISIONAL IRA.

ADAMS, GERRY. PSF MP for
W. Belfast 1983–. Assembly member for W. Belfast, 1982–. Vice-president of Provisional Sinn
Fein, 1978–. b. Belfast, 1949. Barman in Belfast when he became
involved in what Republicans
describe as 'defence work during
the pogroms', and he was believed
by the security forces to be head
of the PIRA in the Ballymurphy
area of W. Belfast when he was
interned in 1971. Released in 1972
to take part in secret London talks
between PIRA and Secretary of
State William Whitelaw, which
gave rise to brief ceasefire. In
resumed campaign, he was
believed by British intelligence
sources to be the Belfast brigade
commander of PIRA, and in 1973
one of three-man group running
PIRA after arrest of Sean MacStiofain, chief of staff. After arrest
with other leading Republicans in
Belfast in 1973, he tried to escape
from the Maze prison. For this, he
was sentenced to eighteen
months' imprisonment and
released in 1976. Both as an internee and a convicted prisoner, he
was in the PIRA compound at the
Maze, but he has repeatedly
denied that he has been a member
of PIRA. In February 1978, he was
charged with membership of
PIRA, but after being remanded
in custody for seven months, he
was freed after the Lord Chief
Justice, Lord Lowry, ruled that
there was not sufficient evidence
for a conviction. He has on several
occasions stressed the need for
increased political action by

Republicans. In June, 1979, he told a Wolfe Tone commemoration ceremony at Bodenstown, Co. Kildare, that the aims of the movement could not be achieved simply by military means, and their failure to develop an alternative to constitutional politics had to be continually analysed. At the 1980 PSF ard-fheis, he said that the British now realised that there could not be a military victory, and it was time that Republicans realised it, too. He had a leading role in deciding policy on the 1981 H-Block hunger strike, and when he topped the poll in W. Belfast in the 1982 Assembly election, he became the dominant NI personality in Provisional Sinn Fein. Tim Pat Coogan, a leading authority on the IRA, called him a 'Shogun-like figure' in Northern Republicanism. He is among those who have campaigned for a more socialist approach by PSF, and when the party dropped federalism from its policy in 1982, it was a further triumph for Adams and his supporters and put him at odds with some leading Southern PSF figures such as Daithi O Conaill. In December, 1982, he was banned by Home Secretary William Whitelaw, under the Prevention of Terrorism Act, from entering GB to speak to Labour MPs and councillors at the invitation of GLC leader Ken Livingstone. But the ban was lifted by the Home Office in June, 1983, when he took W. Belfast in the general election, with a majority of more than 5,000, unseating veteran MP Gerry Fitt. In July 1983, he provoked controversy with a visit to London, where he met some Labour MPs.

ADVISORY COMMISSION. An eleven-member body set up by William Whitelaw MP, as Secretary of State, soon after direct rule to advise him on local legislation and matters generally. It continued until the setting up of the Assembly, and was controversial from the start. Both Unionists and the SDLP boycotted it, although the Secretary of State gave an assurance that it would not usurp the functions of MPs. Members: Sir Robin Kinahan, leading local businessman and one-time Unionist MP; Miss Sheelagh Murnaghan, former Liberal MP for QUB; Prof. Norman Gibson, of the NUU; R. D. Rolston, president of the Confederation of British Industry Council in NI; Mrs Ada Malone, headmistress of Enniskillen Collegiate School for Girls; Norman Kennedy, trade union leader; Tom Conaty, businessman and chairman of the Falls Road-based CCDC; R. B. Price, of Ballymoney, who had been active in local authority and chamber of commerce affairs; James O'Hara, a member (later chairman) of the Housing Executive and first Catholic appointed to former Housing Trust; A. E. Gibson, former president, Ulster Farmers' Union; and John H. Nicholl, vice-chairman of Londonderry County Council, to which he was elected as Nationalist.

AGNEW, FRAZER. Off. U. Assembly member for S. Antrim, 1982–. b. 1942. Newtownabbey Council, 1981–. Chairman, Association of Belfast Orange Unionist Delegates Association.

ALISON, MICHAEL (JAMES HUGH). Minister-of-State, NI Office, 1979–81. b. 27 June 1926. At the NI Office, he was deputy to Secretary of State Humphrey Atkins, and his most arduous period at Stormont was in 1981, when he was responsible for handling the prison situation during most of the H-Block hunger strike. He left NI, however, a month or so before the protest ended. Conservative MP for Barkston Ash, 1964–. Conservative Research Dept., 1958–64; Parliamentary Under-Secretary, Health and Social Security, 1970–4; Minister-of-State, Employment, 1981–. Parliamentary Private Secretary to Mrs Thatcher 1983–.

ALL CHILDREN TOGETHER. An organisation aimed at bringing together Protestant and Catholic children in shared schools, with the cooperation of the Churches and where parents have expressed a wish to have their children educated together. It promoted a parliamentary bill to achieve this object, which was introduced in the House of Lords in June 1977 by the Alliance peer, Lord Dunleath. In parliament, the government supported its general aims, but suggested its withdrawal. It was, however, passed, and got the royal assent on 26 May 1978.

ALLEN, DAVID. VUPP Convention member for N. Antrim, 1975–6. b. 1937. Ballymena Borough Council, 1973–7. A former teacher and active educationalist, be became general secretary of the Ulster Teachers' Union in 1977. In 1982, he claimed that the closure of State-controlled schools in border areas, was threatening many Protestant communities, particularly in Co. Fermanagh, and would result in the border being pushed northwards and eastwards in practical terms.

ALLEN, JOHN ALEXANDER (JACK). Off. U. Assembly member for Londonderry, 1982–. Londonderry City Council, 1967–9 and 1973–81. Mayor, 1975. Vice-chairman, NI Housing Association.

ALLIANCE PARTY. One of NI's main political parties, it prides itself on giving priority to attracting support from both sides of the community. The party was launched in April 1970, and although its initial leadership was drawn largely from people previously unknown in politics, it quickly gained support from a section of Unionists who had backed the Prime Minister, Terence O'Neill, and who felt that Alliance, rather than the OUP, represented their outlook. Although its main base, to start with, appeared to be middle-class, it also absorbed many people who had formerly backed the NILP. It got an early boost in 1972, when three sitting MPs joined it: Phelim O'Neill ex-Unionist Minister; pro-O'Neill member, Bertie McConnell, and Tom Gormley, Nationalist. In its first electoral test, the May 1973 district council elections, it got 13.6 per cent of the votes. This should have secured it more than seventy seats, under the newly-introduced PR system, but in fact it got sixty-three. In the hard-fought Assembly election which followed the next month, it secured 9.2 per cent of the total vote and eight seats. Many of its supporters had hoped for more, but it went on to take part in the crucial negotiations on the power-sharing scheme and in the Sunningdale conference. Two of its members – Oliver Napier, the party leader, and Bob Cooper, the deputy leader – were included in the short-lived Executive government. In the 1975 Convention elections, its share of the vote rose slightly, to 9.8 per cent and it again got eight seats. In the Convention campaign, it called for a strong legislative assembly. It said that both sides of the divided community must be involved at all levels in the government of the province, although it indicated in the Convention itself that it would not object to majority government eventually if the atmosphere improved. It dropped the idea of a Council of Ireland, as envisaged at Sunningdale, saying that it was unnecessary to have such a formal body to achieve practical co-operation with the Republic. Its main policy contribution in the Convention was to outline a scheme for government by committees, elected in proportion to the strength of parties in the Assembly. In the district council elections in 1977, it improved its poll to 14.4 per cent of the total and secured seventy seats. It benefited from transfers, notably from Official Unionists, who had been advised to give their lower preferences to Alliance as a pro-Union party. In the 1979 Westminster election, the party fought all twelve seats, but failed to gain a single seat, despite its prediction

that it would take E. Belfast. Its share of the poll was 11.9 per cent. In the 1979 European election, its candidate was Mr Napier, and his share of first preferences was only 6.8 per cent. In the 1980 Constitutional Conference, it continued to press the case for partnership government. But this did not bring it any dividends in the 1981 council elections, in which it suffered from the polarisation produced by the H-Block hunger strike. Its nine per cent vote was more than five per cent down on the previous council contests. In 1982, it emerged as the party showing most enthusiasm for the 'rolling devolution' initiative. However, its vote in the October Assembly election stayed at nine per cent, but PR worked very appreciably to its advantage, so that it took ten Assembly seats—or twice as many as PSF, which had ten per cent of the vote. But its share of the poll in the 1983 Westminster election fell to 8 per cent, and its hope of taking one or more seats was disappointed. Partly for tactical reasons, it contested only twelve of the seventeen seats.

ALLISTER, JAMES HUGH. DUP Assembly member for N. Antrim, 1982–. b. 1953. LL.B. (QUB). Barrister. European Parliament personal assistant to Rev. Ian Paisley and DUP press officer, 1980–. Joint organiser of OUP–DUP 'Operation, USA' publicity campaign in the US, January, 1982. DUP Assembly Whip, 1982–. In the 1983 Westminster Election he was 367 votes behind the OUP winner in the new East Antrim Seat.

AMERICAN ANCIENT ORDER OF HIBERNIANS.
This Irish-American organisation claims several hundred thousand members, and it figures largely in the annual New York St Patrick's Day parade. In 1978, spokesmen for the AOH in Ireland stressed that the US organisation was entirely autonomous. This arose from controversy, going back to 1972, about the precise attitude of the US body to NI affairs. In 1972, Judge James Comerford, a former president of the American AOH, declared that it 'unequivocally supports the Provisional IRA campaign'. But this was denied by the US National Secretary, William Bartnett, who said that the organisation neither granted financial aid to PIRA nor maintained goodwill contacts with its leadership. When the AAOH held its annual convention in Killarney in July 1978, a resolution which repudiated violence in NI and praised the Irish government's stand on the North was ruled out of order. The motion was stated to have been backed by Senator Edward Kennedy. Later, a spokesman for AAOH stressed that the conference decision was strictly procedural, since the organisation could not support any foreign government. And the spokesman said it was totally opposed to the use of violence as a solution to the NI problem. Argument also arose from a comment by the deputy leader of the SDLP, John Hume, that the AAOH had been writing to US firms, opposing the idea of investment in NI. Mr George Clough, a director of the AAOH, said they did not want to stop US investment in NI, but they wanted equal opportunities in employment there. It organised the 1983 St Patrick's Day parade in New York which provoked controversy because a PIRA supporter, Michael Flannery, founder of NORAID, was chosen to head the parade.

AMERICAN CONGRESS FOR IRISH FREEDOM. An Irish-American organisation, headed by James C. Heaney, a New York lawyer, which campaigns for British withdrawal from NI. In 1969, it ran into criticism both from the NI government and NICRA when it distributed leaflets advising US industrialists against setting up factories in NI. NICRA complained that it had spread 'falsehoods and half-truths'. In 1971 and 1972, it campaigned against internment without trial.

ANCIENT ORDER OF HIBERNIANS. An organisation often regarded as the Catholic equivalent of the Orange Order. It has always been associated with defence of the Catholic faith and promotion of Irish nationalism. Its present title dates from the 1830s, but its origins are traceable from the Catholic insurrection of 1641 through the Whiteboys and the Ribbonmen of the eighteenth and nineteenth centuries. A formidable AOH personality was Joe Devlin, the Belfast Nationalist MP who was active in the early years of this century and became national president. In the 1960s, the national vice-president, the late Gerry Lennon, of Armagh, a Nationalist Senator, had talks with the then leader of the Orange

Order, Sir George Clark, about a possible political settlement. The discussions, known as the 'Orange–Green talks' were unsuccessful. The Order has declined somewhat in recent years, a trend evidently linked with the eclipse of the Nationalist Party. It still has a substantial membership, however, and the AOH hall remains a familiar landmark in many parts of rural Ulster. It is organised in divisions, and its public parades, with bands, banners and sashes superficially resemble those of the Orange Order. They are held on 15 Aug. (the Feast of the Assumption) and sometimes on St Patrick's Day. The leadership decided not to hold any parades between 1971 and 1974 because of the violence. Its national vice-president, Hugh News, of Lurgan, defined its aims in 1976 as 'faith, unity and true Christian charity'. In 1978, he criticised the American AOH which, he said, had no connection with the Irish organisation. His statement followed claims that the AOH in the US had been discouraging investment in NI, a claim denied by spokesmen for the US organisation.

ANDERSON, ALBERT WESLEY. Unionist MP for Londonderry at Stormont, 1968–72. b. 23 July 1907. Mayor of Londonderry, 1963–8. Senior Parliamentary Secretary, Home Affairs, 1971–2.

ANDERSONSTOWN. The district on the western fringe of West Belfast which has been one of the main strongholds of the IRA, and where the Peace People movement was born in 1976. There is a strong republican tradition, so that it became an area of intense confrontation between the PIRA and the security forces, particularly after the introduction of internment. The area has been heavily scarred by the violence, and troops and police have operated from strongly fortified stations. The former RUC station has become a joint police and army centre, and is protected by high walls, steel plates and special netting. There is heavy unemployment, but the government has set up several factories at Kennedy Way in an effort to provide local employment. The local SDLP Convention member, Vincent McCloskey, wrote in May 1976: 'More than any other area, Andersonstown has suffered all the horrors of this undeclared civil war. There is not a street that has not suffered its own private tragedies. There is not a child that cannot recognise the sound of gunfire or the type of weapon being used. The people have been battered from all sides with the propaganda of the various forces but have managed in spite of all to maintain their civilised standards of behaviour.' Loyalists have tended to see it as the heartland of republicanism. Before the launching of the Peace People, after the incident in which three young children died, there were several moves by women in the area to organise peace meetings, and on some occasions they clashed with women supporting the Provisionals. In the 1981 hunger strike, it was the venue of many rallies in support of the anti-H-Block cause, and there were emotional scenes as the funerals of hunger strikers paused on the way to Milltown cemetery.

ANDREWS, SIR JOHN LAW-SON ORMROD. Minister and Leader, NI Senate, 1964–72, in which capacity he frequently acted as Deputy Prime Minister, b. Comber, Co. Down, 15 July 1903, son of second Prime Minister of NI, John Miller Andrews. Unionist MP for Mid-Down, 1953–64, holding office successively as Minister of Health and Local Government, Minister of Commerce and Minister of Finance, before being elected to Senate. Took part in Downing Street talks immediately prior to direct rule, 1972.

ANNON, WILLIAM, DUP Convention member for N. Belfast, 1975–6. b. 1912. Before his adoption as DUP candidate for the Convention, he was chairman of the OUP's Sydenham (Belfast) branch and returned to the OUP in 1983. Belfast City Council, 1977–.

APPRENTICE BOYS OF DERRY. One of the Protestant 'Loyal Orders', which is based on the 'no surrender' action of the thirteen apprentice boys in slamming the gates of Londonderry on the army of King James II at the start of the siege of 1689. Its main parade in the city is held on 12 August to celebrate the relief of the city and the end of the siege, and usually some 10,000 to 12,000 members take part, drawn from all parts of the province and sometimes accompanied by members from Great Britain and overseas. There is a lesser demonstration on 18 December to mark the shutting of the gates. On that occasion, an effigy of Colonel Lundy, an officer who tried to negotiate the surrender of the city at the start of the siege, is burned. This is the origin of the term, 'Lundy', frequently used by extreme loyalists to describe someone whom they regard as having betrayed their cause. Members of the APD can be initiated only within the city walls, and such ceremonies are held in August and December. There were serious riots in the city after the August march in 1969, and parades were banned in 1970 and 1971. In 1972, the APD's general committee decided to call off its parade when it was limited to the Waterside area – that is, the predominantly Protestant east side of the River Foyle. But many Apprentice Boys rallied on the Waterside, and were addressed by one of their number, the Rev. Ian Paisley. The then NI Prime Minister, Brian Faulkner, was expelled from the Order in 1971 for being associated with the parades' ban. Members of the organisation were permitted to parade again within the old walled city in 1975. But they were not allowed to walk round the walls, which had been part of their traditional route because these overlook the mainly Catholic Bogside.

ARDILL, ROBERT AUSTIN. Off. U. Whip in Assembly, 1974, and in Constitutional Convention, 1975–6. b. 1917. As MP for Carrick (1965–9) and Secretary of the '66 Committee (Unionist backbench committee), he was opposed to leadership of Terence O'Neill. He was chairman of the Ulster

NORTHERN IRELAND – A POLITICAL DIRECTORY, 1968–83

Loyalist Association in 1971 and deputy leader of the Vanguard movement in 1972. Before Harry West took over as leader of the OUP in 1974, he was Whip of the Unionist Assembly members who did not accept Brian Faulkner as leader. In the Convention, he was one of the UUUC team of nego-tiatiors with the SDLP, and after the Convention was dissolved he and the Rev. Martin Smyth had private talks with John Hume and Paddy Devlin of the SDLP. The talks did not lead to any agree-ment. In 1977–8, he was one of the party delegation who met the Secretary of State, Roy Mason, and his officials about the possi-bility of some form of interim devolution. Joint Hon. Sec. of Ulster Unionist Council, 1978. He has been associated with the strongly devolutionist wing of the OUP. In 1982, sought unsuccess-fully a party nomination in S. Antrim in the Assembly election.

ARDOYNE. A mainly Catholic area of N. Belfast, adjoining the upper Crumlin Road. There was serious rioting in the district in August 1969, and there has been considerable burning of homes, many explosions, and a variety of violent incidents in the area over the years. In the early 1970s the PIRA was extremely active in the district. In August 1969, there were clashes between local people and the RUC, and with Protes-tants from the nearby Shankill area. Some of the initial violence in August 1969 was attributed by the Scarman tribunal to efforts to tie up the RUC, and so prevent police reinforcements being sent to the Bogside in Derry. The Scarman report mentioned that stones, petrol bombs, and explo-sive devices made from copper tubing had been used in assaults on the police. Scarman also held that Protestants had been responsible for the burning of several Catholic owned pubs in the area on 15 August and for the burning of about twenty houses in Brookfield Street which had been occupied by Catholics before the riots. On the night of 15–16 August, twenty-six civilians suf-fered gunshot injuries and one man was killed. The army moved into the area on 16 August. The Scarman report rejected sugges-tions that the Ardoyne monastery had been used as an arsenal and that priests had been handing out bullets. Referring to the RUC's use of the Browning machine gun, Scarman said these incidents illustrated the unsuitability of this weapon for riot control, and that it was a merciful chance that there was no fatal casualty from Brown-ing fire. In October, 1981, local city councillor Lawrence Ken-nedy, thirty-five, an Ind. Republi-can, was shot dead in a local social club, apparently by Loyalist gun-men. PIRA was active in the area during the 1981 hunger strike, and there were several shootings and riots. A report produced for the local Flax Trust in January, 1983, said support for PIRA and INLA was high in the area, which had been 'abused and abandoned by Government and industry alike'. The report added that male unemployment was over fifty-four per cent among the 8,000 resi-dents, with poverty rampant, twenty-eight per cent of families living in overcrowded conditions and thirty-five per cent of homes lacking basic amenities.

ARMAGH CITY. Ireland's ecclesiastical capital, which was mentioned as a possible venue for a Council of Ireland if it had come into being after the 1973 Sunningdale agreement. With fairly well-defined Protestant and Catholic areas, it has always had a reputation for intense political rivalries. One of the major incidents involving loyalists and civil rights supporters occurred here on 30 November 1968. The police had given permission to the civil rights supporters to have a march through the city centre, but at 2 a.m. the Rev. Ian Paisley and his supporters began to arrive in the central area. By the time the civil rights march had moved off from the fringes of the town, the loyalists had effectively occupied the key junction. Many of them carried walking sticks and clubs, and although they were warned by the police that it was an illegal assembly, they were able to prevent the civil rights march getting into the main thoroughfare. Later, Mr Paisley and one of his supporters, Major Ronald Bunting, were each sentenced to three months' imprisonment for illegal assembly, but they were released early as part of an amnesty. Armagh's main shopping streets have suffered heavily during the PIRA bombing campaign, and there have been many murders in the area, which has become known, together with adjoining areas of Co. Tyrone, as the 'murder triangle'. In December 1972 an Armagh Unionist councillor and member of the Policy Authority,

William Johnston, was kidnapped and murdered. In 1982, Cardinal O'Fiaich and Church of Ireland Archbishop John Armstrong co-operated in promoting a one-day 'at home' festival aimed at improving inter-community relations. Soon afterwards, the shooting dead by the RUC of two local INLA members who had driven through a checkpoint provoked angry controversy.

ARMSTRONG, MICHAEL. Off. U. Convention member for Armagh, 1975–6. b. France, 1924. Fatally injured in car accident, 1982. LL.B. (Cantab.), barrister-at-law. With a strong military background (Captain in Irish Guards 1939–45, and for a time in Allied military government in Germany; district commandant in USC at disbandment; commander, Armagh company UDR 1970–4) he had been Off. U. spokesman on security and hon. sec. of the Ulster Unionist Council.

ARMY. See Security Section (p. 309).

ASSEMBLY. See Election and Government Sections (pp. 286 and 300).

ASSOCIATION FOR LEGAL JUSTICE. A body set up in 1971, it has been active in investigating allegations of ill-treatment against the security forces and in monitoring the reform programme. In 1971, it published a booklet, *Know Your Legal Rights*, setting out procedures to be adopted by persons if they were arrested, subjected to search, or approached to give evidence. It campaigned for an end to political appointments to the judiciary. It strongly opposed internment, and in 1971 co-operated with NICRA in protesting that detainees had been ill-treated by the security forces. In 1974, it opposed the system of extra-territorial courts in NI and the Republic, and in a report in 1974 accused NI courts of showing an anti-Catholic bias in terms of longer sentences for Catholics. In 1974, it also complained that the RUC was using torture to extract confessions of IRA membership. In 1982, it complained that shootings by the security force of suspected terrorists represented 'summary executions', and urged investigations by the European Commission of Human Rights.

ATKINS CONFERENCE. See CONSTITUTIONAL CONFERENCE.

ATKINS, SIR HUMPHREY EDWARD. Secretary of State for NI, May 1979–Sept 1981. b. 12 August 1922. After service in Royal Navy, 1940–8, he developed an interest in politics, and became Conservative MP for Merton and Morden (1955–70) and Spelthorne (1970–). He was Parliamentary Private Secretary to Civil Lord of the Admiralty, 1959–62, and Honorary Secretary of the Conservative Defence Committee, 1965–7. From 1967 to 1979 he served either as an opposition or government Whip, and was government Chief Whip, 1973–4. He was the third former Conservative Chief Whip to become NI Secretary of State, the others being William Whitelaw and Francis Pym. His appointment as NI Secretary was one of the few surprises in Mrs Thatcher's first Cabinet. It became necessary because of the assassination of the Party's NI spokesman, Airey Neave. Like Mr Neave, he was a very close adviser of the new Prime Minister. The upsurge of PIRA violence in August, 1979, led to his increasing RUC strength by 1,000. His most severe test came with the Republican hunger strikes in 1980 and 1981 – the latter resulting in the deaths of ten prisoners, including Bobby Sands, MP. He reflected Mrs Thatcher's uncompromising opposition to the protest, which was still under way when he left office. He tried two unsuccessful political initiatives. The first was a Constitutional Conference at Stormont, January-March, 1980, attended by the DUP, SDLP and Alliance. The Official Unionists boycotted it (see separate entry). And in 1981 he proposed a fifty-member Advisory Council which would consist of nominated members. On leaving NI he became Deputy Foreign Secretary, but he resigned along with the Foreign Secretary at the start of the Falklands crisis in 1982. He was knighted in 1983.

B

BABINGTON, ROBERT JOHN. Unionist MP for North Down, 1969–72. b. Dublin, 9 April 1920. QC. County Court Judge, 1974–. In his 1969 election address, he called for one man, one vote, and in 1970 urged the expulsion from the Unionist Party of those who refused to support government policy. He frequently warned against the dangers of UDI for Northern Ireland, and advised Unionists not to get involved in violence. He complained in 1972 that the IRA ceasefire had resulted in gunmen finding NI a safer haven than the Republic. In 1973, he resigned from the Orange Order 'for personal reasons'. He was a firm backer of Brian Faulkner as Prime Minister, and was closely associated with him in the period immediately after direct rule.

BAILIE, ROBIN JOHN. Minister of Commerce, NI, 1971–2. b. 6 March 1937. Unionist MP for Newtownabbey, 1969–72. LL.B. (QUB). Solicitor, NI Supreme Court, 1961. On the liberal wing of the Unionist Party, he gave up active politics and resigned from Brian Faulkner's 'shadow cabinet' soon after direct rule in 1972. As a Minister of Commerce he had been interested in the possibilities offered to NI by EEC membership, and was among the earliest to urge a cross-border development plan for the North-West, with Common Market support. In 1973, he joined the Alliance Party for a brief period.

BAIRD, ERNEST AUSTIN. Leader of the UUUP, 1977–. b. Ballycampsie, Co. Donegal, 1930. A founder and the first chairman of the Vanguard Movement in 1972, he was closely associated with William Craig until 1976, when, as deputy leader of the VUPP, he disagreed with Craig's advocacy of voluntary coalition with the SDLP, and established the UUUM, dedicated to promoting Unionist unity. In this it failed, and became the UUUP to fight the local government elections in 1977. He polled surprisingly strongly in the Assembly elections in Fermanagh–S. Tyrone in 1973, securing more first-preference votes than either Harry West, who was shortly to become Unionist leader, or John D. Taylor, who had been MP for S. Tyrone in the former Stormont parliament. He was also returned there in the Convention election, but this time he lagged behind Mr West. He was extremely active in the UWC strike in 1974, and was associated with the Rev. Ian Paisley in the Action Council strike in May 1977, which secured much less support. Unsuccessfully contested Fermanagh–S. Tyrone in 1979 Westminster election, and the 1982 Assembly election.

BALLYKELLY BOMBING. See LONDONDERRY.

BALLYMURPHY. The W. Belfast Catholic housing estate which was the centre of serious rioting in 1971 and 1972. In Jan. 1971, trouble on a serious scale continued for five consecutive nights and the Prime Minister, Major Chichester-Clark, declared that the army would not be forced out of its main base there, the Henry Taggard Memorial Hall, by either physical or political pressure. The hall had been repeatedly attacked by crowds with stones and bottles. The security forces claimed that the rioting had been orchestrated by the IRA, and Dr William Philbin, the Catholic bishop, said in Ballymurphy that members of secret organisations had no obligation to obey immoral orders. A group of Ballymurphy women demonstrated at the Bishop's home in protest against the sermon. In Oct. 1971, an arms haul by the security forces included seven Thompson sub-machine guns and a number of rifles and revolvers. Mother Theresa of Calcutta set up a mission in Ballymurphy in late 1971 and stayed there until 1972.

BARNHILL, SENATOR JACK.

Off. U. member of the NI Senate, 1958–71, who was assassinated in his home at Brickfield, near Strabane, Co. Tyrone on 12 December 1971. b. 1904. He was the first politician to be assassinated in the violence which began in 1969, and his death was claimed by the OIRA. They claimed that they had not intended to kill him, but only to destroy his home 'in reprisal for the destruction of working-class homes by the British army'. The IRA said they had shot him during a struggle. The NI Prime Minister, Brian Faulkner, blamed an IRA gang which, he said, had been able to operate from a safe haven in nearby Donegal in the Republic, and he said this gang might have killed five people in the Strabane area in the previous three months. Jack Barnhill was remembered by his fellow Senators as a speaker who laced his Senate speeches with poetic quotations.

BARR, GLEN.

Vanguard Unionist Assembly (1973–4) and Convention (1975–6) member for Londonderry. b. Londonderry, 1932. He was in the LAW and the UDA in 1971, and in 1974 he had the key post of chairman of the Co-ordinating Committee which ran the loyalist strike. The committee included loyalist politicians, the UWC and representatives of Protestant paramilitary groups. During the strike, he commented that it would have been perfectly possible to set up a provisional government. After the stoppage, he led paramilitary spokesmen in talks with the Secretary of State, Merlyn Rees. In October 1974 he was suspended from the UUUC for three months for supporting the VPP candidate in W. Belfast in the Westminster election. In November 1974, as political adviser to the UDA, he took a UDA deputation to Libya for talks with the Libyan government. A Provisional Sinn Féin delegation was there at the same time and there was apparently some contact between them, although both sides denied that there had been any negotiations. Mr Barr said on his return that the possibility of Libyan financial aid to an independent Ulster, and the prospect of Libyan orders for Ulster firms, had been discussed.

(Mr Barr was involved later in negotiations for the sale of NI beef to Libya.) A UDA spokesman said they had been trying to stop Libyan aid for the IRA. The VUPP Executive at first decided to expel Glen Barr over the visit, but later changed his mind, and in the end took no action. In the Convention, he stood by William Craig when VUPP split over the idea of a voluntary coalition, and he was joint leader of the VUPP until February 1978, when it reverted to the status of the Vanguard movement, and ceased to be a political party. He did not follow Mr Craig into the OUP, but took up an independent stance. Involved with UDA again in 1978–9 when he took part in a body known as New Ulster Political Research Group, which produced a plan for an independent NI, and he visited the USA in 1979 with UDA leaders for talks in Washington with leading politicians. In June, 1981, he withdrew from politics when the UDA set up the Ulster Loyalist Democratic Party.

BARRY, PETER. Foreign Minister of Irish Republic, 1982–. b. Cork, August, 1928. He was deputy leader of Fine Gael when he took over as Foreign Minister, and shared responsibility with the Taoiseach, Dr Fitzgerald, for NI matters. Formerly served as Transport Minister and Education Minister. TD, 1969–. Alderman, Cork City Council, 1967–73 (Lord Mayor, 1970–1). In January 1983, he visited NI for talks with local political parties. In March, 1983, he declared that a long-term British presence in Ireland was a barrier to peace.

BAXTER, JOHN LAWSON. Head of the Office of Information Service in NI Executive, 1974. b. Coleraine, Co. Derry, 1940. BA (TCD) LL.M. (Tulane University, New Orleans); qualified as solicitor, 1964 (QUB). He was chairman of N. Antrim Unionist Association, and member of committee which had drawn up Unionist election manifesto, when he was returned from N. Antrim to Assembly in 1973. Strong supporter of Brian Faulkner, and during the lifetime of the Executive pressed for energetic presentation of the administration's case.

BEATTIE, REV. WILLIAM JOHN. DUP Assembly member for S. Antrim, 1982–. b. 1942. Deputy leader of DUP, 1971–80; Party secretary, 1980–3. Minister, Dunmurry Free Presbyterian Church. In April 1970, as a Protestant Unionist, he gained the S. Antrim seat at Stormont from the OUP by a majority of 958 in a by-election. He headed the poll in S. Antrim in the Assembly election, 1973, with 10,126 first-preference votes. Deputy Chief Whip of the United Unionists in Assembly, 1973–4. Re-elected in S. Antrim in Convention election, 1975, and one of UUUC negotiators in talks with the SDLP in the Convention. Lisburn District Council, 1977–. In 1982, INLA placed a bomb at his home near Lisburn, but it was discovered in time and defused.

BEGGS, JOHN ROBERT (ROY). Off. U. Assembly MP for

E. Antrim, 1983–. Assembly member for N. Antrim 1982–. Larne Council, 1973–. Mayor of Larne, 1977–. Originally DUP, but joined OUP in 1982 after being suspended by the DUP for visiting the council at Dun Laoghaire in the Irish Republic in 1981 in defence of DUP policy. First chairman of Assembly's economic development committee, 1983–.

BELFAST. See ANDERSONSTOWN, ARDOYNE, BALLYMURPHY, FORUM HOTEL, FALLS ROAD, MARKETS, NEW LODGE ROAD, PEACE LINE, SANDY ROW, SHANKILL ROAD, SHORT STRAND, STORMONT, TIGER BAY, POPULATION, and RELIGION.

BELL, WILLIAM BRADSHAW. Off. U. Assembly member for S. Antrim, 1982–. b. Belfast, 1935. Served as N. Belfast Convention member, 1975–6. Chairman, N. Belfast Unionist Association, 1973–5. Lord Mayor of Belfast, 1979.

BELL, SIR WILLIAM EWART. Head of the NI Civil Service, 1979–. b. 13 November 1924. M.A. (Oxford). Joined NI Civil Service, 1948. Assistant Secretary, Commerce, 1963–70; Deputy Secretary, 1970–3. Permanent Secretary, 1973–6. Permanent Secretary, Finance, 1976–9. Former Irish rugby international.

BELSTEAD, LORD (JOHN JULIAN GANZONI). Parliamentary Under-Secretary, NI Office, 1973–4. b. 30 September 1932. MA (Oxon.) At the NI Office, he was House of Lords spokesman, and maintained interest in local legislation as Conservative front bencher, 1974–9. Home Office Under-Secretary, 1979–.

BENN, JOHN NEWTON. NI Ombudsman, 1972. Commissioner of Complaints, 1968. b. Burnley, Lancs., 16 July 1908. Before becoming Ombudsman (Parliamentary Commissioner dealing with grievances about administration channelled through MPs) he was Permanent Secretary, Ministry of Education.

BENNETT REPORT. The report produced by a three-man committee, headed by Judge Harry Bennett QC, an English Crown Court Judge, on the interrogation procedures of the RUC, and the operation of the machinery for dealing with complaints. The committee was set up by NI Secretary of State Roy Mason in June 1978, in response to many demands for an official inquiry after an Amnesty International team had inquired into seventy-eight complaints of ill-treatment by persons who had been held at the Castlereagh interrogation centre in Belfast and other centres. The committee, which reported in 1979, went outside its terms of reference to mention that there had been cases where medical evidence had been produced concerning injuries sustained while in police custody which were not self-inflicted. Two of the main recommendations of the committee – that closed-circuit TV should be installed in interview rooms and that terrorist suspects should have access to a solicitor after forty-eight hours – were accepted by the Labour Government and virtually all the remaining forty recommendations were endorsed by the Conservative government. But one government Minister stressed in parliament in May 1979 that only fifteen cases had fallen into the category of injuries sustained while in police custody, and not self-inflicted, out of a total of some 3,000 people who were detained in 1977–8. The Bennett committee was requested by the government to make medical evidence in these cases available to the Director of Public Prosecutions so that he could decide whether any prosecutions should be brought against members of the RUC. The publication of the Bennett report was accompanied by angry controversy about the extent of ill-treatment and two doctors involved at the interrogation centres voiced their concern about ill-treatment.

BIAGGI, MARIO. Democratic Congressman for New York and chairman of the ad hoc Congressional Committee on Irish affairs, 1977–. b. New York, 26 October 1917. LL.B. (New York Law School). Former New York detective. Biaggi has visited Ireland on several occasions. He was in Newry for the protest march held after 'Bloody Sunday' in 1972. In 1978, he was accused by the Taoiseach of the Republic, Jack Lynch, of associating with men of violence when he visited Ireland at the request of the US-based Irish National Caucus. Mr Lynch also complained that the views of the Republic's government had been seriously misrepresented in the US. Biaggi's Congressional Committee announced plans in early 1978 for a peace conference on NI to be held in Washington DC, but the idea was opposed by Senator Kennedy and several other leading Irish-Americans.

BIGGS-DAVISON, SIR JOHN. Conservative front bench spokesman on NI, 1976–9 and chairman of party's NI committee, 1979–. b. 7 June 1918. MA (Oxford). MP for Epping Forest, 1974–; Chigwell, 1955–74. Has had lengthy association with Ulster Unionists, and has spoken frequently at party meetings. He has warned repeatedly of an 'Irish Cuba' on Britain's doorstep. In January 1973 he wrote in *Belfast Newsletter:* 'Civil rights have been used as a front by the fomentors of civil war; social reform as a stepping stone to social revolution. What civil rights are there in Cuba?' In 1980 he suggested loose linkage of UK, Republic of Ireland, Isle of Man and Channel Islands as Islands of North Atlantic. (IONA). Strongly opposed Prior devolution plan in 1982.

BLACK, ALISTAIR. Vanguard Unionist (later UUUM) Convention member for Armagh, 1975–6. b. Lanarkshire, Scotland, 1913. MA Dip.Ed (QUB). Headmaster at Lurgan, Co. Armagh. Chairman of Co. Armagh Committee of UWC, 1974. One of the Vanguard Convention members who refused to support William Craig's idea of voluntary coalition, he became a member of UUUM, later the UUUP, led by Ernest Baird. Stood unsuccessfully as

UUUP candidate in Armagh in the 1982 Assembly election.

BLACK, SIR HAROLD. Last Secretary to NI Cabinet before direct rule. b. 9 April 1914. As Cabinet Secretary, 1965–72, he accompanied three Prime Ministers (O'Neill, Chichester-Clark and Faulkner) to London for talks with British Ministers. He had a key role in reform programme after James Callaghan's October 1969 visit, since he was on three-man steering committee which co-ordinated the work of committees on detailed changes. After direct rule, he was Deputy Secretary in NI Office until his retirement in 1974.

BLACKBURN, RONALD HENRY ALBERT. Clerk of the NI parliament, 1971–2, of Assembly (1973–4) and of Constitutional Convention, 1975–6. b. 9 February 1924. LL.B. (University of London). Served Foreign Office, 1943–6; Stormont Parliamentary staff, 1946.

BLANEY, NEIL. MEP for Connaught–Ulster, 1979–. Independent Fianna Fail TD for Donegal, 1977–. Earlier, TD for North-East Donegal, 1948–77. b. 1922. Neil Blaney succeeded his father, an old IRA man, in North-East Donegal, and has made it a strong power base. With his republican background and his closeness to events in NI, he has regarded himself as a voice of NI nationalism in the Republic. He survived politically his expulsion from the Fianna Fail party in 1970, following his sacking by the Taoiseach, Jack Lynch. Soon after his dismissal from the post of Minister for Agriculture, he was accused of conspiring to import arms illegally into the Republic. But a district court found that he had no case to answer. In the Dail in 1972, he attacked new anti-terrorist legislation and complained that the PIRA was being smeared, although it had arisen from the needs of the time from local defence committees in NI. He has frequently demanded British withdrawal from NI, and has urged that cross-border co-operation should be withheld until this is achieved. Despite his expulsion from Fianna Fail, he topped the poll in North-East Donegal in 1973, and in 1976 a supporter, Paddy Keaveney, gained a Donegal seat from Fianna Fail in a by-election, although he lost it again in the 1977 general election. In earlier years, Blaney was one of the most influential figures in Fianna Fail. He was chairman of the Executive from 1949 to 1951 and joint treasurer from 1968 to 1970. He was Minister for Posts and Telegraphs and Minister for Local Government before becoming Minister of Agriculture. His capacity for local political organisation in Donegal has led to his supporters being dubbed the 'Donegal Mafia' and his appeal in the North West was confirmed when he easily won a seat in the first directly elected European parliament. In Strasbourg he was appointed chairman of a group of independent MEPs. In the Fermanagh–S. Tyrone by-elections in 1981, he supported hunger-striker Bobby Sands, and his successor, Owen Carron.

BLEAKES, WILLIAM GEORGE. Off. U. Assembly member for N. Down, 1982–. b. 1934. Lisburn Council, 1977–. Chairman, Official Unionist Councillors' Association, 1978–. Hon. Sec., N. Down Unionist Association and member of party executive.

BLEAKLEY, DAVID. Minister of Community Relations, April–October 1971. b. 1926. The only NILP member to serve in a NI government, he was appointed to the Community Relations post by Brian Faulkner. He was not then an MP, so his tenure of office was limited to six months. Best-known NILP personality. MP for Victoria, Belfast, 1958–65, and served as chairman of Stormont Public Accounts Committee. Elected in E. Belfast to Assembly and Convention, in both of which he was the only representative of his party. He unsuccessfully contested E. Belfast in the Westminster elections, February and October 1974, and he was also unsuccessful in the 1979 European election, in which he stood as a United Community candidate. Secretary, Irish Council of Churches, 1979–. Chairman, Standing Commission on Human Rights, 1981–.

BLEASE, LORD (OF CRO-MAC). Created Labour life peer, 1978. Opposition spokesman on NI in House of Lords and Labour Whip, 1979–82. b. Cromac, Belfast, 1914. Formerly William (better known as Billy) Blease, he was officer of the NI Committee of the Irish Congress of Trade Unions, 1959–75. He had a key role in securing recognition of ICTU by Unionist government for the first time under Premier O'Neill. In 1974, he faced an arduous task when ICTU was unable to counter the loyalist strike aimed at bringing down the power-sharing Executive. Associated over many years with NILP, and party candidate in four elections in Belfast. NI member, Independent Broadcasting Authority, 1975–9.

'BLOODY FRIDAY'. Friday, 21 July 1972, when PIRA set off twenty-six explosions in Belfast, which killed eleven people and injured 130. Seven people were killed at the Oxford Street bus station, which had been crowded at the time, and four at a shopping centre on the Cavehill Road. Two soldiers were among the dead. Since this was the most devastating day of violence in Belfast up to that time, and many of the injured suffered serious mutilation, the impact on public opinion was enormous, and many observers regarded it as the point at which PIRA had put itself outside the pale of political negotiation.

'BLOODY SUNDAY'. The incident in Londonderry's Bogside on 30 January 1972, in which thirteen people were shot dead by soldiers of the First Parachute Regiment. The shootings occurred on the occasion of an illegal march organised by the Derry Civil Rights Association, and they gave rise to angry controversy. They were denounced by civil rights leaders as 'another Sharpeville'; the Republic's Prime Minister, Mr Lynch, said it was 'an unwarranted attack on unarmed civilians'; the British Embassy in Dublin was burned down by demonstrators, and in the Commons, Bernadette Devlin MP, struck the Home Secretary, Mr Maudling. The Prime Minister, Mr Heath, announced an inquiry into the shootings by the Lord Chief Justice of England, Lord Widgery. That report did not appear until April 1972, but by then the Stormont parliament had been suspended: and the convulsion caused by the affair was regarded as the decisive factor in the decision to impose direct rule from Westminster. Lord Widgery's verdict was a complex one. He held that there would have been no deaths if there had not been an illegal march, which had created 'a highly dangerous situation'. But he also said that it might well be that if the army had maintained its low-key attitude, and had not launched a large-scale operation to arrest hooligans, the day might have passed off without serious incident. Lord Widgery also found that the soldiers had been fired on first, and he said there was no reason to suppose that they would have opened fire otherwise. None of the dead or wounded had been proven to have been shot while handling a firearm or bomb. The verdict was sharply attacked by Derry Catholics, and Mr Lynch said that it showed the need for an international examination of the activities of the British army. Unionist MP Lawrence Orr said it 'exploded some of the myths surrounding the so-called Bloody Sunday'.

BLOOMFIELD, KENNETH PERCY. Permanent Secretary of Department of Economic Development, 1982–. Earlier Permanent Secretary of Commerce (1981–2). Environment (1976–81) and Housing and Local Government (1975–6). b. 15 April, 1931. MA (Oxon.) As Deputy Secretary to the NI Cabinet, 1963–72, he was involved in many of the crucial negotiations linked with the reform programme and the period prior to the abolition of the old Stormont Parliament. Under-Secretary, NI Office, 1972–3, and Permanent Secretary to the power-sharing Executive, January–May, 1974.

BOAL, DESMOND. Unionist MP for Shankill, 1960–71; DUP MP, 1971–2. b. Londonderry, 1929. LL.B. (TCD). One of NI's leading barristers (QC, 1973), he is also one of its most intriguing political figures. As a Unionist MP, he was frequently at odds with the party leadership. He was deprived of the party whip for criticism of Lord Brookeborough as Prime Minister; he was prominent in the backbench revolt against Terence O'Neill as Premier, largely because of his decision to invite Sean Lemass, Taoiseach of the Irish Republic, to Stormont, for unannounced talks; and he was highly critical of the law-and-order policies of the Chichester-Clark and Faulkner governments. In 1966, he lost his post as counsel to the Attorney-General after he had defended the right of Free Presbyterians to protest at the General Assembly of the Irish Presbyterian Church. In 1971, he resigned from the Unionist Party after describing the tripartite talks between Brian Faulkner, Jack Lynch and Edward Heath as 'adding a new dimension of dishonesty' to Unionist politics. Soon afterwards he joined the Rev. Ian Paisley in launching the DUP, of which he became the first chairman. He resigned his Shankill seat immediately following the introduction of direct rule in March 1972, as a protest against Westminster's move. In 1974, after he had given up the chairmanship of DUP, he announced support for a federal scheme in Ireland. He wanted an Irish federal parliament holding the powers reserved to Westminster under the 1920 Act, and the restoration of the Stormont parliament with its old powers. The idea attracted some interest in Dublin, but was generally rejected by Unionists. Paisley joined in the denunciation. In 1977, Boal was involved with Sean MacBride in a chain of contacts between PIRA and loyalist paramilitaries aimed at securing a PIRA ceasefire. Boal's hobby is lone travel in faraway places like China, the Himalayas, and Borneo.

BOGSIDE. See LONDONDERRY.

BOLAND, KEVIN. The Minister for Local Government in the Irish Republic, who resigned from the Lynch government as a protest against the sacking in 1970 of two Ministers – Charles Haughey and Neil Blaney – on the grounds that they had been implicated in the illegal importation of arms intended for NI. b. 1917. Mr Boland claimed later that he had originally offered his resignation in August 1969, when, he said, 'B' Specials in Belfast had led loyalist attacks on Catholic areas, but he had been persuaded by President de Valera to stay in office. After his split with Fianna Fail he set up Aontacht Eireann (the Republican Unity Party), and claimed that the major parties in the Republic had abandoned their republicanism. But he failed in a series of efforts to return to the Dail, and decided to quit active politics in 1976, when he got just over 1,000 votes in a Dublin by-election. In 1974, he sought to have the Sunningdale agreements, reached by the British and Irish governments, declared unconstitutional. This was the agreement which paved the way for the power-sharing Executive in NI. The paragraph to which he took exception read: 'The Irish government fully accepted and solemnly declared that there could be no change in the status of Northern Ireland until a majority of the people of Northern Ireland desired a change in that status'. But in the High Court, Mr Justice Murnaghan held against Mr Boland. He said that this paragraph did not acknowledge that Northern Ireland was part of the United Kingdom, that it was no more than a statement of policy and that the Court should not usurp the functions of the Dail. Mr Boland's appeal to the Supreme Court was dismissed.

BORDER POLL. The constitutional referendum introduced by Westminster to establish the extent to which there is support for the British link and for a united Ireland. The poll replaced the guarantee of NI's position within the UK which resided in the former Stormont Commons and Senate. The poll, intended to be taken every ten years, was first held on 8 March 1973. Questions and votes in favour were as follows:

> *Do you want NI to remain part of the UK?* 591,820
>
> *Do you want NI to be joined with the Republic of Ireland, outside the UK?* 6,463

Other figures: total electorate, 1,030,000; percentage poll, 58.5; spoiled votes, 5,973 (1.0 per cent); percentage of poll for UK link, 97.8; percentage of poll for united Ireland, 1.2; percentage of non-voters, 41.5; percentage of total electorate supporting UK link, 58.0.

The SDLP and most republicans boycotted the poll. The Secretary of State, William Whitelaw MP, said the wishes of the majority would be respected. Unionists welcomed the outcome, and the SDLP said it proved nothing since everyone knew that there was a Protestant majority in NI.

The poll could have been repeated in March, 1983, but Secretary of State James Prior decided against it. He said it would not tell them anything since recent elections had shown that a large majority wanted to remain within the UK.

BRADFORD, REV. ROBERT JOHN. The first NI Westminster MP to be assassinated in the troubles, he had been Off. U. MP for S. Belfast for seven years when he was shot dead by a five-man PIRA squad at a community centre in Finaghy, in his constituency on Saturday, 14 November 1981. b. 1941. Formerly Methodist minister at Suffolk, close to the Lenadoon estate in W. Belfast, a flashpoint in the early period of the violence. Resigned from Methodist Church, 1974. In the 1973 Assembly election, he stood unsuccessfully as a Vanguard candidate in S. Antrim. Keen sportsman and played for House of Commons soccer team. He had been industry spokesman of the Off. U. Parliamentary Party and made a reputation at Westminster as campaigner against pornography. His murder was widely seen as an attempt by PIRA to provoke a loyalist backlash. Some of his friends also regarded it as a bid to silence an MP who had frequently accused Republican paramilitary groups of racketeering. PIRA itself accused him of being 'one of the key people responsible for winding up the loyalist paramilitary sectarian machine'. His death provoked a tense situation and calls by Unionists for better security generally, and a greater effort to protect politicians. Secretary of State James Prior got a hostile reception from a section of the congregation when he attended the funeral service.

BRADFORD, ROY HAMILTON. Unionist member for E. Belfast in Assembly, 1973–4, and head of Department of the Environment in Executive, 1974. b. Belfast, 7 July 1920. B.A. (TCD). Unionist MP for Victoria (Belfast), 1965–72. Parliamentary Secretary, Ministry of Education,

1967. Minister of Commerce, 1969–71; Minister of Development, 1971–2. Strongly criticised British government's initial handling of direct rule. He came into conflict with some Executive colleagues when he suggested that there should be some contact between the British government and the UWC during the loyalist strike in 1974. In 1975, he was an unsuccessful candidate in the Convention election in E. Belfast. He speaks French and German fluently and was active as a broadcaster for both BBC and ITV before entering politics. Has had a long-standing interest in EEC affairs, and chairman of the European Movement in NI, 1977–. In a novel, *The Last Ditch* (1981), he gave a barely fictionalised account of the inside struggle by NI Cabinet in 1972 against imposition of direct rule.

BRADLEY, PATRICK A. Chief electoral officer, NI, May, 1980–. b. 1935. BA (Open University). Has had varied career in civil service both in London and Belfast, including periods at Air Ministry and Local Enterprise Development Unit in NI, and in private industrial management (Chemstrand and Du Pont). Joined Electoral office in NI, 1974.

BRITISH-IRISH INTER-GOVERNMENTAL COUNCIL. The proposed structure for Anglo-Irish consultations which developed from the Thatcher-Haughey summit in Dublin in December, 1980. The idea was finally approved at the Downing Street meeting between Mrs Thatcher and Dr Fitzgerald in November, 1981, although many of the details remained unresolved. The British and Irish Government officials who drafted the plan envisaged a four-tier structure – ministerial, official, parliamentary, with an advisory committee. The Council may be said to have existed since November, 1981, at ministerial and official level, and the London meeting in January, 1982, between NI Secretary James Prior and Irish Foreign Minister James Dooge was the first ministerial get-together under the Council. Initially there seemed to be more enthusiasm for the parliamentary tier in Dublin than in London, where it seemed to be considered as simply a formalising of the regular contacts between interested MPs and TDs. There was the possibility, however, that members of a NI Assembly might be involved, although Unionists continued to say that they would have nothing to do with such a body. In July 1983, both Governments agreed to sponsor an 'Encounter Organisation' to organise high-level Anglo-Irish conferences.

BRITISH LABOUR PARTY. For much of its life, the British labour movement has been inclined to sympathise with Irish nationalism and to regard Ulster Unionism with some hostility. At its 1981 annual conference the party finally committed itself to campaign actively for a united Ireland by consent. Its Nationalist stance has been partly due to the influence of Irish-born people in Great Britain on the Labour and trade union movement, and partly a reaction to the long association between British Conservatism and Ulster Unionism, which was effectively ruptured when a Conservative government suspended the Stormont parliament in 1972. The NI civil rights campaign also attracted considerable support from Labour MPs, notably through the Campaign for Democracy in Ulster. On the left wing of the party, there has been some backing for the 'troops out' movement and general disengagement from NI. At the same time, many British Labour activists have regarded themselves as having more in common with the SDLP than with the NILP, despite the latter's loose association with the British Labour Party. Labour Ministers, however, notably since James Callaghan's visit to NI as Home Secretary in 1969, have sought to strike a fairly even balance between the NI parties, in keeping with the broad consensus policy between the major British parties. The Callaghan government, nonetheless, was accused by the SDLP and by some of its own supporters of adopting an uncharacteristic attitude when it backed extra MPs for NI in 1978 and 1979, since this was a longstanding demand of Unionists. Many critics of the government saw it as yielding to Unionist pressure and seeking to neutralise Unionist votes in the lobbies in the light of the government's minority position. Both the government and the Unionists denied any deal as such, but it became clear just before the fall of the Labour Government in April 1979 that it had been prepared to trade a major inquiry into NI fuel costs for Unionist support. Labour Ministers insisted that they could not oppose extra MPs for NI while retaining Scottish and Welsh representation in their devolution proposals. At its 1979 conference, the party rejected a motion passed originally in 1921 calling for withdrawal from Ireland. In 1982, the Labour Opposition gave general support to the new NI Assembly plan, while pressing for changes to enlarge the Irish dimension. At its 1982 annual conference, the party called for a ban on the use of plastic bullets throughout the UK, despite a warning from its NI spokesman, Don Concannon, that he could not have his hands tied on the issue. The 1983 election manifesto repeated the commitment to Irish unity by consent, and also called for repeal of the Prevention of Terrorism Act and reform of non-jury courts.

BRITISH LIBERAL PARTY. With its backing, historically, for Irish Home Rule, the party tended to give support to the civil rights campaign. Mr Jeremy Thorpe, as party leader, was highly critical of successive Unionist governments in speeches to the National Liberal Assembly and to conferences of the Ulster Liberal Party. In 1971, he suggested dual British and Irish nationality as an approach to the NI problem. On that occasion, the Liberal Assembly at first voted for the replacement of British troops by UN troops, but reversed the decision after an Ulster delegate had protested that this would be a capitulation to gunmen on both sides. The party urged, in particular, PR in Stormont elections and the setting up of a Council of Ireland. It also came out against internment without trial. In 1979, it suggested that NI should have a small advisory committee, elected by PR, as a first step towards the restoration of devolved government. In 1982, it gave general support to the 'rolling devolution' initiative.

BRITISH ULSTER DOMINION PARTY. A small organisation originally launched in 1975 by Professor Kennedy Lindsay under the title Ulster Dominion Group, which changed its name to BUDP in 1977. Professor Lindsay, who was elected to the Convention on the VUPP ticket, submitted a policy document to that body in September 1975, urging that NI should become a self-governing dominion, with the Queen as monarch and with a resident Governor-General. The idea didn't attract any support in the Convention, but it seemed to owe something to the scheme promoted in the 1950s and 1960s by the late William F. McCoy, QC, Unionist MP for S. Tyrone. Both Professor Lindsay and Mr McCoy argued that the suspension of the Stormont parliament in 1972 had demonstrated the weakness of any local devolution system. In 1978, the BUDP was involved in the talks launched by the Apprentice Boys organisation, aimed at securing loyalist unity. About the same time, the BUDP launched a case against the UK in the European Commission of Human Rights, alleging that the plan for PR in the European elections in NI was a breach of the European Human Rights Convention.

BROADHURST, BRIGADIER JOSEPH CALLENDER. Deputy Speaker, Assembly, 1973–4. b. 24 December 1906. UPNI member of Assembly for S. Down, 1973–4, unsuccessful candidate there for Constitutional Convention, 1975. A strong supporter of Brian Faulkner in Assembly. Had a distinguished military career in Middle East, and was Chief of Staff in Arab Legion. Expert on Middle East affairs.

BROCKWAY, LORD. Labour life peer, who has campaigned over many years for more discussion of NI affairs at Westminster. b. Calcutta, 1888. As Archibald Fenner Brockway, Labour MP (latterly for Eton and Slough, 1950–64), he was among the first Labour members to call for reforms in NI. He was involved with the Campaign for Democracy in Ulster, and in 1971 made the first of several unsuccessful attempts in the House of Lords to have a bill passed providing for a Bill of Rights in NI. The measure also suggested PR in elections. He opposed internment without trial, and spoke at one Tyrone anti-internment rally. He was at the centre of the campaign to have the Price sisters moved to Armagh prison, and visited them in prison in England and after they were moved to Armagh.

BROOKEBOROUGH, VISCOUNT. Active member of House of Lords as Conservative Peer and former spokesman of UPNI in the Upper House. b. 9 November, 1922, son of 1st Viscount Brookeborough, Prime

Minister of NI, 1943–63. Represented N. Down in Assembly (1973–4) and Convention (1975–6). As Captain John Warden Brooke, he was Unionist MP for Lisnaskea, Co. Fermanagh, 1968–72. Parliamentary Secretary, Ministry of Commerce, 1969. Additionally, 1970, Parliamentary Secretary, Prime Minister, with responsibility for Government information services. Government Chief Whip, 1971–2. Since the abolition of Stormont, he has been specially concerned with the development of Fermanagh tourism, and in the Lords has concentrated mainly on security issues, farming and EEC matters.

BROWN, WILLIAM. Off. U. Assembly member for S. Down, 1982–. Down Council, 1977–. Farmer; active in Unionism and Orange Order.

BROWNLOW, WILLIAM STEPHEN. Unionist and later UPNI Assembly member for N. Down, 1973–4. b. Winchester, England, 1921. Down County Council, 1969–73. Unsuccessfully contested N. Down Westminster seat, October 1974, and Convention election, 1975.

BRUGHA, RUAIRI. Fianna Fail spokesman on NI affairs, 1973–7. b. Dublin, 15 October 1917, the fourth son of veteran republican Cathal Brugha, who was killed in 1922. Senator, 1969–73 and 1977–81; TD, 1973–7. He has described, in T. P. Coogan's *The IRA*, how he joined the IRA at sixteen, was interned during the war, and how he came to realise that IRA activities had not helped to end parti-

tion. Frequently visited NI as Fianna Fail spokesman. In 1975 he called on Britain to disarm the loyalist paramilitaries. In 1976, he claimed that it was unrealistic to expect Ulster Unionists to abandon their 'not an inch' attitude while Britain was guaranteeing their position. In 1977, he suggested a federal Ireland, independent of Britain, with autonomy for NI. In the 1979 European election, he was an unsuccessful candidate in Dublin.

BRUSH, LT-COL. EDWARD JAMES AUGUSTUS HOWARD. Off. U. Convention member for S. Down, 1975–6. b. Fermoy, Co. Cork, 5 March 1901. Had distinguished army career. Wounded and taken prisoner of war during the British evacuation from France in 1940. Spent three years as POW. After the war he took up farming in Co. Down, was a leading figure in the Territorial Army and became Deputy Lord Lieutenant for Co. Down. He first attracted public attention in 1973, when it was disclosed that over the previous two years he had built up a loyalist paramilitary group known as Down Orange Welfare, which claimed a membership at that time of about 5,000. In the 1974 loyalist strike he was a member of the organising body – the UWC Co-ordinating Committee. In October 1974, he resigned as Deputy Lieutenant for Co. Down. Soon afterwards, there were suggestions that he might lead a new loyalist Home Guard, but this did not materialise. In the 1975 Convention, he represented S. Down, where he was president of the local Off. U Association.

'B' SPECIALS. See Security Section (pp. 304–5).

BUNTING, MAJOR RONALD. A leading loyalist activist in 1968–70. b. 1924. BA (Open University), M.Sc. (Manchester). An ex-regular army officer, he was involved as a mathematics lecturer in promoting local government reform. One of his earliest political activities was to help Gerry Fitt in a Belfast election. In 1968 and 1969, he was a leader of the Ulster Protestant Volunteers and the Loyal Citizens of Ulster, and associated with other loyalist groups opposed to the civil rights campaign. In November 1968, he joined the Rev. Ian Paisley in leading a Protestant rally in Armagh which blocked the path of a civil rights march. Like Mr Paisley, he was jailed for this activity, but he was released quickly under the amnesty called by Major Chichester-Clark when he took over as NI Prime Minister. Bunting was prominent in harassing the PD march from Belfast to Londonderry in January 1969. He broke with Paisley in 1970. His son, Ronald, who was associated with IRSP, was murdered in Belfast in October, 1980.

BURCHILL, JEREMY. Off. U. Assembly member for E. Belfast, 1982–. Representative of same constituency in Convention (1975–6). b. Dublin, 1951. Barrister-at-law. Hon. Secretary, Ulster Unionist Council, and former chairman of Young Unionist Council. Frequent speaker for the party in NI and Great Britain. Conservative Party Executive committee, 1973–4. Stood unsuc-cessfully against Rev. Ian Paisley in N. Antrim at 1979 Westminster election.

BURNS, JOSEPH. Parliamentary Secretary, NI government, 1971–2, and Whip, 1968–9. U. MP for N. Derry, 1960–72. b. Belfast, 19 July 1906 and joined USC at fourteen. In the early 1920s, he worked on farms in Canada and later as a stocks and bonds salesman. Studied at New York University, 1928. Strong traditional loyalist, and prominent in Orange, Black and Apprentice Boys' orders. Chairman of UUAC which organised the loyalist strike of May 1977.

BURNS, THOMAS EDWARD. DUP Assembly (1973–4) and Convention (1975–6) member for S. Belfast. b. Lurgan, Co. Armagh, 1927. Company director, whose firm developed a new building material – rubber concrete – in 1977.

BURNTOLLET. The point in Co. Derry at which the PD Belfast–Derry march was ambushed by militant Protestants on Saturday, 4 January 1969. The marchers, then numbering about seventy and accompanied by eighty police, were attacked by about 200 Protestants using sticks and stones. Several of the marchers were injured, and some were driven into the nearby river. The marchers included two prominent PD figures – Bernadette Devlin and Michael Farrell. The incident gave rise to criticism of the RUC by civil rights spokesmen, who said the police had failed to provide adequate protection and had not acted strongly enough against the Protestants involved. The police pointed out that the marchers had continued through Burntollet despite police warnings. In April 1969 the Minister of Home Affairs, Robert Porter, banned a proposed civil rights march from Burntollet to Altnagelvin after reports to the Minister that firearms might be used against the marchers.

BURROUGHS, RONALD ARTHUR. UK government representative in NI from March 1970 to April 1971. b. 4 June 1917. His period of office covered the growth of both PIRA and loyalist violence and anxious decisions about marches through sensitive areas. He was also concerned in the security arguments between London and Stormont which culminated in the resignation of Major Chichester-Clark as Prime Minister in March 1971. Died 1980.

BUTLER, ADAM COURTAULD. Minister-of-State, NI, Jan. 1981–. b. 11 October 1931 (son of Lord Butler – R. A. Butler). Pembroke College, Cambridge. Took charge initially of the Departments of Commerce and Manpower, and in September 1981 of Agriculture as well. With the recession and the image of the province cutting outside investment, he set up in 1982 a new Industrial Development Board to spearhead the drive for new industry. The establishment of the IDB coincided with the merger of the departments of Commerce and Manpower into the new Economic Development Department for which he took responsibility. In 1982, he negotiated with Republic's government on plan for bringing natural gas from Kinsale to Belfast. After the 1983 election, he became Deputy Secretary of State, and took charge of finance and economic development.

C

CAHILL, JOSEPH. A member of the Provisional Sinn Féin executive, who was among the founders of the PIRA. b. Belfast, 1920. A former carpenter and construction foreman, he was reprieved in 1942 after being sentenced to death with four other men for the killing of a policeman in Belfast. He was Belfast commander of the PIRA for a time before moving to Dublin in 1972. In 1973, he was sentenced to three years' penal servitude for illegal gun-running and IRA membership. In a Dublin court, Cahill and four other men were convicted of attempting to import arms and explosives which had been captured when the ship *Claudia* was intercepted in Waterford Bay on its way from Libya. When the judge described Cahill as the ring-leader in the operation, he replied from the dock, 'You do me an honour'. He was in ill-health when released from prison, and turned his attention to

Provisional Sinn Féin work. For a time, he handled aid for republican prisoners and their families, and later became general secretary of the party.

CALDWELL, TOM HADDEN. Ind. Unionist MP for Willowfield division of Belfast, 1969–72. b. Uganda, 30 June 1921. He won Willowfield as a pro-O'Neill candidate, and unsuccessfully contested S. Antrim in the 1970 Westminster general election. In 1971, he aroused controversy and criticism from Unionists when he met IRA leaders in the Republic in a bid 'to stop the killings'. In 1973, he joined the Alliance Party.

CALEDON. The Co. Tyrone village where the first protest in the 1968 civil rights campaign occurred. Austin Currie, then a Nationalist MP, took possession of a council house on 20 June which he claimed had been improperly allocated to a Protestant single girl by Dungannon Rural Council. He was ejected by police.

CALLAGHAN, JAMES. Labour Prime Minister, 1976–9. Responsible for NI affairs as Home Secretary, 1967–70. b. 27 March 1912. He first became interested in NI affairs in the 1950s, when, with other Labour MPs, he was concerned with studying ways of strengthening the local economy. His tenure at the Home Office saw the province move from being a departmental detail to one of the government's most pressing problems. As the civil rights movement gathered pace in the spring of 1968, he also came under pressure from Labour MPs in the Campaign for Democracy in Ulster. They not only demanded changes in line with those urged by the civil rights demonstrators, but argued that it was wrong for NI MPs to have equal voting rights in parliament when NI issues could not be debated effectively at Westminster. In August 1969, after the serious violence in Londonderry, Belfast and other towns, he was involved, with Prime Minister Harold Wilson, in the decision to send troops to NI to support the RUC. At the end of August 1969, he visited the province for talks with the government and a wide variety of interests. This was the major, visible intervention by the British government in Ulster affairs. Although Mr Callaghan sought to give the impression that electoral, housing and other reforms were being taken on Stormont's initiative, the Home Secretary was clearly the driving force. He returned for a second visit in October 1969, when the new-style RUC emerged, and the 'B' Specials were abolished, in line with the Hunt report. Although he had drawn up contingency plans for direct rule, it fell to the Heath government to implement these. In his book, *A House Divided*, which he wrote while in opposition, and which was published in 1973, he made a number of points. He asked why the RUC had not tried to gain control of Derry's Bogside from the rear in August 1969. He also wrote that if the majority made the Assembly and Executive unworkable, then the UK would be entitled to reconsider her position and her pledges on all matters. He also said that the unity of Ireland could only come about through a freely negotiated voluntary agreement. 'So at the end of the day I would like to see Ireland come together again. If and when it does, it will be a signal to the world that the people themselves have entered freely into a new compact because they are at peace and at ease with one another and recognise how much they have in common.' As Prime Minister, he seemed to be anxious to concentrate on helping the Ulster economy, and gave little priority to political advance, although he stressed on several occasions that there would have to be partnership government. The decision of his government to back extra MPs for NI pleased Unionists and angered the SDLP, who claimed that he was buying Unionist votes to keep his minority government in office. In May 1979, in his first speech as leader of the opposition, he indicated that his party would seek to keep a bipartisan policy on NI and he offered to co-operate with the Conservatives in seeking a political initiative. In 1981, after he had given up the party leadership, he called for an independent NI.

CALVERT, DAVID NORMAN. DUP Assembly member for Armagh, 1982–. b. 1945. Craigavon Council, 1973–. Member, Southern Education and Library Board.

CAMERON COMMISSION. A three-man Commission of Inquiry announced by Capt. Terence O'Neill, as Prime Minister, in January 1969. Its terms of reference were to inquire into the violence since 5 October 1968, to trace the causes of the violence and to examine the bodies involved. The chairman was Lord Cameron, and the other members were Prof. Sir John Biggart and Mr James Joseph Campbell. It sat in private, and the NI Attorney-General gave an assurance that no prosecutions would be brought on the basis of any written or oral evidence to the inquiry. Mr Brian Faulkner, Minister of Commerce, resigned from the government because he disagreed with the decision to establish the inquiry. The Commission's findings were believed to be known to the Home Secretary, Mr James Callaghan, when he visted NI in August 1969, but they were published in early September 1969. The Commission declared that there had been a failure of leadership on all sides, and that the Stormont government had been 'hidebound' and 'complacent'. It gave seven main causes for the disorders. (1) A rising sense of continuing injustice and grievance among large sections of the Roman Catholic population, particularly because of the inadequacy of the housing provision of some local authorities and 'unfair methods of allocation' of houses to perpetuate Unionist control. (2) Religious discrimination in appointments by some Unionist-controlled authorities. (3) Deliberate manipulation of local government electoral boundaries to achieve or maintain Unionist control of local authorities. (4) A growing and powerful sense of resentment and frustration among the Roman Catholic population at the failure of the government to investigate complaints and provide a remedy for them. (5) Resentment, particularly among Roman Catholics, at the existence of the USC as a partisan paramilitary force recruited exclusively from Protestants. (6) Widespread resentment, among Roman Catholics in particular, about the Special Powers Act and (7) Fears and apprehension among Protestants of a threat to Unionist domination and control of government by the increase of the Roman Catholic population. These feelings were inflamed in particular by the activities of the UCDC and the UPV which had provoked a hostile reaction to civil rights claims as asserted by NICRA and later by the PD. The atmosphere thus created was readily translated into physical violence against civil rights demonstrators. The Commission also criticised the RUC, which was said to have been inept on occasions. It said that 'subversive elements' had used the civil rights platform to stir up trouble in the streets.

CAMPAIGN FOR DEMOCRACY IN ULSTER. A London-based group which monitors civil rights in NI and which was especially prominent in pressing for reforms in 1968–9. Although not confined to parliamentarians, it has had the support of up to 100 Labour MPs on occasion, and among those who have held office in it are Lord Fenner Brockway, and Labour MPs Stanley Orme, Paul Rose, and Kevin McNamara. Gerry Fitt, as West Belfast MP, was a frequent speaker at its meetings, which are normally held either at the House of Commons or at the annual conferences of the Labour Party.

CAMPAIGN FOR SOCIAL JUSTICE. An organisation based in Dungannon, which began in January 1964, and which over the next five years mounted a strong publicity campaign in Britain and abroad. Its declared aims were to collect data on injustices in NI and to fight discrimination, especially in employment, housing, electoral practices and boundaries, and public appointments. Its efforts were particularly effective in building up support for the civil rights movement within the British Labour Party. Councillor Mrs Patricia McCluskey, and her husband, Dr Conn McCluskey, of Dungannon, were the members of the twelve-member Campaign committee who became best known as speakers for the group.

CAMPBELL, GREGORY LLOYD. DUP Assembly member for Londonderry, 1982–. Derry City Council, 1977–. Leads DUP group on City Council.

CAMPBELL, ROBERT VICTOR. Unionist member of Assembly for N. Down, 1973–4 and UPNI Convention member for the same constituency, 1975–6. b. Coleraine, Co. Londonderry, 1914. Mayor of Bangor, Co. Down, 1966–70. Member, N. Down District Council, 1973–.

CANAVAN, MICHAEL. Security spokesman of the SDLP, 1974–82. b. Londonderry, 1924. Member for Londonderry in the

Assembly (1973–4) and the Convention (1975–6). Leading figure in the civil rights movement in Derry. Chairman of Derry Citizens' Central Council in 1970, after holding office successively as secretary of the Derry Citizens Action Committee, and a member of the Executive of the Derry Citizens' Defence Association. As SDLP security spokesman, he has paid frequent visits to prisons to check on conditions, and has been active in pressing for stricter precautions against the use of ill-treatment or excessive force by members of the security forces. In particular, he has been highly critical of the use of plastic bullets. In 1982, he expressed his opposition to the new Assembly by refusing to be a candidate in Derry.

CARDWELL, JOSHUA. Unionist Assembly (1973–4) and UPNI Convention (1975–6) member for E. Belfast. b. 1910; died 1982. Belfast City Council, 1952–82. Unionist MP for Pottinger at Stormont, 1969–72. In politics, he concentrated mainly on local issues in E. Belfast, but gave strong support to Brian Faulkner in the controversies over Sunningdale and power-sharing.

CAREY, HUGH. Governor of New York, 1972–. b. 11 April 1919. Associated with Senator Edward Kennedy and other leading Irish-Americans in encouraging US government interest in NI, and in discouraging Americans from giving money gifts to organisations associated with violence in Ireland. Member of Friends of Ireland group. Stayed away from New York dinner for British Prime Minister, James Callaghan, in June 1978, because, according to his spokesman, he wished to protest against British slowness in eradicating violence in NI, and in ending discrimination against Roman Catholics in jobs and housing. In 1979, he tried to set up a New York meeting between Britain and Irish Republic on NI. The idea was accepted by Irish, but rejected by British. On a visit to Ireland in 1981, he said the British Government's attitude to the hunger strike was increasing support for the IRA in the USA.

CARRINGTON, LORD (PETER ALEXANDER RUPERT CARRINGTON). He was closely involved with NI as Secretary of Defence in the Heath government, 1970–4. Leader of Opposition, House of Lords, 1974–9. Foreign Secretary, 1979–82. b. 6 June 1919. He was responsible for big build-up of UDR, but would not agree to radical changes in security tactics being demanded by NI government in early 1971. He flew to Stormont in March 1971 in an unsuccessful bid to persuade Major Chichester-Clark to stay as Prime Minister. In December 1980 he accompanied Mrs Thatcher at Dublin summit which Taoiseach Charles Haughey described as 'an historic breakthrough in Anglo-Irish relations'.

CARRON, JOHN. Nationalist MP for S. Fermanagh, 1965–72. b. Kinawley, Co. Fermanagh, 1909. Was Lisnaskea rural councillor when he succeeded veteran Nationalist Cahir Healy in S. Fermanagh in 1965. In 1949, he unsuccessfully contested Lisnaskea, held by the then Prime Minister, Lord Brookeborough. During the short-lived Opposition Alliance at Stormont in 1969, he was spokesman on community relations.

CARRON, OWEN. Republican MP for Fermanagh and S. Tyrone, 1981–3. PSF member of the NI Assembly, 1982–. b. Macken, Enniskillen, 1953. Trained as teacher at Manchester University, and held a variety of teaching posts in Armagh and Fermanagh, 1976–9. Although he has no Republican family background, he was a founder member and chairman of Fermanagh H-Block committee, and was a member of PSF when he acted as election agent for Bobby Sands in the April, 1981, by-election in Fermanagh and S. Tyrone. When Sands died he was elected as a 'proxy political prisoner' in the August 1981 by-election. He fought on an abstentionist ticket and said he would operate as a full-time constituency MP. In the 1982 Assembly election, he stood as a PSF candidate. In January, 1982, he was arrested while trying to enter the US from Canada, along with PSF colleague Danny Morrison. He lost his Westminster seat in the 1983 election when SDLP intervened to take nearly 10,000 votes and he was succeeded by an Official Unionist.

CARSON, JOHN. Off. U. Assembly member for N. Belfast, 1982–. b. 1933. A Belfast shopkeeper, he was elected to Belfast City Council (1971–.), and High Sheriff in 1978 and Lord Mayor, 1980. MP for N. Belfast, Feb., 1974–9. Pushed up majority in N. Belfast between two 1974 general elections from 10,000 to more than 18,000. The OUP lost seat to DUP when he retired for health reasons in 1979. Repeatedly called for tougher security measures in N. Belfast, and also specially active on housing issues. Voted with Labour Government on crucial confidence vote which led to 1979 election. His independent line, particularly in City Hall politics, has occasionally put him at odds with OUP colleagues.

CARTER, JAMES EARL (JIMMY). US President (Democratic), 1976–80. b. 1 October 1924. In the final stages of his election campaign in October 1976, Mr Carter was widely reported as saying that there should be an international commission on human rights in NI; that the Democratic Party was committed to the unification of Ireland; and that the US could not stand idle on the NI question. His remarks caused the Irish National Caucus (an umbrella group for Irish-American organisations) to call for support for Mr Carter. But there were protests from Unionists in NI, some MPs at Westminster, and spokesmen for the Peace People. There were also demands for clarification from the Irish Republic's government. Mr Carter then sent a cable to Dr Garret Fitzgerald, Irish Foreign Minister, in which he complained that he had been misrepresented in some reports. He stressed that he did not favour violence as a solution to the Irish

Question. He believed in negotiations and peaceful means of finding a just solution which would involve the two communities in NI, and protect human rights which had been threatened. In August 1977, he issued a statement which indicated that there would be economic help for NI if a political settlement could be reached. On 16 March 1978 (the eve of St Patrick's Day) he had a brief meeting at the White House with Mairead Corrigan of the NI Peace People at which he likened the US government's efforts for peace to those of the Peace movement in NI.

CARTER, RAYMOND JOHN (RAY). Parliamentary Under-Secretary, NI Office, 1976–9. b. 17 September 1935. Labour MP for Northfield (Birmingham), 1970 to May 1979 when he lost his seat in the general election – the only member of the Stormont team of Ministers to do so. Initially responsible at Stormont for assisting the Ministers of State in charge of Commerce, Manpower Services and Education. Later took charge of the Environment Department, which covered housing, planning and local government matters. Ran into controversy in 1977 over his unsuccessful attempt to make car seat belts compulsory in NI in advance of Great Britain.

CASTLEREAGH. See BENNETT REPORT.

CATHERWOOD, SIR HENRY FREDERICK ROSS. Conservative MEP, June 1979–. Ulster-born industrialist and chairman (1975–8) of the British Overseas Trade Board, who has put forward a scheme for a political settlement in NI. b. 30 January 1925. In January 1972, he first suggested a Stormont parliament in which the minority would have influence through a system of two-thirds majority voting and offers of government posts to individual members of opposition parties. He repeated the proposal in 1974, when he came out strongly against an independent Ulster, which he said would be 'catastrophic'.

CATHOLIC ANTI-DIS-CRIMINATION. A body active between 1969 and 1974 in opposing prejudice against Catholics in private firms, government departments and institutions generally. It was also involved in pressing for reform of the RUC.

CATHOLIC EX-SERVICE-MEN'S ASSOCIATION. Catholic paramilitary organisation formed after the introduction of internment without trial in the summer of 1971. Its organiser, Mr Phil Curran, quickly claimed to have 8,000 registered members, and it was very active during 1972. It was described as a 'people's army' for the defence of Catholic areas, and although it was unarmed, it claimed to be able to get arms if necessary. Its activities have been mainly in the Belfast area, and entry is not restricted to ex-servicemen in the ordinary sense.

CENTRAL CITIZENS' DEFENCE COMMITTEE. This organisation, based on the mainly Catholic Falls Road in Belfast, brought together in 1969 the various West Belfast defence and community groups operating in Catholic areas. Its first chairman was a leading republican, Jim Sullivan, who was succeeded by a businessman, Tom Conaty. It also brought together local politicians such as Paddy Devlin MP and Paddy Kennedy MP, and the local priest, Father Padraig Murphy. Its first major crisis was over the government demands for removal of the barricades set up during the violent summer of 1969. This entailed talks with the Home Secretary, James Callaghan, and many contacts with the army. There were repeated rows over the RUC and the extent to which the troops could prevent any loyalist attack. In July 1970, the CCDC was engaged in the angry controversy over the thirty-four-hour curfew imposed by the army on a large section of the Lower Falls. It argued that the army operation was unjustified, and particularly criticised the tactics which had led to the deaths of five men during the curfew. It claimed that hundreds of complaints had been filed with the CCDC over the behaviour of the troops, and that any ammunition seized did not begin to compare with arms supplies held in Protestant areas. The CCDC published a special book itemising its case against the army – *Law (?) and Orders, 1970* – but official spokesmen denied an excess of force. During 1970, the CCDC took a strong line against violence. It called for a halt to the throwing of missiles at the army, attacked the shooting of RUC men, and said violence could

harm the cause of justice. With the introduction of internment in 1971 it became involved in the organising of visits to Long Kesh, and in arranging parcels for internees and prisoners. In June 1973, the Committee made a bid to persuade the PIRA to call a ceasefire. PIRA replied eventually that it could not agree to peace at any price. It set out a series of demands – an amnesty for all imprisoned because of the troubles, withdrawal of troops from sensitive areas, declaration of intent to withdraw from Ireland, and agreement by Britain that the Irish people should decide their own future. The CCDC replied that PIRA should show maturity and recognise that peace was the first priority. The general theme of CCDC policy was that Catholics have been treated unfairly by the security forces in comparison with Protestants. In 1973, it put out a 'Black Paper' calling for replacement of the RUC by an 'impartial police force'. William Whitelaw, as Secretary of State, retorted that there was little point in looking back and rehearsing old grievances. The CCDC headquarters were among Falls Road premises bombed in November 1973.

CHANNON, HENRY PAUL GUINNESS. Minister of State, NI Office, 1972. b. 9 October 1935. Has Irish family associations – his mother was a daughter of the second Lord Iveagh, head of the Guinness family. His London home was the venue for the secret meeting between Secretary of State, William Whitelaw, and PIRA leaders in July 1972. Conservative MP for Southend W. 1959–. Trade Minister, 1983–.

CHICHESTER-CLARK, MAJOR JAMES. See under MOYOLA, LORD.

CHICHESTER-CLARK, SIR ROBERT (ROBIN). Unionist MP for Londonderry, 1955–February 1974. b. 10 January 1928. Brother of Lord Moyola, Prime Minister, NI, 1969–71. Chief Conservative spokesman, NI, 1964–70. Minister of State, Employment, 1972–4. Chairman of the Unionist MPs at Westminster, 1971–4. He kept closely in touch with his brother as PM, and in January 1971, he voted against the Conservative government as a protest against what he called the 'ineffectiveness' of the government's security policy in NI. In July 1971, a few weeks before internment was introduced, he threatened to withdraw support altogether unless there was a tougher anti-terrorist policy.

CLARK, SIR GEORGE. President of the OUP Council, 1979–. Member of NI Senate, 1951–72. b. 24 January 1914. Grand Master, Grand Orange Lodge of Ireland, 1957–67. Chairman of Standing Committee of Ulster Unionist Council, 1967–72. Sir George, who had started out in politics as Stormont MP for Dock division of Belfast, attracted interest in the early 1960s when he had talks with the late Gerry Lennon, a Nationalist Senator, about the possibility of improving relations between both sections of the community. The discussions, known as the 'Orange-Green talks', did not have any tangible result. As chairman of the Unionist Standing Committee, he presided at a series of crucial meetings which preceded the resignation of Terence O'Neill from the Premiership. He was a member of the party delegation which made clear to Secretary of State James Prior in 1982 its opposition to 'rolling devolution'. Mr Prior later went to Sir George's home in an unsuccessful attempt to secure an opportunity of speaking to the OUP Executive.

CLOSE, SEAMUS. All. Assembly member for S. Antrim, 1982–. b. 1948. Lisburn Council, 1973–. Chairman, Alliance Party, 1981, and economic spokesman, 1982–. Member of Alliance deputation at the Atkins Conference, 1980. Unsuccessfully fought the Fermanagh and S. Tyrone by-election, August, 1981.

COALISLAND. A village a few miles from Dungannon, with a mainly Catholic population, and suffering heavily from unemployment, and from which the first civil rights march set off for Dungannon on 24 August 1968. The Scarman tribunal mentioned in its report that it had been told that 400 men were without employment out of a total population of 3,000. 'It is not without significance,' said Scarman, 'that the first of the events of the 1968–9 sequence of disturbances began in this little place'.

COLLINS, (JAMES) GERARD. Foreign Minister of Irish Republic, 1982. b. 1938. BA

(UCD). As Foreign Minister in the short-lived Haughey administration in 1982, he was strongly critical of British policy in NI. He said Britain had broken the letter and the spirit of the Anglo-Irish understanding. He also protested that the Republic's government had not been consulted about James Prior's 'rolling devolution' initiative which, he said, had no Anglo-Irish dimension and represented a retreat from power-sharing. As Minister for Justice in Fianna Fail governments 1977–81, he was involved in strengthening border security, although he did not always go as far as British Governments wanted. TD (Limerick), 1967–. Limerick Co. Council, 1974–7. Minister for Posts and Telegraphs, 1970–3.

COMMISSIONER OF COM-PLAINTS. The officer who deals with complaints of maladministration against local authorities and public bodies (see KERNOHAN, HUGH)

COMMON MARKET REF-ERENDUM. In the Common Market poll in June 1975, NI recorded a narrow majority in favour of membership. The result was a surprise, since there had been a strong lobby against membership, involving a large section of Unionism, including MPs like Enoch Powell and the Rev. Ian Paisley. The Northern Ireland Committee of the Irish Congress of Trade Unions had also campaigned against membership. The turnout of 48 per cent was low by local standards. The figures were:

YES	259,251	52.1 per cent
NO	237,911	47.9 per cent
Yes majority	21,340	4.2 per cent

COMMUNIST PARTY OF IRELAND. The party was originally founded on an all-Ireland basis in 1933, but it split during World War II into the Communist Party of Northern Ireland and the Irish Workers' Party in the South. In 1970, the party was re-united at a Belfast conference, with separate area committees North and South. The NI executive members at the time of the merger were: Andrew Barr, Hugh Moore, James Graham, Brian Graham, Mrs Edwina Stewart, James Stewart, Miss Betty Sinclair, Hugh Murphy, Sean Morrissey, and Bill Somerset. Mr Barr and Mr Graham were leading trade unionists, and Miss Sinclair secretary of Belfast trades union council and first secretary of NICRA, of which Mrs Stewart became secretary later. Membership of the CPI at the time of the merger was probably between 400 and 500. The CPI has taken the line that there must be a declaration of independence by the whole of Ireland and that 'it is not in the interests of the Irish people to be part of the monopoly capitalist system'. In 1975, the party called on all paramilitary groups to order a cease-fire, and it also urged the withdrawal to barracks of British troops. No Communist candidate has been returned in any Stormont election, although candidates have stood in Belfast on several occasions. In the 1982 Assembly election two CPI candidates appeared in S. Antrim and S. Belfast; they polled about 400 votes between them and lost their deposits. The Communists have been credited by some writers with exercising a large background influence in the troubles but there is evidence that party members in London, Belfast and Dublin have often been at odds on the NI situation. External broadcasts from Communist countries, notably Russia, China and Albania, frequently attack British policy in Ireland, but the Russian authorities have always rejected suggestions that they have supplied arms to the IRA. OIRA and Official Sinn Féin (now Workers' Party), with a pro-Marxist slant, have had some duplication of membership with the Communist Party.

COMPTON REPORT. The report of the committee set up to investigate allegations that men being interrogated after their arrest on 9 August 1971 – the date of the introduction of internment without trial, had been subjected to brutal treatment. The enquiry was conducted by Sir Edmund Compton; Edgar Fay QC, Recorder of Plymouth; and Dr Ronald Gibson, former chairman of the BMA Council. The Commission, in its report issued in November 1971, found that there had been physical ill-treatment of detainees, but it dismissed charges of brutality. The methods which had been investigated were hooding, exposure to continuous noise, standing against a wall leaning on fingertips, and deprivation of food and sleep. Apart from one man, the detainees involved refused to give evidence, on the grounds that the Commission was sitting in private, and that there would be no opportunity to cross-examine official witnesses. The report was widely criticised both in Britain and in NI, and the Home Secretary, Mr Maudling, announced a new inquiry, under Lord Parker, to consider whether interrogation methods should be changed. Most of the cases before the Compton inquiry eventually went to the European Court of Human Rights.

CONATY, TOM. Chairman of the CCDC (based on Falls Road, Belfast), 1969–74. b. 1930. In 1969, while serving as an ordinary member of the CCDC, he flew to London with a deputation for talks with the Home Secretary, James Callaghan, about plans to protect Catholic areas if the barricades were taken down. He also served on the Peace Committee, a short-lived government-sponsored body set up in 1969. In 1970, he was highly critical of the army curfew imposed over two days on an area of the Falls Road, and in 1971 was a leading opponent of internment without trial. His decision to join the Secretary of State's Advisory Commission after direct rule was attacked by republicans, some of whom demonstrated at his home. In 1974, he issued a strong appeal to the PIRA to call off its campaign of violence, and he said that the Catholic people could not understand why they were carrying it on. He also called on the Republic to provide a guarantee that it would defend NI Catholics in the event of a doomsday situation. In 1975, he stood unsuccessfully in W. Belfast in the convention election on the platform that existing public representatives did not accurately reflect the priorities of the Catholic people.

CONCANNON, JOHN DENNIS (DON). Minister of State, NI Office, 1976–9. b. 16 May 1930. After period as branch official of National Union of Mineworkers, became Labour MP for Mansfield (Notts.), 1966–. Labour Whip, 1968–74. Parliamentary Under-Secretary, NI Office 1974–6. As Minister of State NI, he was responsible for Commerce and Manpower Services. Also acted as Deputy Secretary of State. Active in seeking new industrial investment, notably through trips to US, Germany and Scandinavia. When he left NI Office with defeat of the Labour government in May 1979, he was longest-serving Minister ever in NI Office – over five years. Retained his interest in NI as front-bench spokesman, 1979–. Gave strong backing to Government during H-Block hunger strikes, 1981, and also encouraged 'rolling devolution' initiative in 1982, although pressing for larger Irish dimension. At the 1982 party conference, he was critical of a decision to call for a ban on the use of plastic bullets throughout the UK.

CONN, MRS SHENA E. Off. U. Assembly (1973–4) and Convention (1975–6) member for Londonderry. b. Belfast, BDS (QUB).

CONSERVATIVE PARTY. The British Conservative Party has greatly altered its attitude to NI affairs since 1969. In earlier years, the OUP was considered an integral part of the Conservative Party, usually designated nationally the Conservative and Unionist Party. The link went back to the Home Rule controversies of the nineteenth century when Conservatives aligned themselves with the Unionists against the Liberals and Home Rule. Edward Heath's attitude was decisive in bringing about a change. He veered away from positive defence of the Union above all else, and infuriated Unionists with his suspension of the Stormont parliament in 1972. The break became all but complete when Heath supported the Sunningdale agreement and the great majority in the OUP came out against power-sharing. After the February 1974 election, Unionist MPs adopted a neutral stance in parliament and no longer took the Conservative Whip. In 1977, the Off. U. MPs used their bargaining power to secure support from the Labour government for extra NI MPs. Meantime, the Conservatives moved close to Unionist policy by urging that priority should be given to local government reform. Clearly, Margaret Thatcher was more appealing to Unionists as Conservative leader than Edward Heath – her frequent references to support for maintenance of the Union were particularly acceptable to Unionists, but the SDLP became highly suspicious of Conservative intentions. In their 1979 election manifesto, the Conservative Party suggested a regional council or councils in the absence of devolved government. But this approach was quickly dropped as first Humphrey Atkins and then James Prior tried to get devolved government established. The right wing of the party strongly opposed Mr Prior's Assembly plan in 1982. In April, 1983, the Off. U. Executive voted narrowly to seek restoration of its links with the Conservative Party. The Unionists clearly had in mind the possibility of Tory backing for the return of majority government at Stormont. The Conservative 1983 election manifesto, however, said NI would continue to be offered devolution through the Assembly, but only on the basis of cross-community support. The manifesto also urged a practical working relationship with the Republic without threatening in any way the majority community in NI.

CONSTITUTIONAL CONFERENCE. A conference organised by Secretary of State Humphrey Atkins and held at Parliament Buildings, Stormont, between January and March, 1980. All four main parties were invited, but the Official Unionists declined the invitation. The DUP, SDLP and Alliance delegates met privately under the chairmanship of the Secretary of State. They agreed that there should be devolved government, but while the SDLP and Alliance maintained their position that there should be power-sharing government, the DUP stuck to its demand for majority rule, although it conceded that the minority should have a 'meaningful role'. From outside the conference, the Official Unionists also supported majority Government, with no entrenched powers or privileges for any group. The three parties in the conference were against local government reform without devolved government, and in this they differed from the Official Unionists, who believed that such reform should be pursued in the absence of devolved government – a move to invoke the Government's general election pledge. Since the conference did not deal with security or relations with the Republic, these matters were examined in a parallel conference. With the Conference failing to point to any agreed solution, Mr Atkins, in July, 1980, put forward fresh options for study. One involved an Executive made up of parties achieving a certain measure of popular support and in proportion to their strength. Another envisaged a majority Cabinet balanced by an Assembly Council which would include Opposition parties. Again, there was no common ground, and a further proposal by Mr Atkins for an Advisory Council composed of already-elected representatives was quickly abandoned.

CONSTITUTIONAL CONVENTION. The elected conference of NI parties established by the British government in 1975 to consider – as the government White paper put it – 'what provision for the government of Northern Ireland is likely to command the most widespread acceptance throughout the community there'. It comprised seventy-eight members elected by PR on the same basis as the former Assembly, which had been abolished when the power-sharing Executive fell in 1974. (See *Elections Section* for detailed results). The Convention chairman was Sir Robert Lowry, Lord Chief Justice of NI, (now Lord Lowry) and he had two special advisers, Dr John A. Oliver and Maurice N. Hayes. The Clerk of the Convention was Ronald Blackburn. The fact that forty-seven of the Convention seats were held by supporters of the UUUC indicated that agreement would prove elusive. They were committed to the rejection of power-sharing on the 1973 model. At the same time, the parties of the former Executive – SDLP, Alliance and UPNI – still pressed for partnership. Although the public debates simply underlined these facts, an elaborate programme of inter-party discussions was mounted. The UUUC made it clear that they wanted the restoration to a new devolved government of the powers conferred on Stormont by the original 1920 Act, including law-and-order powers. They also saw minority participation in government as something which would be achieved by inclusion in departmental committees rather than the Cabinet. This approach was firmly opposed by the power-sharing parties. The Vanguard Unionist leader, William Craig MP, made an attempt to break the deadlock by suggesting a voluntary coalition during the emergency – he used the analogy of a wartime coalition at Westminster – but he got no support from his coalition partners and very little within his own party, which split on the issue. Westminster refused

to accept the majority report of the Convention as meeting the criteria of the White Paper. But the Secretary of State, Merlyn Rees MP, recalled the Convention for a further month at the start of 1976 to allow it to think again. He also told the Convention that the government would not agree to extra NI seats at Westminster until a local political settlement had been reached (this attitude was reversed by the Labour government in 1977). The government also held that a formal Council of Ireland was not essential to cross-border co-operation, and that any transfer of law-and-order powers from Westminster (excluding judicial appointments and control of Courts) would have to be gradual. The Convention ended its sittings in March 1976, without finding any agreement acceptable to Westminster.

COOK, DAVID. Deputy leader of Alliance Party, March, 1980–. Assembly member for S. Belfast, 1982–. b. 1944. Lord Mayor of Belfast, 1978–9, and first non-Unionist to hold that office. His election as Lord Mayor was a major political surprise, and arose because two UPNI councillors opposed the outgoing Off. U. Lord Mayor, James Stewart, and gave Cook a two-vote margin. Leader of Alliance group in Belfast City Council, 1973–80. Unsuccessfully contested S. Belfast in 1974 and 1983 Westminster election and in the 1982 by-election.

COONEY, PATRICK MARK. Minister for Justice, Irish Republic, 1973–7, and Defence Minister 1982–. b. 2 March 1931. BA LL.B. (UCD). A solicitor. Mr Cooney was a Fine Gael member of the Dail, 1970–7, when he lost his seat and was elected to the Senate. As Justice Minister in the Cosgrave administration, he took a strong stand against the IRA, and strengthened cross-border security co-operation, notably by improving communications between the Gardai and the RUC. He also negotiated with the British government the reciprocal legislation to enable a person accused of terrorism to be brought to trial on whichever side of the border he was arrested, and introduced the power to hold without charge for seven days, after the assassination of the British Ambassador to Dublin in 1976. He was an unsuccessful candidate in the European elections of June 1979.

COOPER, SIR FRANK. Permanent Under-Secretary, NI Office, 1973–6. b. 2 December 1922. Head of the civil service in the NI Office during a critical period, which extended from the Sunningdale conference through the five-month life of the NI Executive, the loyalist strike of 1974, and over the period of the Convention. He worked under three Secretaries of State – Whitelaw, Pym and Rees. He was no desk-bound administrator, and through a great variety of political and other contacts, was usually aware of the smallest intrigue. He knew in advance of the talks at Feakle between leading Churchmen and PIRA. In 1976, he moved to the Defence Ministry as

Permanent Secretary. When he retired in 1982, he talked of 'organising' the people who had talked to Provisional Sinn Féin. He also said he did not expect a NI solution for a long time, and commented that the British and the Loyalists had never understood each other.

COOPER, IVAN AVERILL. Minister of Community Relations in NI Executive, 1974, and SDLP Assembly member, 1973–4, and Convention member, 1975–6, for Mid-Ulster. b. Killaloo, Co. Londonderry, 1944. First experience in politics as a Young Unionist; member NILP, 1965–8; prominent in civil rights movement from earliest days, and president of the Derry Citizens' Action Committee, 1968–9. MP for Mid-Derry at Stormont, 1969–72; Independent until 1970, then SDLP, of which he was a founder member. Unsuccessfully contested Mid-Ulster in both the February and October 1974 Westminster elections. Has interested himself particularly in cross-border economic development, and promotion of industry at Strabane, one of the province's major unemployment black spots.

COOPER, ROBERT GEORGE. Head of the Department of Manpower Serves in the NI Executive, 1974. b. Donegal, 24 June 1936. Gave up his job in industrial relations to become Alliance Party's first full-time General Secretary, and later deputy leader. Elected from W. Belfast to Assembly, 1973–4 and Constitutional Convention, 1975–6. Head of the Fair Employment Agency set up to investigate allegations of political and religious discrimination in employment, 1976–.

CO-OPERATION NORTH. An organisation based in Dublin, and aimed at fostering friendship and co-operation with NI. Launched in June 1978, with the support of a large number of voluntary bodies, trade unions, commercial companies, professional organisations and State-sponsored companies. Dr T. K. Whitaker, an Ulsterman who was largely responsible for organising the historic Stormont meeting between Sean Lemass and Terence O'Neill in 1965, presided at the inaugural meeting.

CORRIGAN-MAGUIRE, MAIREAD. One of the three founders of the Peace People, she was joint recipient, with her colleague, Mrs Betty Williams, of the Nobel Peace Prize for 1976. b. 1944. Aunt of the three Maguire children whose deaths, when they were struck by a gunman's getaway car, led to the formation of the Peace People. In September, 1981, she married Jackie Maguire, husband of her sister Anne, who died of 'heartbreak' in a suicide in 1980, when she was said to have been seriously depressed by the death of her children and the continuing violence. Has travelled widely in the US and in Europe to advance the movement, and in 1978 she had a brief meeting with President Carter, who later sent her a personal message wishing the movement well. She disclosed in 1977 that she had almost joined the IRA in 1973 because of the behaviour of troops in W. Belfast.

She became chairman of the PP in 1980, when it was affected by internal rows, but in 1981 she returned to the role of an executive member.

CORRIGAN, MAIREAD. See CORRIGAN-MAGUIRE, MAIREAD.

CORRYMEELA. The inter-denominational community centre at Ballycastle, Co. Antrim, which has sought to promote reconciliation by bringing together people of differing backgrounds from both sides of the community. In April 1966, Prime Minister Terence O'Neill voiced his hopes for better community relations when he addressed an audience of fifty prominent Protestants and Roman Catholics at the centre. Seminars at the centre have been attended by leading politicians, churchmen, academics and journalists, as well as by groups from the ghetto areas on both sides.

COSGRAVE, LIAM. Taoiseach of the Irish Republic, 1973–7. b. 13 April 1920. Son of William T. Cosgrave, former Prime Minister of Irish Free State. TD, 1943–81. Leader of Fine Gael, 1965–77. Mr Cosgrave's Ministerial career began as a Parliamentary Secretary in the Inter-Party government of 1948–51, and he was Minister for External Affairs, 1954–7. Chairman of Council of Ministers, Council of Europe, 1955. Chairman, first Irish delegation, UN General Assembly, 1956. His most crucial involvement with NI affairs was as head of the Irish government delegation at the Sunningdale conference in

December 1973. His comments afterwards suggested that he believed that this get-together of British and Irish Ministers and representatives of the pro-power-sharing parties in NI would provide the basis for a permanent settlement. He was personally acquainted with the Chief Executive designate of the NI Executive, Brian Faulkner, both as a politician and as a lover of horses and hunting. And while Mr Cosgrave did not concede that there was any need for amendment of the Republic's constitution (unlike some of his Ministers, particularly Garret Fitzgerald and Conor Cruise O'Brien) he did agree to the clause in the Sunningdale ageement which stated that there could be no change in the status of NI unless the people there desired it. Although Britain would have preferred the Republic to agree to straight extradition of suspected terrorists who had entered the Republic, a compromise was reached, with the joint legislation providing that such a person could be tried on whichever side of the border he was arrested. And broadly, the Cosgrave government's security policies between the Sunningdale period and its election defeat in 1977 were welcomed by Britain. At various meetings with the British government and Common Market summit meetings, Mr Cosgrave pressed for British initiatives to secure partnership government in NI, and what he regarded as fair representation in the new directly-elected European parliament of the minority in NI. His proposal that there should be three NI seats filled on the PR system was eventually adopted by Westminster. Mr Cosgrave visited NI occasionally and one of his longest trips was in 1972 when he spent several days in the province as Fine Gael leader and met a variety of political and other groups.

COSTELLO, SEAMUS. Leader and founder of the Irish Republican Socialist Party until he was shot dead in Dublin in October 1977. b. Bray, Co. Wicklow, 1939. Active in his early years in the republican movement, he was the leader – according to J. Bowyer Bell, in his history of the IRA, *The Secret Army* – of an IRA flying column which was active in NI during the 1956 campaign. He was said to have been responsible for burning down the courthouse in Magherafelt, Co. Derry. During the campaign, he was interned at the Curragh for two years. He opposed the OIRA ceasefire in 1972, and after his expulsion from the IRA established the IRSP. From 1967 he had been active in council politics in Co. Wicklow. In 1975, during the feud between the Official Republicans and the IRSP, he survived an assassination bid in Waterford. Both the PIRA a.d OIRA denied that they had been responsible for his murder. In 1982, INLA accused OIRA of carrying it out. It was the first assassination of a party leader in the history of the Republic.

COULTER, MISS JEAN. Off. U. Assembly member for W. Belfast, 1973–4, and Convention member for the same constituency, 1975–6.

COUNCIL FOR THE UNION.
See MOLYNEAUX, JAMES.

COUSLEY, CECIL JAMES.
DUP Assembly member for N.
Antrim, 1982–. Ballymoney Council, 1981–. Farmer.

CRAIG, WILLIAM. MP for E.
Belfast at Westminster, February
1974–9. b. 2 December 1924. One
of the province's most controversial politicians, he began as an
orthodox Official Unionist, notably active in the Young Unionist
movement. He became MP for
Larne in 1960, and as government
Chief Whip (1962–3) had a key
role in the choice of Cap. Terence
O'Neill as Prime Minister in 1963.
He became Minister of Home
Affairs in the O'Neill government,
and then Minister of Health and
Local Government in July 1964.
When O'Neill set up a new
Ministry of Development to look
after local government reform and
establishment of the new City of
Craigavon, in 1965, Craig took
charge of it. He returned to the
post of Minister of Home Affairs
in October 1966. He became the
centre of intense controversy in
October 1968, when he banned a
civil rights march in Duke Street,
Londonderry – a march which
went ahead on 5 October and led
to a bitter clash between police
and civil rights supporters, who
included several Westminster and
Stormont MPs, among them
Gerry Fitt MP and Eddie
McAteer, then leader of the
Nationalist Party. Batons and
water cannon were used by the
RUC, and the scenes transmitted
on TV, focused world attention
on the NI situation. Craig was
sharply attacked by anti-Unionists
on all sides, but he defended himself vigorously. He denied police
brutality and claimed that the IRA
had been involved in the Derry
march. He also accused the British government of bringing pressure on the NI government to
introduce reforms. He said there
had been financial pressure which
amounted to blackmail. In
December 1968, Captain O'Neill
sacked Craig from the Cabinet.
He said Craig had been attracted
by ideas of a UDI nature and a 'go
it alone' Ulster was a delusion.
Craig now hit out strongly at
O'Neill's tactics, and as a backbencher was a steady critic of what
he regarded as the 'appeasement'
of the enemies of Unionism. He
also assailed the security policies
of Westminster and of the
Chichester-Clark and Faulkner
governments. The disbandment
of 'B' Specials he considered to be
one of the major blunders in this
field. Although he was frequently
at odds with the Rev. Ian Paisley,
they often came together on loyalist platforms. He headed the Ulster Loyalist Association from 1969
to 1972, and on various occasions
mentioned that force might have
to be used to achieve 'normality'.
He led the Unionist pressure
group, Ulster Vanguard, which
was in the forefront of the opposition to the Heath government's
suspension of Stormont and
introduction of direct rule in 1972.
It helped organise a forty-eight
hour loyalist strike against the
move. At that period, Craig
became familiar as the leading
speaker at massive rallies. One of
these was held at Parliament
Buildings to coincide with the last

sitting of the local parliament and Brian Faulkner, as Prime Minister, appeared on the balcony beside Craig – much to Faulkner's embarrassment, it emerged later. In the Assembly election in 1973, he was returned in N. Antrim, some 6,000 votes behind the Rev. Ian Paisley. He forcefully attacked the Sunningdale agreement, and the power-sharing Executive, and converted Vanguard into a full political party. In February 1974, he won the E. Belfast seat at Westminster, and with the other two leaders of what had now become the UUUC – Paisley and Harry West – he was among the top planners of the May 1974 loyalist strike which brought down the three-party Executive. In the October 1974 Westminster election, he strengthened his hold on E. Belfast – his majority was up about 10,000. He headed the poll in E. Belfast in the Convention election in 1975. In the Convention, he caused a major surprise by advocating the idea of a voluntary coalition, including the SDLP, for a limited period. He claimed that this was not power-sharing, which he had attacked in the Assembly. But he got no support from his Coalition partners – the Official Unionists and the Democratic Unionists – and the majority of his own party deserted him on the issue. The breakaway group, under the leadership of Ernest Baird, now called themselves the United Ulster Unionist Movement. When Paisley and Baird backed the loyalist strike in May 1977, Craig stood aside. In 1977, he was appointed to the Council of Europe, on the nomination of the British government,

and as a member of the legal committee he was appointed by the Council to report on human rights legislation in Europe – an assignment which was criticised by some of those associated with the original civil rights campaign. Then, in February 1978, the VUPP ceased to exist as a political party. It reverted to the title Ulster Vanguard, as a pressure group, and Craig remained at its head. In more than one sense, his career had turned full circle. But in the general election of May 1979 he lost E. Belfast to the DUP by sixty-four votes. Six months after the election, he was threatening to resign from the OUP because of its refusal to attend the Atkins conference, and in 1980 there were hints that Vanguard might reappear as a political party. In July, 1981, he urged that James Callaghan's plea for an independent NI should be carefully examined, and soon afterwards he criticised the OUP for failing to respond to Garret Fitzgerald's constitutional 'crusade' which he described as 'very significant'. In November, 1981, he had talks in Dublin with Dr Fitzgerald who, he believed, wanted to be helpful. And the next month he called for a decision to take NI out of the UK by 1983 if the Convention report was not implemented. But the 1982 Assembly election showed that his power base in E. Belfast had all but vanished and he failed to secure election. He stood as a Vanguard Unionist.

CRAIGAVON. The new city in Co. Armagh which embraces the two old-established boroughs of Lurgan and Portadown, both of which have suffered seriously in the PIRA bombing campaign. The Craigavon project was the focus of sharp controversy when it was launched by the O'Neill government in the early 1960s, with a population target of 100,000 by 1981. The opposition parties accused the government of neglecting West Ulster, and especially Londonderry, and providing a new centre for incoming industry at Craigavon, with its mainly Protestant population. In the event, it proved difficult to persuade people to move from Greater Belfast to the new city, despite special grants for new occupiers of public authority and private housing. Apart from bombing in the shopping streets of the two main towns, the area has had many attacks on members of the security forces and sectarian assassinations. In council politics, intense rivalry has developed between the DUP and the OUP. In July 1979, a plan to have a twinning scheme between Craigavon and Santa Rosa, California, was abandoned after protests by Irish-American groups, including the Irish National Caucus. In the 1981 H-Block hunger strike, tension was high in the Lurgan area and there was a row over Republican attempts to rename streets after hunger strikers. At the end of 1982, three policemen were killed by a booby-trap land-mine near Lurgan, and soon afterwards a row developed over the shooting dead by the RUC of three PIRA members who were said to have driven through a checkpoint. In the 1980s, the Council was accused by Fair Employment Agency of anti-Catholic bias.

CREASEY, LT-GEN. SIR TIMOTHY. Army GOC, NI, November 1977–9. b. 1923. After wartime service with Indian troops, he joined the Royal Norfolk Regiment in 1947. His later career included a period as military secretary to the Defence Ministry in 1967–8. He acquired special expertise in anti-guerilla operations as commander of the Sultan's forces in Oman, 1972–5. He was Director of Infantry, 1975–7. In December 1977, he commented that the PIRA was being 'suppressed, contained and isolated'. In August, 1979, he drew criticism from both Unionists and the SDLP when he called in at the Falls Road, Belfast, shop of Provisional Sinn Féin with an army patrol. In a BBC programme in January 1980, he said they were faced in NI with an organised revolutionary force of some five hundred hard-core terrorists. But he did not subscribe to the view that they could not be defeated – 'given the national will' and using all the resources of a modern state.

CROSSMAGLEN. The S. Armagh village regarded as one of the main strongholds of the PIRA. With a population of about 1,000, and situated four miles from the border, it has taken on a legendary quality for republicans, and is more widely identified as defying authority through the lines, 'From Carrickmacross to Crossmaglen, there are more rogues than honest men'. To natives, it is known simply as 'The Cross'. The area has a long history of support for the republican cause, and more than thirty British soldiers were killed by local PIRA units in the three years after internment, mainly through culvert bombs and booby traps on the twisting roads which criss-cross the border. There have been several attacks on the RUC and army posts, and the use by the army of part of the Gaelic football pitch as a helicopter landing pad has particularly angered villagers. In August, 1979, Mrs Thatcher visited the army base during a border tour following the Mountbatten and Warrenpoint killings. In the same year, a memorial to dead Republicans was unveiled in the village and attracted protests from Unionists. On a visit to Crossmaglen in March, 1981, Cardinal O'Fiaich urged PIRA to end violence.

CUBBON, SIR BRIAN CROSSLAND. Permanent Under Secretary, NI Office, 1976–9. b. 9 April 1928. Sir Brian first became familiar with NI problems as private secretary to James Callaghan MP, Home Secretary, in 1968–9. Soon after taking up his Stormont post, he narrowly escaped death when he was travelling in the same car as the British ambassador to Dublin en route to the Dublin embassy, when it was blown up by a landmine and the ambassador and a woman civil servant were killed. Before going to Stormont, he had been deputy secretary at the Home Office and earlier deputy secretary to the Cabinet.

CUMANN na mBAN. The women's section of the IRA, which has always had a significant part in IRA activities. Like the IRA proper, it is illegal in both NI and the Republic. In the PIRA campaign, its members have been used for the gathering of intelligence, reporting on the movements of army and police, and in finding shelter for IRA men. Women have also had a role in the placing of fire bombs, particularly during 1977. The exact strength of the section is uncertain, since it has always relied on the support of sympathisers and relatives of IRA activists.

CUNNINGHAM, LT-COL. JAMES GLENCAIRN. President of the Ulster Unionist Council, governing body of the OUP, 1974. b. 1904. Served in World War II with 8th (Belfast) Regiment, H.A.A., and with 14th Army in Burma. Northern Ireland Senate, 1958–72.

CUNNINGHAM, JOSIAS. Chairman of the executive of the OUP, 1976–9. b. 20 January 1934. MA (Cantab.) Member of a family long associated with Ulster Unionism, and Chairman of S. Antrim Unionist Association, 1974. Chairman of the Belfast unit of the Stock Exchange.

CURRIE, AUSTIN. SDLP Assembly member for Fermanagh and S. Tyrone, 1982–. Head of the department of housing, planning and local government in the power-sharing Executive, 1974. b. Coalisland, Co. Tyrone, 11 October 1939. BA (QUB). Youngest MP ever returned to Stormont when he was elected as Nationalist in 1964 by-election in E. Tyrone (a seat he held until 1972) and he was active, in association with Nationalist leader Eddie

McAteer, in a bid to give the Nationalist Party a more progressive image and a stronger organisational base. In June 1968 he was engaged in the first direct action of the civil rights campaign when he staged a 'sit-in' in a council house at Caledon, Co. Tyrone, as a protest against its allocation to an unmarried woman. He was a regular speaker at civil rights demonstrations and helped organise the first CR march at Dungannon, Co. Tyrone in August 1968. A founder member of the SDLP, he was returned as an SDLP member from Fermanagh and S. Tyrone to both the Assembly (1973–4) and the Convention (1975–6). Chief Whip of the SDLP from 1974 to 1979, when he resigned the post to fight Fermanagh and S. Tyrone unsuccessfully, as Independent SDLP in the 1979 Westminster election. He was defying a party decision not to contest the seat, but he retained his SDLP membership and was the prospective candidate of the party when it again decided to opt out of the 1981 by-elections in the constituency. SDLP North-South spokesman, 1979–82. During the troubles, his home has been attacked several times and his wife was injured on one occasion.

CUSHNAHAN, JOHN. Alliance party Whip in Assembly, 1982–. Assembly member for N. Down, 1982–. b. 1948. B.Ed. (QUB). All. general secretary, 1974–82. Belfast City Council, May, 1977–. Lost N. Belfast in 1979 Westminster election and N. Down in 1983. First chairman of the 1982 Assembly's education committee.

D

DAIL ULADH. The name given to a proposed new nine-county Ulster parliament, which was promoted energetically by Provisional Sinn Fein and PIRA during 1972. A council was set up to promote the idea, and among those also associated with it were Frank McManus, then Unity MP for Fermanagh-S. Tyrone, and Patrick Kennedy, Republican Labour MP at Stormont, as well as some members of the NICRA.

DALY, THOMAS. SDLP Assembly (1973–4) and Convention (1975–6) member for Fermanagh and S. Tyrone. b. Belleek, Co. Fermanagh, 1938. B.A. (QUB). Irvinestown rural district council, 1963–8. Fermanagh Co. Council, 1968–73. Fermanagh District Council 1973–9 (Chairman, 1975–9). Joined SDLP from Nationalist Party in 1973, and announced resignation from public life in February 1979. Brother of Dr Edward Daly, Roman Catholic Bishop of Derry.

DARLINGTON CONFERENCE. A three-day conference on NI affairs held at Darlington, 25–27 September 1972. It was called by William Whitelaw as Secretary of State in a bid to find inter-party agreement on a future form of government for the province. The gathering, held in conditions of tight security at a hotel just outside the town, achieved very little, since only three parties agreed to attend – the Official Unionists, Alliance and NILP. Four other parties – SDLP, Nationalist, DUP and Republican Labour – rejected the invitation for a variety of reasons, and the politicians who did attend couldn't agree on the form of a top tier of government.

DAVIS, IVAN. DUP Assembly member for S. Antrim, 1982–. b. 1937. Lisburn Council, 1973–.

DEMOCRATIC UNIONIST PARTY. Founded in September 1971, by the Rev. Ian Paisley and the then MP for Shankill, Desmond Boal (a leading barrister-at-law), who had been expelled from the Unionist Parliamentary Party. Mr Boal had been a strong opponent of Terence O'Neill as Prime Minister and his views at that time coincided with Mr Paisley's – the new party, said Mr Boal, would be 'right wing in the sense of being strong on the Constitution, but to the left on social policies'. Mr Boal was the first chairman of the party, which took the place of the Protestant Unionist Party, also led by Mr Paisley. The Protestant Unionist Party's first successes were in the two April 1970 by-elections for the NI Commons. Bannside, seat of Terence O'Neill, was won by Mr Paisley, while the Rev. William Beattie gained the S. Antrim seat from an Official Unionist. In the Assembly elections, when it got eight seats (10.8 per cent of first-preference votes)

it opposed power-sharing with the SDLP, and fought both the 1974 Westminster general elections as part of the UUUC. In both elections, Mr Paisley retained the N. Antrim seat, which he had won in 1970. The DUP also contested the 1975 Convention elections in co-operation with UUUC partners. It secured twelve seats (14.7 per cent of first-preference votes). Again in the Convention, it publicly rejected power-sharing, and firmly denied suggestions that it had on occasion privately toyed with some form of partnership with the SDLP. Mr Paisley strongly attacked Mr William Craig's proposal for a voluntary coalition, which would have included the SDLP. In 1977, the withdrawal of the Official Unionists from the UUUC over the issue of an Action Council, which organised the abortive loyalist strike in May 1977, created a new situation for the DUP. Mr Paisley and Official Unionist leaders publicly attacked each other. These exchanges came at the same time as the district council elections, and undoubtedly robbed the DUP of many Off. U. second-preference votes. Nonetheless, the DUP, which employed the slogan 'The Unionist Party You Can Trust', to underline its differences with the Official Unionists, got seventy-four seats (12.7 per cent of first-preference votes). In 1978, the DUP tried to get an agreement with the Official Unionists and the UUUP on how candidates could best be deployed in the coming Westminster elections, but the Official Unionists pointed out that they had no control over local associations in the selection of candidates. Meantime, DUP councillors were involved in controversy over their opposition to Sunday opening of sports and recreational facilities in several areas, and they were able to have their way in Ballymena (Co. Antrim), where they controlled the council. In the May 1979 Westminster election, DUP gained two seats from Official Unionists – E. and N. Belfast – by narrow majorities. The successful candidates were Peter Robinson and John McQuade. Its share of the poll in that election was 10.2 per cent (five seats contested). In the 1979 European election Mr Paisley headed the poll with 29.8 per cent of first-preference votes – a triumph which surprised even the most enthusiastic of DUP supporters. The DUP took a firm anti-EEC line, and polled strongly even in Fermanagh-S. Tyrone, Mid-Ulster and Londonderry, areas where it has not been active to any extent in previous elections. Its run of success was maintained in the 1981 council elections, when its 26.6 per cent first preference vote was more than double that of the previous council election, and even slightly ahead of OUP. But it ran second to OUP in the 1982 Assembly election, getting twenty-one seats and twenty-three per cent of first preferences. In contrast to the OUP, it welcomed the first stage of the 1982 Assembly with mainly scrutiny powers, and it also angered the OUP by supporting James Kilfedder as Assembly Speaker and not the OUP candidate, John Carson. In the 1983 Westminster election, its representation remained at three seats in the re-drawn constituen-

cies. It held N. Antrim and E. Belfast; lost N. Belfast and gained Mid-Ulster. It took 20 per cent of the votes, after making a limited agreement with the OUP by which the DUP were not opposed by the OUP in Foyle, while OUP got a clear run on the Unionist side in Fermanagh and S. Tyrone and Newry-Armagh. In the event, its position was weakened relative to the OUP which got 34 per cent of the votes and eleven seats.

DERRY. See under LONDONDERRY.

DERRY CITIZENS' ACTION COMMITTEE. A body established on 9 October 1968, and made up of five local groups which had helped to organise the civil rights march in Duke Street, Londonderry, on 5 October 1968. Ivan Cooper was chairman and John Hume deputy chairman. The first move by the committee was a sit-down in the Diamond, Londonderry, on 19 October, and the committee also sponsored a massive parade from the Waterside across Craigavon Bridge on 2 November 1968, and supported the People's Democracy march from Belfast to Derry in January 1969. They were also concerned with organising patrols in the Bogside after complaints about RUC behaviour there. They took a petition to Downing Street, calling for police and other reforms.

DERRY CITIZENS' DEFENCE ASSOCIATION. The vigilante group set up in the Bogside area of Derry in July 1969, which took a more militant line than the Derry Citizens' Action Committee. It was involved throughout the period of rioting in August 1969 erecting barricades, mounting patrols, providing first-aid, countering CS gas attacks, and on 24 August it said it had taken control of administration and security behind the barricades of what became known as 'Free Derry'.

DEVLIN, BERNADETTE. See under McALISKEY, BERNADETTE.

DEVLIN, PATRICK JOSEPH (PADDY). SDLP member of NI Executive, 1974, as head of the Department of Health and Social Services, b. Belfast, 8 March 1925 M.Sc (1981). A highly individualistic politician, he has switched party several times. He was in the republican movement from 1936 until 1950, and was interned in Belfast Prison, 1942–5. In 1950, he joined the Irish Labour Party, but moved to the NILP in 1958, and was chairman, 1967–8. In 1970, he became a founder member of the SDLP, and was Chief Whip in the Assembly and chairman in the Convention. But in 1977, he was expelled from the SDLP after he had complained that the party was departing from its previous approach, and reducing the socialist content of its policy. Belfast City Council, 1956–8 and 1973–. MP at Stormont for Falls, 1969–72. Elected to Assembly, 1973–4, and Convention, 1975–6, from W. Belfast, where he had the largest single vote of any candidate in the 1977 district council election. He was a founder member of the NICRA and was closely involved in dealing with the situation in the Falls area in the violence of 1969. When the Convention failed, he

joined his then SDLP colleague, John Hume, in private talks with the Rev. Martin Smyth and Capt. Austin Ardill of the OUP on a possible political settlement. But the effort was unfruitful. He has had a lifelong association with the trade union movement, and became full-time district secretary of the Irish Transport and General Workers' Union in 1976. In 1978, he was among a small group who launched the United Labour Party, and he stood unsuccessfully as the party's candidate in the 1979 European election, claiming that he was the only candidate backing a socialist policy on Europe. In the 1981 council election, he narrowly retained his Belfast City Council seat in the west of the city, but had to leave his home in that area because of threats from Republican extremists. He has written a book describing the fall of the NI power-sharing Executive.

DICKSON, ANNE LETITIA. Leader of UPNI, 1976–81. b. London. Elected as Unionist MP for Carrick in 1969 and strong supporter of Terence O'Neill as Premier. Vice-chairman of Newtownabbey Urban Council, 1967–9. In the Assembly election of 1973, she was elected in S. Antrim without the support of Unionist Party HQ because of a dispute about her selection. She supported the power-sharing Executive, and was also elected to the Convention from S. Antrim in 1975. When Brian Faulkner (the late Lord Faulkner) gave up the leadership of UPNI in 1976, she succeeded him as the first woman leader of a NI political party. In 1979, she unsuccessfully contested N. Belfast in the

Westminster election. In October, 1981, she presided at UPNI's final conference, when it was decided to wind up the party after a series of poor election results.

DIPLOCK REPORT. The report of the Commission, headed by Lord Diplock, which reported in December 1972 that non-jury trials should be introduced for a wide range of terrorist offences. It argued that trials should be held before judges sitting alone, because of the risks of intimidation, for the period of the emergency. The Commission also held that there should be easier admissibility of confessions. The proposals were adopted by the government, and the courts became known as 'Diplock Courts', with a High Court judge sitting for the more serious cases, and a county court judge for the less serious.

DIRECT RULE. See Government Section (p. 294).

DOBSON, JOHN. Government Chief Whip and leader of the Commons at Stormont, 1969–71. b. Lurgan, 7 May 1929. Graduate of TCD. Solicitor. Banbridge Urban District Council, 1961–7. Unionist MP for W. Down, 1965–72. He was one of twelve Unionist MPs who signed a statement in February 1969, saying they would like to see Terence O'Neill replaced as Unionist Party leader.

DONALDSON, LORD (OF KINGSBRIDGE). Parliamentary Under-Secretary, NI Office (and spokesman of the Department in the House of Lords), 1974–6. b. 9 October 1907. A Labour life peer, he took charge of three NI departments – Health and Social Services, Agriculture, and Community Relations – after the reorganisation of the NI Executive in May 1974. He was involved in public controversy mainly because he also had responsibility for prison administration. In November 1974, after a good deal of agitation inside and outside the prison, he agreed to the segregation of loyalists and republican prisoners at the Maze Prison.

DONEGAN, PATRICK SARSFIELD. Defence Minister in the coalition government in the Republic, 1973–7. b. 29 October 1923. TD for Louth, 1954–7 and 1961–77. Senator, 1957–61. As Defence Minister, Mr Donegan took a strong line against the PIRA. In April 1974, he declared that he would be 'tightening up everything' to beat the IRA, and pointed out that the Republic's security forces had reached the highest point for twenty years. There were 11,257 in the Defence Forces and 7,500 in the police. Under his direction, the patrolling of the border was intensified, principally by the use of planes and light armoured cars. Communications were also strengthened between the security forces on either side of the border, although he resisted any direct army-to-army link-up.

DOOGE, JAMES CLEMENT IGNATIUS. Foreign Minister of Irish Republic, 1981–2. Appointed to the Senate in 1981 by the Taoiseach, Dr Garret Fitzgerald, he was surprise choice as Foreign Minister in the Fine Gael-Labour Coalition which took office in July, 1981. Involved with Dr Fitzgerald in negotiations with British Government on setting up of British-Irish Intergovernment Council, and was at first formal meeting of that Council in January, 1982, when he had talks with NI Secretary of State James Prior. Was successively Professor of Civil Engineering in UCC and UCD before taking office.

DOUGLAS, WILLIAM ALBERT BOYD DOUGLAS.

Off. U. Assembly member for Londonderry 1982–. Also served in 1973–4 assembly and 1974–5 convention. OUP Whip in 1982 Assembly. b. 1921. As Limavady district master of the Orange Order, he was prominent in demonstrations against Civil rights meetings in S. Derry in 1969, and in staging loyalist demonstrations in Dungiven, where there were clashes between Orangemen and their opponents on several occasions during 1971. Limavady rural district council, 1960–73.

DOWN ORANGE WELFARE.

Loyalist paramilitary group based in N. Down, and linked with membership of the Orange Order. Formed in 1972, and especially active during the loyalist strike in May 1974, under the leadership of Lt-Col. Brush. Its members were involved in road blocks during the stoppage. The organisation also backed the more limited loyalist strike in May 1977.

DRUMM, MRS MAIRE. Vice-

President of Provisional Sinn Fein (1972–6), who was shot dead while a patient in the Mater Hospital, Belfast, on 28 March 1976. b. 1920. She was assassinated by three gunmen, two of them dressed as doctors, who burst into the ward. An open verdict was returned at the inquest in 1978, and her husband Jimmy Drumm (also a leading figure in Provisional Sinn Fein) protested after the inquest that the army had put about suggestions that she had been killed by the PIRA. This was denied by the army. Although there were many reports suggesting loyalist involvement, a police officer told the inquest that he did not know who the killers were. Mrs Drumm had resigned as vice-president of Provisional Sinn Fein ten days before her death; she said she had done so strictly for health reasons and supported the leadership. She had been acting President of Provisional Sinn Fein in 1971–2 when Ruadhri O'Bradaigh was in prison in the Republic. She herself had been to prison several times – the first occasion was in 1970 when she was accused of inciting people to join the IRA in the Bogside area of Londonderry. In a speech in Belfast in 1975 she spoke of republicans 'pulling down Belfast stone by stone' in defence of political status for prisoners. This led the Secretary of State, Merlyn Rees, to describe her as 'a Madame Defarge sitting by the guillotine'. Roy Mason, Secretary of State at the time of her death, spoke of her murder as 'savage'. In 1978, all sections of the Provisional Republican movement were represented at a ceremony in Milltown cemetery, Belfast, when a memorial to her was unveiled. She had previously requested that she should be buried outside the republican plot. Her husband, Jimmy Drumm, continued to serve on the executive of Provisional Sinn Fein.

DUFFY, PATRICK ALOYSIUS.
SDLP Assembly (1973–4) and Convention (1975–6) Member for Mid-Ulster. b. Stewartstown, Co. Tyrone, 1934. BA., LL.B. (QUB). Solicitor, with extensive business interests. Representative, National Political Front, 1964. Secretary of the Assembly of the Northern Irish People, 1971–2. Cookstown District Council, 1973–. When the NI Executive collapsed in 1974, he urged a joint British-Irish Administration as 'the only means of providing a satisfactory form of government in Northern Ireland'. Unsuccessfully contested Mid-Ulster in 1979 Westminster election. At the party's annual conference in November 1980, he said he could support the five individual demands of the H-Block hunger strikers, but not the idea of bringing them together as political status. He caused some surprise when he declined to be a candidate in Mid-Ulster in the 1982 Assembly election.

DUNGANNON. The South Tyrone town, with a population almost evenly comprised of Protestants and Catholics, which has figured heavily in events since 1968. The first civil rights march was from Coalisland (a nearby predominantly Catholic village) to Dungannon on 24 August 1968. One of the points of community tension in 1968 was the complaint of Catholics that they were denied their fair share of houses by the Unionist-controlled local council. In August 1969, riots flared in the town in the wake of events in Londonderry. The town has suffered greatly from the PIRA bombing campaign, and there have been many sectarian assassinations.

DUNLEATH, LORD (CHARLES EDWARD HENRY JOHN DUNLEATH). Active member of the House of Lords and effectively the voice of the Alliance Party at Westminster. b. London, 23 June 1933, son of Baron and Lady Dunleath. Represented N. Down in 1973 and 1982 Assemblies and in the Constitutional Convention, 1975–6. In 1977, successfully sponsored legislation in the House of Lords to provide for shared schools (for Protestant and Catholic pupils), wherever there is sufficient demand from parents. He also brought forward a Bill to bring divorce law in NI broadly into line with that in Great Britain, which led to the government having similar legislation passed in 1978. Has extensive business interests and is president of the Royal Ulster Agricultural Society. BBC National Governor for NI, 1967–73. Resigned from Alliance Party for a period in 1979–80 to make an unsuccessful bid for NI ITV franchise.

DUNLOP, MRS DOROTHY. Off. U. Assembly member for E. Belfast, 1982–. BA (QUB). Formerly on staff of BBC talks department in Belfast, and later taught in several Belfast schools and in the prison education service, Belfast City Council, 1975–. Deputy Lord Mayor, 1978–9. Chairman. E. Belfast Unionist Association. Granddaughter of Sir Robert Woods, one-time Unionist MP at Westminster for Trinity College, Dublin.

DUNLOP, JOHN. MP for Mid-Ulster, February 1974–83. Originally Vanguard-UUUC; UUUP, 1977–. b. 20 May 1910. Has catering business in Moneymore, Co. Londonderry, and sat in Assembly for Vanguard, 1973–4. Joined Rev. Ian Paisley in support of Unionist Action Council strike in May 1977, and split from Off. U. MPs with the break-up of Unionist parliamentary coalition in 1977. In the 1979 general election, Official Unionists decided not to oppose him in Mid-Ulster. Unsuccessful candidate in Mid-Ulster in 1982 Assembly election.

DUNLOP, STEWART. DUP Convention member for S. Antrim, 1975–6. b. 1946. Founder member of Protestant Unionist Party and DUP, Antrim District Council, 1973–.

DUNN, JAMES ALEXANDER. Parliamentary Under-Secretary, NI Office, 1976–9. b. 30 January 1926. Labour MP, Kirkdale (Liverpool) 1964–81; SDP, 1981–3. A prominent figure in the Merseyside Catholic community and especially active in education and soccer circles. At NI Office, he had special responsibility for Agriculture, Finance, and oversight of public bodies. Absent from NI Office through illness for most of his last year in office. Commons spokesman for SDP during passage of the 1982 devolution measure, to which he gave general support.

DUTCH-NORTHERN IRISH ADVISORY COMMITTEE. This committee, comprising educationalists, churchmen and others in both countries, has sponsored trips to Holland to show how the Netherlands has tackled the problems of religious and other divisions. Delegations of NI politicians to Holland have included an inter-party group in 1973, a further party in 1975, including members of the SDLP, Alliance, NILP and UPNI; a twenty-strong Off. U. deputation, headed by party leader Harry West. The trips have all included the study of law-and-order policy and visits to the Dutch parliament. The committee's 1977 report proposed the development of an adult education centre in the province. Members of paramilitary groups have attended some of the Dutch-based conferences sponsored by the committee.

E

ECONOMY. The province has always had a level of prosperity well below the UK average. Unemployment has tended to be higher and earnings lower, with personal income about seventy-seven per cent of UK average in 1982. At the best of times, the unemployment rate has been fifty per cent above the GB figure, and by 1979, it had reached twelve per cent – twice the UK average – while at the end of 1982, it was over twenty per cent, with the Government predicting a further rise in male unemployment over the next three years. Apart from the disincentive of the violence, employment has been declining over a long period in traditional industries like shipbuilding and textiles, as well as in farming. In 1977 the extensive attractions for new industry (in financial terms, the highest in the EEC) were further improved, and a new independent Economic Council established under the chairmanship of Sir Charles Carter of Lancaster University to advise the Government on ways of achieving more rapid economic growth. It included four independent members, with five from the CBI and five from the NI committee of the Irish Congress of Trade Unions. In 1982, Secretary of State James Prior further streamlined the Government structure concerned with industry and employment. The Commerce and Manpower departments were merged into a new Department of Economic Development, with an associated Industrial Development Board aimed at concentrating the drive to attract outside investment. The new Board was set up at a moment when the province's industrial base was contracting rapidly, after closures or serious cutbacks in several multinationals, such as Courtaulds, British Enkalon and Michelin, and the collapse of the De Lorean sports car project, which had once raised employment hopes in W. Belfast. In March, 1983, Mr Prior announced new measures to help industry, including up to 80 per cent refund of Corporation tax and 100 per cent de-rating of industrial premises. With the limited openings for school-

leavers, it was estimated that forty per cent of Government spending on support of the labour market would be going into youth training projects in 1983-4. The principle has been long established of broad parity in services and in taxation with the rest of the UK, but because of the lower tax yield in NI a substantial Treasury subsidy has been necessary in recent times. This amounted to £74m in 1969-70; by 1973-4 it had reached £314m; by 1975-6, £571m, and by 1978-9 about £860m. According to a Commons ministerial estimate in 1980, only about £1,000m of the £2,300m Government spending in the province was raised through taxation in NI. The total Treasury subvention between 1969 and 1979 was just under £4,000m. This excluded the writing-off in 1978 of NI Electricity Service debts totalling £250m. These figures also left out of account the cost of maintaining the army in NI, which amounted to £409m over the same 10-year period. It can be argued that the military spending involves little extra cost to the Exchequer, however, since a Government reply in the Commons has shown that the cost of keeping troops in NI is lower than in Germany, and not much greater than keeping them in GB. The cost of other law and order services was estimated at £400m for 1983-4. See EUROPEAN ECONOMIC COMMUNITY.

ELTON, LORD (OF HEADINGTON; RODNEY ELTON). Parliamentary Under-Secretary, NI Office, 1979-81. b. 2 March 1930. M.A. (Oxon.). Varied teaching career in comprehensive and grammar schools and as college lecturer, 1962–72. Conservative Whip in House of Lords, 1974–6. Front Bench Conservative spokesman in Lords, 1976–9. In NI Office, spokesman on all subjects in Lords and responsible for the departments of Agriculture and Education. Under-Secretary, Home Office, 1981–.

EMPEY, REGINALD. VUPP (and later UUUM) Convention member for E. Belfast, 1975–6. b. 1947. B.Sc. (QUB). He had been vice-chairman of the Young Unionist Council (OUP) before he joined VUPP, of which he became chairman in 1975. In the Convention, he was secretary of the UUUC's policy committee. Deputy leader, UUUP, 1977–. Unsuccessfully contested E. Belfast in 1982 Assembly election.

ENGLISH, MICHAEL. Chairman of the NI standing committee of MPs at Westminster, 1976–9. b. 24 December 1930. LL.B. (Liverpool). Has an Ulster family background. Labour MP for Nottingham W., 1964–83.

ERSKINE, LORD (OF RERRICK). Governor of NI, 1964–8. b. 14 December 1893. Was jeered by supporters of Rev. Ian Paisley when he attended the General Assembly of the Irish Presbyterian Church in Belfast on 5 June 1966. The protest was said to be against the 'Romeward trend' of the Church. The incident drew condemnation from the then Prime Minister, Capt. O'Neill, who talked of trends towards Nazism and Fascism.

EUROPA HOTEL. See FORUM HOTEL.

EUROPEAN COURT/COMMISSION OF HUMAN RIGHTS. Some interesting decisions affecting NI have been handed down by these interlinked Strasbourg-based bodies. The first of major interest was given in 1978, when, on the application of the Republic's Government, the Court dealt with charges of ill-treatment of internees during 'interrogation in depth'. The Court found that some internees had been subjected to 'inhuman and degrading treatment', but not to torture. Shortly before the 1981 H-Block hunger strike, the Commission (representing the first stage of the procedure) turned down a submission by four H-Block prisoners that their treatment was a breach of the European Convention, although it criticised the 'inflexibility' of the British Government. Two members of the Commission visited the Maze prison when Bobby Sands, MP, was on hunger strike, but Sands refused to follow up a complaint lodged on his behalf by his sister. This was followed by a move by a group of widows of victims of terrorism in NI to persuade the Commission that the Republic's Government was breaching the Convention by not taking adequate anti-terrorist measures. This campaign was organised by Armagh MP, Harold McCusker, and it appeared in early 1983 that the Commission was taking the line that there had been too much delay in making this plea. In 1982, the Commission undertook to investigate a case brought by a Newry woman who claimed that the army had shot her husband in October, 1971, without sufficient justification. In October, 1981, the Court held that the ban on male homosexuality in NI was a breach of the Convention, and in 1982 an Order was introduced to achieve parity in the law with GB.

EUROPEAN ECONOMIC COMMUNITY. The EEC has always been controversial in NI, as the narrow majority in favour of membership underlined. (See COMMON MARKET POLL). Although it was reported that receipts from Brussels at the end of 1982, after ten years of membership, amounted to £342m in grants, £129m in loans and nearly £212m under supplementary measures related to the UK budget rebate, intense arguments still raged in the province as to the extent to which the funnelling of money through Whitehall breached the 'additionality' rule of the EEC. Critics of membership suggested that there was, in effect, a net outflow of money to the Community. A Commons reply in March, 1981, stressed that it was not possible to determine in total how much of the UK's contribution to the EEC could be attributed to NI, nor the full extent of receipts from the Community. But it gave identified receipts up to that time as £136.5m and 'notional attribution of part of NI's share of UK payments' as £166.4m. The Government argument is that EEC money enables public spending in NI to be kept at a higher level than would otherwise be possible. The EEC treats NI as one of five high-priority areas in the Community. When the Commission vice-president, Christopher Tugendhat, spoke in Belfast in January, 1983, he said the Ulster crisis was 'a blot on the entire Community,' and it was obvious after ten years that the EEC had no panacea for NI's problems. But he claimed the EEC had cushioned the impact of the decline of traditional industries like shipbuilding and textiles, while the regional and social funds had grant-aided development of the infrastructure. He also said new possibilities would be opened up if NI people could agree on what the EEC should be doing in the province. An integrated plan for Belfast, linked with a similar project in Naples, had made little progress up to the end of 1982, but EEC budget arrangements indicated that substantial aid might be forthcoming eventually. A proposed £16m payment for Belfast housing had been held up by West Germany because it feared this would create a precedent, but in July, 1983, an urban renewal grant of £19m was finally approved by EEC. The refunds to the UK negotiated by Mrs Thatcher and totalling £212m in respect of NI to the end of 1982 included help for the link road in Belfast for the M1 and M2, and for the new Foyle bridge in Londonderry, as well as housing in both these cities. In 1981, £4.5m was allocated for a scheme to help tourism, communications and small businesses in NI border areas. In farming, the EEC was considering at the start of 1983, the extension of the less-favoured areas scheme, already covering forty-five per cent of agricultural land, to seventy per cent. Because of the EEC's monetary compensation arrangements at the Irish border, there has been heavy smuggling of animals in the early 1980s. One estimate is that 120,000 cattle were smuggled into NI in 1981, with a loss to the Intervention Board of about £5m. The European Parliament (see separate entry) has shown considerable interest in the local economy. In 1980, the EEC opened an office in Belfast, and in January, 1983, thirteen civil servants from NI were on secondment to the Commission staff, which was employing thirty-five NI people in all. NI receipts (including commitments), 1973-83:

Grants – agriculture fund, £21,914,000; regional fund, £139,060,000; social fund, £182,911,000; energy measures, £105,000. Loans: Investment Bank, £128,369,000. Special measures linked to UK refund, £211,748,000.

See EUROPEAN PARLIAMENT.

EUROPEAN PARLIAMENT.

NI has three seats in the Parliament. This allocation derived from a discussion at a European summit meeting in 1976, when the heads of government accepted a proposal from the Irish Republic's government that NI should have one more seat than it was entitled to under UK representation so as to ensure that both NI communities would have a voice in the Assembly. The idea was backed by James Callaghan, for the British Government. In January, 1978, the British Parliament decided that the first direct election should be held on PR in a single NI constituency – a further guarantee of a Nationalist-aligned member. Unionist MPs, who urged a straight vote as in the rest of the UK, had the support of a large section of the Conservative party. The election, on 7 June, 1979, resulted in the return of the Rev. Ian Paisley (DUP); John Hume (SDLP); and John Taylor (OUP), in that order. (See Elections Section). NI was previously unrepresented in the Assembly, except during 1973-4, when Rafton Pounder, Unionist MP for S. Belfast, was included in the British Conservative delegation. In Strasbourg, the three MEPs, despite their other differences, have co-operated in pressing the case for more EEC aid. The most notable example was when Mr Hume, in 1979, put forward a motion calling for a special report on measures to boost the NI economy. He was supported by Dr Paisley and Mr Taylor, and a special survey was carried out by a French MEP, Madame Simone Martin, in 1980. The Parliament backed her report, which called, among other things, for tax exemption for new industries for at least five years, special help for Belfast housing, and a common energy price structure throughout the UK. By early 1983, the Commission had still not given a full response to the report, although it clearly accepted its general approach. And Mrs Thatcher's decision to bring electricity charges in NI broadly into line with those in GB, and a proposal for financial aid for Belfast housing could be seen as a partial reply. The two Unionist MEPs and the SDLP leader have been strongly at odds on whether the Assembly should concern itself with NI political issues. In the autumn of 1982, Mr Hume sought to have special hearings organised by the Parliament's political affairs committee to find ways in which the Community could help end the political and economic crisis in the province. But both Dr Paisley and Mr Taylor attacked the suggestion, saying that it conflicted with a decision by the Parliament in 1981 that it should not become involved in the political and constitutional affairs of NI. In the event, the proposal gave rise to strong opposition from the British Government, with Mrs Thatcher declaring that there would be no co-operation with such an inquiry. But the Bureau of the Parliament authorised the political affairs committee to have a special report prepared by Danish MEP, Neils Haagerup. In May, 1981, the Parliament rejected a motion calling for British 'flexibility' on the H-Block dispute, put forward by two MEPs from the Republic, Neil Blaney and Paddy Lalor, on the ground that it was not competent to intervene in NI, and regretting the more than two thousand deaths in the current violence. But the Parliament passed in 1982 a motion calling for a ban throughout the EEC on the use of plastic bullets, which were at that time a matter of controversy in NI. There is an all-party committee on NI in the Parliament, headed by Danish MEP, Neils Haagerup, which has visited NI to talk to local politicians, but none of the three local MEPs is a member.

Public interest in NI in the activities of the Parliament is evidenced by the large number of local visitors to Strasbourg. See EUROPEAN ECONOMIC COMMUNITY.

EWART-BIGGS, CHRISTOPHER. British ambassador to Dublin, assassinated on 21 July 1976, two weeks after he took up the post. b. 1921. Ewart-Biggs and a young woman civil servant from the NI Office, Judith Cook, died when the ambassador's car was blown up by a land-mine, a short distance from his official residence in Sandyford, Co. Dublin. The assassination gave rise to the declaration of a state of emergency in the Irish Republic, and the introduction of additional anti-terrorist measures. In September 1976, Dublin newspapers reported that a PIRA spokesman had admitted responsibility for the murders. Ewart-Biggs was a colourful personality – 'straight out of P. G. Wodehouse' was a common assessment – and had a distinctive appearance, having worn an eye-patch since he lost his right eye in World War II. A novel which he had written in his early years was still banned in the Irish Republic when he was appointed to Dublin. His wife, Jane (created Life Peer 1978), declared that she had no bitterness towards the Irish people and she joined the Peace People, and also launched a memorial literary prize which is awarded to authors whose works are adjudged to have helped, among other things, towards peace and reconciliation in Ireland.

F

FALLS ROAD. The main Catholic district of Belfast, centred on the thoroughfare which stretches westwards from the city centre to Andersonstown. It runs parallel to the predominantly Protestant Shankill Road, from which it is separated by the Peace Line (or Orange-Green line) erected after riots and house-burnings of 1969. In this area of confrontation there have been many serious incidents during the troubles, and thousands of people moved out of their homes in the summer of 1969 when Protestant militants invaded the area and burned many homes (there were counter-claims on the Protestant side that loyalist homes had been attacked). The IRA has always looked for support to the Falls area, and it was here in the aftermath of the serious violence of 1969 that the PIRA began to assert itself. It was in the Lower Falls in the summer of 1969 that protests were mounted against RUC action in the Bogside area of Londonderry, and the Scarman report criticised the RUC for 'unjustified' firing of a Browning machine gun into Divis flats, which resulted in a young boy's death. The erection of barricades in the area in 1969 gave rise to angry controversy and delicate negotiations between the Falls Road-based CCDC and the government and security forces. These involved, at one point, a deputation to London to meet the Home Secretary, James Callaghan. The barriers were eventually lowered, but their existence brought repeated protests from loyalists, who sometimes erected their own barricades in the Shankill area as a protest. A major problem for the security forces has been the refusal of people in the area to fully accept the RUC, although by 1978 the police were claiming that co-operation was increasing and people in the area were more willing to give information, particularly by way of the confidential telephone. But the Scarman report showed that the policing problem was there even before 1969. It stated that after 1968 RUC foot patrols didn't go into a substantial area in the Falls on foot either late at night or early in the morning. This was the area bounded by the Falls Road, Grosvenor Road, Albert Street and Cullingtree Road. The police, according to Scarman, had code named the area 'Nogoland'. This was virtually the area chosen for the army curfew on 3–5 July 1970, which, according to Catholics, marked the end of the 'honeymoon' with the British army as protectors of the minority. During the curfew, which extended over thirty-four hours (apart from a two-hour shopping break), five civilians were killed, and sixty injured, while fifteen soldiers were injured. The army search during the curfew yielded fifty-two pistols, thirty-five rifles, six automatic weapons, fourteen shotguns, one hundred home-made bombs, a grenade, 250lbs of explosives, about 21,000 rounds of ammunition and 8 two-way radio sets. The operation led to strong protests from NICRA and the

CCDC, and two local politicians, Gerry Fitt MP and Paddy Devlin MP flew to London to complain that the troops had looted, stolen and abused people during the operation – charges broadly denied by the army. Falls Road spokesmen claimed that the army were ignoring much larger supplies of weapons and ammunition in the Shankill area. During the troubles, the Falls has been the venue of some fierce gun battles between the security forces and the PIRA, and of bitter feuds between the PIRA and the OIRA and between the OIRA and the IRSP. Several factories in the area were burnt in 1969, and over the years there have been numerous riots and demonstrations, in many of which buses have been burned and vehicles hi-jacked. The three RUC stations in the area – at Hastings Street, Springfield Road and Andersonstown – have been attacked frequently. Easter parades to the republican plot at Milltown cemetery, where many IRA men are buried, and funerals of members of the republican movement have been occasions of high tension between many residents and the police and army. And the introduction of internment in 1971 and the subsequent civil disobedience campaign further alienated many residents from the authorities. Up to the 1981 hunger strike, the SDLP with its support for constitutional politics, had majority backing in the area, and in 1977, official sources attributed PIRA's decision to regroup and alter its tactics to the disenchantment of local people with violent methods. But there was undoubtedly strong support for the H-Block protest in the Falls Road area, and in wider West Belfast. There were many pro-hunger strike demonstrations, and the vast turn-out for the funeral of Bobby Sands, MP, to Milltown cemetery testified to the growth of Republicanism. PSF's decision to contest W. Belfast at the 1982 Assembly election was a direct challenge to the SDLP, and strong organisational effort and a network of PSF advice centres paid off. Gerry Adams, vice-president of PSF, headed the poll with 25.5 per cent of first preferences, with the total SDLP vote for three candidates standing at 24.5 per cent. Mr Adams was also returned to Westminster in the 1983 general election, unseating Gerry Fitt, who had held the seat since 1966. See CENTRAL CITIZENS' DEFENCE COMMITTEE.

FARREN, SEAN NIAL. SDLP Assembly member for N. Antrim 1982–. SDLP chairman, 1981–. Unsuccessfully contested N. Antrim in 1979 Westminster election. Lecturer in education at NUU.

FAUL, FATHER DENIS. A leading campaigner against alleged ill-treatment of persons arrested for interrogation and of detainees during internment. b. Co. Louth, 1932. A teacher at St Patrick's Academy, Dungannon, he first attracted attention in November 1969, when he declared that Catholics felt that NI's judicial system was loaded against them. The statement was attacked by government ministers and brought a rebuke from Cardinal Conway. His main attacks have been on the army and the RUC Special Branch, but he has also strongly condemned PIRA violence and has called on PIRA, without success, to declare a ceasefire. In March 1977, he described the PIRA campaign of that period as 'spurious in republican terms' and 'directly contrary to Catholic teaching on the sacredness of human life'. As a Maze prison chaplain during the H-Block hunger strikes in 1980–1, he strongly opposed the fasts, but at the same time urged Government reforms to defuse the crisis. The meetings of relatives which he organised in the autumn of 1981 were seen as an important element in bringing the protest to an end. PSF accused him of bringing pressure on relatives to request medical intervention where hunger-strikers had lapsed into a coma.

FAULKNER, LORD (OF DOWNPATRICK). Formerly Brian Faulkner, Prime Minister, 1971–2, and Chief Executive in power-sharing administration, 1974. b. 18 February 1921 and killed in a hunting accident near his Co. Down home in March 1977. His career was the most dramatic and varied of any in Ulster politics. He was the last Prime Minister under the 1920 Constitution, and the first head of a Unionist government to include a Catholic in the Cabinet. In 1974, he led the brief inter-party Executive which embraced Unionists as well as members of the mainly Catholic SDLP and the Alliance Party. First spotted as a potential politician by British Labour Minister, Hugh Dalton, he started out as a traditional Unionist active in the Orange Order (he was a member of the Grand Orange Lodge of Ireland), and he was elected as MP for East Down in 1949. At 28, he was the youngest MP returned to Stormont up to that time. After three years as Government Chief Whip, he became Minister of Home Affairs in 1959 and was active in countering the IRA border campaign. In March 1963 he became Minister of Commerce in the Terence O'Neill government, and even political opponents praised his energetic and successful approach to the attraction of new industry, particularly from overseas. He caused a major surprise in January 1969 when he resigned from the O'Neill government in protest against the setting up of the Cameron Commission to inquire into the causes of the violence. The resignation was obviously a climax to tensions between Faulkner and O'Neill. And when O'Neill resigned as Prime Minister in April 1969, Faulkner failed by only one vote to succeed him. Major Chichester-Clark became Prime Minister and appointed him Minister of Development, with the task of carrying through local government reform and the setting up of a central housing authority. When Chichester-Clark bowed out as Premier in 1971, he finally achieved his ambition to become Prime Minister, easily beating his only challenger, William Craig. In August 1971, he introduced internment without trial, a move which infuriated the opposition, and led to an escalation, rather than a decline, in violence. And in March 1972, what he had confidently predicted would never happen occurred overnight – the Stormont parliament was prorogued. He joined militant Unionists in demonstrating against the action of the Heath government, and he refused to have anything to do with the Commission set up to advise the Secretary of State. Northern Ireland, he declared, would not be treated like a 'coconut colony'. His biggest test came in 1973 when he joined with the SDLP and Alliance parties in the Sunningdale conference and the Coalition Executive. But power-sharing and the cross-border Council of Ireland were too much for the Unionist Party. The loyalist strike brought down the Executive in May 1974. In the Convention election, he tried to bring mainline Unionism behind his UPNI, a breakaway group, but it fared badly in the election. In 1976, he announced that he was quitting active politics. In 1977, he became a Life Peer (he could have had a peerage in 1972), and he confessed that power-sharing had cost him his political life. His autobiography, *Memoirs of a Statesman,* appeared in 1978, fifteen months after his death. His widow, Lady Lucy Faulkner, a BBC Governor, became first chairman of the NI Broadcasting Council in 1981.

FEAKLE TALKS. Secret discussions between Protestant Churchmen, mainly from NI, and Provisional Sinn Féin and IRA representatives in Smyth's Village Hotel, Feakle, Co. Clare, on 9-11 December 1974. The talks were criticised by many Unionists, and

the churches stressed that the clergy taking part had acted only as individuals. The talks were followed by a brief IRA ceasefire, and later by a more extended ceasefire (or truce according to the IRA) which petered out in renewed IRA violence after a few months. The Churchmen involved were: Dr Arthur Butler, C. of I. Bishop of Connor; Dr Jack Weir, then Clerk of the Presbyterian Assembly; Rev. Eric Gallagher, former president of the Methodist Church in Ireland; the Rev. Ralph Baxter (secretary) and Rev. William Arlow (assistant secretary) of the Irish Council of Churches; Dr Harry Morton, secretary, British Council of Churches; Right Rev. Arthur McArthur, moderator of the United Reformed Church in England and Mr Stanley Worrall, former headmaster of Methodist College Belfast, and chairman of NUM. The Provisional Sinn Féin spokesmen included the president, Ruadhri O'Bradaigh; Mrs Maire Drumm, vice-president, and Seamus Loughran, Belfast organiser. The IRA leaders included David O'Connell, chief-of-staff, and at the time regarded as the most wanted man in Ireland, Seamus Twomey and Kevin Mallon. There was a touch of drama during the meeting, since men from the Republic's Special Branch entered the hotel, apparently as a result of a tip-off. But the IRA men had already left. The proposals exchanged between the Churchmen and the Provisionals were as follows:
The Churchmen suggested that the IRA would consider that its requirements prior to a perma-

nent ceasefire were met if the British government issued a policy statement which included the following:

1 HM Government solemnly reaffirms that it has no political or territorial interests in Ireland beyond its obligations to the citizens of Northern Ireland.

2 The prime concern of HM Government is the achievement of peace and the promotion of such understanding between the various sections in Northern Ireland as will guarantee to all its people a full participation in the life of the community, whatever be the relationship of the Province to the EEC, the United Kingdom, or the Republic of Ireland.

3 Contingent upon the maintenance of a declared ceasefire and upon effective policing, HM Government will relieve the army as quickly as possible of its internal security duties.

4 Until agreements about the future government of Northern Ireland have been freely negotiated, accepted and guaranteed, HM Government intends to retain the presence of the armed forces in Northern Ireland.

5 HM Government recognises the obligation and right of all those who have political aims to pursue them through the democratic processes. The PIRA's Army Council sent a point-by-point reply within a few days as follows:

We have considered at length the points you submitted to our colleagues. We wish to make the following observations:

1 It is sovereignty rather than political or territorial interests which is the basic issue. Until HM Government clearly states it has no claim to sovereignty to any part of Ireland, the statement is meaningless. We accept that economic commitments must be honoured.

2 A noble wish with which we concur, but we believe it can only be realised in the full community of the people of Ireland.

3 We feel you are referring to a truce. We see no difficulty in maintaining community peace if a bilateral truce is agreed to between the British Army and the Irish Republican Army. We would welcome discussions with loyalist groups to secure their co-operation in maintaining peace.

4 We accept that following a declaration of intent to withdraw, a limited British Army presence will be maintained while a negotiated and agreed settlement is sought and implemented.

5 It is meaningless to talk about democratic processes while, among other things, 2,000 political prisoners are in jail.

We submit for your consideration and for forwarding to the British Government the following set of proposals:

To provide the basis for a lasting peace, the Republican Movement calls for the implementation of the following measures:

1 The establishment of a constituent assembly elected by the people of Ireland through universal adult suffrage and proportional representation. The assembly to draft a new all-Ireland constitution which would provide for a

provisional parliament for Ulster (nine counties) with meaningful powers. The constitution to be submitted in national referendum within six months of the first meeting of the assembly, and its adoption to require two-thirds support of the total valid poll.

2 A public commitment by the British Government to withdraw from Ireland within twelve months of the adoption of the new all-Ireland constitution. This commitment to entail an immediate end to all raids, arrests and harassment of the population and a withdrawal of troops to barracks.

3 Declaration of amnesty for all political prisoners in Britain and Ireland, and all persons on the wanted list. The amnesty to be given effect by immediate releases and to be completed not later than thirty days prior to the date of the general election for the constituent assembly.

4 On the acceptance of these terms, the Republican Movement would be prepared to order a total ceasefire. A number of matters would require further clarification and elaboration which would be discussed as soon as the ceasefire is established. The Republican Movement for its part would welcome tripartite talks with loyalist and British Army forces to secure their cooperation in the implementation of the ceasefire and the maintenance of community peace.

Finally, having discussed the terms offered by the Church representatives, and found them to be unacceptable, we, the Republican Movement will declare a temporary cessation of activities from midnight on the 22 December 1974 until midnight on the 2 January 1975 to enable the British Government to reply favourably to the counter proposals we have made to them. The cessation will be total and complete providing that

1 British Army raids, harassment and arrests cease for the same period.

2 No show of provocation is carried out by the Crown forces.

3 The reintroduction of the RUC into areas in which they are not acceptable is not attempted. (This includes any of the Crown forces in or out of uniform.)

4 Any breach of these terms will be considered as a refusal to accept the eleven-day cessation, and appropriate action will be taken to protect our people. We wish to have an indication of the British Government's attitude before the 28 December 1974.

The Army Council, Oglaigh na hEireann

December 1974.

On 18 December the Secretary of State, Mr Rees, received five of the Churchmen involved in the Feakle talks to hear the IRA's views. Afterwards, he issued a statement declaring that if there was a genuine cessation of violence there 'would be a new situation to which the British Government would naturally respond'. On 19 December Mr Arlow had a meeting with the IRA chief-of-staff, and the ceasefire over the Christmas and New Year period was ordered by the IRA. But Mr Rees insisted that there could be no deals with the IRA, and although government officials met Provisional Sinn Fein representatives to 'explain' government policy, and special incident centres were set up to allow Provisional Sinn Fein to make quick contact with the authorities so as to safeguard the ceasefire, it was evident by Easter 1975, that the Provisionals felt they weren't getting anything tangible in political terms and the violence crept back steadily. The high hopes which some of the Churchmen had voiced after the Feakle talks had been disappointed, and the affair had proved no more than an interesting exercise in indirect contacts between the British government and the IRA.

FEELY, FRANK. SDLP Assembly member for S. Down, 1982–. Also represented same constituency in Assembly (1973–4) and Convention (1975–6). b. Kiltimagh, Co. Mayo, 1937. BA (UCG) H.Dip.Ed. (Maynooth). Active in ALJ and in Newry civil rights committee, 1968–71. Party delegate at Atkins Conference, 1980.

FENIAN. A term sometimes applied to Catholics by extreme loyalists, but strictly referring to members of the Fenian Brotherhood, active in the nineteenth century in Britain and North America in fighting British rule in Ireland.

FERGUSON, (WILLIAM) RAYMOND. Off. U. Assembly member for Fermanagh and S. Tyrone, 1982–. Comes of a family long associated with Unionism in Fermanagh. Fermanagh Council, 1977–. Chairman of Council, 1981–. Unsuccessfully contested the Westminster seat in the 1979 general election. Solicitor; ex-Ulster rugby player.

FERGUSON, RICHARD. Unionist MP at Stormont for S. Antrim, 1968–70. b. Belfast 22 August 1935. LL.B. Hons (QUB), B.A. (TCD). Member NI Bar (QC), English Bar, and in March, 1983, became first NI barrister called to Republic's Inner Bar. On the liberal wing of the Unionist Party, and a supporter of Terence O'Neill, he resigned from the Orange Order in August 1969. In February 1970, he resigned as MP for health reasons, and in April 1970, his home in Lisburn was damaged by a bomb. He joined the Alliance Party in March 1971.

FIANNA FAIL. One of the two major parties in the Irish Republic, it originated from the wing of Sinn Fein opposed to the Anglo-Irish Treaty of 1921. It first came to power under Eamon de Valera in 1932, and it has been the governing party for most of the period since. It gave way to inter-party Governments headed by Fine Gael in 1948–51, 1954–7, 1973–7, July, 1981–February, 1982; and December, 1982–. In the 1930s it took a number of steps to underline separation from Britain – high protective tariffs, and distinguishing of Irish nationality from British, the abolition of the post of Governor-General. Furthermore, the 1937 Constitution contained articles stating the claim to a united Ireland. These have been regarded by Ulster Unionists as a threat to NI, although Southern spokesmen have always insisted that they seek unity only by consent. A Fianna Fail policy statement in 1975 called for a British declaration of intent to withdraw from NI, but party leader Jack Lynch and his colleagues stressed that it was not comparable with the 'Brits Out' demands of PSF. They said that no time scale was mentioned, and that the aim was to encourage Britain to promote unity in a peaceful way, and not simply to repeat 'negative' guarantees of NI's position. Mr Lynch, who in the early 1960s, as Minister for Industry and Commerce, broke new economic ground by giving preferential tariffs to some NI goods, caused anger in Britain and in NI with his criticism of British security policy in NI in 1969. There were also occasional complaints from Britain that his Government was not taking a sufficiently tough line against PIRA, notably after the Mountbatten murder. When Mr Lynch resigned in December, 1979, his favoured candidate as successor, George Colley, lost out to Charles Haughey. And Mr Haughey gave a new direction to FF's NI policy. He stressed the need for agreement with Britain on NI's future, and clearly saw his December, 1980, summit meeting with Mrs Thatcher in Dublin as a useful step. But FF's relations with Britain worsened as the Thatcher Government felt Mr Haughey had over-played the Dublin meeting, and when he also criticised the Conservative Government's approach to the H-Block hunger strike and failed to back Britain on anti-Argentina sanctions during the Falklands conflict. The 1982 FF Government was also highly critical of Britain's 'rolling devolution'

initiative in NI. In 1983, it supported the Forum for a New Ireland (see separate entry).

FIANNA na h-EIREANN. Youth wing of the PIRA, traditionally used to provide communications, to alert terrorists as to the approach of security forces, and on occasion to stage incidents which might lure troops or police into ambush positions. The security forces claimed that after the introduction of internment without trial, the youth wing was employed increasingly in carrying bombs and in moving weapons. The exact strength of the movement is difficult to determine, but it probably reached several hundred in Belfast in the 1971–2 period, and then declined somewhat as the IRA switched its effort more to small active service units.

FINE GAEL. One of the two main political parties in the Irish Republic. Derives from the pro-Treaty wing of the old Sinn Fein movement. In the 1920s it was known as Cumann na nGaedheal, and formed the first government of the Irish Free State. That administration was headed by W. T. Cosgrave, whose son, Liam Cosgrave, was to become Taoiseach, 1973–7. To many people outside the Republic, particularly NI Unionists and the British public, it has been regarded as taking a softer line than the Fianna Fail Party on NI issues and a united Ireland. But the overall records of the two parties on these matters have differed little in practice. Although de Valera and Fianna Fail rejected the Treaty which led to the setting up of two separate administrations in Ireland, and to the partition of the country, the future Fine Gael party was supported by republicans like Michael Collins and by the underground Irish Republican Brotherhood. Since losing power to de Valera and Fianna Fail in 1932, it has been unable to sustain a government from its own ranks. Out of power in the 1930s, it was allied briefly to Eoin O'Duffy's 'Blue-shirts', a fascist-type group. When one of its leading figures, James Dillon, urged support for the Allies in World War II, he was expelled. The inter-party government of 1948–51, made up of Fine Gael, the Irish Labour Party and the small republican party, Clann na Poblachta, and led by John Costello, broke the last tenuous link with the British Commonwealth. When it came to power, in combination with the Irish Labour Party in 1973, under the leadership of Liam Cosgrave, it had acquired a left-centre image. One of the disappointments of the Fine Gael leadership in that period was the failure of the Sunningdale conference in 1973 to provide a lasting solution in NI. And when Dr Garret Fitzgerald took over as party leader in 1977, after the defeat of the coalition, one of his first moves was to launch a fresh appraisal of policy on NI and Irish unity. In 1979, the party published a scheme for an Irish confederation, but it failed to attract any serious interest among Unionists. The party returned to power after the June, 1981, election, again in coalition with Labour, but as a minority administration dependent on the votes of a few Independents. The Coalition agreed

with the British Government in November, 1981 the setting up of the British-Irish Intergovernmental Council, but soon afterwards it was defeated on its Budget and lost office in the February, 1982, election. Fine Gael was unhappy about the British Government 'rolling devolution' initiative on NI in 1982, but less vehement in its denunciation than the Fianna Fail Government. It was also critical of Taoiseach Charles Haughey's all-out assault on sanctions against Argentina during the Falklands conflict – an attitude which greatly angered the Thatcher Government. When the minority Fianna Fail Government was defeated in the November 1982, election, Fine Gael returned to power, once more in combination with Labour and promised a 'radical new approach' to NI. In 1983, its leader launched the Forum for a New Ireland (see separate entry).

FITT, LORD. As Gerard Fitt MP at Westminster for W. Belfast, 1966–83. Has been Independent Socialist since 1979, when he resigned from the SDLP, which he had led from its foundation in 1970. He broke with the SDLP because of its initial refusal to attend the Constitutional Conference organised by Secretary of State Humphrey Atkins, and his belief that the party was becoming less Socialist and 'more green Nationalist'. Earlier, he was Republican Labour and, still earlier, Irish Labour. b. Belfast, 9 April 1926, he first worked as a soap boy in a barber's shop, and then served with the British merchant navy, 1941–53, and he was in many wartime convoys to Russia. At sea, he educated himself in law and politics and when he left the navy he devoted himself to grassroots politics in his native Dock ward, then a tough and colourful waterfront area. His energy and keen sense of humour – he often referred to his five daughters as the 'Miss Fitts' – soon established him as a personality in local politics. In 1958, he was returned as an Irish Labour member of Belfast City Council, of which he remained a member until 1981, when his anti-hunger strike stance brought about his defeat. In 1962, he entered the NI Parliament, gaining the Dock seat from the Unionists. In 1966, he also won the W. Belfast seat from a Unionist, and his effective use at Westminster of material provided by the Campaign for Social Justice was an important factor in developing British Labour interest in the NI situation. He organised several trips to the province by sympathetic Labour MPs, notably on the occasion of the Londonderry civil rights march on 5 October, 1968, when he received a head injury. During the five-months power-sharing Executive in 1974, he was the Deputy Chief Executive – that is, deputy to Brian Faulkner. He has stood out strongly against PIRA, some of whose supporters attacked his Belfast home in August, 1976. On that occasion, he defended himself, his wife and some members of his family with a gun. He has been a supporter, for the most part, of the Labour Party at Westminster, and his vote was often important to the Wilson and Callaghan Governments. But he abstained in the crucial confidence vote in 1979 which brought down the Labour administration. He was demonstrating, he said, his 'disillusionment' with Roy Mason as NI Secretary. In 1978, he secured the passage of a Private Members' Bill to bring the law in NI on the chronically sick and disabled into line with that in GB. He lost his seat to Gerry Adams, PSF, in the 1983 election, but pulled over 10,000 votes, many of which were believed to have come from normally Unionist and Alliance voters. He had campaigned on an anti-PIRA ticket and his appointment as a Life Peer in 1983 was popular at Westminster, but not with Irish Nationalists.

FITZGERALD, GARRET. Leader of the Fine Gael party in the Republic 1977–. Taoiseach, 1981–March 1982; December, 1982–. b. 9 February 1926. Dr Fitzgerald has probably visited NI more frequently than any other Dublin-based politician. He has close northern family connections for, while his father Desmond was the first Foreign Minister of the Irish Free State, his mother was an Ulster Presbyterian. His ministerial responsibility for NI affairs as Foreign Minister in the Cosgrave government 1973–7 covered the period of Sunningdale, the Assembly and the Convention, so that he was regularly involved in talks with British Ministers on security and political issues affecting the province. He used his influence as Foreign Minister and as EEC president to promote cross-border economic co-operation. After the failure of the

Convention in 1976 he tried to encourage fresh thinking on NI devolution, including an interim scheme, and had fairly regular meetings with most of the NI political groups, other than the DUP. While looking to an eventual United Ireland, he has always stressed the need for full consent within NI and reassurance for Northern Protestants. He disclosed in 1978 that he had told loyalist leaders in NI in 1974 that they would be 'bloody fools' to join the Republic under its existing Constitution. Formerly a lecturer in political economy at UCD he operated extensively as a journalist for British and American publications before going on to the front bench in the Dail. On taking over the Fine Gael leadership in 1977, he emphasised that he would continue to have personal oversight of his party's policy on NI. Following a re-assessment, Fine Gael produced in 1979 a scheme for an Irish confederation. It was clearly intended to open up debate on the future of NI, and while Unionists showed no enthusiasm for the idea they conceded for the most part that it was a sincere effort by Dr Fitzgerald to meet Northern sensibilities. In February, 1980, Dr Fitzgerald said most British politicians would prefer not to have to maintain the link with NI and should say so publicly. When he took office as Taoiseach after the June, 1981, general election, he quickly announced a 'crusade' to make the Republic's Constitution more attractive to NI Protestants. At his London meeting with Mrs Thatcher in November, 1981, the decision to set up a British-Irish Intergovernmental Council (see separate entry) was announced. But that Coalition Government was short-lived. The Fine Gael-Labour administration was dependent on the backing of a few Independents, and their refusal to support the January 1982 Budget led to a further inconclusive election in February and a minority Fianna Fail Government. In the November, 1982, general election, he was once more poised for power as Fianna Fail lost ground, and he took office again in December as head of a Fine Gael-Labour coalition with an overall majority. During that election campaign, he urged the setting up of all-Ireland Courts and an all-Ireland police force to counter terrorism – ideas which brought him into sharp collision with Fianna Fail leader Charles Haughey. Speaking at QUB in January 1983, he said his Government wanted a 'new and dynamic relationship' with both NI communities, the British Government and their European friends in creating a tolerant, compassionate and just society in Ireland. He did not want EEC 'interference' in NI, but he said there was need for international encouragement for some solution that would dissolve the impasse. In March, 1983, he had talks with Mrs Thatcher at Brussels Euro-summit in a bid to restore Anglo-Irish relations. In April, 1983, he launched the Forum for a New Ireland (see separate entry). When Unionists took fifteen of the seventeen NI seats at Westminster in the 1983 election, he urged PR for these contests so as to give more representation to SDLP and Alliance.

He also said PSF's heavy vote in the election could not be ignored.

FITZSIMMONS, WILLIAM K. Minister of Health and Social Services, 1969–72. b. Belfast, 31 January 1909. As Minister of Development in 1967, he drew up statement on reform of local government. Unionist MP for Duncairn, 1956–72.

FLANAGAN, SIR JAMIE. Chief Constable of the RUC, 1973–6. b. 1914. The first Catholic to be appointed police chief, he had been Deputy Chief Constable since November 1970. He had two specially difficult periods as Chief Constable – the UWC strike in 1974 and the PIRA ceasefire in 1975. During the 1974 strike, there was an undercurrent of criticism of the RUC by supporters of the Executive that it did not act vigorously enough against the strikers. During the ceasefire, there were indications of some unrest within the RUC on the ground that they were being required for political reasons to 'go easy' on the PIRA. In the autumn of 1975, there were allegations that the Secretary of State, Merlyn Rees, was anxious to see Sir Jamie sacked, but this was firmly denied.

FOOT, MICHAEL. Leader of British Labour Party, 1981–3. b. 23 July 1913. Deputy leader, Labour Party, 1976–81. MP for Ebbw Vale, 1960–. As leader of the Commons in the Callaghan Government, he pleased Unionists and angered the SDLP when he supported the proposal for a Speaker's Conference on the NI seats, which led to the Boundary Commission recommendation of five extra MPs. When he visited NI in February 1982, to talk to politicians and trade unionists, it was his first trip to the province for twenty-five years, and he stressed mainly the need for more jobs rather than pushing his party's new policy of campaigning actively for a united Ireland by consent. In December 1982, he was critical of the action of GLC leader Ken Livingstone in inviting two PSF Assemblymen, Gerry Adams and Danny Morrison, to London to speak to Labour MPs and councillors. The project was halted by the Home Secretary's decision to exclude both men under the Prevention of Terrorism Act.

FORSYTHE, CLIFFORD. Off. U. MP S. Antrim, 1983–. Assembly member for S. Antrim, 1982–. Newtownabbey Council, 1973–. Mayor of Newtownabbey, 1981–3. Former professional footballer with Linfield and Derry City.

FORUM FOR A NEW IRELAND. The conference of Irish Nationalist parties which had its initial meeting in Dublin on 30 May 1983, with the aim of providing by the end of 1983 a blueprint for a NI settlement. The body was set up primarily at the suggestion of the SDLP, whose leader, Euro-MP John Hume, joined the Republic's leading politicians at the inaugural session in Dublin Castle. The differing attitudes of the Republic's two main political parties to NI and the issue of Irish unity emerged at the opening. The Taoiseach, Dr Garret Fitzgerald, urged consensus and said they must not hold back from examining any structures which would guarantee the two Irish traditions. But Fianna Fail leader, Charles Haughey, was more specific – he wanted the forum to construct a basic position which could then be put to an all-Ireland constitutional conference, convened by the British and Irish Governments as a prelude to British withdrawal. Mr Hume spoke of the need for reconciliation of seemingly irreconcilable differences. Because of their advocacy of violence, PSF were not invited to the conference, and the Workers' Party rejected an invitation. In Northern Ireland, all three parties attending the Assembly also refused to take part. The two main Unionist parties – OUP and DUP – made it clear they would have nothing to do with the forum which they portrayed as a new SDLP tactic to secure a united Ireland. The Alliance Party dismissed the body as 'counterproductive'.

FORUM HOTEL. Formerly the Belfast Europa Hotel, close to Belfast city centre, which was once known as NI's most-bombed building. A bomb which caused considerable damage in 1976 was the twentieth to explode in or near the twelve-storey hotel belonging to the Grand Metropolitan Group. The hotel has been a favourite rendezvous for politicians and journalists during the troubles.

FOSTER, REV. IVAN. DUP Assembly member for Fermanagh and S. Tyrone, 1982–. b. 1943. Free Presbyterian Church Minister, 1967–. Named as local commander in Fermanagh of the 'third force' set up by the DUP in early 1982. Active in Vanguard Movement in early 1970s.

FREELAND, LT-GEN. SIR IAN HENRY (Retd). Army GOC and Director of Operations, NI 1969–71. b. 14 September 1912. Sir Ian, who had been Deputy Chief of the General Staff, 1968–9, was the first GOC to be overall Director of Operations in NI – a situation which arose from talks between the British and NI governments in August 1969, when troops first went on to the streets in support of the RUC. Sir Ian had to cope with a great variety of problems – the 1969 riots and the development of barricades and no-go areas, the erection of a 'peace line' between Catholic and Protestant areas in W. Belfast, and the recurring civil rights marches and loyalist counter-demonstrations. In 1970, he took a tough line with trouble-makers and ran into severe criticism from NICRA and local defence committees in Catholic areas. In April 1970, he warned petrol bombers that they would be shot and in June 1970, that anybody carrying a firearm would be shot without warning. His most controversial operation in Belfast was the Falls Road curfew from 3–5 July 1970. From Friday night until Sunday morning, a large area was sealed off and houses searched intensively. A large cache of arms and ammunition was uncovered, but there was severe violence during which five civilians were killed and sixty injured, while fifteen soldiers were injured. The curfew, which was raised for only two hours on Saturday to allow for local shopping, gave rise to allegations by the NICRA and local MPs that there had been looting, theft and abusive behaviour by the troops. General Freeland denied, however, that there had been any excessive force by the army.

FREUD, CLEMENT. British Liberal Party spokesman on NI, 1976–9. b. 1924. A grandson of Sigmund Freud, father of modern psychology, he supported reconciliation in statements on NI, and sought to maintain all-party approach to NI problems. MP for Isle of Ely, 1973–. Popular journalist and broadcaster.

FRIENDS OF IRELAND. An organisation set up in Washington on 16 March 1981 – the eve of St Patrick's Day – by leading Irish-Americans associated with Sen. Edward Kennedy and Speaker

'Tip' O'Neill. The politicians reaffirmed support for Irish unity, but said it must have the support of the NI majority. They said the US had a constructive role to play in promoting a NI settlement, and they expressed satisfaction that support in the US for violence in Ireland had diminished since they had issued their first St Patrick's Day message in 1977. In 1982, some leaders of the Church of Ireland and the Presbyterian Church criticised the group for not taking enough account of the Unionist viewpoint.

FYFFE, WILLIAM. Unionist MP for N. Tyrone at Stormont, 1969–72. b. Strabane, 1914. A leading local journalist, he strongly argued against the holding of civil rights marches in Strabane, since they tended, he argued, to worsen community relations. Supported Terence O'Neill in 1969 election campaign.

G

GARDINER REPORT. The report of the committee of inquiry, headed by the former Lord Chancellor, Lord Gardiner, which reported in January 1975, on measures to deal with terrorism in NI in the context of civil liberties and human rights. The committee also included Lord MacDermott, former Lord Chief Justice of NI; Alistair Buchan, J. P. Higgins, Kathleen Jones, Michael Morland, and John Whyte. It held that detention without trial was a short-term necessity, and that 'special category' (or political sta-

tus) for convicted prisoners should be ended, with priority being given to a halt on admission of new prisoners to the status. Other points were: the system of non-jury trials for terrorist offences should be continued for the present; that there should be a new offence of terrorism; that the prison building programme should be speeded up; and that an independent means of investigating complaints against the police should be introduced. The committee also said that the normal conventions of majority rule would not work in NI. It said no political framework could endure unless both communities shared in the responsibility of administering, and recognition was given to the different national inheritances of the two communities. Lord MacDermott declined to subscribe to this second point, however, since he said he could not understand what it meant.

GASTON, JOSEPH ALEXANDER. Off. U. Assembly member for N. Antrim, 1982–. b. 1928. Ballymoney Council, 1973–. Chairman, N. Antrim Unionist Association. Was part-time member of UDR for seven years until he lost a leg from IRA booby-trap bomb.

GIBSON, SIMPSON. DUP Assembly member for N. Down, 1982–. Ards Council, 1977–. Vice-chairman of DUP and secretary of the Unionist Forum, an 'umbrella' group of the Unionist parties.

GILLILAND, DAVID. Chief Information Officer, NI Office, at Stormont, 1972–. b. Londonderry, 1927. Journalist on the *Londonderry Sentinel* and *Belfast Telegraph* before joining the NI Government Information Service in 1956. Principal official spokesman at Stormont since he became press secretary to Lord Moyola as Prime Minister in 1969, and by 1982 had served under six Secretaries of State. Has visited the US regularly to brief officials and journalists.

GILMOUR, SIR IAN HEDWORTH JOHN LITTLE. Conservative spokesman on NI, 1974–5. b. 8 July 1926. Conservative MP

for Norfolk Central, 1962–74; Chesham, 1974–. Lord Privy Seal (Deputy Foreign Secretary), 1979–81. Sir Ian was closely involved with security policy in NI between 1970 and 1974, since during this period he rose from Under-Secretary in the Defence Ministry to Secretary for Defence. As opposition spokesman on NI from June 1974 until early 1975 he gave strong support to the Labour government's Convention initiative, and he warned that if it failed the dangers could be very great. Before he was sacked from the Government by Mrs Thatcher in 1981, he was member of Cabinet group discussing a NI initiative.

GLASS, JOHN BASIL CALDWELL. Deputy leader of the Alliance Party, 1976–80. b. Co. Leitrim, Irish Republic, 1926. LL.B. (QUB) A leading Belfast solicitor, he was the first chairman of the Alliance Party and president, 1972–4. Represented S. Belfast in both the Assembly (1973–4) and the Convention (1975–6), but unsuccessful candidate there in the 1982 Assembly election. Alliance Chief Whip, 1973–6, and Deputy Chief Whip of NI Executive, 1974. Unsuccessfully contested S. Belfast in the October, 1974 Westminster election, but got more than 11,000 votes. Belfast City Council, 1977–81. Party vice-chairman, 1983–.

GLENDINNING, WILL. All. Assembly member for W. Belfast, 1982–. Belfast City Council, 1977–. Leader of Alliance group in City Council and party spokesman on housing.

GOODHART, PHILIP CARTER. Parliamentary Under-Secretary, NI Office, 1979–81. b. 3 November 1925. Conservative MP for Bromley, Beckenham, 1957–. Former Fleet Street journalist. Has served on many British delegations, including UN General Assembly, NATO Assembly and Council of Europe. As chairman of Conservative Party's Committee on NI, 1976–9, he was only Minister appointed to Stormont by Mrs Thatcher who had close knowledge of NI issues. Responsible in NI Office for Department of the Environment.

GORMLEY, THOMAS COLUMBA. MP at Stormont for Mid-Tyrone, 1962–72 (Ind. Nationalist until 1972, when he became one of first three members of Alliance Parliamentary Party). b. Claudy, Co. Derry, 29 July 1916. Strabane rural council, 1947. Tyrone Co. Council, 1950–73.

GOULDING, CATHAL. Chief-of-staff of OIRA, 1969–. b. Dublin, 1922. Comes of strong republican family, and his record in IRA goes back to World War II, during which he was interned by the Dublin government. He was involved in revival of IRA organisation after the war, and in 1953, while working as a house painter in England, became associated with Sean MacStiofain, who was later to become chief-of-staff of PIRA. They, together with another man, were sentenced to eight years imprisonment for an arms raid on Felstead School in Essex in 1953. By 1967 he had become a power in the IRA, and

in an address at that period put forward the Marxist views which were later to become associated with Official Sinn Fein and the OIRA. In 1972, he led the OIRA in declaring a ceasefire, and he was strongly critical of the PIRA bombing campaign. In an interview with *Pravda* in 1972, he said the Provisional bombings were inhuman acts in moral terms, and provocative in political terms. He made no comment when allegations were made in a Dublin magazine in 1982 that OIRA was still involved in murders and large-scale armed robberies. The Workers' Party (formerly Official Sinn Fein, the political wing of OIRA) dismissed the charges as 'muck'.

GOWRIE, EARL. (Alexander Patric Greysteil Ruthven), Minister of State and Deputy Secretary of State, September 1981–3. b. 26 November 1939. Educated Eton and Oxford. Member of a Southern Irish Protestant family, he came to NI with James Prior, with whom he had served as Minister of State at the Employment Department. As Minister reponsible for prisons, he was closely involved in the later talks on the 1981 H-Block hunger strike. He occasionally stirred controversy – for example, by urging joint British and Irish citizenship for NI people. In 1982, he commented that the Government's plans for 'rolling devolution' might take twenty or thirty years to mature. In 1983, he described PIRA leadership as 'very intelligent, very sophisticated.' After the 1983 election, he left NI to become Minister for the Arts.

GRAHAM, EDGAR SAMUEL DAVID. Off. U. Assembly member for S. Belfast, 1982–. b. 1954. Barrister and law lecturer, QUB. Chairman, Ulster Young Unionist Council, 1981–. Hon. Sec., Ulster Unionist Council 1982. Has written two pamphlets for his party's Devolution Group, and responsible for legal submissions to European Commission of Human Rights on behalf of widows of terrorist victims through special unit set up by Harold McCusker, MP. First chairman of Assembly's finance and personnel committee, 1983–.

GRAHAM, GEORGE. DUP Assembly member for S. Down, 1982–. b. 1947. In 1975, he was the first DUP member elected to Newry and Mourne Council. In 1981, the SDLP-controlled council elected him as chairman, despite his opposition to cross-border co-operation.

GRAHAM, BRIGADIER PETER WALTER. Commander, UDR, May, 1982–. b. 1937. Had considerable army experience in NI before joining UDR; served two years as brigade major with the 39 Infantry Brigade, and later commanded 1st batt., Gordon Highlanders, during two year stay at Holywood barracks. Has served in Kenya, Borneo and with BAOR.

GREEN, DESMOND GEORGE RENNIE. VUPP (and later UUUM) Convention member for N. Down, 1975–6. b. 1914. North Down District Council, 1973–. Mayor, 1979. As chairman of the Ulster Special Constabulary Association (organisation of ex-'B' Specials, of which he was former district commandant), he was involved in the loyalist strike in 1974, and in later efforts to set up a new 'home guard'. In 1974, he claimed that more than 30,000 people had registered their names as possible members of such a 'third force', but the idea was never accepted by the government. Some members of his organisation were believed to be involved in the unofficial 'Ulster Service Corps', which mounted patrols in some rural areas in early 1977. Stood unsuccessfully as UPUP candidate in N. Down in 1982 Assembly election.

GREY, LORD (OF NAUNTON). The last Governor of NI. b. Wellington, New Zealand, 15 April 1910. LL.B (Auckland University College) and Hon. LL.D (QUB). A barrister and solicitor in New Zealand, he entered the British Colonial Service. Deputy Governor-General Nigeria, 1967. Governor, British Guiana, 1969. Governor, Bahamas, 1964. Governor, NI, 1968–73. The post of Governor was abolished under the legislation which provided for an Assembly elected by PR and the constitutional duties of Governor were absorbed by the Secretary of State. The ending of the Governorship was strongly criticised by Unionists who regarded it as a weakening of the link with the British Crown. After leaving NI, he maintained his interest in the province, notably as Chancellor of NUU.

H

H-BLOCKS. The Maze Prison cell blocks – so called because of their shape – which were designed to accommodate terrorist-type prisoners with the ending of special-category status. The term 'H-Block' went round the world in the spring of 1978 when some 300 republican prisoners, campaigning for political status or the restoration of special-category status, decided to step up their existing campaign of wearing only a blanket. They refused to wash, or leave their cells, or use the toilet facilities, and the walls of many of the cells were covered with excreta. They also smashed up cell furniture. For the PIRA, the protest had the effect of attracting world-wide publicity, and the British government attempted to counter it by claiming that if the prisoners would only accept the normal prison discipline they would be able to enjoy the facilities of one of the best-equipped prisons inntwestern Europe. The Roman Catholic archbishop of Armagh, Dr Tomas (now Cardinal) O'Fiaich, urged the British government in August 1978 to do something to deal with the 'inhuman conditions' at the Maze, but the then Secretary of State, Roy Mason, ruled out any change of policy. In late 1978 and early 1979, the government stepped up its publicity drive against the H-Block protesters since they obviously feared that the republican campaign was making some impact in the United States, notably among Irish-Americans, and possibly stimulating financial aid to republican funds. For the first time, journalists were allowed inside the Maze Prison to describe the conditions, although they were not allowed to talk to the protesters. In 1980, the Republican prison protest took a more dramatic turn, with the arrival of the mass hunger strike. On 27 October, seven prisoners – 6 PIRA and one INLA – at the Maze began fasting in support of the demand that, among other things, they should be allowed to wear their own clothes and be excused prison work. The British Government, through Secretary of State Humphrey Atkins, insisted that there could be no concession which could be regarded as permitting political status, although he argued that the Government were prepared to talk about improvements in conditions on purely humanitarian grounds. In October, 1980, the Government announced that all male convicted prisoners would be allowed to wear official-issue, civilian-type clothing, but it emerged quickly that this would not be seen by the protestors as meeting the 'own clothing' demand and many people sympathetic to the prisoners' cause criticised the Government for stopping short of conceding on the clothing issue. This phase of the hunger strike ended in some confusion on 18 December 1980. With one PIRA prisoner, Sean McKenna, close to death, the prisoners said they had abandoned their fast because of a message from Mr Atkins and a thirty-

NORTHERN IRELAND – A POLITICAL DIRECTORY, 1968–83

four page description of prison conditions which had been shown to them. On 25 Jan. 1981, however, Bobby Sands, twenty-six-year-old newly-elected leader of the PIRA prisoners, claimed that moves for gradual co-operation between the prisoners and the administration had broken down. On 1 March 1981 – fifth anniversary of the start of phasing out of special category – Sands began fasting on his own, and thus launched a campaign which was to drag on for seven months, provoking a political crisis in both NI and the Republic, and intense controversy in many parts of the world. In the course of the protests ten hunger-strikers died – seven from PIRA and three from INLA. Sands, who had been elected MP for Fermanagh-S. Tyrone in the April 1981 by-election, died first on 5 May, after sixty-six days without food (see separate entry). His funeral from Twinbrook, West Belfast, to Milltown cemetery, was an impressive display of Republican strength, with some seventy thousand people attending. The others who died were:

Francis Hughes (twenty-five), PIRA, on 12 May after fifty-nine days.

Raymond McCreesh (twenty-four), PIRA, on 21 May after sixty-one days.

Patsy O'Hara (twenty-three), leader of INLA prisoners, on 21 May after sixty-one days.

Joe McDonnell (thirty), PIRA, on 8 July after sixty-one days.

Martin Hurson (twenty-seven), PIRA, on 13 July after forty-six days.

Kevin Lynch (twenty-five), INLA, on 1 August after seventy-one days.

Kieran Doherty (twenty-five), PIRA, elected TD in Cavan-Monaghan in the June general election, on 2 August after seventy-three days.

Thomas McElwee (twenty-three), PIRA, on 8 August after sixty-five days.

Michael Devine (twenty-three), INLA, on 20 August after sixty-six days.

Basically, it was a battle of wills between the prisoners and the British Government. Outside the prison, the campaign for the 'five demands' (own clothing, no prison work, freedom of association, extra recreational facilities and more visits and letters, and restoration of remission lost on protests) was spearheaded by the National H-Block/Armagh Committee, and strongly backed by Provisional Sinn Fein. But there was much sympathy for the hunger strikers in the general Nationalist-Catholic sector of the community. This often fell short of support for political status, and in common with much Dublin opinion, concentrated on British 'intransigence'. Certainly Mrs Thatcher gave a strong lead against any concessions while the hunger strike continued, and during a visit to Belfast on 28 May she remarked that the protest 'might well be the last card' of the PIRA campaign. British information services abroad stressed the rejection by the European Commission of Human Rights of a claim by four prisoners that their treatment had breached the European Convention of Human Rights. Britain also argued that the Maze prison was one of the most modern in western Europe, and prisoners were failing to take advantage of its facilities. But the recurring deaths, the tense atmosphere and a high level of violence spurred a great variety of individuals and organisations to try their hand at reconciliation. The Roman Catholic Church was involved at many levels. In the early stages, the Papal envoy, Monsignor John Magee, Ulster-born personal Secretary to Pope John Paul, talked with Sands in an unsuccessful bid to persuade him to abandon the protest. Cardinal Tomas O'Fiaich and the Bishop of Derry, Dr Edward Daly, had several meetings with Government Ministers. They urged that clothing and work should be optional, and apparently were disappointed at an early stage that the Government did not concede 'own clothing', as they had been led to believe it would. When Raymond McCreesh and Patsy O'Hara died in May, the Cardinal warned that the Government would 'face the wrath of the whole Nationalist population' if it failed to modify its 'rigid stance'. The Irish Commission for Justice and Peace (a sub-committee of the Irish Bishops' Conference) had a series of lengthy talks with Michael Alison, the Minister-of-State in charge of prisons up to September 1981. The Commission was optimistic about an end to the protest in July, when it produced an elaborate package of reforms, but it evidently misjudged the Government's attitude. Father

Denis Faul, a prison chaplain, was also closely involved, particularly in the final stages of the hunger strike, when he organised meetings of relatives of those still fasting. In Dublin, both Charles Haughey and Garret Fitzgerald, as successive heads of Government, tried unsuccessfully to persuade Mrs Thatcher to soften her approach, as did SDLP leader John Hume, at a meeting with the Prime Minister. In July, the Irish Government also failed in a bid to enlist the interest of President Reagan, at least publicly. The European Commission of Human Rights, and the International Red Cross were also briefly involved. The hunger strike had widespread repercussions in terms of violence and a political spin-off both in NI and the Republic. During the protest, sixty-one people died in violent incidents in NI. Fifteen RUC men – twelve regulars and three reservists – along with eight soldiers and seven UDR members died in bombings and shootings. Five of the soldiers died on 19 May in a landmine explosion near Camlough, home village of hunger striker Raymond McCreesh. Thirty-four civilians were killed, including seven people (two of them girls of eleven and fourteen) who died as a result of injuries inflicted by plastic bullets fired by the police or army. In the Republic, the most serious violence occurred in Dublin on 18 July, when some two hundred people were injured during a riot, when Gardai prevented an H-Block march passing the British Embassy. As for the political effects inside NI, the by-election victory of Sands and then of his election agent, Owen Carron, in Fermanagh-S. Tyrone, were a reminder that the passions of an across-the-board Nationalism could still be aroused. The by-elections also served to weaken the British argument that the protest enjoyed very little public support. In the Council elections of May 1981, the atmosphere also resulted in hardened attitudes reflected in many of the results. The impact on Southern Irish politics was also far-reaching. The return of two Maze prisoners as TDs – hunger striker Kieran Doherty in Cavan-Monaghan, and Paddy Agnew in Louth – and the substantial vote for H-Block nominees was seen as playing a major part in the defeat of the Fianna Fail Government in the June 1981 general election. The nine H-Block candidates took nearly forty thousand first preference votes. In Britain, Mrs Thatcher had broad support in Parliament for her refusal to make concessions, and a MORI poll in May suggested that ninety-two per cent of English and Welsh voters rejected political status. Opposition politicians such as Labour's Don Concannon and Liberal leader David Steel visited the Maze, but saw no scope for Government concessions. Only about fourteen Labour backbenchers were sympathetic to the H-Block cause. When James Prior became Secretary of State in mid-September, there were clear signs that the hunger strike had lost its impetus. Already, the relatives of four hunger-strikers had intervened to ensure that they were fed under medical supervision. Nonetheless, Mr Prior's first commitment outside Government offices was a three-hour visit to the Maze prison within four days of taking over, and he saw two of the hunger strikers, although he did not talk to them. On 29 September, Lord Gowrie, Minister of State and deputy to Mr Prior, who had now taken responsibility for prison matters, repeated that no concessions would be made to prisoners until the protest ended. The six remaining hunger-strikers now became aware that their relatives would intervene to save their lives, and this was the factor which finally brought an end to the long-drawn-out bid to secure political status. On the afternoon of Saturday 3 October, the six men still fasting agreed to take food. Three days later, the Secretary of State announced that all prisoners would be allowed to wear their own clothing at all times. At the same time, protesters would have fifty per cent of lost remission restored. But the Government refused to meet the demand for an end to prison work and for free association, although it hinted at some improvement on these points. Unionists protested strongly at the clothing and remission moves, and Republicans who had heavily backed the protest consoled themselves with the claim that the overall result of the hunger strike had been to give international recognition to the prisoners' political status. And in 1982, the demand for segregation of Republican and Loyalist prisoners, which had seemed a minor element in 1980–1, suddenly began to be pressed by both sides. There was some political support for the idea outside the prison, even from parties opposed to political status, and the proposal was backed by Belfast City Council. Loyalist interests claimed that their prisoners were being assaulted by Republicans. The Government showed itself opposed to segregation in principle and hinted at collusion between Republican and Loyalist prisoners to achieve separation.

HAILSHAM, LORD (OF ST MARYLEBONE). Formerly Quintin McGarel Hogg, concerned with NI as Shadow Home Secretary, 1966–70 and Lord Chancellor, 1970–4, and 1979–. b. 9 October 1907. A former Conservative MP for Oxford, he has held a variety of government posts, including leader of the House of Lords. His father's family were Lowland Scots who were settled for more than a century at Lisburn, Co. Antrim. Lord Hailsham strongly backed James Callaghan as Home Secretary in his efforts to get reforms in NI in 1969. At that period, he suggested some radical changes in Anglo-Irish relations which created unease among Unionists. In 1969, he urged a Treaty of perpetual friendship, binding Great Britain, Northern Ireland and the Republic. Such a treaty, he said should involve a recognition of the border as a fact of the situation of indefinite duration; a human rights convention placing the rights of minorities in all three territories on a judicially enforceable, and not simply political, footing. In 1971, he created controversy with a suggestion that people accused of serious bombings should be charged with treason, which would carry the death penalty. In 1974, he urged the setting up of a 'Council of the Islands' which would bring together England, Scotland, Wales, Northern Ireland, the Irish Republic, the Channel Islands, and Orkney and Shetland. He said that unless all these components prospered, none could prosper, and he suggested that it was the failure to recognise this dimension that was largely at the bottom of the 1974 Loyalist strike in NI. But he also argued that the extreme Protestant viewpoint in NI had not assisted those who wanted to maintain the Union. As Lord Chancellor in the Thatcher Government he was said to be the most vocal member of the Cabinet committee which considered the issue of NI devolution.

HALL-THOMPSON, MAJOR ROBERT LLOYD. Leader of Assembly, 1973–4, and Chief Whip in Executive. b. 9 April 1920. First elected to Stormont in 1969 as pro-O'Neill Unionist in Clifton. Son of former Stormont Education Minister and grandson of MP for N. Belfast at Westminster. With split in Unionism he joined Brian Faulkner in UPNI and represented the party in Convention. Wide variety of public interests, and heavily involved in horse racing and breeding.

HARTE, PATRICK DONAL. Fine Gael spokesman on Security and Northern Ireland, 1977–81. b. 1932. Elected to the Dail as a Donegal deputy in 1961, and served on Dail committee reviewing the Republic's Constitution.

Minister-of-State, 1981–2. Throughout the troubles, he has sought to promote peace in NI, and has maintained close contacts with a wide variety of interests, including paramilitaries. In early 1982, he complained that Donegal was being used increasingly as a terrorist base by PIRA and INLA, following a number of large seizures of arms and explosives in areas of the county adjoining the border.

HARVEY, CECIL. Chairman of the UUUP, 1977–80, but joined DUP in 1981. b. Belfast, 1918. An ex-member of the OUP, he was elected in S. Down as a Vanguard Unionist to the Assembly, 1973–4. In the Convention, 1975–6, he was chief whip of the Vanguard Party, and represented his party on the business committee. With the split in Vanguard on the issue of a voluntary coalition, he opposed the idea and became member of the UUUM, led by Ernest Baird. When the UUUM became a separate political party as the UUUP in 1977, he was appointed chairman of the new party, and was its prospective candidate for the Westminster S. Down seat in opposition to sitting MP, Enoch Powell, whom he backed in the October 1974 election and unsuccessfully opposed in the 1983 election. Active in the Rev. Ian Paisley's Free Presbyterian Church.

HATTERSLEY, ROY SYD-NEY GEORGE. Minister of Defence (Administration), 1969–70 and mainly responsible for detailed planning for setting up UDR. b. 28 December 1932. B.Sc.Econ. (Hull). Labour MP for Sparkbrook (Birmingham), 1964–. Visited NI for 'Operation Motorman', 1972, as Labour Defence spokesman. In 1978, as Prices Secretary, asked Prices Commission to make informal investigation of higher prices in NI. Shadow Home Secretary, 1980–.

HAUGHEY, CHARLES JAMES. Taoiseach (Prime Minister) of Irish Republic, December, 1979–July 1981; March–December, 1982. b. Castlebar, Co. Mayo, 16 September 1925. B. Comm, B.L. (UCD). One of Republic's ablest, wealthiest and most colourful politicians, he has a NI background and is regarded as a 'hardliner' on Northern issues. His parents came from Swatragh, Co. Derry, and from families with a strong Republican tradition. His father, Sean, was second-in-command of the northern division of the IRA. He joined Fianna Fail in Dublin in 1948, and in 1951 married Maureen Lemass, daughter of former Fianna Fail Taoiseach Sean Lemass. After two years in Dublin Corporation, he was elected to the Dail at the third attempt in 1957 in Dublin North-East, an area which has provided him with a strong constituency base over the years. He was Minister for Justice, 1961–4, and Minister for Agriculture, 1964 to 1966, when he was a strong contender for the Fianna Fail leadership, but eventually withdrew from the contest and gave his support to Jack Lynch. He was at the centre of gun-running allegations at the height of the NI troubles in 1970. As Finance Minister he was sacked by Lynch, and later charged with conspiracy to import arms and ammunition illegally. But he and three others were acquitted. He returned to office in the Lynch Government elected in 1977, taking over the Health Ministry. In December 1979, he succeeded Lynch as Taoiseach and Fianna leader, but the Parliamentary Party vote was indicative of Haughey's inability to win general acceptance within Fianna Fail. He defeated George Colley (Lynch's deputy and his favourite for the post) by 44–38. On taking over as head of Government, he voiced his opposition to all the activities of PIRA, undertook to maintain all existing security measures, and named peaceful reunification of Ireland as his first political priority. At his party's annual conference in Dublin in 1980, he declared that the Stormont Constitutional Conference, then under way, could not provide a conclusive settlement. He envisaged the British and Irish Governments working together to find a solution. 'For over sixty years now,' he said, 'the situation in Northern Ireland has been a source of instability, real or potential, in these islands. It has been so because the very entity itself is artificial . . . In these conditions, violence and repression were inevitable.' This approach dominated his thinking on NI during both his terms of office as Taoiseach. Unlike his Fine Gael opposite number, Garret Fitzgerald, he was not prepared to modify those parts of the Constitution which were attacked by Unionists, and he saw no merit in any kind of internal settlement in NI. Thus, he considered the

Anglo-Irish talks as the key to the situation. His summit talks with Mrs Thatcher in Dublin in December 1980 were particularly gratifying, since the British Prime Minister and three Cabinet colleagues (Secretaries for Foreign Affairs and Northern Ireland and the Chancellor of the Exchequer) agreed to a communiqué which he described as 'an historic breakthrough'. There were to be joint studies into a wide range of subjects and the 'totality of relations between the two countries,' and the possibilities of new institutions. The ground was laid for the British-Irish Intergovernmental Council (see separate entry) which finally emerged the next year. But Mrs Thatcher dismissed any idea of a federal status for NI and her government were obviously worried at the intense anger which the Dublin package aroused among Unionists, many of whom talked of a 'sell-out' and an attempt to revive the Sunningdale plan. This led Mrs Thatcher to repeat the NI constitutional guarantee on every possible occasion, and she also rejected any idea of concessions to the H-Block hunger strikers for which Mr Haughey pressed. In the event it was probably the appearance of anti-H-Block candidates which led to the downfall of the Haughey administration in the June 1981 election. And when he got back to power in 1982 as the leader of a minority Government, he had a further policy clash with Britain, since he was opposed to EEC sanctions against Argentina over the Falklands. In this situation, there was little surprise that NI Secretary James Prior went ahead with his 'rolling devolution' initiative in 1982 without consulting the Dublin Government about the details. Indeed, Mrs Thatcher rubbed in the point by saying that Britain had no obligation to consult the Republic about NI affairs. So Mr Haughey denounced the initiative as 'unworkable'. London, however, apparently found nothing to complain about in Mr Haughey's anti-terrorist policy. In the November 1982 election campaign, he firmly opposed suggestions by Dr Fitzgerald that there should be an all-Ireland Court and cross-border police force to deal with terrorism, and he sought to portray much of British political opinion and the media as interfering in an Irish election by expressing a preference for Dr Fitzgerald. The election was certainly a severe blow to Mr Haughey since it gave a Fine Gael-Labour Coalition a secure majority and he left office with Anglo-Irish relations at almost an all-time low. Unionists in NI took the change calmly, with some of them saying that they preferred the certainty of Mr Haughey's Republicanism to Dr Fitzgerald's subtlety. The SDLP looked for the restoration of a strong bipartisan policy on NI in Dublin. This emerged to the extent that Mr Haughey joined Dr Fitzgerald in supporting the Forum for a New Ireland (see separate entry).

HAUGHEY, DENIS. SDLP Assembly member for Mid-Ulster, 1982–. Chairman of the SDLP, 1973–8. b. Coalisland, Co. Tyrone, 3 October 1944. B.A. (Hons) in political science and modern history (QUB). Active in university as member of New Ireland Society, and in civil rights movement as first chairman of Tyrone Civil Rights Association. Joined SDLP on its formation, and unsuccessful in two Westminster elections – Fermanagh-S. Tyrone in February 1974 and Mid-Ulster 1983. Also failed in Convention poll in N. Antrim in 1975. SDLP delegate to Socialist International and bureau of Confederation of Socialist Parties of EEC. In 1980 became full-time assistant to party leader John Hume in his work as MEP, and International Secretary of the party.

HEATH, EDWARD RICHARD GEORGE. Conservative Prime Minister, 1970–4 and opposition leader, 1965–70 and 1974–5. b. 9 July 1916. There were three decisive points in Edward Heath's policy towards NI as Prime Minister and Conservative leader. Firstly, he switched the emphasis of Tory policy away from positive support of the Union. In November 1971, he said: 'Many Catholics in Northern Ireland would like to see Northern Ireland unified with the South. That is understandable. It is legitimate that they should seek to further that aim by democratic and constitutional means. If at some future date the majority of the people in Northern Ireland want unification and express that desire in the appropriate constitutional manner, I do not believe any British government would stand in the way. But that is not what the majority want today.' Secondly, he moved swiftly to suspend Stormont in March 1972, in the wake of 'Bloody Sunday' in Londonderry, defying the advice of the NI Premier, Brian Faulkner, and risking a loyalist backlash. Thirdly, he brought all his Prime Ministerial power to bear at the Sunningdale conference in December 1973, to get the power-sharing administration established. The previous August he made a two-day visit to NI during which he urged politicians to get on with the job of making the Assembly work. There could be no justification for delay, he said. On that occasion, he made one of his few gestures to Unionism when he attended the Belfast memorial service for the former Prime Minister, Lord Brookeborough. Earlier visits to NI were in December 1971 (essentially a pre-Christmas visit to the Army), and on 16–17 November 1972, when he was pondering the scope of the British political initiative. One of his most surprising comments was made in Dublin in September 1973, after talks with Mr Cosgrave and other Ministers. In a BBC interview, he mentioned the possibility of NI being fully integrated with Great Britain. After protests from Harold Wilson, the opposition leader, and many sections of NI and Dublin opinion, he claimed that he was not advocating integration as a solution. In his *Memoirs of a Statesman,* the late Brian (Lord) Faulkner quotes Mr Heath as saying in the critical pre-direct rule talks at Downing Street that NI should have a county council or Greater London Council-type administration. Visiting Belfast in January, 1983, he described himself as 'the best friend Ulster ever had'.

HENDRON, JAMES. Alliance Convention Member for S. Belfast, 1975–6. b. Belfast, 1931. Solicitor. Founder member and ex-chairman of the Alliance Party. His brother, Dr Joseph Hendron, was SDLP Convention Member for W. Belfast.

HENDRON, JOSEPH GERARD. SDLP Assembly member for W. Belfast, 1982–. b. Belfast, 1932. M.B. (QUB) General medical practitioner in Falls Road area of Belfast and former ship's surgeon. Was a Convention member for W. Belfast, and his brother, James, was an Alliance Convention member for S. Belfast. Chairman of the SDLP Constituency Representatives, 1980–. In the 1983 Westminster election, he was runner-up to Gerry Adams, who won the seat for PSF, but Gerry Fitt blamed him for his loss of the seat since he said Dr Hendron was unable to attract the non-Nationalist support which had gone to him (Mr Fitt).

HERMON, SIR JOHN. Chief Constable of the RUC, Jan. 1980–. b. Larne, Co. Antrim, 1929. He had been in the RUC for twenty-nine years when he was appointed Chief Constable, having risen through the ranks. In 1963, when he became a head constable, he was also the first RUC officer to go to Bramshill police training college in England. In 1966, he was district inspector in charge of the Cookstown area, and in the following year chief superintendent and the RUC's first training officer in charge of the training centre at Enniskillen. By 1976, he was deputy chief constable (operations) and when he went on attachment to Scotland Yard in 1979, he was widely tipped for the top post. As Chief Constable, he has faced a wide variety of challenges – the revival of street violence in the 1981 hunger strike, sharp criticism from some Unionists, and even some discontent with his policy within the local police federation. When the Rev. Ian Paisley launched his 'third force' at the end of 1981, Sir John gave a strong warning that no private army would be allowed to usurp the authority of the police or army. At private conferences, he has proved a highly articulate defender of the RUC, and has been a strict disciplinarian apparently unworried by his detractors. He has claimed increasing Catholic support for the RUC, and worked amicably with his opposite number in the Republic. In 1982, he welcomed the appearance of informers or 'super-grasses' among the paramilitaries as a 'new dimension' and rejected suggestions that they had emerged because of police blackmail and financial inducements.

HERRON, TOMMY. Vice-chairman and leading spokesman of the UDA, who was found shot dead at Drumbo, near Lisburn, in September 1973. b. 1937. An open verdict was returned at the inquest. UDA leaders dismissed the idea of a serious political motive, ruling out both IRA and Protestant paramilitary involvement. They suggested that 'cranks', bitterly opposed to Herron, had been responsible. He

stood unsuccessfully as a Vanguard Unionist candidate in the Assembly election in 1973.

HESLIP, HERBERT. Off. U. member for S. Down in the Assembly (1973–4) and Convention (1975–6). b. Ballinaskeagh, Co. Down, 1913. For many years a leading figure in Unionism and local government in S. Down. Member of Down Co. Council, 1966–73. Banbridge District Council, 1973–. Vice-president, Down Orange Welfare. Deputy Speaker of NI Assembly, 1973–4. Farms near Banbridge and is active in several farming organisations.

HILLERY, DR PATRICK JOHN. President of Irish Republic, 1976–. b. 2 May 1923. B.Sc. M.B. B.Ch., B.A.O. (UCD). Dr Hillery made his most dramatic intervention in NI affairs on 6 July 1970, as the Republic's Minister for Foreign Affairs. He drove secretly to Belfast and appeared on the Falls Road. He had not consulted the British government, and there was an angry protest from Britain's Foreign Secretary, Sir Alec Douglas-Home. He said it was a 'serious diplomatic discourtesy' and would add to the difficulties of those working for peace. Mr Jack Lynch defended the visit, saying that there was fear on the Falls and it was vitally important that it should not be exploited by subversive elements. Dr Hillery was Foreign Minister, 1969–73, and earlier Ministerial posts were: Education (1959–65); Industry and Commerce (1965–6), and Labour (1966–9). He was EEC Commissioner for Social

Affairs, 1973–6, and one of his earliest EEC announcements was that concerning the setting up of an EEC office in Belfast.

HOLDEN, SIR DAVID CHARLES BERESFORD. Head of the NI Civil Service and permanent secretary, Department of Finance, 1973–6. b. 26 July 1915. Educated at King's College, Cambridge. Joined the NI Civil Service in 1937, and after retirement in 1976, served for a year as Director of the Ulster Office in London.

HOLLYWOOD, SEAN. SDLP candidate who lost by 3,567 votes to Enoch Powell (Off. U.-UUUC) in S. Down in the Westminster election, October 1974. b. 1945. B.A. (QUB) Caught attention as main opponent to Enoch Powell in heavily publicised campaign. His strong showing in a constituency where the Unionist majority had often reached 10,000 to 20,000 clearly owed much to his ability to pull over some votes of Unionists unhappy at Mr Powell's candidature. Newry and Mourne District Council, 1973–7. Unsuccessful SDLP Convention candidate in N. Down, 1975. In 1978, he was at variance with the party on the power-sharing issue.

HOUSE, LT-GEN. SIR DAVID. Army GOC, NI 1975–7. b. 8 August 1922. General House took over in NI when the PIRA ceasefire was petering out. One of his major tasks was to deal with the outbreak of violence in S. Armagh, including the killing of ten Protestant workers in a mini-bus in January 1976. This led to the introduction of the undercover Special Air Service into S. Armagh, and soon afterwards it was permitted to operate anywhere in NI, mainly to counter sectarian assassinations. Sir David adopted a low profile during his command, and in 1977 he left the army to become Black Rod in the House of Lords.

HOWELL, DAVID. Parliamentary Under-Secretary, NI Office, 1972–3. b. 18 January 1936. Energy Minister, 1979–81; Transport Minister, 1981–3. Conservative MP for Guildford 1966–. After a short period in the economic section of the Treasury, he was leader writer and special correspondent of the London *Daily Telegraph*, 1960–4. As director of the Conservative Political Centre, he had a hand in drafting the party's 1964 election manifesto. At the NI Office, he had charge of the departments of Finance, Commerce and Agriculture.

HULL, WILLIAM (BILLY). Chairman of LAW, 1969–73. b. Belfast, 1912. Member NILP, 1948–73. A stocky figure, he became well-known as a voice of Protestant workers at the height of the violence. He left the NILP in protest against Harold Wilson's attitude to NI. He had helped organise the Workers' Committee for the Defence of the Constitution, which preceded LAW, and as convenor of shop stewards at the Belfast shipyard engine works, was one of a small group which organised LAW throughout the Province to the point it claimed about 100,000 members. After the murder of three Scottish soldiers in Belfast in early 1971, he led a march of 9,000 engineering workers to Unionist headquarters – a protest which was regarded as one of the main factors which led to the resignation soon afterwards of James Chichester-Clark from the Premiership. He was also involved in planning the forty-eight-hour loyalist strike when Direct Rule was introduced in 1972. Although it surfaced briefly from time to time, most of LAW's supporters linked up with the UWC in early 1973, when Billy Hull differed with some of the other leaders on tactics.

HUME, JOHN. SDLP MEP for NI, 1979–. Leader, SDLP, Nov. 1979–. MP for Foyle 1983–. Assembly member for Londonderry, 1982–. Head of Commerce Department in power-sharing NI Executive, 1974, and deputy leader, SDLP, 1973–9. b. Londonderry, 18 January 1937. M.A. (Maynooth). An ex-teacher, he first came to political prominence in the civil rights movement in Londonderry in 1968, and was vice-chairman of the Derry Citizens' Action Committee, 1968–9. In the Stormont general election of February 1969, he was returned as MP for Foyle, unseating the Nationalist leader, Edward McAteer. During the election campaign he urged the establishment of a social democratic party. He was a founder member of the SDLP in 1970, and soon emerged as the party's chief policy-maker. He was elected to the Assembly, 1973–4, from Londonderry and was heavily engaged in the negotiations with the Secretary of State, William Whitelaw, and in the Sunningdale conference, which led to the setting up of the Executive. As head of the Commerce department, he was deeply involved with the economic problems thrown up by the loyalist strike in 1974. He fought the Londonderry seat unsuccessfully in the Westminster election of October 1974. He was returned to the Convention for Londonderry, and after the failure of the Convention joined his then party colleague, Paddy Devlin, in private but unavailing talks with Austin Ardill and the Rev. Martin Smyth, Official Unionists, on a possible political settlement. He then became active in liaising with politicians in Europe and the US, and in 1977 he became part-time adviser on consumer affairs to the EEC Commissioner, Richard Burke. This entailed considerable travel within the Common Market area. As a fluent French speaker, he became a regular contributor to TV and radio programmes on Ireland, broadcast from France. In 1978, the main political parties in the Republic took up in principle his plea that they should seek to spell out in detail their intentions on eventual Irish unity. He suggested at the same time that more thought should be given to a federal solution. In 1978, he was unanimously selected as the SDLP candidate for one of the three NI seats in the 1979 European direct elections. He fought a vigorous campaign, essentially on EEC issues, but claimed that the new parliament would lead to co-operation between MEPs from NI and the Republic, and would form a 'healing process' in Irish affairs.

On the first count, he secured 140,622 votes, or 24.5 per cent – that is, just short of the quota. He had more votes than the combined total of the two Official Unionists, and the poll was a record one for the SDLP. He was elected on the third count, with 146,072 and became a member of the socialist group in the European Assembly, and a member of the Assembly's regional committee. Mr Hume succeeded Gerry Fitt, MP, as party leader. Mr Fitt had resigned because of the initial refusal of the SDLP to attend the 1980 Constitutional Conference promoted by Secretary of State Humphrey Atkins, and also because he argued that the SDLP had abandoned a Socialist approach and become simply a Nationalist party – a contention hotly denied by Mr Hume. Mr Hume later claimed that at the Atkins conference, the SDLP had proposed that power-sharing government should be limited to ten years, and he said it was clear that Unionists were totally opposed to partnership government. Mr Hume again cited Unionist opposition to power-sharing as one of the reasons for rejecting the 'rolling devolution' scheme put forward by Secretary of State James Prior in 1982. Dubbing the plan 'unworkable,' he also complained that the Irish dimension was far too limited. During the passage of the legislation, Mr Hume urged that a Parliamentary tier of the Anglo-Irish Inter-Governmental Council should have responsibility for security, civil rights and 'identity'. In the event, he led the SDLP into the October, 1982, Assembly elections, with a boycott of the Assembly itself and called for a 'Council for a New Ireland,' which would bring together politicians from the Republic and NI to draw up a realistic Irish unity blueprint. The proposal led to the Forum for a New Ireland (see separate entry). After the polls, he said the assembly was 'dead as a dodo'. In the European Parliament in 1980, he spearheaded a new economic initiative for NI, which was supported by the other two local MEPs, and which led to a special EP report on ways of strengthening the local economy. In March 1982, he was one of President Reagan's guests at a St Patrick's Day lunch in the White House, at which the Republic's Prime Minister, Charles Haughey, was guest of honour. Mr Hume used the occasion to explain SDLP policy to Congressional leaders. In 1983, he pressed in European Parliament for an inquiry by its political affairs committee into NI's economy and political situation. The idea was adopted, despite opposition from the British Government and Unionists. In the 1983 Westminster election, he won easily the new Foyle constituency – the first time a non-Unionist had got a Westminster seat in the Londonderry area since the establishment of NI.

HUNGER STRIKE. See H-BLOCKS.

HUNT REPORT. The report produced by the committee headed by Lord Hunt which led to far-reaching reforms in the NI security forces in 1969. The report recommended an unarmed RUC and replacement of the controversial USC by a new part-time force under the Army GOC (it emerged as the UDR), as well as the setting up of a Police Reserve. The proposal for ending the USC was strongly criticised by many Unionists, and led to serious rioting in Protestant areas of Belfast. It was welcomed by those who had supported the civil rights campaign.

Convention election, he said he would share power in government only with those who supported the link with Great Britain. Sentenced to one month's imprisonment after incidents in November 1968 in Armagh, following the civil rights march and loyalist counter-demonstrations there. Expelled from Orange Order for criticism of leadership. Unsuccessfully contested 1982 Assembly election in Armagh.

HUTCHINSON, DOUGLAS. DUP Assembly (1974–5) and Convention (1975–6) member for Armagh. b. Richhill, Co. Armagh, 1918. One of the Rev. Ian Paisley's most active supporters, he was on Armagh Rural Council, 1953–73, and Armagh District Council, 1973–. Former member, USC. In

HUTTON, NORMAN. General secretary of the OUP, 1974–83. b. 1943. A former businessman, he was responsible for planning the party's election campaigns, and was heavily involved in carrying through constituency reorganisation to deal with the five extra Westminster seats.

I

ILLEGAL ORGANISATIONS. See Security Section (page 316) for list of bodies proscribed under the Emergency Provisions Act.

INDEPENDENT ORANGE ORDER. A relatively small organisation which was originally a breakaway from the main Orange Order. It was founded in 1903 after a row over a Belfast by-election in which the Off. U. candidate was defeated by a shipyard worker, T. H. Sloan. When Sloan was expelled from the Orange Order he and his friends set up the Independent Orange Order. It took a distinctive line, calling on its members to 'hold out the right hand of fellowship to

those who, while worshipping at other shrines, are yet our countrymen'. It holds its own 12 July demonstrations, some of which have been addressed by the Rev. Ian Paisley, who broke with the main Order in 1962. In 1982, the Rev. Martin Smyth, MP, as head of the main Order, said he hoped that the official and independent Orange Orders would eventually reunite. He said the two were already working in close harmony in Co. Antrim.

INDEPENDENT UNIONIST GROUP. See PROGRESSIVE UNIONIST PARTY.

INTEGRATION. The idea of complete absorption of NI into the UK, without any regional self-government. Such a status for the province was not supported by any group in the Constitutional Convention in 1975–6, but after the collapse of the Convention, a section of Unionism seemed to be resigned to the prospect, provided that NI was given parity with Great Britain in representation at Westminster and two-tier local government on the same basis as the mainland. The decision of the Callaghan government in 1978 to back between four and six extra MPs for the province was interpreted by the SDLP as a lurch towards integration. The British government continued to insist, however, that it was still working for devolution, and to this end was maintaining a separate statute book for local legislation during what it regarded as temporary direct rule.

IRISH ASSOCIATION FOR CULTURAL, ECONOMIC AND SOCIAL RELATIONS. Founded on an all-Ireland basis in 1938 to bring together people of differing religious and political views. Idea originated with late Maj. Gen. Hugh Montgomery, of Fivemiletown, Co. Tyrone, and its first president was the liberal-minded Lord Charlemont, a former NI Education Minister. The Association was largely inactive during World War II. Since then it has organised regular addresses by leading politicians, academics and journalists.

IRISH DIMENSION. A term which came into popular usage in 1973, when the Conservative government published its Green Paper on NI. It was used to denote the desire of the bulk of the Catholic minority for an eventual united Ireland. It was a counter-balance to the British Dimension, the term used to describe the Unionist attachment to Britain. It found expression in the plan for a Council of Ireland, which emerged in the Sunningdale Agreement, and which attracted the fierce opposition of loyalists. The scheme foundered with the collapse of the power-sharing Executive in 1974. One theory is that the phrase was coined by a civil servant making notes at the Darlington conference in 1972.

IRISH INDEPENDENCE PARTY. A party launched in 1977 which sought a British withdrawal from NI to prepare the way for negotiation of the province's future status in Ireland. The main initial tactic of IIP appeared to be to seek agreed anti-Unionist candidates in Westminster elections. The leading figures in the new group were former Unity MP for Fermanagh-S. Tyrone, Frank McManus, and Fergus McAteer, the Derry Nationalist and son of former Nationalist leader, Eddie McAteer, who had also expressed support for some move towards independence. Its main support was drawn from W. Ulster, N. Antrim, and S. Down, and it attracted the interest of several Independent and Nationalist Councillors. In the Westminster election in May 1979, it ran four candidates, and secured 3.3 per cent of the total vote, with the best showing by Pat Fahy in Mid-

Ulster with a vote of 12,055. Soon afterwards, Mr Fahy was appointed party leader, with Mr McManus deputy leader, and Mr McAteer, chairman. The party improved its share of the vote to 3.9 per cent in the 1981 council elections, but opted out of the 1982 Assembly elections because of its intense opposition to the 'rolling devolution' scheme. It failed, however, with a campaign to persuade Nationalists generally to boycott the Assembly elections.

IRISH LABOUR PARTY. The Republic's third-largest political party. In the early 1960s, it was linked to the NILP for a time through a Council of Labour. In 1972, it backed the SDLP policy statement, 'Towards a New Ireland'. While it was in coalition government with Fine Gael, 1973-7, there were some differences of emphasis on NI within the party. One of its Ministers, Dr Conor Cruise O'Brien, was highly critical of the articles in the Constitution claiming all-Ireland jurisdiction. At the 1978 party conference, Frank Cluskey, who succeeded Brendan Corish as leader in 1977, criticised Jack Lynch's comments on NI as likely to help the 'godfathers' of the IRA. Michael O'Leary, Mr Cluskey's successor (who joined Fine Gael in 1982) maintained close contact with the NI parties. The party decided, however, not to invite the SDLP to send representatives to its 1982 conference. Dick Spring, newly-elected leader, who became deputy to Dr Garret Fitzgerald in the Fine Gael-Labour Coalition which took office in December, 1982, said he strongly favoured a consensus policy on NI among the Republic's main parties. He also backed the Forum for a New Ireland.

IRISH NATIONAL CAUCUS. The American umbrella group for the majority of Irish-American organisations. It embraces the Gaelic Athletic Association and the AOH, Irish county associations, and scores of local bodies in New York, Boston, Philadelphia, and other US cities with strong Irish-American links. In 1978, sent a three-man inquiry team to NI, headed by its national co-ordinator, Father Sean McManus (brother of ex-MP Frank McManus), which urged a 'peace forum' on NI in Washington and reported to this effect to the ad hoc NI Congressional Committee. The visiting team had talks with the IRA, UDA, UVF and some other loyalist organisations, and said that paramilitary organisations must be included in any search for a solution. In 1978, Jack Lynch, as Taoiseach of the Irish Republic, attacked the Caucus for giving support to the PIRA, but spokesmen of the Caucus have insisted that it has no connection with any organisation outside the USA, and that it has been cleared of any suspicion of support of violence by FBI and other inquiries. In the 1980 Presidential election, it claimed as a victory the call for Irish unity in the Democratic platform. But it failed to get any commitment from the Republicans, and was clearly disappointed by the election of Ronald Reagan. The Caucus was active during the H-Block hunger strikes in 1980 and 1981, in support of the protesters, and Father McManus went on hunger strike in Washington for several days. It took a strong anti-British line over the Falklands war in 1982.

IRISH NATIONAL LIBERATION ARMY. Military wing of the IRSP. An illegal, ruthless and probably not very large paramilitary group which has been responsible for many acts of violence in NI, and to a lesser extent in GB and the Republic since 1975. Its initial strength probably derived from ex-OIRA members angry at the OIRA ceasefire in 1972, and it is believed to have gained recruits from PIRA during its ceasefire in 1975, when its members were active in the feud between OIRA and the IRSP. One of its first acts was to kill OIRA commander Billy McMillen in Belfast in April, 1975. Its main support has come from the Lower Falls and Markets areas in Belfast, and from parts of Co. Derry, notably S. Derry. Many of its attacks have been on members of the security forces, but it first attracted world attention when it claimed to have placed the car bomb which killed Conservative NI spokesman, Airey Neave, at Westminster in March, 1979. In a statement issued through a Belfast office of IRSP it said that he had been specifically selected for assassination because of his 'rabid militarist calls for more repression against the Irish people'. INLA also said that its primary aim was to secure a British military, political and economic withdrawal from Ireland, and it denied that it was a cover group for PIRA. In fact, PIRA members tend to talk of INLA as 'wild men'. It was declared illegal throughout the UK in July, 1979, when NI Secretary Humphrey Atkins told parliament that it was engaged in violence and contacts with terrorist groups abroad. Government security experts claimed that it was getting arms, including the Russian AK-47 rifle, from the Middle East. In the succeeding years, INLA stepped up its activities. It was said to be responsible for nearly thirty deaths in NI in 1982. Seventeen of these were caused by the bombing on 6 December of the 'Droppin' Well' pub disco in Ballykelly, Co. Londonderry. Eleven of the victims were off-duty soldiers stationed nearby and most of the others local people. It was the second highest death-toll in any incident during the troubles, being exceeded only by the Warrenpoint bombing in 1979. In the 1981 H-Block hunger strike, three INLA prisoners died. In the later stages of the protest, Belfast IRSP councillor Sean Flynn said they could not replace hunger strikers at the same rate as previously, since INLA had only twenty-eight prisoners against PIRA's 380. (See H-BLOCKS) A period of internal disagreement coincided with the hunger strike, and the injuring of Harry Flynn, press officer of the IRSP, in a machine-gun attack in Dublin was believed to be associated with the feud. The differences were apparently patched up as the operation of informers gave rise to mass arrests of INLA members in 1982. In July, 1982, the IRSP publication, *Starry Plough*, denied that there was any split between IRSP and INLA and it also said that the INLA structure had been reformed with a new chief of staff from NI. In September, 1982, it brought strong criticism from residents in the Divis flats in the lower Falls Road area of Belfast, when it set off a bomb which killed two local boys of eleven and fourteen and a soldier. The flats were regarded as one of INLA's main strongholds. In the 1980s it has carried on a campaign against loyalist politicians. In a statement in September, 1982, INLA said certain Unionist politicians were on a 'hit list' because they had been responsible for inciting the murders of seven hundred innocent Catholics over the previous ten years. In January, 1981, it claimed to have shot dead E. Belfast loyalist John McKeague. In March, 1981, it shot and seriously wounded Belfast UDA councillor Sammy Millar at his Shankill Road home. In October, 1981, it killed a senior Belfast UDA man, Billy McCullough, in retaliation, it said, for recent loyalist murders of Catholics. In May, 1981, it placed a powerful blast incendiary bomb at the Lisburn home of DUP Assembly member Rev. William Beattie but it was detected before it went off. Soon afterwards, it shot and seriously wounded Belfast DUP councillor Billy Dickson (an Assembly candidate) at his home. In January, 1983, the Republic's Government proscribed the organisation, which meant that conviction for membership could result in up to seven years' imprisonment. The organisation was said to have committed 'particularly vicious outrages' both north and south of the border and in London. In the Republic, INLA was suspected of the murder of a Garda in Co. Dublin in early 1982. In September that year it blew up the radar station at Schull, Co. Cork, and it was also thought to have carried out a series of armed robberies in the Republic during 1982. On 25 November 1981, an INLA bomb exploded at a British army camp at Herford, W. Germany, but caused no injuries. A similar bomb failed to explode at the British Consulate in Hamburg the day before.

IRISH NORTHERN AID COMMITTEE. The US-based committee, established in 1969, for the declared purpose of providing funds for the relief of families deprived of wage-earners because of the struggle against Britain. The body has been at the centre of angry controversy since its inception. The money raised – possibly around four million dollars by 1982 – has been handled in Ireland by people associated with Provisional Sinn Fein, and there have been frequent allegations that some of the money is siphoned off, either in Dublin or in the US, for the purchase of arms for PIRA. NORAID spokesmen have denied this, and PSF has retorted that PIRA has its own means of raising money. British and Irish Government Ministers, on visits to the USA, have warned people not to help NORAID. Dr Garret Fitzgerald, when Irish Foreign Minister, told Americans that every dollar given to agencies like NORAID contributed to the killing of Irish people. The organisation is thought to have over a hundred local groups in centres with substantial Irish-American populations, such as New York, Boston, Philadelphia, and Chicago, and it makes no secret of its bitterly anti-British stance. In 1977, the organisation was required, as a result of a case brought by the Justice Department, to register as an agent of PIRA under the Foreign Agents' Act. Although this meant that it had to give more detailed information about its activities, it was not a serious obstacle to its operations. NORAID claims that the money it raises is distributed through PSF in Dublin and the Green Cross in Belfast. The organisation got a big fillip from the H-Block hunger strike in 1981, when its income was around 400,000 dollars – about four times the average. In November, 1982, the chairman and founder of NORAID, eighty-year-old Michael Flannery, was one of five men acquitted in New York of conspiracy to supply arms to PIRA. The accused pleaded successfully before a jury that the CIA were aware of the activities of their supplier, and were involved in monitoring the supply of arms to PIRA. Mr Flannery, an IRA man in the 1920s, said that while he had not been personally involved in gun-running to PIRA, such activity would have his blessing. He also denied that NORAID money had been used for buying arms. Mr Flannery was at the centre of controversy when he was chosen to head the New York St Patrick's day parade in 1983. It sent a large delegation to NI in 1983 for the internment anniversary in August.

IRISH REPUBLICAN ARMY. See under OFFICIAL IRA and PROVISIONAL IRA.

IRISH REPUBLICAN SOCIALIST PARTY. Formed December 1974 and for the most part a breakaway group from Official Sinn Fein, that is, some who disagreed with the political approach of the Republican Clubs and the OIRA ceasefire. Possibly a few dissidents from Provisionals, unhappy at their freshly declared ceasefire, also switched to the IRSP. By March 1975, they were claiming some 700 members in Belfast. Their best-known personality at that time was former Mid-Ulster MP Mrs Bernadette McAliskey, who with other leaders, insisted that it did not have a military wing. Its founder was Seamus Costello, who was shot dead in Dublin in 1977. At first, it seemed that the group would fight elections, with Mrs McAliskey a possible candidate for the Convention. They decided, however, to boycott the election, saying that there would be no political advantage in putting forward candidates. It claimed that any convention solution could only be in the interests of British imperialism. In early 1975 there was a bitter feud between the OIRA and the IRSP, with claims of assassinations on both sides. When Cathal Goulding, chief-of-staff of the OIRA, spoke at the funeral of Sean Fox of the OIRA in Belfast's Milltown cemetery in February 1975, he supported the OIRA claim that Fox had been shot by the IRSP. And he described the IRSP as 'a few misguided and confused malcontents'. The feud was a particularly vicious one, and involved shootings both north and south of the border. A leading Official Republican in Belfast, Billy McMillen, shot dead in Belfast in April 1975, was said to be one of the victims. At one point, the IRSP temporarily disbanded its Belfast organisation and a Dublin Senator, Michael Mullen, acted as intermediary in a bid to stop the inter-factional shootings. When it was registered as a political party in the Republic in May 1975, it claimed nearly 400 members in NI. In September 1975, it denied any link with the South Armagh Republican Action Force, which had claimed killings at an Orange Hall in Newtownhamilton. But in 1976, 1977 and 1978, the security authorities alleged that the IRSP's military wing, the Irish National Liberation Army, had been responsible for several murders and attempted murders. In December 1977 there were clear indications that the IRSP was moving closer to Provisional Sinn Fein, many of whose members attended Seamus Costello's funeral in October. INLA claimed in 1982 that Costello had been shot by a member of OIRA. Certainly, the 1981 hunger strike brought closer co-operation with PSF, although the IRSP has always regarded itself as being to the left of the Provisionals. In the 1981 council elections, it took two seats in Belfast, but, unlike PSF, it opted out of the 1982 Assembly election. In May, 1983, several leading members were accused of terrorist offences arising from the evidence of an informer.

J

JELLICOE REPORT. See Security Section.

JOHN, BRYNMOR THOMAS. British Labour Party spokesman on NI, June 1979–80. b. 18 April 1934. LL.B. (London). Solicitor. Labour MP for Pontypridd, 1970–. Parliamentary Under-Secretary, Defence, 1974–6; Minister of State, Home Affairs, 1976–9. Defence spokesman, 1980–.

K

KANE, ALAN JAMES. DUP Assembly member for Mid-Ulster, 1982–. b. 1958. Barrister. Cookstown Council, 1981–. Party's law reform spokesman, 1982–.

KELLY, MR JUSTICE. Judge of the NI High Court, 1973–, and Attorney-General of NI, 1968–72.

b. 10 May 1920. LL.B Hons (TCD). QC, 1958. Unionist MP for Mid-Down at Stormont 1964–72, and senior Crown Counsel in Tyrone, Fermanagh and Armagh before becoming Attorney-General. He had a key role as law officer of the NI government in the civil rights period and in the months preceding the imposition of direct rule. In a debate in the NI Commons in 1969, he stated that Westminster had the power to interfere with the powers of the NI parliament, but that it would be against convention to do so. But he stressed that law was stronger than convention. In May 1971, he was accused by opposition MPs of showing political bias in ordering court prosecutions. But an opposition motion to this effect was rejected by twenty-five votes to nine. In 1983, he presided at a trial of 38 people implicated in PIRA terrorism by 'Supergrass' Christopher Black and passed sentences totalling 4,000 years.

KENNEDY, EDWARD. One of group of Irish-Americans who have been keenly interested in NI situation, b. 22 February 1932, brother of late President John F. Kennedy. Senator Kennedy's attitude to NI has altered with the growth of PIRA violence. In October 1971, he spoke in Congress in support of a motion calling for the immediate withdrawal of British troops and the calling of a conference of all parties for the purpose of establishing a united Ireland. He argued that this was the only realistic way to bring peace, but his remarks were strongly criticised within NI, especially by Unionists and the Alliance Party. US official spokesmen stressed that Senator Kennedy was not reflecting US government policy. But he repeated his plea for withdrawal of troops in 1972, saying that they had become a symbol of Protestant supremacy, and he vigorously attacked internment without trial, which he regarded as discriminating against Catholics. When the power-sharing Executive fell in 1974, he described it as a tragedy for the cause of peace in Ulster, and said Britain could not yield to the tactics of extremists. He followed up these comments with repeated advice to Irish-Americans not to give moral or financial support to terrorists. In 1977, he joined with other Irish-American leaders to sponsor a call for peace in NI, and he was among those who urged President Carter to promise US economic aid for the province in the event of a political settlement. The President did this in August 1977. He took a strong united Ireland line during his unsuccessful campaign for the Democratic presidential nomination in 1980. He was one of the founders in 1981 of the Friends of Ireland group made up of leading Irish-American politicians. And in 1983 was one of the sponsors of a Senate motion calling for a united Ireland.

KENNEDY, JOHN ANDREW DUNN. Clerk to the NI Assembly, 1982–. b. Londonderry. Barrister-at-law. Served on NI Parliamentary, (1962–72), Assembly (1973–4) and Convention (1975–6) staffs. Head of Office of Law Reform, Stormont, 1976–82.

KENNEDY, PATRICK. Republican Labour MP for Belfast Central 1969–72. b. 1943. Became leader of Republican Labour Party when Gerry Fitt MP left in 1970 to head the newly-formed SDLP. He had been prominent in opposition protests against the Unionist government in 1969, and in support of the civil rights campaign. In June 1969, he declared that if extreme Unionists were going to police their side of Belfast, 'we must do something to police our end of the city'. In September 1969 he flew to London in CCDC deputation for a meeting with the Home Secretary, James Callaghan, to discuss the tension over demands for removal of barricades in W. Belfast. In 1970, he refused to join the SDLP, and in July 1971, he withdrew from Stormont, and soon afterwards introduced Joe Cahill as leader of the PIRA at a Belfast news conference. He failed to secure election to the Assembly in 1973 as a candidate in W. Belfast.

KEOGH, MICHAEL. Nationalist MP for S. Down, 1967–72. When editor of the former Newry weekly newspaper, *The Frontier Sentinel,* he retained the seat for the Nationalist Party in a by-election in 1967, with a majority of 5,627 over a Unionist candidate. In the 1969 general election, when no Unionist stood, his majority over a PD candidate was 220. In 1972, he took a strong line against IRA bombing in Newry, which he said was hitting severely at community relations in the town.

KERNOHAN, THOMAS HUGH. Ombudsman and Commissioner of Complaints, NI, 1980–. b. 11 May 1982. In this dual investigatory role, he deals with complaints about administrative failures both in Stormont departments and in council affairs. Official (latterly Secretary) of NI Employers' Association, 1953–80. In August, 1982, a Westminster select committee praised Mr Kernohan's work and said he seemed to be 'trusted equally by all sectors of the population'. He said 'most heartache' was caused by decisions of the Environment Department, particularly in planning matters.

KIDD, SIR ROBERT HILL. Head of the NI Civil Service, 1976–9. b. 3 February 1918. B.A., B.Litt. (TCD). Served in army in World War II. Joined NI Civil Service in 1947; second secretary in Department of Finance, 1969–76, with rank of permanent secretary. In 1980, he carried out a review of NI's industrial incentives. Active in Co-operation North movement.

KILFEDDER, JAMES ALEXANDER. MP for N. Down, 1970–. (OUP, 1970–9; UPUP, 1979–.) Speaker, NI Assembly, 1982–. b. Kinlough, Co. Leitrim, 16 July, 1928. BA (TCD). Gave up his London barrister's practice when he entered Parliament. He was MP for W. Belfast, 1964–6, and during that time he was for a period secretary of the Unionist MPs, and of a number of Conservative committees, including that on NI. He has always pursued a highly individualistic course, and in 1977 he parted from the other Official Unionist MPs at Westminster, complaining that Enoch Powell was dictating policy. In early 1979, he finally broke with the OUP after an exchange of letters with party leader Harry West. In the 1979 election, he was opposed by Clifford Smyth for the OUP, but held the seat easily. Apparently, his devotion to constituency work has been the key to his success, since he was able to beat off an earlier challenge in February 1974 election, when Roy Bradford stood against him as a Pro-Assembly Unionist. He topped the poll in N. Down in the Assembly contests of 1973 and 1982, and also in the Convention election. His first preference vote in 1973 of 20,684 was the largest of the whole election. In the 1979 Euro-election which he fought as 'Ulster Unionist', he got over 38,000 first preference votes, and on the sixth count he was runner-up to John Taylor (OUP), last of the three successful candidates. In 1979, he founded the Ulster Progressive Unionist Party, but the party name was changed to Ulster Popular Unionist Party in 1980 because of confusion with the PUP. Although he was critical of the 'rolling devolution' scheme, he accepted nomination as Speaker of the 1982 Assembly. He was elected by DUP and All. votes, with the OUP opposing, and his Speaker's salary of £18,000, together with his Westminster salary, made him the UK's best-paid politician. In the 1983 Westminster election, he held off without the use of posters a strong challenge from OUP and Alliance in the reduced N. Down constituency.

KINAHAN, CHARLES. Alliance Convention member for S. Antrim, 1975–6. b. Belfast, 1915. Brother of Sir Robin Kinahan, Unionist MP for Clifton at Stormont, 1958–9. Unsuccessfully contested S. Antrim Westminster seat in February and October 1974. Vice-chairman, Alliance Party, 1978–. Antrim Borough Council, 1973–.

KING, GENERAL SIR FRANK DOUGLAS. Army GOC, NI, February 1973–August 1975. b. 9 March 1919. He arrived in NI at a time when sectarian assassinations were running at a high rate. But his most testing time came in 1974, when the loyalist strike, which led to the downfall of the power-sharing Executive, posed new problems for the army. Some Executive Ministers and many opponents of the stoppage accused the army of not moving swiftly in the first few days of the strike to dismantle UDA and other loyalist barricades. There were also complaints that the army was reluctant to take on oil distribution when petrol supplies were halted by the strikers, and disappointment that the army did not have the expertise to run the power stations. There was a widespread belief that General King was not anxious that troops should become involved in strike-breaking activities. After he left NI, he said in an interview that 'if you get a large section of the population which is bent on a particular course, then it is a difficult thing to stop them taking that course'. The General also provoked controversy in April 1975, when he said in a speech in Nottingham that the phased release of internees could help the IRA. Since the statement came at a moment when the IRA ceasefire was showing signs of petering out, and politicians were preparing for the Convention elections, the comment was highly unwelcome to the government. It pleased loyalists, dismayed the SDLP, and brought the remark from Provisional Sinn Fein that the army wanted to show the British government who was boss. General King claimed that his words had been taken out of context, since what he meant was that 'in a cease-fire situation it is obviously necessary to take steps to bring about a situation of normality without lowering our guard'.

KIRK, HERBERT VICTOR. Minister of Finance, 1966–72. b. Belfast, 5 June 1912. A chartered accountant, he was earlier Minister of Labour and Minister of Education, and an influential figure in Unionism for many years. Was a member of Brian Faulkner's team at the Darlington and Sunningdale conferences, but he didn't seek re-election after the Stormont parliament was suspended.

KIRKPATRICK, THOMAS JAMES (JIM). Off. U., Assembly member for S. Belfast, 1982–. b. 1937. Ex-UDR officer.

L

LAIRD, JOHN. Off. U. member for W. Belfast in Assembly, 1973–4, and Convention, 1975–6. b. 1944. Succeeded his father, Dr Norman Laird, as Stormont MP for St Anne's, Belfast, in a by-election in 1970. At 26, he was then the youngest MP at Stormont. Chairman, Young Unionist Council, 1970. Topped the poll in W. Belfast in both the Assembly and Convention elections. In the Assembly, he opposed power-sharing and led an unsuccessful demand for renegotiation of the Sunningdale agreement. Joint honorary secretary of the Ulster Unionist Council, 1976–8. Established his own public relations agency when Convention wound up.

LARKIN, AIDAN JOSEPH. SDLP Assembly member for Mid-Ulster, 1973–4. b. Cookstown, Co. Tyrone, 1946. M.A. (QUB). Barrister; formerly teacher. Magherafelt District Council, 1973–.

LENIHAN, BRIAN JOSEPH. Foreign Minister, Irish Republic, 1979–81 and in 1973. A prominent Fianna Fail politician, his second period at the Foreign Affairs Ministry gave him responsibility for NI matters at a crucial time. He held a variety of Cabinet posts between 1964 and 1973, and was a member of the European Assembly, 1973–7.

LENNON, JAMES GERALD (GERRY). Opposition (Nationalist) leader in NI Senate, 1965–71. b. 1907, died 1976. He was the longest-serving Nationalist Senator, having entered the House in 1944. In 1962 and 1963, he had several meetings with the Grand

Master of the Orange Order in Ireland, Sir George Clark, in an effort to remove what he termed 'the stigma of religious discrimination in NI'. The 'Orange-Green talks' did not produce any significant result. He was national president of the AOH for the last year of his life.

LIDDLE, LIEUT.-COL. GEORGE. Imperial Grand Master of the Orange Order, 1982–. b. 1901. Colonel Liddle was associated in his youth with the formation of the Ulster Special Constabulary ('B' Specials) in Co. Fermanagh. He was later in charge of the force in the county, where he was prominent in both Unionism and Orangeism. He succeeded the Rev. Martin Smyth, MP, as Imperial Grand Master. At the time of his appointment he was grand master of the Order in Fermanagh. He served for many years on the Ulster Unionist Council.

LINDSAY, KENNEDY. VUPP Assembly (1973–4) and Convention (1975–6) member for S. Antrim. b. Saskatchewan, Canada, 1924, B.A., Ph.D. (TCD, Edinburgh, London). Held university appointments in Canada, US, UK, West Indies and in Nigeria, and during an Assembly debate he donned a Nigerian ceremonial robe to make a point. In the Convention, he launched the Dominion Party, and stood unsuccessfully in district council elections in Newtownabbey in 1977. In the 1982 Assembly election, he was an unsuccessful UUUP candidate in S. Antrim.

LOGUE, HUGH. SDLP Assembly member for Londonderry, 1982–. Also represented the constituency in the 1973–4 Assembly and the 1975–6 Convention. b. Londonderry, 1949. SDLP Executive 1970–3, and chairman SDLP policy committee, 1971. NICRA Executive, 1971–2. Economic Affairs spokesman of SDLP, 1975–. In 1974, he called for disbandment of the UDR because, he said, many of its members had supported the loyalist strike. After the collapse of the Executive in August 1974, he said that a statement of British disengagement would end the uncertainty and desperate political vacuum. After the winding up of the Convention, he was active in political journalism. Unsuccessfully contested Londonderry in 1979 Westminster election. Member of the Irish Commission for Justice and Peace which had important role in the H-Block hunger-strike controversy in 1981.

LONDONDERRY or **DERRY**. The city where the civil rights demonstration in Duke Street on 5 October 1968, put the movement on the TV screens and front pages of the world's press. The dual name of the city epitomises its eventful history. The name Derry is based on the original Irish and tends to be favoured more by Catholics; the name Londonderry remains official despite moves in the City Council in 1978 and 1983 to have it changed to Derry. The official title denotes the British connection and the role of the City of London companies in the development of the city. It has been symbolic for loyalists since

Protestants defied King James II in the siege of 1689. Local conditions were a key issue in the civil rights controversy. One of the reforms demanded was the abolition of the Corporation, dominated by Unionists because ward boundaries had been drawn in a manner which meant that a Unionist minority was able to secure a majority in the City Council. One of the earliest reforms granted by the O'Neill government was the replacement of the Council by a nine-man Development Commission. This reform was announced only a month or so after the Duke Street demonstration. The march route had been heavily restricted by the government, but some 200 people, including Opposition MPs from Stormont, a few British Labour MPs, civil rights leaders and local civil rights groups, defied the ban. TV film of the event showed the attempts of the RUC to prevent the march and the ensuing confused confrontation in which police batons and placard poles were intermingled with bleeding faces. The publicity spin-off for the civil rights movement was astonishing. It was highly damaging to the NI government and an embarrassment to the British Labour administration, headed by Harold Wilson, whose sympathies were largely with the marchers. There is no doubt that the event caused Britain to put heavy pressure on Stormont for reforms. But it was not until 1969, and after even larger civil rights demonstrations in the city, that Derry came to play a decisive role in reducing the power and authority of the NI government. The riots which blew

up on the edge of the Catholic Bogside in the wake of the Protestant Apprentice Boys' 12 August march led to British troops being introduced in the streets. The barricades went up in the Bogside and the adjoining Catholic area, Creggan, and behind them the PIRA planned bombing and other missions which caused substantial damage to the city. The existence of 'Free Derry', as extreme republicans termed it, raised tensions in loyalist areas, and there were many sectarian killings in the city and county. The refusal by the authorities to agree to an impartial inquiry into the shooting dead by the army of two Derrymen – Seamus Cusack and Desmond Beattie – on 8 July 1971 led to the withdrawal of the SDLP from Stormont. The SDLP contested the official explanation that Cusack was shot when he was seen to raise a rifle against troops and Beattie when he was about to throw a nail bomb. The 'Bloody Sunday' affair, in which thirteen civilians were shot dead by paratroopers on the edge of the Bogside on 30 January 1972, was one of the incidents which precipitated direct rule from Westminster. At the end of July 1972, the security forces mounted 'Operation Motorman' to end the no-go areas and moved in strength into the Bogside and Creggan, with little more than token resistance from PIRA. With the reform of local government in 1973, the Development Commission was replaced by a district council, in which PR gave anti-Unionists a majority. In 1978, as a result of a special Derry-Donegal survey, EEC money became available to help finance a second bridge across the river Foyle and to improve the harbour and road and telephone links with Donegal. There were still occasional terrorist attacks, but by 1978 there was some easing of traffic checks at the approaches to the old walled city. But tension rose sharply during the 1981 hunger strike, and in that and the following year there were many deaths arising from PIRA and INLA activity. There was also intense controversy over deaths caused by the operations of the security forces, notably through the use of plastic bullets. But 6 December, 1982, brought the heaviest death-roll in any incident in the county during the troubles. Seventeen people died in the bombing of the 'Droppin' Well' pub disco at Ballykelly. Eleven were soldiers stationed nearby, and most of the civilian victims were from Ballykelly itself. INLA claimed the attack, and mentioned that warnings had been given to pubs serving members of the security forces. The INLA warning was repeated a few weeks after the bombing. It was generally believed that the bombing had been carried out by INLA members from S. Derry, an area where the organisation was known to have some support. The SDLP took control of the City Council after the 1981 council elections, but Provisional Sinn Fein got a boost in the 1982 Assembly election, when its best-known Derry city figure, Martin McGuinness was returned. With some 9,000 unemployed in the city, the Government announced in 1982 an 'enterprise zone', with special inducements for investment,

while work went ahead on the second Foyle Bridge. In the 1983 general election, the area got its first non-Unionist MP at Westminster since NI was established. SDLP leader and Euro-MP John Hume took the new Foyle seat, embracing Derry City and part of Tyrone, including Strabane. See DERRY CITIZENS' ACTION COMMITTEE and DERRY CITIZENS' DEFENCE ASSOCIATION.

LONG, CAPT. WILLIAM JOSEPH. Minister of Home Affairs, December 1968–March 1969, a period which included the eventful PD march from Belfast to Londonderry. b. Stockton-on-Tees, England, 23 April 1922. Stormont MP, 1962–72, and held a number of junior posts before becoming Minister of Education in 1969. Minister of Development, 1969.

LONG KESH. See Security Section (p. 313).

LOWRY, LORD. As Sir Robert Lowry he was chairman of the Constitutional Convention, 1975–6. b. 30 January 1919. QC, 1956. Lord Chief Justice of NI, 1971–. Sir Robert presided over the Convention's public sittings, and behind the scenes, with the assistance of advisers, he tried to reconcile the conflicting views of the political parties on the type of administration which would prove viable. Notably, he had a scheme prepared for voluntary coalition, as distinct from imposed power-sharing. The circumstances which had given rise to the document proved a major point of controversy, and on the United Unionist side only Mr William Craig and a few of his supporters were attracted to the idea. Despite the failure of the exercise, Sir Robert's efforts were praised on all sides of the Convention. Raised to peerage in 1979. PIRA made an unsuccessful bid to assassinate him at Queen's University, Belfast, in March, 1982. Four shots were fired, and one injured a QUB professor.

LOYAL CITIZENS OF ULSTER. A small militant group which first appeared in Londonderry in October 1968. Its leader, Major Ronald Bunting, threatened that it would hold a meeting on the city walls to coincide with a sit-down in Guildhall Square below by supporters of the Derry Citizens' Action Committee. But the counter-demonstration was banned by William Craig, as Minister of Home Affairs. In January 1969, it announced a counter-demonstration to a PD march in Newry, but it didn't proceed with its plan. The LCU appeared at a variety of loyalist demonstrations in 1968 and 1969.

LYNCH, JOHN (JACK). Fianna Fail Taoiseach of Irish Republic, 1966–73 and 1977–9. b. Cork, 15 August 1917. Hon. LL.D. (TCD and NUI); Hon D.O.L. (University College, N. Carolina). Began as civil servant in Department of Justice, 1936, and called to Bar, 1945. TD for Cork Constituencies 1948–81. Junior Minister, 1951–4. Minister for Lands, 1951; Minister for Gaeltacht, 1957; Minister for Education, 1957–9;

Minister for Industry and Commerce, 1959–65; Minister for Finance, 1965–6, when he succeeded Sean Lemass as Taoiseach. As Minister for Industry and Commerce he developed improved economic relations with NI, and had talks with Brian Faulkner, NI Commerce Minister, at the same period as Sean Lemass's historic trip to Stormont in 1965. He brought in special preferential tariffs for some NI goods. As Taoiseach, he had talks at Stormont with Prime Minister Terence O'Neill in 1967, and his car was snowballed at Stormont by supporters of the Rev. Ian Paisley. During the early years of the NI violence, his words and actions became a matter of intense controversy in the province. Many Catholics looked to him for moral and sometimes material support. Unionists blamed him for what they termed 'interference in the internal affairs of the United Kingdom'. During the violent clashes in the Bogside area of Derry, he said in a broadcast, on 13 August 1969, that it was evident that the Stormont government was no longer in control of the situation. 'Indeed, the present situation is the inevitable outcome of the policies pursued for decades by successive Stormont governments. It is clear also that the Irish government can no longer stand by and see innocent people injured and perhaps worse'. He called for a UN peacekeeping force and said he had asked the British government to see that 'police attacks on the people of Derry should cease immediately'. Mr Lynch also announced that army field hospitals would be set up at points along the border to treat people who did not wish to go to hospitals in NI. The Scarman report on NI troubles said of Mr Lynch's statement: 'There is no doubt that this broadcast strengthened the will of the Bogsiders to obstruct any attempt by the police to enter their area, and to harass them by missile and petrol bomb attacks, whenever they appeared on the perimeter'. The NI Premier, Major Chichester-Clark, reacted angrily. He said he had heard the broadcast with indignation, and he would hold Mr Lynch personally responsible for any worsening of feeling which his 'inflammatory and ill-considered remarks' might cause. In 1970, during what became known as the 'arms trial crisis', Mr Lynch sacked two Ministers, Charles Haughey and Neil Blaney, who were later acquitted of charges of being involved in arms deals. Mr Lynch also rejected suggestions that Fianna Fail had been involved in the setting up of the PIRA. He rejected, too, a claim by Mr Blaney that twenty-five senators and deputies in Dublin had given their guns for use in NI. In 1973, he lost the general election, which he said he had called partly because of the NI situation. In 1975, Fianna Fail's policy statement, calling on the British government to declare its commitment to an ordered withdrawal from NI, brought angry protests from many quarters. In Britain and in NI, and to some extent in the Republic, he was accused of adopting PIRA policy. This Mr Lynch hotly denied, and in 1977 he scored a surprise election triumph over the Fine Gael-Labour coalition, led by Mr Cosgrave. He got an unprecedented twenty-seat majority in the Dail. Some tension developed in relations between London and Dublin. British Ministers throught he could do more to tighten cross-border security and they argued that the Lynch government was discouraging a political settlement by stressing Irish unity too strongly. At the 1978 annual conference of Fianna Fail in Dublin, he announced a special party group to study North-South relations. At the end of 1978 he tried unsuccessfully to persuade the British government to join the new European Monetary System so as to avoid problems in cross-border currency. In September, 1979, in the wake of the murder of Earl Mountbatten, he had talks in London with Mrs Thatcher on ways of strengthening cross-border security. Improvements were agreed, mainly in the communications field, but Mr Lynch ruled out in advance two moves sought by the British security forces: the right of the British army to 'hot pursuit' of suspected terrorists across the border, and permission for RUC detectives to interrogate persons held in the Republic. Towards the end of 1979, pressure built up against Mr Lynch in his own party, and in December he gave way to Charles Haughey as party leader and Taoiseach, and in 1981 also gave up his Dail seat.

LYNCH, SEAMUS. Regional chairman and national vice-president of the Workers' Party (formerly Official Sinn Fein nationally and Republican Clubs in NI), 1978–. b. 1945. Belfast City Council, 1977–81. Unsuccessfully defended his council seat in N. Belfast in 1981, and he also failed to secure election in the constituency in the 1979 and 1983 Westminster elections and the 1982 Assembly election.

M

McALISKEY, JOSEPHINE BERNADETTE. Ind. Unity MP for Mid-Ulster, April 1969–February 1974. b. Cookstown, Co. Tyrone, 23 April 1947. Final-year psychology student at QUB, 1969. As Bernadette Devlin, she first came to prominence in the civil rights campaign as a member of the PD movement. She took part in the student demonstrations in Belfast in the summer of 1968, and in all the major NICRA marches that year in Dungannon, Armagh, and in Duke Street, Derry, on 5 October. She was also in the Belfast–Londonderry PD march in January 1969, when it was attacked by militant loyalists at Burntollet. She lost her first election, when she stood against Major Chichester-Clark (who was soon to become Prime Minister) in S. Derry in March 1969. But the next month she won a by-election in Mid-Ulster for Westminster, defeating the Unionist candidate (widow of the former MP) by 4,211 votes in a poll of 92 per cent. She became the youngest woman ever to be elected to Westminster, and the youngest MP for 50 years. She took her seat on her twenty-second birthday. It was, she said, 'the arrival of a peasant in the halls of the great'. Her sponsors were Gerry Fitt MP, and Labour MP Paul Rose, chairman of the Campaign for Democracy in Ulster. Ignoring tradition, she made her maiden speech an hour after taking her seat. In it, she attacked the Unionist government of Capt. O'Neill and said an extreme, but possible solution would be the abolition of Stormont. The Home Secretary, James Callaghan, spoke of her 'brilliance' and said he looked to the day when she might be standing at the government despatch box. Conservative MP, Norman St John Stevas said that not since the days of F. E. Smith had the House listened to such an electrifying maiden speech. Newspapers hailed her triumph, not only as the voice of the NICRA, but of the student generation. The maiden speech was sandwiched between lunch with the Government Chief Whip and dinner with Lord Longford. But soon Bernadette Devlin was to make very different headlines. In the 'battle of the Bogside' in Londonderry in August 1969, she became the focus of world attention. The slight, five-foot tall MP was to be seen encouraging the Bogsiders to raise their barricades against the police. The report of the Scarman tribunal had described how she was involved in 'inconclusive' telephone conversations from the Bogside to

Major Chichester-Clark (then Prime Minister) and Lord Stonham (Minister of State, Home Office) at the height of the violence on 13 August 1969. Of that same day, Scarman also noted: 'She was seen in the afternoon to be actively defending the Rossville Street barricades, taking missiles up to its defenders, and shouting encouragement to them. In the morning, she led a flag party to the high flats where she unfurled at one end of the roof the 'Starry Plough' flag of the Connolly Association.' Bernadette Devlin now became to her admirers 'an Irish Joan of Arc', and to at least one Unionist MP (Stratton Mills) a 'mini-skirted Castro'. In August 1969, she made a trip to the US during which she raised more than £50,000 for relief in NI, but the distribution of the money aroused intense controversy. Thirteen charges were brought against her over the Bogside incidents, and civil rights supporters accused the NI government of bringing the charges for political reasons. In December 1969, she was sentenced to six months' imprisonment at Derry Magistrates Court for incitement to riot and obstruction and disorderly behaviour. Her counsel, Sir Dingle Foot, told the court that she had acted from the highest motives. Her appeal and an attempt to take the case to the House of Lords were both rejected. She went to Armagh prison in June 1970, after she had increased her Mid-Ulster majority to nearly 6,000 in the general election. When she was jailed, there were protest marches and demonstrations in many parts of

NI and a protest march in London. In July 1971, she announced that she was going to have a baby. Newspaper opinion was divided. Some papers praised her courage and her insistence that her private life was her own; one critical paper said she seemed to have become a lost leader. In January 1972, she punched the Home Secretary, Reginald Maudling, in the Commons. She accused him of lying about the events of 'Bloody Sunday' in Derry, in which thirteen people had died. The scene was unprecedented in recent history, and she said later that the reaction to it showed a lot about the English. It had created more popular outrage than the Derry shootings, she said. In April 1973, she married Michael McAliskey, a schoolmaster, at a quiet, early morning ceremony. Once again, it was an event on her birthday – her twenty-sixth – and the wedding was at a Catholic church near her home town of Cookstown. In the February 1974 general election, she lost her Mid-Ulster seat. The intervention of the SDLP split the anti-Unionist vote, and a Vanguard Unionist, John Dunlop, was returned. She had now moved closer to the Official Republicans, and relations with the SDLP were extremely strained. In 1973, Gerry Fitt, the SDLP leader, had described her as an 'irrelevancy' and after the Mid-Ulster result, she attacked the SDLP as a party of 'quitters' and 'political gangsters'. The old unity of the civil rights movement had vanished, and she also moved away from the Official Republicans to help found the IRSP at the end of 1974.

When the 1975 feud developed between the OIRA and the IRSP, she strongly denied that the IRSP had a military wing. On a lecture tour in the US in 1976, she attacked the Peace People as 'dishonest', since, she said, they were asking women to accept peace at any price. She also said she was not going to tell the PIRA to stop fighting. They were fighting British imperialism in the only way they knew how, she said. In the 1979 European election she championed the republican prisoners engaged in protests at the Maze Prison to secure political status, but Provisional Sinn Fein made it clear that it was not supporting her, and it urged voters to boycott the election. She fought a vigorous campaign after a period of relative political inactivity, but was eliminated on the third count, although she managed to save her deposit. On 16 February 1981 she and her husband were seriously injured when they were shot in their home at Derrylaughan, near Coalisland, by Loyalist gunmen. The shootings took place in front of their three children. An army patrol arrived quickly, and Mrs McAliskey later acknowledged the value of emergency treatment given by the soldiers. In 1980 and 1981 she was the main spokesman of the National H-Block Committee, and in September, 1981, she was expelled from Spain when she arrived to speak at an H-Block meeting in the Basque country. But she managed to slip into Spain again from France, and addressed a meeting without being apprehended. In 1982, she stood unsuccessfully in both the Republic's general elections as PD candidate. She contested Dublin North Central, Mr Haughey's constituency. She has described her early life in her book, *Price of My Soul*, published in 1969.

McALLISTER, JAMES. Sinn Fein Assembly member for Armagh, 1982–. b. Crossmaglen, S. Armagh, 1944. Both his parents' families were deeply involved in Republicanism, and his own activity in the movement dates from the early 1960s. After a period in England, he resumed his interest in 1974, and was PRO of the S. Armagh Hunger Strike Action Committee in 1981, and then became chairman of Sinn Fein in S. Armagh.

McAREAVEY, DANIEL. General secretary SDLP, 1975–80. b. 1926. A former agricultural journalist, he was organiser of SDLP for eighteen months before becoming general secretary. Died March, 1980.

McATEER, EDWARD. Leader of the Nationalist Party at Stormont, 1964–9. b. Coatbridge, Glasgow, 1914. A civil servant from 1930 until 1944, when he started his own accountancy business. He was returned unopposed as Nationalist MP for Mid-Derry in 1945, and again in 1949. He represented Foyle from 1953 until 1969, when he lost to John Hume. He was on Derry Corporation from 1952 until 1958. Early in his career he published a blueprint for civil disobedience entitled 'Irish Action', but in the civil rights campaign he frequently urged moderation. He accepted the role of official opposition at Stormont in 1965, and he often said that much of the trouble might have been avoided if Unionists had offered concessions at that period, and he brought his own brand of wit and sarcasm to parliamentary proceedings. His late brother, Hugh McAteer, was at one time chief-of-staff of the IRA, and staged an escape from Crumlin Road prison in Belfast. In 1977, Eddie McAteer indicated support for the newly-established IIP.

MacBRIDE, SEAN. The Nobel Peace Prize winner of 1974 and international jurist and diplomat, who was involved in peace talks in 1977 aimed at securing a paramilitary ceasefire in NI. b. 27 January 1904. MacBride was among the most prominent IRA leaders in the 1920s and 1930s. He was reputedly chief-of-staff for a time, and was imprisoned three times between 1918 and 1930. He urged a concentration on constitutional action during the 1940s and became leader of the republican party, Clann na Poblachta, and a member of the Dail, 1947–58. He was Minister for External Affairs in the inter-party government, 1948–51. He was Assistant UN Secretary-General and UN Commissioner in Namibia 1973–4, and returned to Dublin when he left this post. In 1977, he was awarded the Lenin Peace Prize. In that year, he tried, without success, to get agreement between loyalist and IRA paramilitaries in NI. These talks also involved Desmond Boal, the NI lawyer and former Unionist MP and first chairman of the DUP. The con-

tacts were made in great secrecy and did not involve face-to-face talks between the two sides. Churchmen were used to some extent as intermediaries. Despite his early involvement with the IRA, he has stressed his opposition to the PIRA campaign. He summed up his view by saying that there were injustices in NI, but they were not unbearable and there were probably other ways of remedying the situation. It was disclosed in British Cabinet papers released in January 1980, that MacBride had a meeting at Stormont in 1949 with the then Prime Minister, Lord Brookeborough. But MacBride said there had been no negotiations as such.

McCANN, EAMONN. Civil rights activist. b. 10 March 1943. Expelled from QUB 1965, when reading psychology. President of university 'Literific' Society and vice-president of Labour Club. One of the organisers of civil rights march in Londonderry, 5 October 1968. As chairman of Derry Labour Party, unsuccessfully contested Foyle in Stormont 1969 general election and Londonderry in 1970 Westminster election. Active in 'battle of the Bogside' in Derry and author of *War in an Irish Town.* His Foyle campaign included a demand for take-over of all vacant property suitable for housing accommodation. Later, he took up journalism in Dublin.

McCARTNEY, ROBERT. Off. U. Assembly member for N. Down, 1982–. b. 1936. A native of the Shankill area of Belfast, he was a QC and one of NI's most successful barristers when he caught the political limelight in 1981 with a sharp attack on the Rev. Ian Paisley, whom he dubbed a 'fascist'. In October, 1981, he led a delegation of NI lawyers and businessmen in talks with Taoiseach Dr Garret Fitzgerald, on his 'constitutional crusade'. In August, 1982, as chairman of the OUP's newly-formed Union Group, he visited the USA and in a speech to the Irish Forum in San Francisco described as 'simplistic and dangerous nonsense' the idea that Ireland's problems would be solved if only the British left.

McCLOSKEY, VINCENT. SDLP Assembly (1973–4) and Convention (1975–6) member for S. Antrim. b. Belfast, 1920. Formerly National Democratic Party. Lisburn Rural District Council, 1968–73.

McCLURE, WILLIAM JAMES. DUP Assembly member for Londonderry, 1982–. Was Convention member for the same constituency, 1975–6. b. 1927. Founder member of DUP, chairman (1974) of the party's Londonderry Association. Party chairman, 1978–. Coleraine Council, 1973–. Past Grand Master of Independent Orange Order.

McCONNELL ROBERT DODD (BERTIE). Alliance Assembly (1973–4) and Convention (1975–6) member for N. Down. b. Bangor, Co. Down, 1921. Blinded in World War II, during army service, he served on Bangor Borough Council, 1958–73, and N. Down Council, 1973–.

MP for Bangor in NI parliament, 1969–72; elected as pro-O'Neill Unionist and joined Alliance Party in 1972 as one of first members of Alliance Parliamentary Party. President, Alliance Party, 1976.

McCREA, RAYMOND STUART. DUP Assembly member for S. Belfast, 1982–. b. 1945. Belfast City Council, 1977–. Leader, DUP group on City Council, 1981–.

McCREA, REV. (ROBERT THOMAS) WILLIAM. DUP MP for Mid-Ulster, 1983–. Assembly member for Mid-Ulster, 1982–. b. 6 February 1948. A Free Presbyterian Minister prominent in Loyalist politics since 1971, when he was sentenced to six months' imprisonment for riotous behaviour in Dungiven, Co. Londonderry. Widely known as a Gospel singer. Chairman, United Loyalist Front, 1972. Magherafelt Council, 1973–. Chairman, DUP, 1976. Housing Executive Board, 1979–80. Unsuccessfully contested S. Belfast by-election 1982. His 1983 election majority in mid-Ulster of 78 was the smallest of the election in NI.

McCULLOUGH, RAYMOND. Off. U. Assembly member for S. Down, 1982–. Vice-chairman, Banbridge Council, 1981–. On Executive of Official Unionist Party; hon. sec., S. Down Unionist Association; and on committee, Grand Orange Lodge of Ireland.

McCUSKER, JAMES HAROLD. Off. U. MP for Upper

Bann, 1983–. MP for Armagh, 1974–83. Assembly member for Armagh, 1982–. Deputy leader, Official Unionist Party, 1982–. b. 7 February 1940. A teacher and later production manager, he was Secretary and Whip of the Unionist Coalition MPs, 1975–6. Active in pressing for tougher security measures in S. Armagh. Voted with the Labour Government in crucial confidence vote which led to the defeat of the Callaghan Government and the 1979 general election. He held off a challenge from the DUP in that election, and in the 1982 Assembly election topped the poll in Armagh with 19,547 votes. In 1981, he was responsible for setting up a unit based at Official Unionist headquarters which sought to persuade the European Commission on Human Rights that border security had not been adequate in terms of British or Irish effort, and that widows of innocent victims of the violence should be regarded as suffering a deprivation of human rights.

McDONALD, JAMES. SDLP Assembly member for S. Antrim, 1982–. b. 1930. Craigavon Council, 1973–. First SDLP deputy mayor of Craigavon, 1979. Unsuccessfully contested Convention election in S. Antrim, 1975.

McFAUL, KENNETH. DUP Assembly member for N. Antrim 1982–. Was Convention member for same constituency, 1975–6. b. 1948. Carrickfergus Council, 1973–. Mayor of Carrickfergus, 1981–3. Formerly in Protestant Unionist Party.

MacGIOLLA, TOMAS. President of the Workers' Party and its predecessor, Official Sinn Fein, January 1970–, and earlier president of Sinn Fein, 1962–70. He presided at the Dublin meeting at which the walk-out of the future Provisional members occurred. b. 1924. B.A., B.Comm. (UCD) TD, 1982–. Has frequently visited NI, particularly to speak in support of Republican Clubs candidates. In 1972, he was cleared of a charge of membership of the OIRA. In that year, he was twice deported from Britain, but in 1976, the Home Secretary, Roy Jenkins, resisted Conservative demands that he should be expelled. On that occasion, he addressed a private meeting of MPs at the House of Commons, which had been arranged by Labour MP Joan Maynard. Unsuccessfully contested the 1979 European election in Dublin.

McGONAGLE, STEPHEN. Parliamentary Commissioner for Administration (Ombudsman) and Commissioner for Complaints, 1974–9. Irish Senator, 1983–. b. Londonderry, 1914. Leading local trade unionist before appointment as Ombudsman; district secretary of the Irish Transport and General Workers' Union and president of the NI Committee of Irish Congress of Trade Unions, 1972. He became vice-chairman of Londonderry Development Commission in 1969, but resigned in August 1971, as a protest against the introduction of internment without trial, in line with the withdrawal of many leading Catholics from public appointments. Chairman of Police

Complaints Board set up in 1977 to independently investigate complaints against the RUC, but resigned from this post in 1983, after Unionist protests that it was inconsistent with membership of Irish Senate. In 1982, presided at initial, short-lived inquiry into homosexual scandal at Kincora boys' home in E. Belfast. Irish Labour Party delegate to Forum for a New Ireland, 1983.

McGRADY, EDWARD KEVIN. SDLP Assembly member for S. Down, 1982–. Also served in Assembly (1973–4) and Convention (1975–6). b. Downpatrick, Co. Down, 1935. Head of Department of Executive Planning and Co-ordination in NI Executive, 1974. Downpatrick Urban Council, 1961–73 (chairman, 1964–73); Down District Council, 1973–, (chairman, 1974–5). Mr McGrady was particularly critical of Secretary of State Merlyn Rees after the fall of the Executive. He said that a remark by Mr Rees that he had not expected the Executive to endure showed the 'duplicity and dishonesty' of British policy. Unsuccessfully contested S. Down in 1979 Westminster election. Chief Whip, SDLP, 1979–. Unsuccessfully stood against Enoch Powell in S. down in 1979 and 1983, when he failed by only 548 votes. Chief Whip, SDLP, 1979–.

McGUINNESS, JAMES MARTIN. Sinn Fein Assembly member for Londonderry, 1982–. b. Bogside area of Londonderry, 1950. An active Republican since 1969, he was a member of the top-level IRA delegation which met NI Secretary William Whitelaw in London, July, 1972. Has been imprisoned on several occasions both in NI and the Irish Republic. In 1981, gave the oration at funeral of IRA hunger-striker Francis Hughes in Bellaghy, Co. Derry.

McGURRAN, MALACHY. Chairman of the six-county executive of Republican Clubs and vice-president of Official Sinn Fein from 1970 until his death from bone cancer in July 1978. b. Lurgan, 1938. Active in the 1956 IRA campaign and interned for a time. Unsuccessfully contested the Convention election at Armagh, and the October 1974 Westminster election in same constituency. Craigavon District Council, 1977–8.

McIVOR, WILLIAM BASIL. Education Minister in Executive, 1974. b. 17 June 1928. LL.B. (QUB) Barrister, 1950. Unionist MP for Larkfield, 1969–72. Minister of Community Relations, 1971. After direct rule, he dissociated himself from Unionist attacks on the Secretary of State, William Whitelaw. One of the Unionist team at the Sunningdale conference, December 1973. As head of the Education Department in the power-sharing Executive, he announced the scheme for shared schools for Protestant and Catholic pupils wherever there was sufficient parental support, but the scheme was never implemented owing to the short life of the Executive. Resident Magistrate, 1976–.

McKAY, JOHN ALEXANDER. Off. U. member of Convention

(1975–6) for Fermanagh and S. Tyrone, b. 1945.

McKEAGUE, JOHN DUNLOP. A leading Belfast Loyalist who was shot dead by an INLA gunman in his E. Belfast shop in January, 1982. b. 1930. First came to prominence as chairman of the Shankill Defence Association, 1969–70. He stood unsuccessfully as Protestant Unionist candidate for Belfast Corporation by-election in Victoria in 1969, and as an Independent in N. Belfast at the 1970 Westminster election. He was often described as a founder of the Loyalist paramilitary group, the Red Hand Commandos, but always denied that he was involved with the organisation. He was cleared in 1969 of charges of conspiracy to cause explosions. In October 1969, sentenced to three months' imprisonment for unlawful assembly. In 1971, his elderly mother was burned to death, when his shop and flat in E. Belfast were set on fire by petrol bombs. *Loyalist News,* the paper run by McKeague, said she had been 'murdered by the enemies of Ulster'. In the same year he and two others were the first persons to be accused under the Incitement to Hatred Act, after they published a *Loyalist Song Book.* The jury disagreed at the first trial and they were acquitted at the re-trial. In 1976, as a member of the ULCCC, he was prominent in advocating independence for NI and in 1977 became spokesman for the Ulster Independence Association.

McKEE, JACK. DUP Assembly member for N. Antrim, 1982–. b. 1944. Larne Council, 1973–. Leader of DUP on Larne Council, 1981–.

McKEOWN, CIARAN. One of the three founders of the Peace People in 1976. b. Londonderry, 24 December 1949. Graduated in philosophy at QUB, 1966, and in that year president of the Students' Union. President of Union of Students of Ireland, 1967. On Belfast staff of *Irish Press,* (Dublin), before joining Peace People full-time in 1976. In 1977, awarded scholarship worth £4,000 a year by Norwegian government to help with peace work and the writing of articles for the Norwegian Institute for Peace Research. Director and editor of *Fortnight,* NI current affairs magazine, for a period during 1977. Editor Peace People newspaper, 1978–9. Resigned from Peace People Executive, 1980, and returned to journalism as a freelance.

McLACHLAN, PETER. UPNI Assembly member for S. Antrim, 1973–4. b. 1937. In 1977, he became a full-time official of the Peace Movement and was elected Chairman when the original leaders stood down from the Executive in 1978. He resigned from this post in February 1980, and became Secretary of the Belfast Voluntary Welfare Society. Worked in a great variety of posts – teacher, civil servant at Stormont and Westminster, secretary to the Youth Orchestra of Great Britain, personal assistant to Fleet Street newspaper Chief Cecil King – before taking charge of NI desk at Conservative Central Office in 1970. Parliamentary lobbyist at Westminster, 1972–3. In the Assembly he was one of Brian Faulkner's closest advisers, particularly during the Sunningdale conference. But he declined a post in the Executive, arguing that he would be better employed as a backbencher and in building up UPNI. Stood unsuccessfully in Westminster election in E. Belfast in 1974 and in Convention election in S. Antrim in 1975. Specially interested in penal reform and community groups and chairman of NI Federation of Housing Associations, 1977.

McMANUS, FRANCIS JOSEPH (FRANK). Unity MP for Fermanagh and S. Tyrone, 1970–4. b. Enniskillen, 16 August 1942. B.A., Dip.Ed. (QUB). Chairman of Fermanagh Civil Rights Association, 1968–71, and leading speaker at civil rights demonstrations throughout the province. Chairman, Northern Resistance Movement, 1972. Chairman, Comhairle Uladh (republican-orientated, 9-county forum), 1972. Leading figure in Unity Movement which contested a variety of elections, and in 1977 one of founders of IIP of which he became deputy leader in 1981. In 1971, sentenced to six months imprisonment for defying a parade ban in Enniskillen. In same year, cleared of charge relating to IRA documents. Injured by one of four shots fired at him in September 1973. Has written extensively on civil rights issues. Irish representative of US-based Irish National Caucus, 1976–.

McMASTER, STANLEY EDWARD. Unionist MP for E. Belfast, 1959–74. b. 23 September 1926. Barrister in practice in London. Lecturer in company law, Regent Street Polytechnic. Was active as MP in pressing the claims of Belfast shipyard and aircraft factory, both in his E. Belfast constituency.

McNAMARA, KEVIN JOSEPH. Chairman of the Labour Party's NI committee at Westminster, 1974–9. b. 5 September 1934. Labour MP for Hull N., 1966–74 and Hull Central, 1974–. Co. Down family background. Leading figure in Campaign for Democracy in Ulster.

McQUADE, JOHN. DUP MP for N. Belfast, 1979–83. b. 1912. Ex-docker, ex-soldier, ex-boxer, he has been for many years one of the best-known personalities on the Protestant Shankill Road in Belfast. Unionist MP for Woodvale at Stormont, 1965–72, he broke with the Unionist Parliamentary Party in 1971, and resigned as MP when Stormont was suspended in 1972. He then joined the DUP, and was returned as a DUP Assembly member for N. Belfast, 1973–4. When the Assembly was prorogued in May 1974, he refused to take his salary and donated it to a holiday fund for old people. In February 1974, he unsuccessfully contested W. Belfast as UUUC candidate. He then broke with the DUP but rejoined in 1979, and with a split in the Unionist vote, gained N. Belfast from the Official Unionists by a majority of just under 1,000 in a seven-cornered contest. He retired at the 1983 election.

MACRORY, SIR PATRICK. Chairman of the review body which produced the plan for local government reform in NI, 1970. b. 11 March 1911. A barrister-at-law, Sir Patrick was a director of a variety of top companies and a member of the NI Development Council, 1956–64. The Macrory proposals produced a great deal of controversy. They were strongly attacked by existing councillors, and supported by the NICRA. They were accepted by the Chichester-Clark government, and the twenty-six district councils which replaced the former complex structure were first elected in 1973. Apart from the councils, the scheme provided for area boards for education, library and health services which were strongly attacked by Unionists on the ground that the majority of members of the boards were nominated by the government rather than elected representatives. The disappearance of the Assembly removed what was intended to be the top tier of local government, and this has been dubbed the 'Macrory gap'. In 1978, the Conservative opposition suggested that Sir Patrick should be recalled by the government to consider a new top tier of local government – something that was being demanded by Unionists but opposed by the SDLP who argued that it would mean Unionist dominance of councils again, as in the pre-1973 period.

McSORLEY, MRS MARY KATHERINE. SDLP Assembly member for Mid-Ulster, 1982–. Magherafelt Council, 1977–. Executive member, Association of Local Authorities.

MacSTIOFAIN, SEAN. Chief-of-staff of the PIRA, 1970–2. b. Leytonstone, London, 17 February 1928. John Edward Drayton Stephenson's adoption of an Irish background and dedication to IRA aims were apparently due to the influence of his mother, who claimed to be a native of Belfast. After National Service with the RAF (he became a corporal), he joined some London-Irish associations and, presumably, the IRA. In 1953, he and 2 other men – one of them Cathal Goulding, who was later to become chief-of-staff of the OIRA – were sentenced to 8 years imprisonment for stealing 108 rifles and eight Bren guns from the cadet armoury of Felstead School in Essex. After his release in 1959, he travelled to Dublin (the first time he had been in Ireland) and became salesman for an Irish language organisation. By this time he was a fluent Irish speaker. He soon became immersed in IRA intelligence work, and he devoted his organisational skill to the building up of the PIRA after the split in the republican movement. At the height of the PIRA campaign, he made many secret trips to NI, but he was believed to be interested in moving over eventually to the political side of the Provisionals. In 1972, in one of his few public statements, he said he was interested in peace, but not peace at any price, and the British must first agree to the basic IRA aims. In November 1972, he was arrested in Co. Dublin soon after he had recorded a controversial interview with RTE journalist, Kevin O'Kelly. Jailed for 6 months for IRA membership. IRA made an unsuccessful bid to free him when he was taken to a Dublin hospital on hunger strike. In Jan. 1973, he ended the 57-day hunger strike after PIRA leadership stated that it was 'serving no useful purpose'. He then ceased to be PIRA chief-of-staff. At end of 1981, resigned from PSF after its ard-fheis had shown a majority opposed to the 'Eire Nua' federal policy. In March, 1983, he appealed for a PIRA ceasefire.

MAGINNIS, JOHN EDWARD. Unionist MP for Armagh, 1959–February 1974. b. Tandragee, Co. Armagh, 7 March 1919. Served in RUC, 1939–45. Group Secretary Ulster Farmers' Union, 1956–9. Stood unsuccessfully as UPNI candidate in Armagh at the Convention election.

MAGINNIS, KEN. Off. U. MP for Fermanagh and S. Tyrone, 1983–. Assembly member for same constituency, 1982–. b. 1938. Teacher. Formerly served in Ulster Special Constabulary ('B' Specials), and was later part-time major and company commander, UDR, for 11 years. Official Unionist security spokesman, 1982–. First chairman of Assembly's security committee, 1983–. Dungannon Council, 1981–. Unsuccessfully contested Fermanagh and S. Tyrone by-election, Aug. 1981, but had 7,000 plus majority in 1983 election when SDLP competed for Nationalist vote.

MAGUIRE, M. FRANCIS (FRANK). Independent MP for Fermanagh-S. Tyrone, October, 1974–81. b. 1929, died 5 March 1981. A publican, he was active in the Republican movement and was interned for nearly two years in the late 1950s. As an MP, he took a special interest in the welfare of Irish prisoners in English jails. He came close to practising the Abstentionist policy so often favoured by Republicans, and rarely attended at Westminster and still had not made a maiden speech at the time of his death. But he did support the Callaghan Government in some key divisions, and his absence from the final vote of confidence contributed to its defeat. In the 1979 election, he increased his majority and his death gave rise to the by-election in which hunger striker Bobby Sands was elected.

MAGUIRE, PAUL. All. Assembly member for N. Belfast, 1982–. Lecturer in law, QUB, and party spokesman on legal affairs. Party adviser at Stormont Constitutional Conference, 1980.

MALLON, SEAMUS. Deputy leader of SDLP, 1979–. b. Markethill, Co. Armagh, 1936. Elected Assembly member for Armagh in 1982, but disqualified on grounds that he was a member of the Republic's Senate. Former Co. Armagh gaelic footballer and head teacher. Prominent in civil rights campaign and chairman, Mid-Armagh Anti-Discrimination Committee, 1963–8. Armagh Council, 1973–. Represented Armagh in both the 1973–4 Assembly and the 1975 Convention. Unsuccessfully contested Armagh in Westminster elections, October, 1974, and 1979. He succeeded John Hume as SDLP deputy leader in 1979. Earlier, he had been chairman of the SDLP in the 1973 Assembly and chairman of constituency representatives, 1977–9. His appointment to the Republic's Senate by Taoiseach Charles Haughey in June, 1982, was a major surprise. It meant that he was ineligible to sit in the 1982 Assembly, and Mr Mallon protested that the situation highlighted the 'incongruity' of British political involvement in Irish affairs. Despite the SDLP decision not to attend the Assembly, he was unseated in an Election Court on a petition brought by Armagh MP, Harold McCusker. From 1979–82, he was party spokesman on relations with Westminster, and in 1982 took over as law and order spokesman. His failure in 1983 Westminster election to take the new seat, Newry-Armagh, was a disappointment for his party.

MANSFIELD, EARL, Minister-of-State, NI Office, 1983–. b. 7 July 1930. (Heir, Viscount Stormont.) Minister-of-State, Scottish Office, 1979–83. Member of British delegation to European Parliament, 1973–5. Opposition spokesman in House of Lords, 1975–9. Apart from being departmental spokesman in the Lords, he took responsibility for agriculture in NI Office.

MARKETS. A district close to the centre of Belfast, where there were many bombing and shooting incidents in 1969–70. At the start of the troubles, OIRA had a strong presence in the area, and after 1972 it was largely displaced by INLA, which continued to be active in the area in the early 1980s. The population has been greatly reduced by redevelopment.

MARTIN, (THOMAS) GEOFFREY. Head of EEC Office in Belfast, 1979–. b. 26 July 1940. B.Sc. Hons. (QUB) President of the National Union of Students, 1966–8. Diplomatic staff, Commonwealth Secretariat, 1974–9. After the Dublin summit of December, 1980, he suggested that the EEC could provide 'a useful institutional relationship' in the future strategy of Anglo-Irish relations, and that the European dimension could have a growing importance in NI affairs.

MASON, ROY. Secretary of State for NI, September 1976– May 1979. b. 18 April 1924. As a boy of fourteen he went down the mines in his native Barnsley, Yorkshire, and remained in the coal industry until 1953, when he became Labour MP for Barnsley. Labour Party spokesman on Defence, Home Affairs and Post Office, 1960–4. Minister-of-State, Board of Trade, 1964–7. Minister of Defence, Equipment, 1967–8. Minister of Power, 1968–9. President of the Board of Trade, 1969–70. Secretary for Defence, 1974–6. His appointment to Stormont was unexpected, and regarded by many non-Unionists as indicating a tougher direct rule regime than that of his predecessor, Merlyn Rees. Some SDLP members suggested that he would be concerned only with a military solution. He was also handicapped in some quarters by a statement which he had made as Defence Secretary in April 1974: 'Pressure is mounting on the mainland to pull out the troops. Equally, demands are being made to set a date for the withdrawal, thereby forcing the warring factions to get together and hammer out a solution'. The comment caused alarm in the three-party NI Executive, and the Deputy Chief Executive, Mr Gerry Fitt, flew to London to seek clarification from the Prime Minister, Mr Wilson. In a statement after a Cabinet meeting, the Prime Minister said the troops would stay in the front line against terrorism, and a statement from the Defence Ministry said Mr Mason did not intend to suggest any change of policy. At the same time, he was responsible for military initiative in NI: the introduction of units of the controversial SAS in S. Armagh in 1976. As Defence Secretary, he called an early morning meeting of his top advisers and presented the plan to Mr Wilson, who accepted it immediately as an answer to some horrific murders in the area. At Stormont, Mr Mason was helped by three factors: his experience of the army role during his previous two years at the Defence Ministry; a more friendly attitude towards him by the Conservative opposition than Mr Rees had enjoyed; and the tendency for violence to decline, notably from the loyalist side. In his early months in the province he ran into criticism from the media because of an attempt to introduce voluntary censorship of news of 'sensitive

terrorist incidents'. He wanted to bring in the equivalent of the Whitehall 'D' notice system which is designed to discourage the dissemination of information likely to be damaging to national security. He was also opposed to the BBC and ITV broadcasting interviews in support of allegations of ill-treatment directed against the RUC. This was clearly part of a psychological approach. At his initial news conference in September 1976, he spoke of the IRA 'reeling'; at the end of the year the 'net was tightening on the terrorist'; and by the end of 1977, the 'corner is being turned in the war against the terrorists'. Certainly, the security forces achieved major successes in terms of arrests during 1977, and there was a distinct drop in the level of killings and bombings. But at the end of 1977, with a fireman's strike, the PIRA mounted a new incendiary bomb campaign, which caused heavy damage. And the IRA said Mr Mason was being a 'fool' to predict their defeat. One of the important changes which he made in security policy during 1977 was to increase the covert tactics of the army, and the Special Air Service was allowed to operate throughout the province. Other features of his security approach were to enlarge the role of the RUC and UDR (more 'Ulsterisation' of security is the local phrase). At the start of 1978 he also aimed to switch a larger section of the army locally from men on four-month tours to units which would remain on a long-stay basis, that is for two years. In 1977, he had a substantial political success in defeating the efforts of the UUAC to repeat the triumph of the 1974 UWC strike. During that year he also made two attempts to get some movement towards a political settlement. After talks with the various parties in February and March, he reported to parliament that there was little sign of bridging the divide. Towards the end of the year he had more talks on the possibility of 'interim devolution', but these rapidly petered out. Roy Mason also put emphasis on bringing forward controversial legislation during direct rule – a regime which he claimed was 'positive, compassionate and caring'. Legislation was brought forward to bring the laws on divorce and homosexuality into line with those in Great Britain – both measures took effect after some delay – and the government committed itself to comprehensive education. A move to make car belts compulsory in advance of Great Britain proved abortive. The courts system in the province was substantially reformed. The short pipe-smoking Secretary of State forcefully projected his dominant personality in the local scene. He was often at his Stormont or Whitehall desk at 8 o'clock in the morning. His recreation might be listed in *Who's Who* simply as 'work – provided one can keep on top of it', but he admitted to one major hobby: designing neckties. And, according to his ex-driver, his two favourite topics were life in the mines and Barnsley bitter.

MATES, MICHAEL JOHN. Conservative MP for Petersfield and chairman of the Anglo-Irish all-party committee at Westminster, 1979–. b. 9 June 1934. Served with army in NI as lieut. colonel. Secretary of Conservative backbench committee on NI, 1974–9; vice-chairman, 1979–81. Frequent visitor to NI, and has differed strongly from right-wing MPs on Conservative NI Committee, who were critical of the James Prior initiative.

MAUDLING, REGINALD. As Home Secretary, responsible for NI affairs at Westminster, 1970–2. b. 7 March 1917, died February 1979. Conservative MP for Barnet, 1950–79. When he took over from Mr Callaghan when the Conservatives returned to power in 1970, he made it clear that he would continue to support reform moves in NI. But with the Prime Minister, Mr Heath, concerning himself closely with NI matters, Mr Maudling's influence was secondary. His relaxed approach also brought criticism within NI when he stated in March 1971 that the London and Stormont governments were in agreement on security, and shortly afterwards, the NI Premier, James Chichester-Clark, resigned leaving little doubt that he was dissatisfied with Westminster's approach to law and order. Best remembered in NI for having coined the phrase 'acceptable level of violence'. The remark drew a strong protest from the NI government despite his denial that he was in any way complacent. He backed the decision of the Faulkner government to introduce internment without trial in August 1971.

MAWHINNEY, BRIAN STANLEY. Ulster-born Conservative MP for Peterborough, 1979–. b. 26 July 1940. B.Sc. (QUB); M.Sc. (University of Michigan); Ph.D. (University of London). Active in Conservative Party's NI Committee, and in 1980 put forward proposal for a NI Assembly with limited powers initially, which has been widely seen as the inspiration for the 1982 'rolling devolution' plan. Author of *Conflict and Christianity in Northern Ireland* (1976).

MAWHINNEY, GORDON. All. Assembly member for S. Antrim, 1982–. b. 1943. Specialist in valuation and rating. Formerly on party Executive.

MAZE PRISON. See Security Section (p. 313).

MELCHETT, LORD (PETER ROBERT HENRY MOND). Minister of State and House of Lords spokesman, NI Office, 1976–9. b. 24 February 1948. B.A. (Cantab.); M.A. (Keele). Government Whip, 1974–5, Parliamentary Under-Secretary, Trade, 1975–6. Chairman, government working party on pop festivals, 1975–6, and has described himself as a punk rock fan. Responsibilities at NI Office: departments of Education and Health and Social Services; also probation, court services; youth matters. His strong support of comprehensive education proved controversial in NI.

MILLAR, FRANK. Ind. U. Assembly member for N. Belfast, 1982–. Was Ind. Loyalist member of the 1973–4. Assembly and

UUUC member of the Convention (1975–6). b. Belfast, 1925. Former shipyard worker and shop steward. Founder member, Belfast Protestant Action, 1956–64. Belfast City Council, 1972–.

MILLAR, FRANK. General secretary, OUP, January 1983–. b. Belfast, 1954; son of Ind. U. Assembly member, Frank Millar. Press officer, Young Unionist Council, 1972–3. Research officer for Off. U. MPs at Westminster, 1977–81. Press officer to OUP in Belfast, 1981–3, before becoming youngest-ever general secretary of the party.

MILLS, PETER. Parliamentary Under-Secretary, NI Office, 1972–4, with special responsibility for agriculture. b. 1921. Conservative MP for Torrington, 1964–.

MILLS, WILLIAM STRATTON. MP for N. Belfast, 1959–74. b. 1 July 1922. One of a group of Unionist MPs – styled a 'truth squad' by the party – who visited the USA and Canada in August 1969, to counter statements by Bernadette Devlin MP. He had served on several Conservative Party committees, including the Executive of the 1922 (backbenchers') Committee, and as vice-chairman of the NI Committee. But in February 1971 he voted against the Heath government as a protest against its 'inadequate security policy' in NI. After the introduction of direct rule, he expressed the view that any future Stormont Assembly should not be dominated by one party, and should not have control of security. This was unwelcome to many

Unionists, and when he failed to persuade the party's Standing Committee in 1972 that members of Vanguard should be expelled, he resigned from the party. He continued to sit at Westminster, initially as an Ind. Unionist and then as an Alliance MP from 1973 until the February 1974 general election, when he was not a candidate.

MINFORD, NATHANIEL (NAT). Speaker of the NI Assembly, 1973–4. b. 1913, died 1975. Unionist MP for Antrim, 1960–72. Leader of the Commons, 1971–2. Elected to Assembly from S. Antrim.

MINORITY RIGHTS GROUP. A Catholic pressure group established in Belfast in 1971 to represent minority views outside parliament. It was under the chairmanship of Tom Conaty, who was also chairman of the CCDC. It included some Catholic priests, together with professional and business people and trade unionists.

MITCHELL, DAVID BOWER. Parliamentary Under-Secretary, NI Office, Jan., 1981–3. b. June 1928. Cons. MP for Basingstoke, 1964–. He took charge of the Environment Department at Stormont – the department which has the most wide-ranging responsibilities, taking in much of local government, housing and planning, the 'enterprise zones' in Belfast and Londonderry and the Belfast integrated operation, for which EEC aid has been sought. Parliamentary Under-Secretary, Transport, 1983–.

MITCHELL, ROBERT. Unionist MP for N. Armagh, 1969–72. b. 1912. Lurgan Borough Council, 1957–73; Coleraine Council, 1977–. Captain Mitchell, as secretary of the Unionist Backbenchers' Committee, 1971–2, was often critical of the government's law-and-order policies.

MOLYNEAUX, JAMES HENRY. Leader of the Official Unionist Party 1979–. MP for Lagan Valley, 1983–. MP for S. Antrim, 1970–83. Assembly member for S. Antrim, 1982–. b. 27 August 1920. He was Whip and Secretary of the Unionist Coalition MPs from March to October, 1974. He had been defeated by Harry West in a contest for the party leadership in Jan., 1974, but he succeeded Mr West as leader of the Coalition MPs when Mr West lost his seat in October 1974. Mr Molyneaux held this post until the break-up of the Coalition in 1977, and he continued as leader of the Official Unionist MPs. Vice-president of the Ulster Unionist Council, deputy grand master of the Orange Order, and Sovereign Commonwealth grand master of the Royal Black Institution. His early period of leadership was marked by the adoption of a neutral stance at Westminster, in contrast to the party's former close association with the Conservative Party. He had a leading role in persuading the Callaghan Government to give NI more MPs. In early 1977, he advocated some form of interim devolution, but his critics within Unionism accused him of seeking integration rather than full devolution. When he took over the party leadership in 1979, the party was somewhat demoralised by the triumph of the Rev. Ian Paisley in the European election. But he vigorously defended the OUP decision to stand aside from the Atkins conference at Stormont in 1980, and seemed to be determined to build a more broadly-based leadership and to tighten party organisation at the grass-roots. At the same time, he tried to project himself to a greater extent through the media. Despite this, the DUP achieved a small lead in votes over the OUP in the 1981 council elections, and this was followed by some rumblings against his leadership. In the run-up to the 1982 Assembly elections, he was active in Parliament and outside, warning that the Prior plan was a serious threat to Unionism. He pressed one argument repeatedly – that the 'rolling devolution' Assembly could not produce majority rule government since it basically sought to re-establish the Sunningdale formula, both in terms of power-sharing Government and a new cross-border institution. At the end of 1981, he announced the setting up of a Council for the Union 'to defeat the drift towards a united Ireland, as indicated by the Anglo-Irish talks'. It attracted some support from outside the OUP and from right-wing Conservative MPs, and held a conference in Belfast in 1982. In his speech at the Royal Black Institution demonstration at Scarva in 1982, he commented that 'certain not-so-loyal Crown servants' had not been surprised by the murder of the Rev. Robert Bradford.

James Prior described it as an 'appalling charge' and referred it to the Chief Constable. In the 1982 Assembly election, he led his party to a modest victory – the OUP took five more seats than the DUP, and achieved a three per cent swing in votes from the DUP as compared with the 1981 council elections. His own first preference vote of 19,978 in S. Antrim was the largest of the whole election. In the 1983 Westminster general election, he tried to establish an electoral pact with DUP in marginal seats, but largely failed. His majority in the 1983 Westminster election in the new seat, Lagan Valley, was more than 17,000 and the OUP achievement in taking eleven NI seats in that election, putting it ahead of the SDP, strengthened his position as leader. Privy Councillor, 1983–.

MORGAN, WILLIAM JAMES. Off. U. Assembly (1973–4) and Convention (1975–6) member for N. Belfast. b. 1914. MP for Old-park (Belfast) at Stormont, 1949–58. MP for Clifton (Belfast) at Stormont, 1959–69. Minister of Health and Local Government, 1961–4. Minister of Labour, 1964–5; Minister of Health and Social Services, 1965–9; NI Senate, 1970–2. Took strong line against the Council of Ireland proposal during Assembly debate on Sunningdale proposals, and on this issue transferred support from Mr Faulkner to Mr West in May 1974.

MORRELL, LESLIE JAMES. Head of the Department of Agriculture in NI Executive, 1974. b. Enniskillen, 1931. B.Agr. (QUB). Farms near Coleraine and active in Royal Ulster Agricultural Society. Assembly member for Londonderry, 1973–4, but failed there in Convention election, 1975. Deputy Leader of UPNI, 1974–81. Londonderry County Council, 1969–73. Coleraine district council, 1973–.

MORRISON, DANIEL GERARD (DANNY). Sinn Fein Assembly member for Mid-Ulster, 1982–. b. 1953. A former internee; charge of IRA membership was dropped in 1979. Became well-known through TV appearances during the 1981 H-Block hunger strike, since he was nominated by Bobby Sands, MP, as external spokesman for the prisoners. Sinn Fein director of publicity and editor, *An Phoblacht/Republican News*, 1981–. His comment at 1981 annual conference of Sinn Fein about Republicans having 'an Armalite in one hand and a ballot-paper in the other' has become a familiar phrase to illustrate Sinn Fein's increased electoral activity. In January, 1982, he was arrested when trying to enter the US from Canada, with Owen Carron, MP. In December, 1982, he was banned by the Home Secretary from entering Britain when invited by GLC leader Ken Livingstone to speak to Labour MPs and councillors in London. In the 1983 Westminster election, he pushed up PSF vote in Mid-Ulster and was only 78 votes behind the DUP winner.

MORRISON, GEORGE. VUPP (and later UUUM) Convention member for S. Antrim, 1975–6.

b. 1924. A founder member of the Vanguard Unionist Party, he is a former chairman of the Lisburn branch. In the row over William Craig's plan in the Convention for a voluntary coalition between Unionists and the SDLP, he opposed Mr Craig and became a member of UUUM, later the UUUP, led by Ernest Baird. Lisburn Borough Council, 1973. Joined OUP, 1983.

MORROW, ADAM JAMES. (ADDIE), All. Assembly member for E. Belfast, 1982–. Castlereagh Council, 1973–. Deputy mayor of Castlereagh, 1981. Party spokesman on agriculture.

MOYLE, ROLAND DUNSTAN. Minister of State, NI Office, 1974–6. b. 12 March 1928. Son of late Baron Moyle, a Labour peer. M.A., LL.B. (Cambridge). Barrister-at-law. In the NI Office, Mr Moyle took charge of the departments of Education and Environment after the collapse of the NI Executive.

MOYNIHAN, DANIEL PATRICK. US Senator (New York State), 1977–. b. 16 March 1927. Associated with Senator Edward Kennedy and other Irish-American politicians in urging peace in NI and in setting up the Friends of Ireland group in 1981. In June 1979 he said he hoped to see Ireland united, and that American interest in NI was consistent. 'I hope it will not be supposed that we will be everlastingly patient,' he said. He also attacked the PIRA as a 'band of sadistic murderers'.

MOYOLA, LORD. Formerly James Chichester-Clark, Prime Minister of NI, May 1969–March 1971. b. 12 February 1923. Returned unopposed as Unionist MP for S. Derry in 1960; again unopposed in 1965, but had to fight off a challenge from Miss Bernadette Devlin (PD) in 1969. Unionist Chief Whip in 1963, leader of the Commons, 1966, and succeeded Harry West as Minister of Agriculture in 1967. On 23 April 1969, he resigned from the O'Neill government, following speculation that he might become Premier if Captain O'Neill resigned. He gave as his reason for resignation the timing of the 'one man, one vote' reform, although he said he was not against the principle of the reform. Five days later, O'Neill stood down, and on 1 May 1969 Chichester-Clark was elected Prime Minister by seventeen votes to sixteen over Brian Faulkner. One of his first acts was to order an amnesty for those convicted of or charged with, political offences since the previous October. The Rev. Ian Paisley was among those released from prison. But neither this gesture, nor an appeal to opposition MPs to join in a declaration that Ulster was at peace and would remain so, brought any response. The demands for reform were intensified, and the violence grew to a climax in August 1969, when the serious rioting in the Bogside area of Londonderry and in Belfast forced the Chichester-Clark government to ask for troops to be sent to help maintain order. The situation led to angry exchanges between Major Chichester-Clark and Republic's Prime Minister, Jack Lynch. Mr Lynch had called for UN intervention, moved army field hospitals to the border, and arranged special camps in the Republic to accommodate people who had fled their homes in NI. Chichester-Clark attacked Mr Lynch for 'inflammatory and ill-considered' comments. The entry of British troops subtly changed the position of Chichester-Clark and his government. At Downing Street talks with the Prime Minister, Harold Wilson, the Ulster Premier agreed that the army GOC should be director of security operations. At Downing Street, Wilson gave a TV interview in which he indicated that the USC (the 'B' Specials) would be phased out. This was denied by Chichester-Clark and his Ministers, but by October the USC was on the way out, the RUC was being disarmed, and the Inspector-General of the RUC, Mr Anthony Peacocke, had been succeeded by Sir Arthur Young. It was all extremely embarrassing for Chichester-Clark, who argued, however, that the new UDR would essentially fill the role of the USC. The Home Secretary, James Callaghan, who had ministerial responsibility for NI, had, in the meantime, twice visited the province to encourage reforms such as anti-discrimination measures, action to ensure fair housing allocations, and to improve community relations. The Ulster Premier now had to face a double threat – a loyalist backlash, reflected in wide-spread violence, including shooting and the erection of barricades in loyalist areas, and on the other side, the obvious growth of the IRA, with rioting in republican areas, which produced a threat from the GOC, General Freeland, that troops might shoot to kill. Besides, he had to face the loss of two Stormont seats to the Rev. Ian Paisley and his deputy, the Rev. William Beattie, and in June 1970, the election which brought the Conservatives back to power also returned Mr Paisley to Westminster. Early July brought a fierce gun battle in the Falls Road area between the army and IRA snipers after soldiers had begun to search houses in the area. A three-day curfew was clamped on the Falls area, and more than 100 fire-arms and some 20,000 rounds of ammunition were found by soldiers. But the continued existence of republican 'no-go' areas made many Unionists furious with Chichester-Clark. Groups of paramilitaries mushroomed in loyalist areas of Belfast. At the same time, the PIRA emerged, and the murder of three young Scottish soldiers in Belfast in March 1971 was the signal for a new loyalist campaign demanding Chichester-Clark's resignation. On 18 March, the Premier flew to London for talks with Mr Heath and other Ministers. He pressed for some dramatic security initiative, but Mr Heath would only authorise an extra 1,300 troops, and many Unionists regarded this as derisory. Chichester-Clark was believed to have pressed for, among other things, saturation by the security forces of areas which he considered were dominated by the IRA. Some of his colleagues wanted internment without trial. Two days later, he resigned from the Premiership, after the

Defence Secretary, Lord Carrington, had flown to Belfast for special talks with the NI Cabinet. In a statement, he repeated his view that some further security initiative was needed. He also said: 'I have decided to resign because I see no other way of bringing home to all concerned the realities of the present constitutional, political and security situation.' He was succeeded by Brian Faulkner, who had run him so close in the leadership vote nearly two years before.

MURNAGHAN, SHEELAGH, MARY. Only Liberal MP to sit in NI Parliament. b. Dublin, 26 May 1924. LL.B. (QUB). Irish hockey international. A barrister-at-law, she was MP for QUB, 1961–9, and prominent in pressing for reforms, notably the introduction of PR voting in NI. Member of NI Advisory Commission and Community Relations Commission, 1972–3. Serves as chairman of Industrial and National Insurance Tribunals. Associated with a great variety of bodies, including United Nations Association, Protestant and Catholic Encounter, and a committee devoted to finding sites for the settlement of itinerants.

MURRAY, HARRY. Chairman of the Ulster Workers' Council during the loyalist strike in May 1974. b. 1921. A Belfast shipyard shop steward, he announced the decision of the UWC to mount the stoppage which brought about the collapse of the power-sharing Executive. He was a leading spokesman of the strikers throughout the stoppage. But after the fall of the Executive, he split with the loyalist paramilitaries. At an Oxford conference on NI in July 1974 he ran into criticism from loyalists when he said that he would talk to the IRA on condition that they put down their guns and bombs. He said his own methods had proved the best in the end since he had brought a country to a standstill in five days when the IRA had not been able to do it in five years. In July 1974, he resigned from the UWC and said that both communities would have to be brought together, and he proposed to devote himself to promoting peace. In 1975, he stood unsuccessfully as an Alliance candidate at a district council election in Bangor, Co. Down, but he said later that he had not actually joined the Alliance Party. In 1982, he was involved in an effort to re-form the UWC as an organisation campaigning for jobs and worker unity, and free of any paramilitary links.

N

NAPIER, OLIVER JOHN. Alliance Assembly member for E. Belfast, 1982–. Leader of Alliance of which he was one of the founders, and earlier prominent in the NUM. b. 11 July 1935. LL.B. (QUB). Belfast solicitor. Elected in E. Belfast to both the Assembly (1973–4) and Constitutional Convention (1975–6). Took a prominent role in the Sunningdale Conference in 1973, and became Head of the Office of Law Reform in the power-sharing Executive. Has travelled extensively in Britain and abroad, explaining the Alliance approach. Belfast City Council, 1977–. In the 1979 Westminster election, he stood unsuccessfully in E. Belfast, where the Alliance Party had high hopes of gaining the seat. But although he polled strongly, the seat went to DUP and he was in third place. He had another disappointment in the 1979 European election, in which he secured fewer than 40,000 first-preference votes, under 7 per cent of the total. He headed his party delegation in the Atkins conference at Stormont in 1980, pressing the case for partnership Government, and gave strong support to the 'rolling devolution' initiative in the 1982 Assembly election campaign. In the 1983 Westminster election in E. Belfast, he again ran third despite party hopes that he might capture the seat.

NATIONAL DEMOCRATIC PARTY. A political party formed in 1965 which operated mainly in the Greater Belfast area until 1970. It developed from the National Unity movement established in 1959 to press for reform of the Nationalist Party. National Unity organised a conference at Maghery, Co. Armagh, in April 1964, which gave rise to a 'National Political Front'. This included Nationalist MPs and 'new frontier Nationalists' who sought a more democratically organised party. But the NPF collapsed after only five months, since there was disagreement about party organisation, and the provisional council of the NDP complained that the Nationalist MPs hadn't consulted them before deciding not to contest the Fermanagh-S. Tyrone seat. The 'new frontier' Nationalists then set up the National Democratic Party which had a high proportion of teachers in its ranks. It produced a variety of discussions papers, notably on economic matters, but had little electoral success. When it was wound up, its members had a strong influence within the newly-established SDLP.

NATIONAL H-BLOCK/ ARMAGH COMMITTEE. The committee which publicised throughout the world the case for political status for Republican prisoners in the Maze and Armagh prisons during the 1980–81 hunger strikes. The committee, which covered a wide spectrum of Nationalism, operated with such skill that it created serious problems for the British information services in the US, Canada, Europe, and many other areas. Its chairman was Father Piaras O'Duill, and its main spokesperson Mrs Bernadette McAliskey. The committee supplanted the Relatives Action Committee which operated in the initial phase of the campaign. See H-BLOCKS.

NATIONALIST PARTY. Deriving from the old Irish Parliamentary Party, it was the main vehicle of anti-partition politics until the civil rights campaign developed in 1968–9. For much of its existence, it was very locally based, and there was a good deal of clerical influence within it. In the 1960s, under the leadership of Eddie McAteer, there was an attempt to give it a more radical image and a more centralised character, but the more dynamic approach of the civil rights movement proved to have greater popular appeal. Much of its support went over to the SDLP, and one of its MPs, Austin Currie, was a founder of the SDLP.

NEAVE, AIREY MIDDLETON SHEFFIELD. Conservative spokesman on NI, 1975–9. b. 23 January 1916; killed by car bomb as he drove out of House of Commons car park, 30 March 1979, an event which cast a shadow over the start of general election campaign. B.A. (Hons) Oxford, Barrister-at-law. Notable army record in World War II. Wounded and taken prisoner by Germans in France, 1940, and first British officer to escape from Colditz POW camp, 1942. Attached after the war to British War Crimes Executive and served indictments on Goering and other leading war criminals tried at Nuremberg. Conservative MP for Abingdon, 1953–79. Masterminded campaign for election of Margaret Thatcher as Conservative leader, and headed her private office from 1975 until his death. Between 1975 and September 1976, he was extremely critical of government security policy in NI, but took a more friendly attitude when Roy Mason succeeded Merlyn Rees as Secretary of State in 1976. He claimed that increased army covert operations and other measures to tighten security were due to Conservative prompting. Often critical of British media which, he argued, over-publicised the IRA and magnified faults of security forces. In early 1978, his speeches and notably his reference to power-sharing as being 'no longer practical politics' caused Unionists to look on him with more friendly eye, and the SDLP to see his policy as a retreat from that of Edward Heath and William Whitelaw. In particular, he urged the setting up of regional councils in NI. Responsibility for his murder was claimed by the Irish National Liberation Army, and it led to strict new rules restricting the movements of visitors to Westminster.

NEESON, SEAN. All. Assembly member for N. Antrim, 1982–. Carrickfergus Council, 1977–. Chairman, Alliance Party, 1982–. Party spokesman on transport and energy. History teacher.

NEILL, IVAN. Speaker of NI House of Commons, 1969–72. b. Belfast 1 July 1906. B.Sc. Econ. (QUB). MP for Ballynafeigh (Belfast), 1949–72. Minister of Labour and National Insurance, 1950–61; additionally, Minister of Home Affairs, August–October, 1952. Minister of Education, 1962. Minister of Finance and leader of Commons, 1964–5. (Resigned from Government, 1965.) Minister of Development, 1968. Alderman and councillor, Belfast City Council, 1964–70.

NEWE, GERARD BENEDICT. Minister of State in Prime Minister's Office, NI government, 1971–2. b. Cushendall, Co. Antrim, 5 February 1907, died November 1982. M.A. (QUB), D.Litt. (NUU). Dr Newe was the only Catholic to serve in a NI government during the fifty-one years operation of the Government of Ireland Act, 1920. Dr Newe was invited by the Prime Minister, Mr Faulkner, to join the government to help promote better community relations, and his acceptance of the appointment caused misgivings among some of his co-religionists. Dr Newe made it clear that he was not and never had been, a member of the Unionist Party. He said he wanted a friendlier relationship between both parts of Ireland. He believed that people must have the right to work peacefully for a united Ireland, if they wished, but he recognised the social and economic benefits for NI of the link with Britain. Dr Newe was regional organiser and secretary to the NI Council of Social Service, 1948–72. Founder member of PACE (Protestant and Catholic Encounter).

NEW IRELAND GROUP/MOVEMENT. See ROBB, JOHN.

NEW LODGE ROAD. District adjoining Antrim Road in N. Belfast, which has been regarded as a stronghold of PIRA. Centre of demonstrations and hi-jacking when Provisionals are active.

NEWMAN, SIR KENNETH LESLIE. Chief Constable of the RUC, 1976–9. b. 1926. Served with Palestine Police, 1946–8 and with London Metropolitan Police, 1948–73. Became Commander at

New Scotland Yard, 1972, in charge of the community relations branch. Senior Deputy Chief Constable, RUC, 1973–6. As Chief Constable of the RUC, he was responsible for setting up regional crime squads to deal with terrorism and for closer intelligence liaison with the army. His period as Chief Constable was also marked by the introduction of the policy known as 'primacy of the police' which gave the RUC a more dominant role in security relative to the army. But there was also continuing criticism of RUC interrogation practices, criticism which Sir Kenneth attacked as 'less than fair'. But a number of reforms were introduced in the area of interrogation. (See BENNETT REPORT). On leaving the RUC he became Commandant of the Police Staff College at Bramshill and in 1982 Metropolitan Police Commissioner.

NEWRY. The 'frontier town' in S. Down with a mainly Roman Catholic population, which demonstrated strong support for the civil rights movement in 1968 and 1969. There was a riot in the town on 11 January 1969 when some police vehicles were set on fire and others pushed into the canal. Ten members of the RUC and twenty-eight civilians were injured and there was much damage to shops. Spokesmen for NICRA and PD deplored the violence and said it would not help the civil rights movement. In August 1969, there was prolonged rioting and severe damage to public buildings and private property. The Scarman tribunal found that an action committee had planned the takeover of the town, but that it had been foiled by skilled police work and lack of public support. The introduction of internment in 1971 brought further violent scenes. In October 1971, the shooting dead by the army of three youths who had failed to halt was followed by burning and looting on a large scale. The town suffered several bomb attacks, notably during 1971. The biggest protest march was held on 6 February 1972, after 'Bloody Sunday', but did not result in any serious trouble. In August, 1972, the Newry branch of NICRA made a strong appeal to PIRA to call off its bombing campaign. But PIRA remained active in the area, and there was some evidence that local units of OIRA were slow to observe the ceasefire called by their leaders in 1972. Despite occasional violent incidents, there have been considerable efforts in the 1980s to develop tourism and to counter the continuing heavy local unemployment. In 1981, the SDLP-controlled Newry and Mourne Council appointed a DUP chairman.

NEWS, HUGH. SDLP Assembly member for Armagh, 1982–. Also represented the constituency in the 1973–4 Assembly and the 1975–6 Convention. b. Lurgan, 1931. Publican and pharmaceutical chemist. Lurgan Borough Council (Independent Citizens' Association member), 1964–7. Craigavon District Council 1973–. National vice president, AOH, 1974.

NEW ULSTER MOVEMENT. A movement which developed in

early 1969 to urge moderation and non-sectarianism in politics and to press for reforms. It was among the first groups to call for a Community Relations Commission, a Central Housing Executive and the abolition of the USC. In a pamphlet in 1971 (*The Reform of Stormont*) it put forward proposals for power-sharing in government and later that year urged the suspension of the Stormont parliament. Many of its early members (it claimed a membership of 7,000 in 1969) became active in the Alliance Party. Its first chairman, Brian W. Walker, became Director of Oxfam in 1974, and he was succeeded by Dr Stanley Worrall CBE, former headmaster of Methodist College Belfast.

NEW ULSTER POLITICAL RESEARCH GROUP – See ULSTER LOYALIST DEMO-CRATIC PARTY.

NICHOLSON, JAMES. Off. U. MP for Newry-Armagh, 1983–. Assembly member for Armagh, 1982–. Armagh Council, 1975–. Secretary-organiser, Mid/South Armagh Unionist Association, 1973–. He took the new seat of Newry-Armagh in the 1983 Westminster election against the odds when the overall Nationalist majority was split between SDLP and PSF, and the DUP backed him.

NO-GO AREAS. The term coined for the districts behind the barricades between the summer of 1969 and July 1972, where para-military groups, rather than the forces of law and order, tended to hold sway. The most notable such areas were the Bogside in Londonderry – Free Derry – and parts of W. Belfast, although similar enclaves existed in other places. The term persisted for some time after the barriers had come down, and even after the 'Motorman' operation by the security forces on 31 July 1972, which sought to re-establish official control in such areas. Although most of the 'no-go' areas were PIRA dominated, loyalists on occasions set up their own 'no-go' areas, particularly in the Shankill-Woodvale district of Belfast, through the agency of the UDA. Some of these moves were designed to pressurise the government to act against the republican 'no-go' areas. Even in 1979, some loyalists continued to see a 'no-go' element in the refusal of the government to allow the deployment of the UDR in republican districts.

NORAID. See IRISH NORTHERN AID COMMITTEE.

NORTHERN IRELAND CIVIL RIGHTS ASSOCIATION. The body established in January 1967, which spearheaded the civil rights campaign. Its constitution was similar to that of the London-based National Council for Civil Liberties, whose secretary, Tony Smythe, attended the inaugural meeting in Belfast. Its initial committee comprised Noel Harris (chairman), of the Draughtsmen and Allied Trades Association; Dr Con McCluskey (vice chairman), of the Campaign for Social Justice; Fred Heatley (treasurer), of the Wolfe Tone Society; Jack Bennett (information officer), of the Wolfe Tone Society; Michael Dolley (QUB); Ken Banks (DATA); Kevin Agnew (republican); Miss Betty Sinclair (Belfast Trades Council); Joe Sherry (Republic Labour Party); John Quinn (Ulster Liberal Party); Paddy Devlin (NILP); Terence O'Brien (unattached); and Robin Cole (chairman of Young Unionist Group at QUB), co-opted. The basic aims of NICRA were: one man-one vote in council elections; ending of 'gerrymandered' electoral boundaries; machinery to prevent discrimination by public authorities and to deal with complaints; fair allocation of public housing; repeal of Special Powers Act; and disbanding of 'B' Special. NICRA's initial impact was in organising protest marches. The first was held at Dungannon on 24 August 1968, on the suggestion of Nationalist MP, Austin Currie, who had already staged a sit-in at a house in nearby Caledon because he objected to the allocation of the house to a single woman by the Unionist-controlled council. Some 4,000 people singing 'We shall Overcome' marked this first NICRA event, but it was the next march in Londonderry, on 5 October 1968, which put the civil rights campaign in the world headlines and on TV. The march in Derry's Duke Street had been banned, and several leading opposition figures, including Gerry Fitt MP and Nationalist leader Eddie McAteer MP, were injured in a clash with the RUC. Lord Cameron, in his report, found that they had been batoned without justification or excuse, although

Mr Fitt's conduct was described as 'reckless and wholly irresponsible'. The Duke Street affair, in which eleven policemen and seventy-seven civilians were hurt, made a big impression internationally and particularly on Labour opinion in Britain. It brought strong pressure from the Wilson government on Stormont to introduce reforms. The NICRA campaign was attacked by Unionists as a front for the IRA. The Cameron Commission held that while there had been evidence that IRA members were active in the association, there was no sign that they were dominant or in a position to control or direct the policy of NICRA. The Official Republican content of NICRA increased as time went on, and its role also changed as reforms were conceded. With the arrival of internment, it was engaged in promoting a civil disobedience campaign, which led to widespread withholding of rent and rates. The setting up of the power-sharing Executive led to some alienation from the SDLP. During the Convention, it was active in pressing for a Bill of Rights. It also became a point of contact for outside bodies interested in civil rights and the intermittent allegations of ill-treatment of suspects by the RUC.

NORTHERN IRELAND LABOUR PARTY. The party which has aimed at attracting pro-British socialists in recent times, but which has had little electoral success. Although there had been Labour candidates in earlier elections, the party itself dates from

1924. It remained essentially neutral on the Border issue until 1949. In that year, a party conference came out firmly for the link with Britain, and this stand gained it more Protestant support, but made it more difficult for it to attract Catholic votes. And the formation of the SDLP, now affiliated, like the NILP, to the Socialist International, added to its difficulties. Although it has enjoyed close contacts with several British-based trade unions, in the fragmented state of local politics it has not been able to achieve any formal link with the NI Committee of the Irish Congress of Trade Unions, comparable to that between the British Labour Party and the TUC. It has also had a fluctuating relationship with the British Labour Party. It has had grants from the British party on an annual basis, but not continuously, and often, particularly in the 1960s, its Westminster candidates have been given endorsement by the British Labour Party leader. Party opinion has been divided on whether it should cease to exist and request the British party to operate fully in NI. But the British party has never shown any serious interest in doing so. The peak of the party's success was in the 1950s when it had four MPs at Stormont, all for Belfast constituencies. But by 1970, when the party's MP for Falls, Paddy Devlin, was one of the founders of the SDLP, it was reduced to one MP (Mr Vivian Simpson) and it also won only one seat in both the Assembly and Constitutional Convention (David Bleakley). In the 1977 district council elections it fought on a narrow front, got one seat, and 4,732 first preference votes: 0.8 per cent of the total. In the 1981 council elections, it also held one seat (in Ards). The party has never won a Westminster seat, although it amassed nearly 100,000 votes throughout the province in 1970, and it has often polled strongly in the shipyard constituency of E. Belfast. In the Assembly contests, it supported power-sharing, but after the collapse of the Executive it opposed both a Council of Ireland and formal power-sharing. With the failure of the Convention, it suggested that local politicians should concentrate in the short-term on improving direct rule from London. In the 1979 Westminster election it ran three candidates in Belfast, but secured only 4,411 votes (0.6 per cent of the total vote) and all three candidates lost their deposits. It had been expected that the party would be wound up at a special conference in 1982, which showed that it had only a handful of active members and very little money. But a decision was deferred, although it did not run a candidate for the 1982 Assembly elections – the first time it was unrepresented in a local election since its formation.

O

O BRADAIGH, RUADHRI. President of Provisional Sinn Fein, 1970. b. 1932. An ex-technical school teacher, he was a TD for a period in the 1950s, being elected for Sinn Fein on an abstentionist ticket in Longford-Westmeath. He is also believed to have been chief-of-staff of the IRA for two periods before the organisation split at the end of 1969. In 1973, he was sentenced in Dublin to six months' imprisonment for IRA membership. He was the first person to be prosecuted under the provision of the Republic's Offences Against the State Act, which allows a court to convict on the evidence of a senior Garda officer that a person is a member of a proscribed organisation. He brought a certain organisational flair to the central direction of PSF, and energetically promoted the federal 'Eire Nua' policy. He opposed the dropping of this policy in 1981, telling the ard-fheis: 'Don't swop a policy for a slogan.' He has been active in building up contacts with revolutionary groups abroad, and in opposing the EEC, and obviously regretted the PSF decision not to contest the 1979 European Parliament election. He took part in the Feakle talks with Protestant churchmen in 1974.

O'BRIEN, CONOR CRUISE. Irish politician and journalist. b. 3 November 1917. B.A., Ph.D. (TCD). In his many-sided career, he has often spoken out on NI, and took a strongly individualist viewpoint as Irish Labour Party spokesman when he was elected to the Dail in 1969, and later as Minister for Posts and Tele-graphs, in the coalition government of 1973-7. He was defeated in the Dail general election in 1977, but was then elected to the Senate from TCD. He resigned from the Senate in 1979. In his earlier career he had been in the Irish diplomatic service from 1944 until 1961, and in 1961 represented the UN Secretary-General in Katanga. He was Vice-Chancellor of the University of Ghana, 1962-5, and Professor of Humanities at New York University, 1965-9. His general theme on NI has been that repeated calls from the Republic for a united Ireland are counter-productive, and may even encourage violence. In opposition after the defeat of the coalition government in 1977, he resigned from the Irish Labour parliamentary party so that he could be free to speak on NI. At a conference on NI at Oxford University in September 1977, he argued forcibly that opinion surveys showed that there was not a majority in the whole of Ireland in favour of Irish unity – a claim which was hotly contested inside the Republic. As Minister for Posts and Tele-graphs, he banned broadcasts by illegal paramilitary organisations and Provisional Sinn Fein. In his book, *States of Ireland* (1972), he suggested that the NI civil rights campaign had failed to make use of its victories and allowed itself to be used as a spring-board for the re-emergence of the IRA. From 1978 to 1980 he was editor-in-chief *The Observer*, London, and then continued as columnist.

O CONAILL, DAITHI. A leading strategist of the Provisional republican movement, 1972–. b. Cork, 1937. He is believed to have joined the IRA at the age of eighteen, and he was wounded in the 1956 IRA campaign. In 1958, he escaped from the Curragh camp in the Republic, where he had been interned. During the break, he hid for hours in a trench which had been covered by blankets camouflaged to look like grass. He worked for a time as a teacher of building and woodwork at Ballyshannon, Co. Donegal, vocational school. In 1960, he was sentenced to eight years imprisonment for carrying a gun and ammunition with intent to endanger life, but he served only three years. In 1971, he narrowly avoided capture when Interpol set up a big search operation after a consignment of Czech arms had been found at Amsterdam airport. He had been travelling with a companion, Maria McGuire, who later fled to England and described her IRA experiences in a book. He was said to have invented the car bomb, and by April 1973, when he slipped through a police and army security net to give an oration in Milltown cemetery, Belfast, he was believed to have become chief-of-staff of the PIRA. In a TV interview in 1974, he stated – as he did on many other occasions – that there would be no end to the IRA campaign until the British made a declaration of intent to withdraw from NI. By 1974, he was a vice-president of Provisional Sinn Fein, and he was among the IRA leaders who talked to Protestant churchmen at the secret meeting in Feakle, Co. Clare – the meeting which led to the 1975 IRA ceasefire. His arrest in Dublin during the ceasefire was presented by the Provisionals as a bid by Dublin to end what the IRA called a 'truce'. He was sentenced to twelve months imprisonment for IRA membership, and was again arrested in July 1976, coincidentally on the same day as the British ambassador in Dublin, Christopher Ewart-Biggs, was killed in a landmine explosion. After his release in 1977, he appeared to be absorbed by political work, but there were strong Unionist protests when he slipped into Derry at Easter 1978 to address a republican ceremony, just as he had done four years earlier. In the 1981 general election in the Republic, he was active in supporting the H-Block candidates, and in the February, 1982, election, he was PSF's director of elections. In one respect, though, his influence waned in the 1980s. He had encouraged some contacts with Protestant paramilitaries, and had seen the 'Eire Nua' federal policy as a concession of sorts to loyalists. But his arguments were swept aside by NI delegates at the 1981 ard-fheis who brought about the defeat of the federal idea. Soon after the PIRA bombings in London, in July, 1982, he threatened more bombs in Britain when he spoke at a rally in Monaghan.

O'DONOGHUE, PATRICK. SDLP Assembly member for S. Down, 1982–. Also represented S. Down in the 1973 Assembly and

the 1975 Convention. b. Castle-wellan, Co. Down, 1930. Deputy Speaker in the 1973 Assembly and SDLP spokesman on education. Down District Council, 1973–. Active in ALJ and GAA. In a speech in Galway in 1974, he suggested that the British had recognised that they could not solve the Irish problem and that 'the long, complex and dangerous business' of British disengagement had already begun.

OFFICIAL IRISH REPUBLICAN ARMY.

The term 'Official IRA' dates from the beginning of 1970 when the split in the republican movement meant that there were now two branches, the Officials and the Provisionals, each comprising an IRA, or military wing, and a political counterpart, Sinn Fein. In Northern Ireland, the 'Officials' are often dubbed the 'Stickies', because of their practice of sticking on coat lapels their Easter lily during the annual commemorations of the 1916 Easter Rising in Dublin. OIRA appears to have been largely inactive since the summer of 1972 when it declared a ceasefire. It represented those militant republicans who remained loyal to Cathal Goulding as Chief of Staff, when the movement divided on the issue of parliamentary action during the December 1969–January 1970 period. There was majority support in the IRA at the end of 1969 for switching to political action – that is, seeking to have candidates elected to the parliaments in Dublin, Belfast and London on a leftist, broadly Marxist policy. Clearly, Goulding and many of his associates felt that the lack of public support for the IRA border campaign in 1956–62 suggested that republicans generally wanted more emphasis on strictly political action even if it meant a break with the traditional IRA policy of regarding all existing parliaments as irrelevant to the struggle for power. But those who sought this new approach failed to secure a two-thirds majority at the Dublin conference of Sinn Fein in January 1970. At that point, the Provisionals walked out of the meeting and since they went off to hold a meeting in Kevin Street, Dublin and established their HQ there, they were initially known as Kevin Street Sinn Fein to distinguish them from the Officials who, for similar reasons, were frequently described as Gardiner Place Sinn Fein. Each side claimed to be the true inheritor of 1916, and the OIRA said later that it had been able to hold 70 per cent of the total of IRA volunteers when the PIRA broke away. In NI, the IRA strength in 1970 was probably about 600, and mainly in Belfast. All the indications, however, are that PIRA rapidly outstripped the Officials in number. Notably in the Belfast republican areas, the Provisionals built on the strength of local defence committees and were widely accepted as the defenders of the people against loyalist attacks. The OIRA also had to face the taunts of the new 'Provos' that it was totally unprepared in the Belfast violence of 1969. The truth of the matter seems to be that a handful of veteran IRA men were involved in the Falls area in resisting loyalist assaults in 1969. The OIRA also insisted that the split in the movement had been engineered by Fianna Fail agents so that a separate IRA would develop in the North and outside the Republic. Certainly, the tension between Officials and Provisionals was intense in 1970-1, and in March 1971, there was a fierce gun battle between the two groups in the lower Falls area of Belfast. One man was shot dead and several wounded, with the British army standing carefully aside. A ceasefire was quickly negotiated in this inter-IRA struggle, but there were to be many more clashes between the two groups. In Belfast and many other centres, the annual Easter parades to cemeteries with republican dead were split into separate Official and Provisional efforts. The OIRA was still involved in violence in early 1971. It bombed a Shankill Road public house in Belfast in April. But Cathal Goulding's warning that PIRA tactics were likely to bring internment without trial in NI proved to be justified. And although OIRA, like PIRA, had been keeping many of its members away from their usual haunts, a good many key PIRA members were rounded up in the dawn swoop on 9 August 1971. PIRA claimed that only thirty of its members had been arrested, but this was probably a serious under-estimation. OIRA suffered, though, from the handicap that many of its activists were people who had a record in the IRA earlier and thus figured in Special Branch lists. Internment, however, created extra problems for OIRA, since it stirred up hostility towards the British authorities and the NI government on a

massive scale. It was an emotion more geared to PIRA strategy than to the politically orientated approach of Cathal Goulding and his friends. Violence became much more the order of the day for OIRA. In December 1971, it killed Unionist Senator Jack Barnhill in Strabane, and burned the Rostrevor home of the Stormont Speaker, Ivan Neill. In February 1972 – that is, immediately after 'Bloody Sunday' in Londonderry – it claimed responsibility for an explosion at the Aldershot (Hampshire) headquarters of the Parachute Regiment. Seven people were killed, including five women canteen workers. Also in February it mounted an assassination attempt on Unionist government Minister John Taylor in Armagh. He was hit by six bullets, and had his jaw shattered. In March 1972 Cathal Goulding and three other men were charged in Dublin with membership of an illegal organisation, but they were freed after the prosecution had applied for the charges to be struck out. When direct rule of NI from Westminster was announced at the end of March, OIRA announced that it would continue the struggle. In April 1972, OIRA was responsible for a spate of violence in Belfast, including many attacks on RUC stations. These were in response to the shooting dead by soldiers of Joe McCann, one of OIRA's most revered leaders. Even members of the Provisionals turned out in a separate parade among the 5,000 people at McCann's funeral. In May 1972, OIRA admitted that it had shot dead Ranger William Best, of the

Irish Rangers Regiment, home on leave in Derry. They said it was a reprisal for crimes by the British army, but it brought angry protests from many Bogside women and calls for OIRA to leave the Bogside and Creggan areas. On Monday, 29 May 1972, OIRA announced a ceasefire. It said it was doing so in accordance with the wishes of the people it represented in NI, although it reserved the right to act in self-defence and to defend areas attacked by British troops or 'sectarian forces'. This ceasefire followed an anxious meeting of the OIRA leadership from all thirty-two counties of Ireland, including some women who were said to be local OIRA commanders. It was stated that the decision had been taken by an overwhelming majority. Goulding seems to have argued that the PIRA bombing campaign could only increase sectarianism. He also claimed that PIRA would soon be forced to call a ceasefire as well, but this prediction was only partially borne out, for the PIRA ceasefire which came soon afterwards was short-lived. The Goulding policy was to seek to develop class politics, and to secure more joint action with Protestants on issues such as housing. This concentration by OIRA on community politics meant that it tended to coalesce completely in most areas with the Republican Clubs – that is, the NI equivalent of Sinn Fein (the Workers' Party) of the Republic. The feud with PIRA has tended to raise its head from time to time, and frequently on the prison front. In 1973, there was trouble between PIRA and OIRA prisoners in Crumlin Road

prison in Belfast, and in 1974, after clashes at the Maze prison, twenty-one OIRA men there were moved to Crumlin Road prison for ten days. Of course, they made common cause on occasional anti-internment protests and worked together to some extent in the Catholic areas of Belfast to reduce hardship during the loyalist strike in 1974. OIRA guns were brought out again in the spring of 1975, when it was involved in a bitter struggle with the newly-formed IRSP. There were deaths and injuries on both sides in Belfast, and a suspicion among the security forces that the IRSP had drawn some recruits from PIRA members who were doubtful about their ceasefire. In April, 1982, the Dublin magazine, MAGILL, claimed that OIRA was still active, well-armed, and engaged in recent years in murders, robberies and intimidation. It also alleged that Seamus Costello, leader of the IRSP, had been killed by a senior member of OIRA in 1977. The magazine added that £2 million had been taken in armed robberies since 1972, and that one major bank robbery had been carried out in NI immediately before the Republic's general election in June, 1981. It also asserted that almost all the hundred or so members of OIRA, including several of its leaders, were members of the Workers' Party. A spokesman for the WP dismissed the allegations as 'muck' and the WP president, Tomas McGiolla (elected a TD in the November, 1982 election), said he had no knowledge of the continued existence of OIRA, and certainly they had no association with any military organisation. In July, 1982, INLA claimed that OIRA had provided information for 'loyalist death squads' which had resulted in the deaths of three Republican activists in Belfast – Miriam Daly, Ronnie Bunting and Noel Little. INLA also said it had murdered Jim Flynn in Dublin after they had been informed by former OIRA members that he had murdered Seamus Costello. In May, 1983, the Republic's Justice Minister, Michael Noonan, said he could confirm that OIRA was still in existence. Its continued activity in NI was also reported by the RUC.

OFFICIAL SINN FEIN. See WORKERS' PARTY.

OFFICIAL UNIONIST PARTY. See ULSTER UNIONIST PARTY.

O'HANLON, PATRICK MICHAEL, Chief Whip of the SDLP in Assembly, 1974.' b. Drogheda, 8 May 1944. B. Comm. (UCD). Active in civil rights campaign and MP for S. Armagh, 1969–72. Founder member of the SDLP, and during Assembly period was member of several party delegations in talks with the Republic's government. Ran unsuccessfully in Armagh in Convention election in 1975 and 1982 Assembly election.

O'HARE, PASCHAL JOSEPH. SDLP Assembly member for N. Belfast, 1982–. b. 1932. Belfast City Council, 1973–. Solicitor. A founder member and former Executive member of the SDLP, he stood unsuccessfully in the 1975 Convention election and the 1979 Westminster election.

O'KENNEDY, MICHAEL. Foreign Minister of the Republic, 1977–9. EEC Commissioner, 1981–2. b. 21 February 1936. MA (NUI) Barrister and classical scholar. Fianna Fail Senator, 1965–9; TD, 1969–81. Minister of Transport and Power, 1973; Minister of Finance, 1979–81. As Foreign Minister, he was the member of Mr Lynch's Government most closely involved with NI affairs, and he was an early advocate of the idea of an all-Ireland Court to deal with terrorism. He was also specially interested in cross-border economic co-operation, and maintained this interest as EEC Commissioner. As Foreign Minister, he was closely involved with the EEC-backed Derry-Donegal schemes. In August, 1979, while President of the EEC Council of Ministers, he urged early efforts to break the NI 'political log-jam' through informal talks between the British and Irish Governments and the NI parties. In October, 1979, he reached agreement in London with NI Secretary Humphrey Atkins on secret anti-terrorist measures.

OLDFIELD, SIR MAURICE. Chief Security Co-ordinator, NI, from 1979 until his death in 1980. b. 16 November 1915. Sir Maurice, who retired from the Foreign Office in 1977, held a great variety of diplomatic posts, including counsellor in Washington, but his real fame rested on his post as head of the Secret Intelligence Service (MI6) between 1965 and 1977. The NI appointment was said to be aimed at increasing pressure on terrorists and bringing them to justice. It followed reports that the army was anxious to see more co-ordination of the security effort and that there were differences between army and RUC chiefs. There were official denials that the appointment reduced the status of the Secretary of State, Humphrey Atkins.

OLIVER, JOHN ANDREW. Chief adviser to chairman of Constitutional Convention, 1975–6. b. Belfast, 1913. B.A., Ph.D. (QUB). Entered NI Civil Service in 1936 and rose to be Permanent Secretary in Development Ministry in 1970, and Housing Department, 1974. Retired from civil service in 1976, and books include an analysis of NI's constitutional options, *Ulster Today and Tomorrow* (London 1978).

OMBUDSMAN. Popular title for Parliamentary Commissioner for Administration, who deals with complaints of maladministration against Stormont Departments. The office was established in 1969, and parallels the Office of Commissioner of Complaints. See KERNOHAN, HUGH.

O'NEILL, LORD (OF THE MAINE). Prime Minister of NI, 1963–9. b. 10 September 1914. Captain Terence O'Neill has a real Anglo-Irish background – among his ancestors were the ancient Ulster O'Neill family, and the English Chichesters. When, in 1963, Lord Brookeborough resigned after twenty years as Prime Minister, O'Neill had been Finance Minister for seven years and seemed the natural successor. He quickly made it clear that he

was set on a reformist course: firstly, in terms of stronger cross-border economic links; and secondly, in trying to accommodate the political ambitions of an increasingly educated Catholic community. In January 1965, he sprang a surprise with an unannounced visit to Stormont of the Republic's Prime Minister, Sean Lemass. Even the majority of his Cabinet colleagues were not told of the meeting in advance, and the trip angered right-wing Unionists, always suspicious of Southern motives. The Rev. Ian Paisley attacked the visit in what can be seen as the start of his 'O'Neill must go' campaign. The extremist UVF emerged on the loyalist side, and the civil rights campaign built up to the torrent of protest reached in 1968. The violent scenes at the civil rights march on 5 October 1968 went round the world on TV and made a tremendous impression on the Prime Minister. He saw that reforms must be pressed forward, and in this he clashed with those who shared the view of the Home Affairs Minister, William Craig, that the civil rights agitation was an expression of republicanism, encouraged by the IRA. In December 1968, O'Neill sacked Craig, and made it evident that he regarded him as an advocate of UDI. He warned against the growth of a 'Protestant Sinn Fein' and appealed to the protest marchers to get off the streets. At the end of 1968, he announced a five point programme of reforms – a points system for housing allocations, an Ombudsman, the ending of the company vote in council elections a review of the Special

Powers Act, and the setting up of the Londonderry Development Commission. In London, the British Prime Minister, Harold Wilson, spoke of Captain O'Neill being 'blackmailed by thugs' and he warned that there would be a re-appraisal of NI's position if he was overthrown. In the event, Captain O'Neill decided to challenge his Unionist critics in a general election in February 1969. But this 'cross-roads election', as he termed it, was extremely confused. He took the gamble of endorsing pro-O'Neill candidates who, in many cases, were opposing the official nominees of the local Unionist associations. Although his leadership was confirmed by the Unionist Parliamentary Party after the election, with twenty-three MPs voting for, Brian Faulkner against, and William Craig abstaining, the election left a legacy of bitterness throughout Unionism. Also, the pressure for change from the civil rights movement was intensified. On 28 April 1969, O'Neill resigned as Prime Minister and was succeeded by James Chichester-Clark, who had resigned from the O'Neill government five days before. In the House of Lords, he has spoken frequently on NI issues. In comments on the 1968–9 period, he has said that the troubles in NI had to happen, and that Westminster only acted when there was trouble. But for trouble, he said in a 1978 radio interview, Britain would probably still be in India. He supported the 1974 power-sharing project, but he insisted that there had been two mistakes – an over-elaborate cross-border Council of Ireland,

and the withdrawal from Stormont of Secretary of State William Whitelaw before the new administration got under way.

O'NEILL, PHELIM. See LORD RATHCAVAN.

O'NEILL, THOMAS P. ('TIP'). Speaker of US House of Representatives, 1974–. b. 1912. One of group of Irish-American politicians, including Senator Edward Kennedy, who have sponsored NI peace appeals and warned Americans against giving aid to funds which would support violence in Ireland. The O'Neill Trust, set up in May 1978, was designed to channel the private contributions of Americans to encouraging employment in both parts of Ireland. President Carter has praised his efforts to secure reconciliation in NI, and Jack Lynch, former Taoiseach of the Irish Republic, has described him as a 'true friend of Ireland'. In April 1979, he paid a brief visit to NI with other Congressmen, and met leaders of the main political parties. In a speech in Dublin he urged the new British government to launch a political initiative in NI and complained that the NI question had been made a 'political football' at Westminster – a comment which brought heated denials from Labour politicians and Mrs Thatcher. He was associated with the Friends of Ireland Group set up in US in 1981.

OPERATION MOTORMAN. Code name of the security forces' operation in the early hours of 31 July 1972, to clear barricades in 'no go' areas in Londonderry and

Belfast. Some 21,000 troops, together with 9,000 mobilised UDR men and 6,000 members of the RUC, were involved. In Derry, 1,500 troops with armoured cars and other vehicles swept into the Bogside and Creggan areas. Resistance was confined to minor sniping and two people were killed by the army. There had been talk previously of at least one hundred deaths if the areas were reoccupied. There was little resistance in Belfast republican areas, and loyalists helped to dismantle their own barricades which they claimed were simply a response to the existence of republican 'no-go' areas. The Secretary of State, William Whitelaw MP told a news conference that the operation had been designed to 'remove the capacity of the IRA to create violence and terror'. Shortly before he spoke, six people were killed in Derry village of Claudy when three car bombs exploded. It was immediately assumed to be an IRA reply to 'Motorman', although the IRA denied responsibility. Wanted IRA men apparently got out of the barricaded areas before the troops arrived.

ORANGE ORDER. The largest Protestant organisation in NI, where it probably has between 80,000 and 100,000 active members, with between 4,000 and 5,000 members in the Republic. The Loyal Orange Institution owes its character to the victories of King William III (William of Orange) in the religious wars of the late seventeenth century. Its annual twelfth of July demonstrations at more than twenty centres in NI celebrate King William's victory over King James at the Battle of the Boyne. It was formed in September 1795, in Co. Armagh, after a clash between Protestants and Catholics at the 'Battle of the Diamond'. Its lodges were based on those of the Masonic Order. Although one of its main objectives is the defence of the Protestant succession to the British throne, its relations with London have often been strained. The Order fiercely resented the ban on Orange processions in the 1860s, and it was widely defied. The Order took on a distinctly Unionist flavour when Home Rule threatened. The effective beginning of the Unionist Party was a meeting of seven Orangemen, elected as MPs, at Westminster in January 1886. The Unionist-Conservative link was forged in the opposition to Liberal plans for Irish Home Rule. A leading Conservative, Lord Randolph Churchill, 'played the Orange card' when he told an anti-Home Rule rally in Belfast's Ulster Hall: 'Ulster will fight and Ulster will be right'. That link between the two parties remained strong until Edward Heath suspended Stormont in 1972. Orangemen didn't want the devolution accorded to NI in 1921, but once the state had been established, they defended it energetically and attacked any idea of a link-up with the South. Most Ministers in Unionist governments were Orangemen, and the controversial B Specials, the auxiliary police force which many Unionists regarded as Ulster's army, were almost exclusively Orangemen. While the defence of civil and religious liberty is a prime Orange aim, it attacked the civil rights movement as republican or communist inspired. The imposition of direct rule and the scheme for power-sharing between Protestants and Catholics in government got little support from Orangemen. The Order remains close to the OUP, although the ties have been loosened a little by the fragmentation of Unionism. And throughout the violence the Order has been calling for tougher security policies, particularly against the IRA, and its leaders have claimed that it has exercised a restraining influence on loyalists. When the Order's World Council met in Belfast in 1976 there were representatives present from ten countries – NI, the Republic, England, Scotland, USA, Canada, New Zealand, Australia, Ghana and Togoland. The then Imperial Grand Master (now Irish Grand Master), the Rev. Martin Smyth, MP, said at the time that there were plans to set up lodges in South Africa and Sweden. There is a lodge at the House of Commons founded originally by James Craig, NI's first Prime Minister, and in the past military lodges existed in places like Hong Kong, Singapore and Egypt. The Grand Secretary, Walter Williams, reported in 1982 that there had been a forty-eight per cent increase in membership in Africa in the previous three years. The World Council, meeting in Belfast in 1985 – 190th anniversary of the founding of the Order – will be discussing plans to celebrate in Belfast in 1990 the 300th anniversary of the battle of the Boyne. The senior branch of the Order is known as the Royal Black Institution (it is headed by OUP leader James Molyneaux, MP) and it is also closely associated with the Apprentice Boys of Derry, with membership often overlapping. There are also women's and junior branches.

ORANGE VOLUNTEERS. A loyalist paramilitary group started in 1972 with about five hundred members and closely linked with the Vanguard movement. Its members was restricted to Orangemen and ex-Servicemen, and it frequently provided stewards at rallies addressed by William Craig. In 1974, when it was thought to have grown to about 3,000 members, it was involved in setting up road blocks and in communications during the loyalist strike. It was represented by Bob Marno on the UWC Coordinating Committee. It also supported the more limited loyalist strike in May 1977.

O'REILLY, JAMES. Nationalist MP for Mourne, 1958–72. He was whip for his party in the later days of the Stormont parliament, frequently spoke on farming issues. In 1964, he unsuccessfully promoted a bill to establish an Ombudsman in NI. In the 1971 census, he refused to complete his return, and went to prison rather than pay a fine. He said he was protesting against 'biased administration of justice'.

ORME, STANLEY. Minister of State, NI Office, 1974–6. b. 5 April 1923. Soon after he was elected

Labour MP for Salford W. in 1964, Mr Orme visited NI at the invitation of Mr Gerry Fitt, the W. Belfast MP, to study the local situation in company with several other Labour MPs. In his book, *A House Divided* James Callaghan noted that these MPs had persistently attempted to open up the NI problem, but 'they found great difficulty in doing so'. Soon afterwards, when the Campaign for Democracy in Ulster was formed at Westminster, Mr Orme became associated with it, and was a strong critic of Unionist administrations. He opposed internment without trial, and in 1973 told an audience in Dublin that he believed in the eventual reunification of Ireland. He was at that time a front-bench Labour spokesman, and prominently associated with the left-wing *Tribune* group of MPs. When he was appointed to the NI Office in 1974, the move was immediately criticised by Unionists. The OUP, in a statement, questioned whether he could deal with NI matters impartially in view of the 'somewhat partisan' opinions which he had aired previously. Friction with the Unionists was increased when he took up a highly critical attitude towards the UWC strike in May 1974. As the Minister responsible for economic affairs, he had charge of the Departments of Commerce and Manpower Services, and made several overseas trips in a bid to find new industrial investment. He was Minister of Social Security, 1976–79.

ORR, CAPTAIN LAWRENCE PERCY STORY (WILLIE). Leader of the Unionist MPs at Westminster, 1954–74, and MP for S. Down, 1950–74. b. Belfast, 16 September 1918. Son of a former Dean of Dromore, he was Unionist organiser in S. Down before becoming the first MP for the newly created constituency. Former Imperial Grand Master of the Orange Order, he revived the Orange Lodge (LOL 1688) in House of Commons in 1955. He was an officer of many Conservative committees during his long career in parliament. In August 1974, he announced he would not be standing again, and supported Enoch Powell as his successor.

OVEREND, ROBERT. Initially VUPP and later UUUM Convention member for Mid-Ulster, 1975–6. b. 1931. A farmer and pedigree livestock dealer, prominent in the Orange Order and Apprentice Boys of Derry. Unsuccessful UUUP candidate in Mid-Ulster in 1982 Assembly election.

OWN GOAL. The term used by the security forces for an incident in which a terrorist has blown himself up.

P

PAISLEY, MRS EILEEN. Wife of the Rev. Ian Paisley. DUP Assembly (1973–4) and Convention (1975–6) member for N. Belfast. b. Belfast. Belfast City Council, 1973–5. In 1982, she was a member of a joint OUP–DUP publicity team visiting the US. She stood in for her husband, who had been refused an American visa.

PAISLEY, REV. IAN RICHARD KYLE. Democratic Unionist MEP for NI, June 1979–. MP for N. Antrim, 1970–. Assembly member for N. Antrim, 1982–. Leader of DUP, 1971–. b. 6 April 1926. Son of a Baptist minister, he is reputed to have started preaching at the age of sixteen. In 1951, he started a Free Presbyterian Church in the Ravenhill Road area of Belfast, where he later erected his large Martyrs' Memorial Church. But it was in 1963 that his interest in political action developed. He organised a march to the Belfast City Hall to protest against the lowering of the Union flag to mark the death of Pope John. And when the parade was the first loyalist march to be banned under the Special Powers Act, he persisted with his plan. He was fined £10, and said he would go to prison rather than pay the fine. But the fine was paid anonymously, and Paisley alleged that it had been paid by the government. In 1964, during the Westminster general election campaign in W. Belfast, he made a big issue of the display of a tricolour flag in the window of the republican head-quarters in Divis Street, adjoining the Catholic Falls Road. He threatened to have a march to Divis Street if the police didn't remove the flag. The RUC broke into the premises and removed the flag. The flag was later replaced, and when the police returned, serious rioting broke out. These incidents established a pattern of protest which he was to employ in many different circumstances. The visit of the Republic's Prime Minister, Sean Lemass, to Stormont in January 1965 gave him a new and potent campaign issue. He insisted, with his booming oratory, that the threat of a united Ireland had been opened up by the 'treachery' of the Prime Minister Capt. O'Neill. The 'O'Neill must go' drive was pursued at rallies and meetings. In June 1966, he infuriated O'Neill by having a march to the general assembly of the Presbyterian Church in Belfast to protest against its 'Romeward trend'. The Governor, Lord Erskine, and church dignitaries, had abuse shouted at them outside the hall, and in parliament, the Prime Minister deplored what he called 'tendencies towards nazism and fascism'. The Premier also accused Paisley of having associations with the UVF, something which Paisley firmly denied. But Paisley had now set up two organisations – the Ulster Constitution Defence Committee and Ulster Protestant Volunteers – which were to figure frequently in counter-demonstrations during the civil rights campaign. One of the largest demonstrations which Paisley and his supporters mounted against a civil rights march was in Armagh on 30 November 1968. He and Major Ronald Bunting arrived in Armagh early in the morning and, with their supporters, blocked the town centre, forcing the civil rights demonstrators to cut short their parade. Paisley and Bunting had to serve six weeks' imprisonment for unlawful assembly. The resignation of O'Neill in April 1969 brought the comment from Paisley that he had 'brought down a captain and could bring down a major as well'. The major, of course, was Major Chichester-Clark, who succeeded O'Neill. Paisley's chance to challenge the new government came in April 1970, when by-elections were held in two Co. Antrim seats – Bannside (former seat of Captain O'Neill) and S. Antrim. Paisley won the Bannside constituency and his colleague, the Rev. William Beattie, the S. Antrim seat. It was a double blow to the government and, two months later, Paisley achieved another parliamentary success – he gained the N. Antrim seat in the Westminster election. In 1971, he set up the Democratic Unionist Party to replace the Protestant Unionist Party. Towards the end of 1971, he angered many Unionists by predicting direct rule from Westminster, despite denials from London and by the Prime Minister, Brian Faulkner. At that period, he seemed to be keen on integration of NI with Great Britain, with a Greater Ulster Council at Stormont. And his concentration on attacks on the 'theocratic'

nature of the Republic's constitution gave rise to suggestions that Paisley was softening a little in his attitude towards the South – an impression which he moved quickly to dispel. The Sunningdale conference aimed at setting up the power-sharing Executive was Paisley's next major target. He claimed that, by excluding his party from full participation in Sunningdale, the Government had gone back on its White Paper promise. And he and his supporters now adopted a wrecking approach towards the Assembly. On 22 January 1974, he and several of his loyalist colleagues were removed bodily from the Chamber after they had refused to give up the front-bench seats to the new Executive members and had mounted a noisy protest. Paisley himself was carried out by eight uniformed policemen. In February 1974, he increased his N. Antrim majority in the general election from under 3,000 in 1970 to some 27,000. Although he was abroad when the loyalist strike started in May 1974, he soon became deeply involved with the message, 'This is one we can't afford to lose'. He, together with Harry West and William Craig, represented the UUUC leadership in the strike committee, and his oratory was employed frequently at the anti-Executive rallies at Stormont and elsewhere. With the fall of the Executive, he was active in calling for new elections. These were granted in terms of the Constitutional Convention, and in the Convention, Paisley served on UUUC deputations which met the Alliance Party. There were conflicting assessments of his position in the Convention. Some Official Unionists said he had been more conciliatory in private than in public towards some form of partnership government. His public stance was certainly one of full support for the majority Convention report. After the Convention was wound up, it was clear however, that his relations with many Official Unionists were strained. Paisley and Ernest Baird backed a United Unionist Action Council, designed to take a more militant line towards direct rule and in favour of tougher security. But the Official Unionists opted out, and refused to back a loyalist strike called in May 1977, with the support of the loyalist paramilitaries. The strike was only a shadow of the 1974 affair, and Paisley's prestige undoubtedly suffered. It also meant a break with the Off. U. MPs. The Scarman report has dealt with the suggestion that Paisley had been largely responsible for the disturbances of 1969. It said: 'Those who live in a free country must accept as legitimate the powerful expression of views opposed to their own, even if, as often happens, it is accompanied by exaggeration, scurrility and abuse. Dr Paisley's spoken words were always powerful and must have frequently appeared to some as provocative: his newspaper [*Protestant Telegraph*] was such that its style and substance were likely to rouse the enthusiasm of his supporters and the fury of his opponents. We are satisfied that Dr Paisley's role in the events under review was fundamentally similar to that of the political leaders on the other side of the secta-

rian divide. While his speeches and writings must have been one of the many factors increasing tension in 1969, he neither plotted nor organised the disorders under review and there is no evidence that he was a party to any of the acts of violence investigated by us.' The European election in June 1979, was seized by Paisley as an opportuntiy to demonstrate that he had more popular support than the Official Unionists. And since his party had gained two seats from the OUP in the May general election, he was well placed to stage a successful campaign. He travelled the six counties, attacking the EEC as both disastrous in economic terms and as a threat to Protestantism. In the event, he headed the poll easily, with more than 170,000 votes, or just under 30 per cent of first preferences, and 80 per cent ahead of the total OUP vote for two candidates. He claimed that the election gave him a mandate to speak for the NI majority in any political negotiations, and to answer criticisms at Strasbourg by MEPs from the Republic. At the first session in Strasbourg in July, 1979, he intervened twice. On the opening day, he was the first MEP to speak, apart from the acting president, when he protested that the Union flag was flying the wrong way up outside the Parliament Buildings. Later, he interrupted Jack Lynch (president in office of the European Council), saying that he was protesting against the Republic's refusal to sign the European Convention on Terrorism. In the European Parliament, he was appointed member of the Energy Committee and an alternate member of the Political Affairs Committee. In July, 1979, he strongly attacked any suggestion that Pope John Paul II should enter NI during the Irish Papal visit in September. Dr Paisley's campaigning in the early 1980s was directed at some familiar targets. In 1980, he castigated the OUP for failing to take part in the Atkins conference, in which the DUP stood out against power-sharing. His other main assaults were on the Anglo-Irish contacts and Government security policy. The Thatcher-Haughey meeting in Dublin in December, 1980, with its launch of joint studies by the British and Irish Governments was presented by the DUP leader as a threat comparable to that faced by Edward Carson and Ulster loyalists in 1912. He accused Mrs Thatcher when he met her privately of 'undermining' NI's constitutional guarantee, a contention which she angrily repudiated. In February, 1981, he organised a demonstration involving five hundred men who paraded late at night on a Co. Antrim hillside, brandishing gun licences. This dramatic gesture was followed by a new 'Ulster declaration' on the lines of the original Covenant, to be signed by loyalists as a protest against the Thatcher-Haughey 'conspiracy'. It was linked to eleven 'Carson trail' rallies, culminating in a march to Stormont on 28 March, attended by some thirty thousand people. Meantime, he was suspended from the Commons for five days for calling Secretary of State Humphrey Atkins a 'liar' when MPs discussed the murder of Sir Norman Strong and his son. He rejected suggestions that the 'Carson trail' was a stunt associated with the May 1981 council elections. In these elections, however, the DUP put itself marginally ahead of the OUP in total votes. After the assassination of S. Belfast MP, the Rev. Robert Bradford, in November, 1981, he was involved in another Parliamentary scene. He and his two party colleagues, Peter Robinson and John McQuade, were ordered out of the Commons by the Speaker when they noisily interrupted Secretary of State James Prior as he was giving the Government's reaction to the killing. At that point, he was promoting a vigilante 'Third Force' to protect loyalists, and it was claimed that five thousand members of the force paraded at a rally in Newtownards on 23 November which was addressed by Dr Paisley. That was the day designated by Unionists as a 'day of action' to demand a tougher security policy. Many Protestants stopped work and OUP and DUP leaders spoke at separate rallies. In early December, 1981, he claimed that the 'Third Force' had 15,000–20,000 members, and was organised on a county basis. Soon afterwards, some Irish-American Congressmen headed by Senator Edward Kennedy urged the State Department to withdraw his US visa in the light of his recent activities. Just before Christmas, the visa was withdrawn, on the ground of the 'divisiveness' of his recent statements and actions so that he was unable to visit the US in January 1982, on a joint DUP-OUP publicity operation. He made the best of it, however, since he travelled to Canada, and got on to the US national TV networks from Toronto, while his wife read his speeches in the US. James Prior's 'rolling devolution' initiative in 1982 was a further occasion for friction between the DUP and OUP. The DUP leader shared with the OUP dislike of the 'cross-community support' condition attached to devolved government. But he argued that it was the last chance in his lifetime to secure devolved government at Stormont, and that the initial scrutiny powers could be a powerful check on direct rule. He was disappointed, however, by the election results, since the OUP took twenty-six Assembly seats to the DUP's twenty-one. He took over the chairmanship of the Assembly's agriculture committee, and to those who marvelled at his spread of commitments, taking in Strasbourg and Westminster, he explained that he would give up his Westminster seat if devolved government was achieved. He also found time to protest on the ground during the Pope's visit to Britain. In 1983, his N. Antrim seat was cut in half by redistribution, but he held it by a 13,000 plus majority.

PARKER COMMITTEE. The committee, headed by Lord Parker, which reported in 1972 on the methods used in interrogating detainees in NI. The committee was particularly concerned with the 'five techniques' which were held by the European Court of Human Rights in January 1978, to amount to inhuman and degrading treatment, but not to torture. Lord Parker and John Boyd-Carpenter held that the methods could be justified in exceptional circumstances, subject to certain further safeguards. But the third member, Lord Gardiner, said he did not believe such measures were morally justifiable, whether in peacetime or even in war against a ruthless enemy. The Prime Minister, Mr Heath, told MPs that the five techniques − hooding, wall-standing, subjection to noise and deprivation of food and sleep − would not be used again, and the decision was welcomed by Mr Wilson for the opposition.

PASSMORE, THOMAS. Off. U. Assembly member for W. Belfast, 1982−. b. 1931. Grand Master of Orange Order in Belfast and chairman of Woodvale Unionist Association. His father was murdered by PIRA.

PATTEN, CHRISTOPHER FRANCIS. Parliamentary Under-Secretary, NI Office, 1983−. b. 12 May 1944. St Benedict's School, Ealing; Balliol College, Oxford. Director, Conservative Research Department, 1974−9. Cons. MP for Bath, 1979−. At the NI Office he took charge of Environment and Health and Social Services.

PATTEN, JOHN HAGGIT CHARLES. Parliamentary Under-Secretary, NI Office, 1981−3. b. 17 July 1945. Cambridge University. Fellow of Hertford College, Oxford, 1972−. Cons. MP for Oxford, 1979−. Oxford City Council, 1973−6. Took charge of Department of Health and Social Services at Stormont, and spokesman in

Commons for those matters for which Lord Gowrie had responsibility, such as finance and police and prison administration. Parliamentary Under-Secretary, Department of Health in London, 1983–.

PEACE LINE. The barrier erected by British troops between the Roman Catholic Falls area and the Protestant Shankill area in Belfast in September 1969. Sometimes known as the Orange-Green line, it was erected because of the violent disturbances in the district in the summer of 1969. In 1982, the height of the barricades was increased after complaints of missiles being thrown over them, and the Department of the Environment announced that an £80,000 brick wall would be built on part of the line.

PEACE PEOPLE. The peace movement established in August 1976, and inspired by the deaths of the three Maguire children, who had been struck by a gunman's getaway car in the Andersonstown area of Belfast. It was founded by Betty Williams, Mairead Corrigan, and Ciaran McKeown, and Mrs Williams and Miss Corrigan were awarded the 1976 Nobel Peace Prize. The movement was initially marked by large rallies in Belfast and other centres in NI, and rallies of supporters in London, Dublin, and various places abroad. The movement has had strong financial support from Norway, and substantial aid from Germany, the US and several other countries. It has defined its aim as 'non-violent movement towards a just and peaceful soci-

ety'. In 1977, it began to switch its effort from large meetings to small groups, particularly in areas of confrontation, and to encourage increased community effort, better recreational facilities and, in some cases, the establishment of local industry. It has created a good deal of controversy, since its leaders have been critical of established politicians. It has set up its own forum for discussion – the Peace Assembly – which brings together annually delegates from its groups throughout the province to debate current social and political issues. In February, 1980 there was serious internal dissention, although not apparently on policy. Mrs Williams resigned for family reasons, and she settled in the US in 1982. Peter McLachlan, who had become chairman of the movement in 1978, also left in 1980. Mairead Corrigan then became chairman, and held this post until 1981, when she was succeeded by Mrs Pat Johnston, although she remained on the Executive. Ciaran McKeown, who resumed his journalistic career as a freelance, was succeeded as editor of the movement's newspaper by Steve McBride. Most of the movement's activities have survived internal divisions, and there is continued strong emphasis on youth work, including a football league and summer camps in Norway for mixed religious groups. On the political side, the movement has been active in campaigning for reform of emergency legislation and in opposing secrecy in the Anglo-Irish talks. But, broadly, conventional politicians have paid little attention to the movement. (See separate entries on founders.)

PEACOCKE, JOSEPH ANTHONY. The last head of the RUC to hold the title of Inspector-General, who was criticised by the Scarman Tribunal for his handling of the situation in the riots of August 1969. b. 1908; died November 1975. He joined the RUC as a cadet in 1932, and became Inspector-General in February 1969. But he held the post only until October 1969, when he was succeeded by Sir Arthur Young with the rank of Chief Constable. The direction of the RUC had been one of the controversial aspects of 1969, and he was widely blamed for not having called for army assistance before 14 August. The Scarman report said Mr Peacocke had acted in August as though RUC strength were sufficient to maintain the public peace. 'It was not until he was confronted with the physical exhaustion of the police in Londonderry on the 14th and in Belfast on the 15th that he was brought to the decision to call in the aid of the army. Had he correctly appreciated the situation before the outbreak of the mid-August disturbances, it is likely that the Apprentice Boys' parade [in Derry] would not have taken place, and the police would have been sufficiently reinforced to prevent disorder arising in the city. Had he correctly appreciated the threat to Belfast that emerged on 13 August he would have saved the city the tragedy of the 15th. We have no doubt that he was well aware of the existence of political pressures against calling in the army, but their existence constituted no excuse, as he himself recognised when in evidence he stoutly and honourably asserted that they did not influence his decision.' This reference to 'political pressure' related to the point that entry of the army to the streets would involve the British government in a reappraisal of the whole position of the Stormont administration.

PENDRY, TOM. Parliamentary Under-Secretary, NI Office, October 1978–May 1979. b. 10 June 1934. Labour MP for Stalybridge and Hyde, 1970–. Opposition Whip, 1971–4. Government Whip, 1974–7. Delegate, Council of Europe, 1973–. Appointed to NI Office to look after Departments of Finance and Agriculture owing to illness of James Dunn MP.

PENTLAND, JOHN WESLEY. DUP Assembly member for N. Down, 1982–. Member of former Lurgan Borough Council and Deputy Mayor in early 1960s. Well-known as spokesman of travel agents in NI.

PEOPLE'S DEMOCRACY. A radical leftist group, which had its beginnings at QUB on 9 October 1968. After a student march to Belfast city centre to demand an impartial inquiry into police brutality in Londonderry and the repeal of the Special Powers Act and the Public Order Act, among other things, a committee of ten was established at the inaugural meeting. Apart from the repeal of what it regarded as repressive legislation, it also urged one man, one vote, with the re-drawing of electoral boundaries, and action to outlaw discrimination in jobs and housing allocations. Its best-known original members were Bernadette Devlin, Kevin Boyle and Michael Farrell. Its most dramatic move was a four-day march from Belfast to London-derry, starting on 1 January 1969, with between forty and seventy people taking part. The project was attacked as provocative by loyalists, and it was harassed by extreme elements at various points. The most serious incident was near Burntollet Bridge, in Co. Derry, when the marchers were ambushed by some 200 loyalists. Stones and sticks were used in the assault and thirteen students had to have hospital treatment. The affair gave rise to angry recrimina-tions, and criticism of the RUC by civil rights spokesmen. In the February 1969 Stormont general election, PD tried its appeal at the polls. None of its eight candidates was successful, but it got a total of 23,645 votes and the PD nominee was only 220 behind the National-ist in S. Down. In 1972, it put out a detailed policy statement, propos-ing a secular, all-Ireland republic, with the dissolution of both the existing states. It said there was no point in submerging the North in the 'gombeen state' in the South. It also called for the disbanding of the RUC and UDR. PD has fre-quently campaigned in close asso-ciation with Provisionals but they have hit out at PD from time to time. In 1974 they criticised it as 'weak and pseudo-revolutionary'. After a ten-year absence from elections, it secured two council seats in Belfast in the 1981 local government contests. It expressed total opposition to the 1982 'rolling devolution' initiative, but put up its two councillors – Fergus O'Hare and John McAnulty – in W. and N. Belfast in the Assembly election. They got fewer than 500 votes between them. Mrs Ber-nadette McAliskey stood unsuc-cessfully as PD candidate in the 1982 general elections in the Republic.

PLASTIC BULLET. See Secur-ity Section (p. 315).

POOTS, CHARLES BOUCHER. DUP Assembly (1973–4) and Convention (1974–5) Member for N. Down. b. 1929. Member, Lisburn District Coun-cil 1973–. Unsuccessful candidate for Stormont Iveagh seat, 1969. Treasurer, Hillsborough Free Presbyterian Church. In the Assembly, in January 1974, he was suspended for a day for calling Chief Executive Brian Faulkner 'a lying tramp'. Stood unsuccessfully in N. Down in 1982 Assembly election.

POPULATION. Preliminary results of the 1981 Census showed NI's total population dropping for the first time in a century. The total was 1,488,077, but non-returns estimated at 74,123 were not taken into account in this total. These were due partly to the efforts of Republican supporters of the hunger-strike to disrupt the count. The 1971 Census total was 1,536,065. The Registrar-General estimated that there was a net out-ward migration of 10,000 people a year. Belfast's population dropped by more than 100,000, but there was a rise of more than 50,000 in the number of people living in Greater Belfast and adjoining towns, reflecting the movement of population due to redevelopment. Belfast had an increasing proportion of people of pensionable age – 18.4 per cent compared with 15 per cent in 1971. The proportion of pensionable age in NI as a whole had risen to 14.5 per cent as compared with 13.3 per cent in 1971.

PORTER, SIR ROBERT WILSON. Minister of Home Affairs, 1969–70. b. Londonderry, 23 December 1923. LL.B. (QUB). QC, 1965. Unionist MP for QUB 1966–9, Lagan Valley, 1969–72. Minister of Health and Social Services, 1969. Known to his friends as 'Beezer' and one of the strongest supporters of Terence O'Neill as Prime Minister. In the Chichester-Clark government, he took part in the crucial Downing Street talks in August 1969. He often argued that Unionism could no longer operate on the 'no surrender' approach, or 'stand still while the rest of the world is changing'. In June 1972, he resigned from the Unionist Party because Mr Faulkner, as Prime Minister, had associated himself with the Vanguard movement in attacking direct rule. He claimed that Unionism was being seen as a Protestant right-wing party. He joined the Alliance Party soon afterwards and resumed his Bar practice, occasionally acting as Deputy Recorder of Belfast and frequently as a prosecuting counsel in terrorist cases. County Court judge, 1978–.

POUNDER, RAFTON JOHN. Unionist MP for S. Belfast, 1963–74. b. Belfast, 13 May 1933. Chartered accountant; internal auditor, QUB 1962–3. Parliamentary Private Secretary to Conservative Industry Minister, 1970–1. Member, UK delegation, European Parliament, 1973–4. Staff of EEC Commission (1974–6) working on scheme for Court of Auditors to check Common Market spending and counter abuses. Defeated by UUUC candidate in S. Belfast, February 1974. Secretary, NI Bankers Association, 1977–.

POWELL, JOHN ENOCH. Unionist MP for S. Down, October 1974–. b. 16 June 1912. M.A. (Cantab.) Enoch Powell had been Conservative MP for Wolverhampton S.W., 1950–74. Minister of Health, 1960–3, and an internationally-known personality before he became interested in Ulster affairs. He displayed his Unionist sympathies intermittently for some years, notably by addressing party meetings in the Province before his break with the Conservatives left him without a seat in parliament. So his entry to active NI politics in 1974 was seen as being of mutual benefit to the Unionists and to Mr Powell. He had been out of the Commons for some six months when he was selected as Unionist candidate in S. Down, and the Unionists saw him as a controversialist with the ability to project their case in Great Britain at a time when Unionist stock was particularly low there. They were disappointed, however to find that his majority in October 1974 over the SDLP candidate in S. Down was only three and a half thousand in a seat which normally yielded Unionist majorities of 10,000 or more. But in the circumstances of direct rule, his mastery of parliamentary and Whitehall procedure was a real asset to the UUUC, particularly since several of their MPs were new to Westminster and didn't have any Stormont experience. Mr Powell's support for Labour in the election was an embarrassment to many Unionists who believed that despite Mr Heath's suspension of Stormont, every effort should be made to restore the former Conservative-Unionist partnership – a belief which was strengthened when Mrs Thatcher took over as Conservative leader. Mr Powell's tactics were, however, to extract as much advantage as possible from the narrowly-balanced parliament, and he pointed to the Labour government's acceptance of the case for more NI seats at Westminster as one of the key gains. He was also regarded on all sides in NI as basically an integrationist who had little time for the revival of a strong devolved government at Stormont, but he answered this point by saying that he always stuck to the letter of his election manifesto. On the Common Market issue, his unwavering opposition reflected the majority view in Unionism. As S. Down MP he has shown little friendliness towards the Republic, which he has always described as a foreign state. He questioned, among other things, the right of the Republic's citizens to enjoy equal voting rights in Britain. By having a house in S. Down and by intensive canvassing he sought to dispel the 'carpetbagger' image, and when he came to fight his second election in S. Down in 1979, he substantially increased his majority. He was also helped by the fact that the Bill to give NI five extra MPs had been put on the statute book, and it was accepted that Enoch Powell had played a major part in the campaign to achieve increased representation. In 1982, he mounted a major attack on the Prior 'rolling devolution' initiative. He saw it as closely tied up with the Anglo-Irish talks, which he regarded as an 'Anglo-American plot' to secure a united Ireland within NATO. Undeterred by Government denials, he spoke vigorously against the devolution Bill both inside and outside Parliament, and reinforced the efforts of Conservative right-wing critics during the committee stage of the measure by some skilful filibustering. But Mr Powell proved to be one of the most forceful Parliamentary supporters of Mrs Thatcher during the Falklands operation. He was among leading politicians to whom she accorded a personal briefing on the crisis, and there were Conservative MPs who thought he should be back on the Front Bench. In 1982, at age 70, he was re-selected as candidate by S. Down Unionists. In the 1983 election, he survived in S. Down despite the handicaps of boundary changes favouring the SDLP and opposition from the DUP. A PSF vote of more than 4,000 blunted the SDLP challenge and gave him a majority of 548.

PRIOR, JAMES MICHAEL LEATHEM. NI Secretary of

State, September, 1981–. b. 11 October 1927. Educated Charterhouse and Pembroke College, Cambridge. Cons. MP for Lowestoft, 1959–83. MP for Waveney, 1983–. Employment Secretary, 1979–81. His appointment to NI came after repeated rumours that he was favourite to succeed Humphrey Atkins but that he had told Mrs Thatcher he would prefer to resign rather than leave Employment. At the time he was known to have qualms about Government economic policy, and to be high on the Prime Minister's list of Cabinet 'Wets'. He was also reckoned to be a possible future challenger for the Conservative leadership. In the end, he deferred to the Prime Minister's wishes. It was his duty, he said, to put the nation first, and he seems to have been concerned with the 'international dimension' of the NI job. Mrs Thatcher also allowed him to remain on the influential Cabinet Economic Committee, and to take three of his close political friends to NI with him – Lord Gowrie, Nicholas Scott and John Patten. In his first Stormont statement, he said he was prepared to lay his political reputation 'on the line' in a bid to secure a political settlement. His immediate challenge was the H-Block hunger strike, which had already led to the deaths of ten Republican prisoners. It was however, petering out as next-of-kin of those close to death sought medical intervention, and within a month PIRA and INLA bowed to the inevitable. Mr Prior announced only one substantial concession when the protest ended – the right of all prisoners to wear their own clothes at all times. But the easing of tension was followed by a new upsurge of violence and the murder of the Rev. Robert Bradford, MP for S. Belfast. He was now brought face to face with Loyalist wrath – notably at Mr Bradford's funeral – and calls from Official and Democratic Unionists for a tougher security policy. The DUP-sponsored 'third force' appeared at several rallies, and Ian Paisley mounted night-time demonstrations on lonely hillsides to dramatise his campaign. But Mr Prior continued to pursue the possibilities of political advance, despite the obvious lack of agreement on how devolution could be achieved. His first thoughts were directed to the setting up of a local administration to which he would appoint Ministers rather like a US President. But he abandoned this quickly for what became known as 'rolling devolution.' (see Government section). He got little encouragement for his gradualist approach. Both main Unionist parties were obsessed by fears of new pressure for power-sharing and the shadow of the new British-Irish Intergovernment Council (see separate entry). The DUP, though, were more enthusiastic than the OUP about the Assembly's scrutiny powers. The SDLP were sharply critical of what they saw as the absence of any firm assurances on power-sharing and an Irish dimension. The major Dublin parties were equally unfriendly to the proposals, and Mr Prior had to face strong criticism from the Conservative far Right during the passage of the legislation in the spring of 1982. At the same time, Mr Haughey's refusal to back sanctions against Argentina during the Falklands crisis brought Anglo-Irish relations to a new low. But despite this unhappy context, Mr Prior pressed on with the initiative, and the 20 October 1982 poll found the SDLP fighting the election, but committed to boycotting the Assembly. This was clearly disappointing for Mr Prior, who was also unable to take any comfort from the achievement of PSF in getting five seats and 10 per cent of the votes in contesting a Stormont election for the first time. He saw the Assembly start with 49 Members present – 26 OUP; 21 DUP; 10 All.; 1 UPUP; and one Independent Unionist. The 14 SDLP and 5 PSF members stayed away. He sought to boost the Assembly's prestige by addressing it on security policy within three weeks of its first meeting, but it was evident that a host of questions hung over this latest British initiative. Mr Prior had the satisfaction, however, of having the Assembly Plan supported in the 1983 Conservative manifesto. There had been some doubts as to whether he would return to NI after the 1983 election, but Mrs Thatcher acceded to his request for a further period in the province.

PRIVY COUNCIL. The Privy Council in the province has been suspended since direct rule. In the old Stormont parliament all Cabinet Ministers were appointed to the Privy Council for life, and the Cabinet formed the Executive Committee of the Council. Some senior judges were also admitted to the Council, which met at the Governor's residence at Hillsborough. Ex-Cabinet Ministers have been permitted to retain the title. Ministers in the power-sharing Executive of 1974 had no Privy Council membership.

PRO-ASSEMBLY UNIONISTS. The name given to Unionists who supported the approach to partnership government in the government's White Paper. When the NI Executive collapsed in 1974, many of them moved to UPNI or the Alliance Party.

PROGRESSIVE UNIONIST PARTY. Started in Belfast Shankill Road area in 1978 as the Independent Unionist Group, becoming PUP in 1979. Alderman Hugh Smyth, an Ind. Unionist member of the Convention, was among the founders; he stood unsuccessfully in W. Belfast in the 1982 Assembly election. It urged in a statement in June, 1978, that there should be a devolved administration based on a 153–seat parliament, with departments run by committees elected by the parliament, which would have power to co-opt non-voting members from outside. The party tried unsuccessfully to take part in the Stormont Constitutional Conference in 1980.

PROTESTANT ACTION. See ULSTER PROTESTANT ACTION GROUP.

PROTESTANT AND CATHOLIC ENCOUNTER. An organisation established in 1968 to bring together people of differing religious and political affiliations so as to promote harmony and goodwill. It aims at the creation of a 'social order based upon justice and charity, and enlivened by mutual respect and understanding . . .'. It is run by a central council, bringing together churchmen, academics, and others, and has groups in many towns and villages. It works through conferences, social events, and a magazine.

PROTESTANT TASK FORCE.
Believed to be a small group involved in assassinations of people it claimed were associated with the IRA. In press interview in November 1974, an unofficial spokesman of the organisation in Mid-Ulster stated that they had murdered twenty-eight people in two months. He also said that the PTF had no scruples in dealing with republicans, was restricted to ex-Servicemen, and unconnected with any leading loyalist paramilitary group.

PROTESTANT UNIONIST PARTY.
The party led by the Rev. Ian Paisley which gave way to the DUP in 1971. The term, 'Protestant Unionist' was used by four candidates in the Belfast Corporation elections in 1964. PUP nominees stood unsuccessfully in the 1969 Stormont election, and its first successes were achieved in April 1970, when Mr Paisley and the Rev. William Beattie won the Bannside and South Antrim by-elections. In June 1970, Mr Paisley won N. Antrim in the Westminster election as a Protestant Unionist.

PROVISIONAL IRISH REPUBLICAN ARMY.
The Provisional IRA, the dominant element in the NI violence, dates effectively from December 1969. In that month, the IRA Army Council voted by three to one to give at least token recognition to the three parliaments – Westminster, Dublin and Stormont. This switch in policy ran directly against the traditional abstentionism and physical-force policy of the IRA. It was too much for the more militant members, who split off to create the PIRA. The break was mirrored in Sinn Fein, the political counterpart of the IRA. When the Sinn Fein Ard Fheis (annual convention) met in Dublin in January 1970, there was a majority for a change in policy, but not the necessary two-thirds majority. So the new Provisionals walked out of the meeting in the Intercontinental Hotel to set up their organisation in Kevin Street, Dublin. There were now two IRAs – Provisional and Official – and the same applied to Sinn Fein. Events in NI, and particularly in Belfast, meant that the PIRA was better placed than the Officials to attract public support in the Northern ghettoes. For the IRA, so far as it existed in Belfast in the violent summer of 1969, had little credibility. Falls Road Catholics complained that it was unable to prevent the burning of Catholic homes. 'IRA – I Ran Away' was scrawled on some walls in West Belfast. The Scarman Commission, which investigated the early troubles, said that the main difference between the Derry Citizens' Defence Association, which had some IRA mem-

bers, and the IRA in Belfast was that the DCDA was ready while the IRA in Belfast was not. Scarman also found that while there was IRA influence in the 1969 riots in Belfast, Derry and Newry, the IRA did not start or plan the riots, and that the evidence was that they were taken by surprise and did less than many of their supporters felt they should have done. But Stormont was convinced that there was a strong IRA influence in the civil rights campaign. The point was made many times by William Craig, as Minister of Home Affairs. Scarman published a letter from the head of the RUC Special Branch to the Minister of Home Affairs, dated 18 August 1969. This claimed that at the end of May 1969 members of Republican Clubs controlled two-thirds of the Executives of all local Civil Rights Associations in NI, while six of the fourteen members of the NICRA Executive were from the republican movement. The Special Branch head also stated that the Citizens' Defence Committees which had developed in Belfast, Derry, Newry, Lurgan, and other towns were all IRA dominated, and that IRA units in these areas had been making hundreds of petrol bombs and some grenades. They were also instructing people in the use of petrol bombs through the citizens' defence committees. Thus, the situation in NI was highly favourable to the Provisionals, who attracted not only many young recruits but a high proportion of veterans of former IRA campaigns, and one survivor of the 1916 Easter Rising in Dublin – the late Joe Clarke. The Pro-

visionals were short of both arms and ammunition at the start of 1970, but friendly sources in Dublin provided some, others were shipped in secretly from Britain and the continent. The guns which they got from the Republic were, of course, sometimes intended for the local defence committees. And the charging in the Republic in 1970 of two Cabinet Ministers (Charles Haughey and Neil Blaney) with illegal dealing in arms was seen by PIRA chiefs as having a valuable publicity spin-off, even if both Ministers were later cleared. The Provisionals duplicated the military organisations of the former IRA. In Belfast, for example, there was a commander and brigade staff, and three battalions: 1st, covering Upper Falls, Turf Lodge and Andersonstown; 2nd, Ballymurphy and Clonard; and 3rd, the Markets area. By mid-1970, PIRA strength overall was believed to be around 1,500, including 800 in NI, divided roughly as follows: Belfast, 600; Derry, 100; other areas, 100. The growing Provisional strength was reflected in the big increase in violence in 1970 compared with 1969. Twenty-three civilians and two RUC men died during the year. There were 153 explosions compared with eight in 1969, and it was reckoned that all but twenty-five of these were the work of PIRA. Street violence also remained at a high level in 1970, and the security forces held that much of it could be traced to inspiration by PIRA. PIRA further stepped up attacks in 1971. It was held responsible for most of the 304 explosions between January and July. In July alone there were ninety-four. In February 1971, General Farrar-Hockley, Commander of Land Forces, named five men as leaders of the PIRA in Belfast, and blamed them for recent rioting. They were Francis Card, William McKee, Liam Hannaway and his son, Kevin, and Patrick Leo Martin. About the same time, the army blamed the Provisionals for organising attacks by children, and claimed that the PIRA were using petrol bombs, grenades and rifles against the troops. In the early part of 1971, a bitter feud went on between the PIRA and OIRA and there was much of what the authorities termed inter-factional shooting. The murder in Belfast of three young Scottish soldiers in March 1971 brought strident loyalist demands for the use of internment without trial against PIRA. The army and police began to lean heavily on PIRA suspects. Billy McKee, the Belfast commander, was arrested in March. His successor, Joe Cahill, held a news conference in Belfast in the summer of 1971, much to the discomfiture of the government and security chiefs. At that period, the leading figures in the top PIRA leadership were Sean MacStiofain, English-born chief-of-staff, and Daithi O'Connell. In July 1971, there was a big round-up of people believed to be connected with both wings of the IRA. It was designed to secure information for the coming internment operation. Government intelligence was satisfied that most of the thirty people killed up to 9 August 1971 – the date of the start of internment – had been victims of PIRA. They comprised eleven soldiers, two policemen and seventeen civilians. The European Court of Human Rights report on the ill-treatment of some of the IRA suspects interned in August 1969 stated: 'Prior to August 1971, the intelligence obtained by the police had failed to provide anything but a very general picture of the IRA organisation.' The internment move was designed to sweep up activists and sympathisers of the IRA. Of the 454 originally taken into custody, 350 were interned, and it was evidently the government's belief that the operation would deprive the Provisionals of their more experienced people and damp down the violence. But the reality was otherwise: the use of internment alienated a huge section of the Catholic population, increased support for PIRA, and violence was intensified. From the date of internment (9 August) to the end of 1971, the count of violence was: 143 persons killed (including forty-six members of security forces); 729 explosions; 1,437 shooting incidents. Security forces put the great bulk down to PIRA, and loyalists were accused of only one killing. At this point, PIRA had assembled a great diversity of weapons, despite the uncovering of a Czech arms deal in Amsterdam in October 1971. Apart from the old stand-by of the IRA, the Thomson sub-machine gun (the 'Chicago piano') it had also some US-made M1 carbines and Garard rifles, and a variety of .303 rifles and German and American pistols. It was using the car bomb, the nail bomb (usually a beer can containing nails wrapped in explosive), and the hold-all bag bomb, often left outside business premises. It had also displayed ingenuity in producing small incendiary devices which could easily be hidden in shops. Two popular types were the cigarette packet incendiary, and the device in which a contraceptive acted as a fuse, with the detonation achieved by acid burning through the rubber. The existence of internment made it easier for the Provisionals to get funds from abroad, particularly from Irish-Americans, many of whom had a basic hatred of all things British and were easily persuaded that the PIRA were a 'liberation army'. Provisional Sinn Fein has always insisted that money coming from US funds has been used for relief of dependants of IRA prisoners and similar purposes, but it is certainly the British view that cash for weapons, and even some weapons themselves, have been smuggled to Ireland by special IRA couriers. The Provisionals were also helped by the non-acceptability of the RUC in many Catholic areas, and they got a new boost at the start of 1972, when thirteen people were shot dead by the army in Derry on what became known as 'Bloody Sunday'. In March 1972, Provisional Sinn Fein launched its 'Eire Nua' policy – a scheme for four provincial parliaments in Ireland – which was also linked with demands for the abolition of Stormont, a declaration of intent of British withdrawal, and a full amnesty for all political prisoners. PIRA ordered a three-day ceasefire in association with this policy, but they called it off because they had not got a British response and arrests had been continued by the

security forces. In fact, there were 900 internees at the end of March 1972, when direct rule was imposed from London, and they were all held because of alleged IRA involvement. But the closing down of the Stormont parliament was not enough to induce PIRA to drop its campaign. Its determination to fight on was announced after a Dublin meeting in April which was said to have been attended by representatives of every active service unit. On 29 May 1972, the OIRA declared a ceasefire, which was still in operation in 1983. Exactly four weeks later, PIRA began a truce of its own, but it lasted only thirteen days. The collapse occurred after a row about housing in Belfast. Two days before the ceasefire ended, a party of PIRA leaders were flown secretly to London for talks with the Secretary of State, William Whitelaw MP. It seemed like a bid by the Provisionals to move away from military action but the talks were unproductive. The restart of the PIRA campaign produced a massive upsurge in violence. For July 1972 alone there was an unprecedented tally of violence: seventy-four civilians and twenty-one members of the security forces killed, nearly 200 explosions and 2,800 shooting incidents. Throughout 1972 there had also been a mounting toll of sectarian assassinations carried out, for the most part, by loyalists. Faced with this two-pronged campaign, the government decided to move against the no-go areas. But few PIRA men remained in the W. Belfast republican areas or in the Bogside area of Londonderry, since the government's intentions had been signalled well in advance. The second half of 1972 was a period of strong pressure on the Provisionals both in NI and in the Republic, and there were sporadic incidents involving members of the PIRA and OIRA. A leading Belfast PIRA man, Martin Meehan, was recaptured in Belfast in August – he had escaped from Belfast Prison at the end of 1971. Documents seized by the security forces in Belfast were claimed to reveal a good deal about the PIRA structure in the city. One document was said to have recommended that any PIRA volunteer questioned by the authorities and released should be suspended from duty for a month to guard against collaboration. It was also stated about the same time in *An Phoblacht*, the Provisional newspaper, that of the forty-four PIRA members killed since 1969, eighteen had been executed for mistakes or for giving information to the security forces. In the final months of 1972, the PIRA chief of staff, Sean MacStiofain, was much in the news. In October he got through a security screen to attend the Provisional Sinn Fein Ard Fheis (annual conference) in Liberty Hall, Dublin, where he declared that there would be no easing off in the campaign of violence. But in November 1972, MacStiofain was captured after he had given an interview to the Republic's Broadcasting Authority, RTE. He was charged with IRA membership and then went on hunger strike, and an unsuccessful attempt was made to rescue him from a Dublin hospital. With Ruadhri O'Bradaigh, president of Provisional Sinn Fein, held in December 1972 for alleged IRA membership, there were rumours that MacStiofain was seeking a larger political role. The British government was claiming that it was getting truce 'feelers' from the PIRA, despite denials by the organisation. There was a leadership crisis in PIRA when MacStiofain abandoned his hunger strike. He was thought to have been succeeded by a three-man council made up of Daithi O'Connell, Joe Cahill and Gerry Adams, a Belfast Provisional who was one of the deputation flown secretly to London in July 1972 to meet Whitelaw. At the end of 1972, Whitelaw said in London that 1,000 IRA men had been arrested and convicted during 1972 and the organisation's command structure greatly weakened. There were also signs that PIRA was finding difficulty in getting conventional explosives because of the clamp-down in the South. The weed-killer chemical, sodium chlorate, was figuring increasingly in IRA weapons. At the beginning of 1973, Martin McGuinness, who was sentenced to six months' imprisonment in Dublin for IRA membership, told the court that he had been an officer in the Derry brigade of the IRA for two years. In fact, he had been regarded by the security forces as the leading PIRA figure in the Bogside. At this period, PIRA continued its attacks alongside loyalist violence on a substantial scale. Official estimates suggested that between 1 April 1972 and 31 January 1973, PIRA was responsible for about 300 deaths, including some 120 members of the security forces. In the case of 'factional' or 'sectarian' assassinations, PIRA was blamed for thirty-four and the loyalists for seventy. Throughout 1973, when the total of deaths was 250 – 171 civilians and seventy-nine security forces – the pattern of PIRA bombing and shooting of soldiers and policemen was continued, while the loyalists concentrated on the shooting of Catholics. In February PIRA warned the UDA that it would take 'ruthless action' against it to halt sectarian killings, but there is no clear indication as to how far this threat was implemented. On the political side, PIRA called for the rejection of the British government White Paper which led to the Assembly system, and it also called for a boycott of the 1973 council elections. It made threats against Aldergrove Airport (reinforced by two small bombs) which led to introduction of exceptional security measures. In May 1973, Joe Cahill was sentenced to five years' imprisonment arising from gun-running charges associated with the vessel *Claudia*, seized off Waterford with a cargo of arms and ammunition from Libya. (In 1982, Colonel Gadaffi of Libya was still voicing 'moral support' for PIRA, although he denied that he was supplying them with arms.) In May, 1973, the government published figures of IRA casualties going back to 1969. They claimed that 123 IRA men had been killed. PIRA admitted that it had lost ninety-nine men, and said the British claim was 'outlandish'. In 1974, there was some falling off in PIRA violence. In part, this was believed to be due to

a desire to encourage the loyalists to make the running against the government in their opposition to the Sunningdale agreement and power-sharing. In particular, PIRA called off most of its campaign for the period of the loyalist strike in May which brought down the power-sharing Executive. But PIRA had its own internal troubles at this time, with apparently a major leak of information to the security forces. A coup for the authorities was the uncovering in the select Malone Road area of Belfast of the brigade HQ of PIRA in the city. In a flat, and posing as a businessman, was Brendan Hughes, the brigade commander, and one of his aides. About the same time, several other key figures in PIRA in the city were also picked up, and stocks of bomb parts were seized. In the Commons, the Prime Minister, Mr Wilson, referred to documents seized at the Provisionals' HQ which, he said, were a 'specific and calculated' plan to take over certain areas of Belfast by creating inter-sectarian hatred, chaos, violence and hardship. The areas to be taken over were said to include loyalist districts like Woodvale and Sandy Row, together with key buildings, such as Telephone House, the gas works, BBC and UTV. PIRA admitted that the plans had been drawn up some time before as a doomsday contingency. The end of 1974 was a period of mixed fortunes for the Provisionals. On one hand, they came under greater pressure after the passing at Westminster of new and tougher anti-terrorist legislation in the wake of the Birmingham bombings. On the other, their leaders became involved in secret talks with Protestant churchmen in Feakle, Co. Clare. PIRA immediately came under suspicion for the bombings which resulted in the deaths in November of nineteen people in two Birmingham pubs. The Provisionals denied that they had been responsible. A spokesman for PIRA noted that there had been a claim by a group calling itself 'Red Flag 74' that it had carried out the bombings. The spokesman said that while they did not know anything about this group, they were satisfied that it was not connected with the republican movement. But there were later PIRA statements promising an inquiry into the bombings, although no result of such an investigation was ever issued. Meantime, six men had been jailed for life for the Birmingham bombings. Two priests – the Rev. Denis Faul of Dungannon, and the Rev. Raymond Murray, of Armagh – argued in a book, *The Birmingham Framework* (July 1977), that these six men were innocent. The immediate effect of the Birmingham tragedy was to unite parliament in support of the Prevention of Terrorism Act, which declared the IRA illegal in Great Britain, allowed suspects to be held without charge for up to seven days, and permitted the expulsion of people to either NI or the Republic. The upshot of the Feakle talks with churchmen was that there was a flurry of talks at mid-December. The Secretary of State, Merlyn Rees, met some of the churchmen to hear the Provisionals' demands, which

included a call for a declaration of intent of British withdrawal. (Six months later, one of the churchmen, the Rev. William Arlow, claimed that the government had told the Provisionals that the army would be withdrawn if the Convention broke down – a claim denied by Rees.) There was also a lengthy secret meeting of the PIRA Army Council, and its chief-of-staff, Daithi O'Connell, met Mr Arlow in Dublin. The only public response from the British government was a comment by Rees that they would naturally respond to any genuine cessation of violence. PIRA then announced a ceasefire from 22 December to 2 January 1975, to give the government time, they said, to consider their proposals. In an atmosphere in which many politicians, and particularly the loyalists, were highly suspicious of what was going on, the government insisted that there was no question of negotiations with PIRA. But there were meetings between government officials and members of Provisional Sinn Fein. So the ceasefire was extended first to 16 January and then to 10 February when an open-ended ceasefire was announced. It said this was being done in the light of the discussions which had taken place with British officials to ensure that there was no breakdown of a new truce. It emerged that the plan to monitor the ceasefire involved the setting up of 'incident centres' manned by Provisional Sinn Fein in Catholic areas of Belfast and Londonderry and other major towns. These would be in instant contact with government officials with the object of avoiding a breakdown of the ceasefire through misunderstanding about individual incidents. There was a great deal of scepticism about the operation. Loyalists feared 'Provo policing', the SDLP were worried that the Provisionals were being given new credibility through ready access to government; and Official Republicans saw signs of co-operation with the RUC through 'Royal Ulster Provisionals', a charge which PIRA were quick to deny. Not all the PIRA activists put away their guns; some joined the IRSP which was engaged in a feud with the OIRA. In March 1975, the Belfast sisters, Dolours and Marion Price, sentenced for the London car bombings, were moved from Durham Jail to Armagh Prison – a decision which was seen as a definite gesture by the government towards the PIRA ceasefire. The ceasefire became more fragile, and more controversial, as time went on. At the beginning of July, four soldiers were killed in an ambush in S. Armagh, and the Secretary of State told parliament that one of the key questions was whether the Provisionals could control their followers. By mid-August, the number of soldiers killed still stood at four during the ceasefire period, compared with nineteen in the same period of 1974, but the total of civilian deaths had risen by twenty-six to 119, and since the increase was entirely accounted for by a rise in the number of Protestants murdered (fifty-seven), the security forces suspected that some of the PIRA effort had been switched to revenge killings of loyalists in view of the continued assassinations of Catholics. There were also murmurings from loyalist politicians at what they saw as a deliberate policy by the security forces of turning a blind eye to Provisionals who had returned to their old haunts in W. Belfast. Notably, there was confusion as to whether Seamus Twomey, a former PIRA commander in the city, was still on the wanted list. There were reports that he had been spotted by an army patrol in W. Belfast, but had got away in a taxi, and there was a claim by the Rev. Ian Paisley that an army intelligence report showed that Twomey was not to be arrested. The implication seemed to be that, with the suspension of the detention process at the start of the ceasefire in February, Provisionals were only being arrested where specific charges could be brought against them. One of the imponderables of the situation was the extent to which PIRA had been preparing during the ceasefire for a new onslaught. Certainly, it had gone to the length of establishing a new 4th battalion in Belfast. In September six men were killed during a raid on an Orange Hall at Tullyvallen, in South Armagh. Although the raid was claimed by the 'South Armagh Republic Action Forces', this was treated by the authorities as a cover for PIRA. Indeed, S. Armagh, which Secretary of State Merlyn Rees had described as 'bandit country', was never effectively covered by the ceasefire. How far this was due to lack of control by the PIRA Army Council was never very clear. In November 1976, it was claimed that PIRA had carried out twenty-one killings in the area during the nine months of the ceasefire. In that month three soldiers were killed in a S. Armagh border dug-out by PIRA and two soldiers were killed by an explosion. Outside S. Armagh, September had brought eighteen PIRA explosions in one day throughout NI. In November the Government closed the incident centres, but Provisional Sinn Fein claimed that contacts continued with the government and that there was still a 'truce situation'. On 5 December the Secretary of State ordered the release of the last seventy-five detainees, among them fifty-seven members of the PIRA. The 1975 security figures reflected the ceasefire in several respects. The thirty deaths of members of the security forces compared with fifty in 1974; the number of shooting incidents was down from 3,206 to 1,803; and the total of explosions from 685 to 399. Then, 1976 opened with the shooting dead by PIRA of ten Protestant workers, when their bus was ambushed in S. Armagh. The incident on 5 January on the Whitecross-Newry Road, was not claimed by PIRA, but British security forces insisted that it had been carried out by a PIRA unit based in the Republic. The killings were, apparently, a reprisal for the murder of five Catholics in two separate incidents in Co. Armagh the previous day. With many Catholics in S. Armagh voicing their fears of loyalist vengeance, the British government announced that men of the Special Air Service (SAS) would be sent into the area. Although there had been many reports of

SAS units operating earlier, these had always been denied by the British authorities. In February the ceasefire finally came to an end, with the death in prison in England of IRA hunger striker. Frank Stagg. His death provoked widespread violence in NI. In March PIRA made a mortar attack on Aldergrove airport. The mortars were fired from a lorry, but fell short of the main terminal building, and did no real damage. In April, the arrival of James Callaghan as Prime Minister was the signal for more PIRA attacks on troops. During the month, five part-time UDR men died. In May, there was a further round of bombing, which was repeated in August at the time of the internment anniversary. Two events then occurred which created problems for PIRA chiefs. The Peace Movement got off the ground in Belfast, and probably accounted in part for an increased flow of information to the security forces. And in September Roy Mason, who had been Defence Secretary, succeeded Merlyn Rees as NI Secretary. He had a reputation for toughness, and while his immediate claim that PIRA were 'reeling', caused some problems for him, he was obviously intent on stepping up army undercover activity against the paramilitaries. He also permitted the SAS to operate anywhere in NI. By late autumn, he claimed in parliament that 690 members of PIRA had been charged since the start of the year, that is, more than twice the total (320) in 1975. The weight of police and army intelligence was directed to cataloguing the movements of suspected terrorists and their life-style, contacts, 'safe-houses', and general tactics. But if the Mason approach was proving effective, it did not prevent a sharp rise in the level of violence in 1976, mostly by PIRA. The number killed was 297, an increase of fifty. Twenty-nine soldiers died, as against nineteen in 1975, and twenty-three RUC members against eleven in 1975. The total of 766 explosions was roughly double the 1975 figure. In 1977, there were signs that the pressure by the security forces on PIRA was beginning to tell. It was also apparently short of explosives, and the car bomb had all but vanished. In February however, PIRA activated an earlier threat when it killed three businessmen and injured four others. In April, active service units, believed by the authorities to be striking out from cross-border bases, were blamed for six deaths, with twenty serious injuries, in Londonderry, Fermanagh and Armagh. At Easter, the feud between PIRA and the OIRA also flared up again. The response of PIRA to growing undercover police and army activity was to mount a large-scale reorganisation. The effect of this seems to have been to substitute very small active service units – possibly with only two or three members – for its larger companies. The Army Council of PIRA was no doubt surprised to find all thirteen members of an active service unit arrested in a single operation in Strabane, Co. Tyrone, in September. These small units allowed PIRA to secure tighter screening of recruits, since one aspect of the

undercover effort of the army was undoubtedly to achieve penetration of PIRA ranks. It is also likely that the new tactics were based on the 'need to know' principle – that is, probably only one member of a bombing unit would be informed in advance of the actual target. The organisation had also come to rely largely on the small incendiary device, with only a very limited explosive content. Increased 'knee-cappings' – shooting through the knees as a punishment – reflected a growing effort by PIRA to deal with members who were careless and to increase 'policing' in republican areas by dealing with those whom they termed 'petty criminals'. The end of 1977 brought a serious loss for PIRA – the recapture in Dublin of Seamus Twomey, its chief-of-staff. The total of soldiers killed by PIRA in 1977 was twenty-nine – the same figure as in 1976 – but violence generally had dropped sharply, and the total death toll was down to 112. PIRA began 1978 with an atrocity which horrified even its own sympathisers, and which it rapidly acknowledged to have been a mistake. On 17 February fire bombs were used to attack the La Mon House restaurant, near Comber, Co. Down, while it was crowded with about 500 people attending two social functions. Twelve people died instantly in the blaze, and twenty-three were badly burnt. Following the attack, the security forces clamped down heavily on Provisional Sinn Fein, and mounted a big effort to prove that it was working closely with PIRA. Meantime PIRA prisoners in the Maze Prison staged a protest against the withdrawal of special category status for those convicted of politically motivated crimes. They refused to leave their cells to wash or go to the toilet. In August 1978, PIRA was blamed by the security forces for a series of bomb attacks on British army barracks in West Germany. There was no immediate confirmation from PIRA, although some of the bombs were said to be of the type favoured by PIRA. On 21 September PIRA bomb attacks destroyed the terminal building at Eglinton airfield, and caused other extensive damage. In November the organisation murdered the deputy governor of Belfast prison, Albert Miles, and bombed the centres of many towns and villages; on 30 November explosives and fire bombs were set off in fourteen centres. At the same time, PIRA warned that it was 'preparing for a long war'. In November the Intelligence Staff of the Defence Ministry concluded that PIRA was still a force to be reckoned with. The Ministry's report, which was regarded as top secret, apparently fell into PIRA hands in May 1979, because it had been in a mailbag stolen in England. The leak of the report was obviously an embarrassment to Ministers. It predicted that PIRA would have the manpower to sustain violence during the next five years and that it would show 'more precise targeting and greater expertise'. And it said that the calibre of members of ASUs did not support the view that they were merely 'mindless hooligans'. It suggested that the Provisional leadership was committed to a long campaign of attrition, and events in the first

half of 1979 indicated that it had settled on striking at a variety of targets – shops, offices, hotels, security installations – and keeping up its assault on members of the security forces and prison officers at about the same level as in 1978. PIRA's activities in the early 1980s became more diffuse, since some members were diverted to promoting the hunger strike campaign and the efforts of H-Block and PSF candidates in Dail elections in 1981 and 1982, and PSF nominees in the 1982 NI Assembly election. This increased political involvement seems to have had full PIRA backing, and its muscle was obviously an element in strengthening anti-H-Block demonstrations, particularly the closing of business premises in Republican areas. The organisation had also to cope with the appearance of informers on a large scale, so that 1982 became known as 'the year of the supergrass.' It was symptomatic of the seriousness of the leak of information and consequent arrests that PIRA let it be known in early 1982 that there would be an amnesty for informers who made themselves and the extent of their disclosures known. This contrasted with the established PIRA practice of killing informers. But there are signs that the 1981 hunger strike brought extra recruits and resources and an increase in Republican solidarity. Army intelligence sources had reported in 1980 that PIRA strength could be 'measured in tens' and in the same year ex-GOC Sir Timothy Creasey talked of 500 hard-core terrorists overall in the province. But the deaths of ten hunger-strikers, seven of them PIRA and including Bobby Sands, MP, undoubtedly spurred support from US Republicans and other sympathisers in Europe and elsewhere. And PIRA chiefs were obviously impressed by the arguments of people like Gerry Adams (PSF vice-president and W. Belfast Assemblyman, 1982) that the Republican movement must have an increasing political content, with no prospect of 'Brits out' being achieved in the foreseeable future. Two PIRA prisoners in the Maze won Dail seats in the June, 1981 election. They were hunger-striker Kieran Doherty (Cavan-Monaghan), who later died from his fast, and Paddy Agnew (Louth) (see H-BLOCKS). In the 1980s, PIRA's NI campaign has been extremely varied. Russian RPG rockets (handled with varying confidence), the M-60 machine-gun, car and beer-keg bombs and landmines with plastic, gelignite and more inferior explosives, homemade mortars, and more sophisticated incendiaries incorporating silicon chips – all these have figured in assaults. Much of PIRA's effort in this period was directed against the security forces, but there were also attacks on property and two coal-boats, the *Nellie M* and *St Bedan*, were sunk in Lough Foyle. Some 42 deaths were believed to have resulted from PIRA attacks in 1982. But the assassination which attracted most attention was that of the South Belfast Official Unionist MP, the Rev. Robert Bradford, shot in November, 1981, at a community centre in Finaghy. He was the first Westminster MP

for a NI seat to be killed in the troubles. PIRA accused him of being 'one of the key people responsible for winding up the loyalist paramilitary sectarian machine'. In March, 1982, it made an unsuccessful bid to assassinate Lord Chief Justice Lord Lowry at Queen's University, Belfast. Immediately before that there was a lull in PIRA activity, and a PIRA spokesman admitted in March, 1982, that they had supply and other problems. These no doubt included difficulties in getting explosives across the border, with the stepped-up operations of anti-terrorist units in the Republic. In 1981 and 1982, these units uncovered many arms and explosives dumps in counties Cavan, Monaghan and Donegal. The PIRA spokesman admitted to six land-mine failures in a row, and said that for every operation which was successful perhaps half a dozen did not come off. The spokesman also pointed out that a snowfall halted all operations, since volunteers would otherwise give away their movements. In mid-November, 1982, three PIRA members were shot dead by the RUC near Lurgan when they were alleged to have driven through a check-point. The incident provoked much controversy and allegations that the RUC was operating a new 'shoot to kill' policy. This was denied by the authorities, although they admitted to the existence of specialised RUC anti-terrorist units. The Lurgan shootings came two weeks after three RUC men had been killed by a PIRA land-mine in the area. The extent to which PIRA should mount attacks in GB has always been a matter of debate within the organisation. The result has been intermittent action there which has probably added greatly to the detection problems of the anti-terrorist squads. But PIRA chiefs are obviously attracted by the greater publicity attached to such incidents. In October, 1981, it placed a bomb in the car of Maj-Gen. Sir Stuart Pringle, Commandant General of the Royal Marines, at his London home, as a result of which he lost a leg. The next month and on the eve of its assassination of the Rev. Robert Bradford, MP it seriously damaged with a bomb the London home of Sir Michael Havers, the Attorney-General, although no one was injured. On October 10, 1981, it set off a nail bomb outside Chelsea barracks in London which killed a woman and injured 23 soldiers and 17 civilians. But PIRA bombings in London on July 20, 1982, were much more spectacular, and clearly intended to dispel suggestions by the security forces that they were a waning force. Attacks by nail bombs on the Household Cavalry at Hyde Park and an army band at Regent's Park left ten soldiers dead and some 50 people injured, both soldiers and civilians, while seven army horses also died in the Hyde Park bombing. Mrs Thatcher denounced the attacks as 'callous and cowardly'. PIRA claimed they were in pursuit of self-determination under the UN Charter. More bombings in Great Britain were threatened by PSF vice-president Daithi O'Connell at a rally in Monaghan in August, 1982. Several PSF spokesmen mentioned in 1983 that PIRA was

dropping punishment shootings (kneecappings). Although the organisation was suffering from the operation of 'supergrasses' in 1983, it declared (25 March) that it would not call a ceasefire until there was a British withdrawal from NI.

PROVISIONAL SINN FEIN. The political counterpart of PIRA, which dates from January, 1970, when the split occurred in the republican movement. At the annual conference, or ard-fheis, in Dublin, the dispute centred on whether Sinn Fein should drop its long-standing policy of non-recognition of the parliaments in Belfast and Dublin. Those against recognition called themselves the Provisionals – an echo of the 'Provisional Government' of 1916 – and they walked out to set up their own organisation with headquarters in Kevin Street, Dublin. There was another important point of difference between the two groups. Those who remained in what became known as Official Sinn Fein (eventually the Workers' Party) inclined to a Marxist approach. PSF's policy is rooted in the demand for British withdrawal from NI, usually expressed in the slogan, 'Brits out'. Originally, it favoured a phased withdrawal and Ruadhri O'Bradaigh, who became its president in 1970, defended this approach on the grounds that they did not want a sudden British pull-out which could create a Congo situation. But its 1980 ard-fheis committed the party to calling for immediate British withdrawal. At the 1981 ard-fheis it effectively abandoned its initial policy of a federal Ireland, with parliaments for each of the four provinces, which it called 'Eire Nua'. This issue produced bitter debate, since the change was spearheaded by the NI leaders, headed by vice-president Gerry Adams, while leading southern figures such as O'Bradaigh and Daithi O'Conaill, a vice-president argued for the status quo. The federal idea was seen by its supporters as a gesture to NI loyalists, but the new NI leaders of PSF were in no mood for compromise and the change was sealed at the 1982 ard-fheis. In 1981, PSF also decided to take up any seats won in council elections in NI. This removed an anomaly, since the party was already contesting local elections in the Republic. After the 1979 local elections, it held 30 seats on 26 councils in 14 counties, and a member was chairman of Galway Co. Council. (During the 1956 IRA campaign, the former Sinn Fein took four Dail seats on an abstentionist basis, one being held by O'Bradaigh). But PSF decided eventually against contesting the 1979 European election, although some of its leaders were in favour of doing so. Increasingly, however, there was pressure from within PSF to seek elected status, even if on an abstentionist basis, since one of the party's obvious aims was to supplant the SDLP as the main voice of NI Nationalists. In the early 1980s PSF's total membership is believed to have been around 5,000, with 400 branches (or cumainn) throughout Ireland. It is a registered political party in the Republic, but its spokesmen have been denied access to TV and radio there.

This ban was first imposed by the Coalition Government of 1973–7, and the then Minister for Posts and Telegraphs, Dr Conor Cruise-O'Brien, defended it on the ground that PSF was essentially a front for the PIRA. This ban was continued by successive governments, including those of Fianna Fail, and it survived a PSF challenge to its constitutionality in the Courts in 1982. In NI, a long-standing ban on Sinn Fein was raised by the British Government in 1974 in the hope that it would contest the 1975 Convention elections. But it decided to ignore these contests, although Albert Price, father of the Price sisters (who had been convicted of the London bombings in 1973) supported PSF policies when he stood unsuccessfully as an Independent in W. Belfast in the February, 1974, Westminster election. At this period, Mrs Maire Drumm was the leading PSF personality in Belfast, as a vice-president. She was murdered by loyalists in the city's Mater Hospital in 1976. Senior Belfast members of PSF were involved in talks with British officials in 1975, and party members manned the seven 'incident centres' set up to monitor the PIRA ceasefire and maintain contact with the NI Office. Although the British Government insisted that the officials were doing no more than explaining British policy and were not engaged in negotiations, the exercise brought sharp criticism from Unionist and other politicians in NI who claimed that it tended to give credibility to PSF. There is no bar to dual membership of PSF and PIRA, and most leading people in Sinn Fein have had a background associated with PIRA or the earlier IRA. Normally, at least one member of the PSF Executive, or ard-comhairle, is on PIRA's army council. In Belfast, PIRA statements are put out through the Sinn Fein office via telex to the media. Far from retreating from support for the campaign of violence, PSF spokesmen have increasingly insisted that political action cannot succeed in itself in the NI situation in advancing its aims. At the 1982 ard-fheis, it was decided that all future PSF candidates must give their 'unambivalent' support to the 'armed struggle'. At the 1981 ard-fheis, PSF's director of publicity, Danny Morrison, articulated the policy in these words: 'Who here really believes that we can win the war through the ballot-box? But will anyone here object if, with a ballot paper in this hand and an Armalite in this hand, we take power in Ireland?' Morrison was speaking at a point where two IRA prisoners in the Maze had secured election in the Republic's general election of June, 1981 – hunger striker Kieran Doherty (who fasted to death), in Cavan-Monaghan; and Paddy Agnew in Louth. PSF joined other anti-H-Block elements in that campaign, but PSF alone was unable to repeat these successes in the February, 1982, election. In NI, the hunger strike apparently brought Sinn Fein more lasting gains. In Fermanagh-S. Tyrone, it had backed PIRA hunger-striker Bobby Sands in his successful campaign in the April, 1981, by-election for Westminster. And a rank and file member of

PSF, Owen Carron, was elected as an abstentionist to fill the vacancy created by Sands' death. The October, 1982, Assembly election found PSF urging initially a boycott of the new institution and the election, but it also committed itself to fighting the election on an abstentionist ticket if a general Nationalist boycott could not be achieved. In the event, SDLP's decision to run candidates, but not to attend the Assembly, seems to have benefited PSF, which ran 12 candidates. Many Nationalists apparently saw PSF as representing a more dynamic boycott policy at a time when there was intense polarisation in the community. The outcome for PSF was highly gratifying in terms of its overall 10 per cent vote, but it might have expected to get more than the five seats which it actually won, since Alliance, with fewer votes, had got ten seats. Nonetheless, it was a breakthrough, and encouraged Sinn Fein to talk of fighting as many as possible of the 17 new Westminster seats. The first major controversy sparked off by the election came in December, 1982, when two of the successful PSF Assembly candidates, Gerry Adams (W. Belfast) and Danny Morrison (Mid-Ulster) were invited to London by GLC leader Ken Livingstone to explain their policies. Both were banned from Great Britain by Home Secretary William Whitelaw under the Prevention of Terrorism Act. The ban also applied to Derry Assembly member, Martin McGuinness. Mrs Thatcher claimed that the ban had been imposed for security and not political reasons. The

1983 Westminster election was broadly successful for PSF. It did not make a net advance in terms of seats, since it gained only W. Belfast and lost Fermanagh and S. Tyrone, but it achieved its target of 100,000 votes and had a percentage poll of 13.4 – three per cent more than in the 1982 Assembly election. It also failed by only 78 votes to win Mid-Ulster. The W. Belfast victory attracted attention for two reasons – it led to unseating of colourful MP, Gerry Fitt, who had held the seat for 17 years, and it was secured in face of strong warnings from the Catholic Church against supporting a group committed to backing PIRA violence.

PYM, FRANCIS LESLIE. Secretary of State for NI, November 1973–February 1974. b. 13 February 1922. Conservative MP for Cambridgeshire, 1961–. Defence Secretary, 1979–82;

Foreign Secretary, 1982–3. On taking office as Secretary of State, he was immediately plunged into the vital Sunningdale conference, but in the event, the Prime Minister, Mr Heath, and his predecessor as NI Secretary, William Whitelaw, were more directly involved in the negotiations which led to the setting up of the three-party power-sharing Executive on 1 January 1974. He was, however, involved in the Stormont ceremony of the swearing-in of the new Executive Members. Shortly afterwards, there was an IRA threat to kill him because he had interned a Derry man. He had no real opportunity to make his presence felt in NI since the Conservatives were defeated in the February 1974 general election, and he was succeeded by Labour's Merlyn Rees. In opposition, he was, successively, spokesman on devolution and foreign affairs.

R

RATHCAVAN, LORD (formerly PHELIM ROBERT HUGH O'NEILL). First Leader of the Alliance Parliamentary Party, 1972–3. b. 2 November 1909. One of Ulster's most individualist politicians, he switched from the Unionist Party to the Alliance Party shortly before direct rule was declared in 1972, and with two other MPs formed the first Alliance group at Stormont. The cousin of Terence O'Neill (Prime Minister, 1963–9) and son of first Lord Rathcavan, (first Speaker at Stormont and for many years MP for N. Antrim at

Westminster) Phelim O'Neill rarely toed the party line, and often treated Ministers scornfully in the former Stormont House of Commons. He described his politics as 'left-wing Conservative'. He was Unionist MP for N. Antrim at Westminster from 1952 to 1959, and Stormont MP for N. Antrim, 1969–72. He was Minister of Education in NI government in 1969 and Minister of Agriculture, 1969–71. He led the Alliance delegation at the Darlington conference in 1972. He was expelled from the Orange Order in 1958 after attending a Catholic service held during a community week in Ballymoney. He vigorously defended his decision to switch to Alliance. He said that whether they liked it or not, both the Unionists and the SDLP were sectarian parties. He succeeded to the title in 1982, when his father died aged 99.

REAGAN, RONALD. President of the US, 1981–. b. 6 February 1911. Another of the many US Presidents who can claim Irish ancestry. His great-grandfather, Michael O'Regan, left Ballyporeen, on the Tipperary-Cork border, during the Irish potato famine in the 1840s. The family went first to the Peckham area of London, and later to Illinois. Although his parents were married in a Roman Catholic Church in Fulton, Illinois, his Protestant mother brought him up in her faith. President Reagan has carefully avoided any deep entanglement with the Irish issue. Although the Republic's Prime Minister, Charles Haughey, was among St Patrick's Day lunch guests at the White House in 1981, the President did not endorse Mr Haughey's bid to make Irish unity a stated objective of US foreign policy. In his St. Patrick's Day statement, the President 'took note' of the violence and suffering in NI, and the importance to the US of a 'peaceful, just and swift solution'. He also urged all Americans to avoid giving money to groups where it might end up in the hands of those who were perpetuating violence. While welcoming the Anglo-Irish initiative, the President made it clear in a letter to Irish Prime Minister

Garret Fitzgerald on 1 December 1981, that his administration had no position on the question of Irish reunification. He said it was not for the US to chart a course others must follow, and that if solutions in NI were to endure, they must come from the people who lived there. President Reagan also appears to have taken no action on a plea by the Irish Government in July, 1981, that he should intervene with Britain over the H-Block hunger strike. In 1982, there appeared to be some difference of emphasis between Mrs Thatcher and the President over the Republic's role in NI. While the President saw it as having a role in a settlement, Mrs Thatcher insisted that Britain had no obligation to consult the Republic on NI affairs.

RED HAND COMMANDOS. A loyalist paramilitary group launched in 1972, and declared illegal in 1973 at the same time as the Ulster Freedom Fighters. It was believed by the security forces to be involved in sectarian assassinations. In April 1974, the RHC in Fermanagh and S. Tyrone sent a letter to a local newspaper saying that it would shoot five Roman Catholics for every Protestant killed in border areas. When Secretary of State Merlyn Rees met loyalist paramilitaries on 7 August 1974, it was stated that the UVF delegate also spoke for the proscribed RHC. It announced a ceasefire four days later, but said it reserved the right to defend loyalist lives and property. In a booklet published in November 1974, it said a sovereign Ulster parliament must protect the link with Great Britain. In January 1978, there was further evidence of its association with the UVF – a statement from a Prisoners' Council representing both organisations at the Maze Prison contained a threat not to do prison work if special category status was not restored. There was a telephone claim that it had murdered John McKeague, the E. Belfast loyalist, in January, 1982, but the INLA claim was generally accepted. McKeague always denied reports that he had been a founder member of the RHC.

REES, MERLYN. Secretary of State for NI, March 1974–September 1976. b. 18 December 1920. Labour MP for Leeds S., 1963–. When he arrived at Stormont, Merlyn Rees had been Labour Party spokesman on NI affairs for two years. He had been to NI with James Callaghan in 1969, and as a teacher he was familiar with Irish history. He was immediately faced with a crisis. The same February general election which had brought Labour to office and Rees to Stormont had also given the UUUC eleven of the twelve NI seats at Westminster. And the loyalists were not slow to claim the result as a landslide against the whole existence of the new three-party power-sharing Executive at Stormont which had taken office on 1 January. For the UUUC were pledged to fight the Sunningdale agreement, on which the Executive was based. Their main slogan was 'Dublin is just a Sunningdale away', indicating their opposition not only to Unionists joining the SDLP in government, but to any

cross-border Council of Ireland. With nearly 60 per cent of all votes secured by anti-White Paper candidates, and more than 50 per cent of these by loyalists alone, it was easy for the UUUC to present the outcome as a vote of no-confidence in the Executive. At the same time, the PIRA stepped up its bombing campaign, and made it more difficult for Mr Rees to accelerate the phasing out of internment. Then, on 13 May 1974, he faced his biggest test. Loyalists, led by the Ulster Workers' Council, which brought together politicians and paramilitary leaders, as well as some key shop stewards, mounted what they called a 'constitutional stoppage'. With loyalist paramilitary groups backing the strike, together with power workers, much of industry came to a standstill. And, with many accusations of intimidation directed against the strikers, Mr Rees was under intense pressure to use troops to keep power stations going and to maintain essential supplies. The Executive, whose morale was already shaken by the election result, was urging Mr Rees to adopt a much tougher line against the strikers. But while he refused to negotiate with the strike organisers, Mr Rees and the British government were obviously cautious about using the army directly to help break the strike. And this attitude clearly reflected the senior army view that 'the game wasn't worth the candle'. Mr Rees also appears to have been doubtful about the capacity of the Executive to survive in any event. And with vital services, particularly sewerage, threatened, the Unionist members resigned on the fifteenth day of the strike, and direct rule was resumed. The Secretary of State told MPs that NI now needed a breathing space. He also called the loyalists 'Ulster Protestant Nationalists'. On 4 July 1974, Mr Rees announced a new initiative – an elected Constitutional Convention to work out a political settlement. And during that summer he resisted strong pressure from Unionists for a new 'Home Guard' or 'Third Force' to supplement the efforts of the RUC and UDR. In mid-September he had talks with the Dublin government aimed at improving cross-border security co-operation. But the SDLP were clearly unhappy with Mr Rees; the party's deputy leader, John Hume, said in October that he had lost all credibility. In November 1974, came the horrific Birmingham public-house bombings in which nineteen people died and 182 were injured. Mr Rees was immediately involved in bringing in the new Prevention of Terrorism legislation so far as it affected NI. The effect was to allow people to be deported from Britain to both the Republic and NI and after protests that this would turn NI into a 'Devil's Island', Mr Rees took power to expel people from NI to the Republic. There was also power to hold a suspect for seven days without charge. Oddly enough, the tightening of security laws coincided with a meeting in early December 1974 between Churchmen and Provisionals (both IRA and Sinn Fein) at Feakle, Co. Clare – a meeting which was kept secret until it had ended and which was widely criticised by loyalists. But it offered

Mr Rees a pause in the IRA violence. After a brief stop over Christmas, the Provisionals declared a ceasefire on 10 February 1975. The Feakle talks had produced a document which the Churchmen involved conveyed to Mr Rees. But Mr Rees insisted that the IRA demands (including a call for a declaration of intent of British withdrawal) would not be considered by the government, although 'a genuine and sustained cessation of violence over a period would create a new situation'. Nonetheless, the ceasefire got a degree of official co-operation. Mr Rees authorised the setting up of seven 'incident centres' manned by Provisionals so that they could make contact easily with government officials. The purpose was to prevent a small incident developing into a threat to the ceasefire. But the exercise was regarded with great suspicion by loyalists, and the army, apparently, weren't happy about it either. The Secretary of State was evidently activated by the hope that the Provisionals might become 'politicised' as a result of the facility, which he had also granted them, of direct talks, if not negotiations, with government officials. But the Provisionals showed no interest in the Convention elections in 1975, and more importantly, these elections gave the UUUC a decisive overall majority. This ruled out any prospect of a repeat of the power-sharing experiment. By the summer of 1975, the IRA ceasefire was no more than a technicality. The overall total of deaths in 1975 was 247. This included an estimated 144 deaths arising from inter-factional or sectarian assassinations, many of them carried out by loyalists. However, in the last days of 1975 Mr Rees set free the last of those detained without trial. And in 1976 he witnessed the final collapse of the Constitutional Convention, and the death toll increased yet again. In September Mr Rees moved to the post of Home Secretary, and was succeeded by the Defence Secretary, Roy Mason. As Shadow Home Secretary in August, 1979, he declared that PIRA could not be defeated militarily, and that any attempt to reintroduce internment would be 'a grave error of judgment.' Under Michael Foot's leadership he was initially Shadow Energy Minister and in 1982, took up the new Shadow Cabinet post of industry and employment co-ordinator.

REFORMS. The changes which have taken place outside the security field as a consequence of the civil rights campaign and the developing situation, include: The closing down of the former Stormont parliament in March 1972, and the introduction of direct rule from Westminster (interrupted only by the five-month tenure of the NI Executive in 1974); the acceptance of the principle of one man, one vote and the use of PR for all elections except those for Westminster; the dismantling of the system of local government (with county boroughs, county councils, and borough, urban and rural councils) and its replacement by area boards to cover health, education, libraries, etc, with twenty-six district councils with very limited powers; the set-

ting up of a central Housing Executive to look after all public housing, which was formerly split between councils and a public Housing Trust; the establishment of a Community Relations Department and Community Relations Commission (both subsequently dropped); the appointment of a Standing Commission on Human Rights, and the creation of an Ombudsman and Commissioner of Complaints to inquire into charges of maladministration by government departments and other public bodies (the posts have been merged); the setting up of a Fair Employment Agency to guard against religious or political discrimination in employment. In 1980, divorce laws were brought into line with those in GB, and in 1982 the laws on homosexuality were treated similarly after they had been condemned by the European Court of Human Rights. The effect of the latter change was to remove the total ban on male homosexuality, and this reform failed to get the support of any of the NI MPs. The DUP strongly campaigned against a change, and the Catholic Church also voiced opposition to the new laws.

REID, RICHARD. DUP Convention member for Mid-Ulster, 1975–6. b. 1922. Cookstown District Council, 1973–. Founder member of the DUP.

RELIGION. There are scores of religious sects in NI, but the 1981 Census figures provided less information about the religious breakdown than the previous Census in 1971. On that occasion just under 10 per cent of the population did not disclose their religion, but the 1981 figures for Belfast showed 20.6 per cent of people in the city refusing to answer the question and 18 per cent for the whole of NI. In 1971, the NI totals for the largest denominations were: Roman Catholic, 477,919 (31.4 per cent); Presbyterian, 405,719 (26.7 per cent); Church of Ireland, 334,318 (22.0 per cent); Methodist, 71,235 (4.7 per cent); Baptist, 16,563 (1.1 per cent); Brethren, 16,480 (1.1 per cent); Congregationalist, 10,072 (0.7 per cent); Free Presbyterians (Church headed by Rev Ian Paisley), 7,337 (0.48 per cent); and Unitarians, 3,975 (0.2 per cent). The 1981 Census returns for Belfast produced more than 70 denominations and sects, with more than 60,000 failing to state any affiliation, and 328 describing themselves as agnostics and 255 as atheists. The overall Belfast figures showed about two-thirds Protestant, and one-third Catholic. The main figures were: Roman Catholic, 77,037; Presbyterian, 59,673; Church of Ireland, 58,987; Methodist, 17,473. The other 21,000 were distributed among a great variety of minor and mainly Protestant sects, but including 344 Jews and 131 Hindu. For the province as a whole, 414,532 gave their religion as Catholic, while the figures for the main Protestant denominations were: Presbyterian, 339,818; Church of Ireland, 281,472; and Methodist, 58,731. Other denominations totalled 112,822. Population experts reckoned that the Catholic percentage had now risen to around 39. But there were doubts as to whether the question on religion would be repeated in the next Census. Health Minister John Patten commented that the information obtained on religion was of very little value in the light of public response.

REPUBLICAN CLUBS. See WORKERS' PARTY.

REPUBLICAN LABOUR PARTY. Founded in Belfast in 1960, mainly on the initiative of Gerry Fitt, then MP for Dock at Stormont. It supported a non-violent republicanism, linked to socialist objectives, and when Fitt was elected to Westminster for W. Belfast in 1966, he supported the British Labour Party in the lobbies. Its activities were almost entirely confined to Belfast. Mr Fitt was joined at Stormont by the MP for Falls, Harry Diamond, who had represented the constituency under various labels, including Eire Labour and Socialist Republican. But in the 1969 general election, Diamond lost his seat to Paddy Devlin of the NILP – a loss compensated for by Paddy Kennedy's gain of the Belfast Central seat. In that election, the RLP ran five candidates, and got 2.4 per cent of the total vote. The party was active in the civil rights campaign, but it split in 1970 when Fitt assumed the leadership of the newly-formed SDLP. When Kennedy withdrew from Stormont in 1971, the party also withdrew its six councillors from Belfast Corporation, and it was heavily engaged in the civil disobedience campaign directed against internment without trial. Kennedy's failure to win a seat in

W. Belfast in the 1973 Assembly election marked the disappearance of the RLP as an effective force.

RICHARDS, SIR (FRANCIS) BROOKS. NI Security Co-ordinator, 1980–2. b. 18 July 1918. Cambridge University. After a long career in Diplomatic Service, Sir Brooks was Deputy Secretary in Cabinet Office, 1978–80. Second holder of NI security post, succeeding late Sir Maurice Oldfield, former head of MI6.

RICHARDSON, SIR ROBERT FRANCIS. Army GOC, NI, 1982–. b. 2 March 1929. Commanded 39 Infantry Brigade in NI, 1974–5. Army's director of manning, 1980–1. In March, 1983, he said it was important to reduce the role of the army to the point where it was seen by everyone as supporting the civil power, and not the visible embodiment of that power.

ROBB, JOHN. Founder of the New Ireland Group in 1982, and earlier the New Ireland Movement. Irish Senator, 1982–. b. 1932. As a Protestant Ulsterman and a surgeon at the Royal Victoria Hospital in Belfast in the early 1970s, he was so moved by the results of the bombing that he began campaigning for a new approach to local problems. His proposals have included a period of negotiated independence for NI, so that North and South, as equals, could seek to work out a new relationship to each other and to Britain. He has also suggested separate referenda in GB and in the Republic to show their real attitudes to NI. He says he was greatly influenced by the philosophy of Gandhi during a visit to India and by seeing Mother Teresa of Calcutta visiting a Belfast woman blinded by the violence and who was the mother of eight children. His appointment by Charles Haughey to the Irish Senate in April, 1982, caused some surprise, and one of his first acts there was to call for cross-border extradition arrangements. In the same year, he was chairman of the New Ireland Group, launched on a broader basis than the NIM. Member of RTE Authority, 1973–7.

ROBINSON, PETER DAVID. Deputy leader of the DUP; MP for E. Belfast, 1979–. Assembly member for E. Belfast, 1982–. b. 1948. His career has epitomised the rise of the DUP. In 1975, he became general secretary of the party and was an unsuccessful candidate that year in the Convention election in E. Belfast. But two years later, he was on Castlereagh Council, and in 1979 gained a surprise victory in E. Belfast at the Westminster election, when he unseated William Craig, Off. U., by 64 votes in a five-cornered fight. He became deputy to the Rev. Ian Paisley in 1980, and has enthusiastically supported the various DUP campaigns, notably against Anglo-Irish talks in early 1981, and at the end of that year when he was associated with the 'third force' and demands for tougher security. With his two party colleagues, he was suspended from the Commons in December, 1981, in the row arising from the assassination of the Rev. Robert Bradford, MP. In the 'rolling devolution' controversy in 1982, he was a staunch supporter of the first phase of the Assembly – that is, its scrutiny powers – and he headed the poll in E. Belfast in the Assembly election. In the Assembly, he became first chairman of the Environment Committee.

RODGERS, MRS BRID. General Secretary of SDLP, 1981–. Irish Senator 1983–. Party chairman, 1978–80. Advisory Commission on Human Rights, 1977–80. Formerly on Southern Education and Library Board.

ROSE, PAUL BERNARD. Labour MP for Blackley, Manchester (1964–79.) and chairman of the Campaign for Democracy in Ulster, 1965–73. b. 26 December 1935. LL.B. Hons. (Manchester). He led many deputations of MPs to see Ministers in the early days of the civil rights campaign, and frequently visited NI on fact-finding trips. In 1973, he resigned as chairman of CDU, since he believed that the Government White Paper met the immediate aims of the campaign.

ROSS, STEPHEN. Liberal Party spokesman on NI, June 1979–. b. 1926. Liberal MP for Isle of Wight, February 1974–.

ROSS, WILLIAM. Off. U. MP for East Londonderry, 1983–. MP for Londonderry, 1974–83. b. 4 February 1936. Farms at Dungiven, Co. Londonderry, and agricultural spokesman of the Off. U. Parliamentary Party, 1974–. Secretary of the local Unionist

Association before entering parliament. In April 1982, he resigned from the National Union of Conservative and Unionist Associations and three of its committees as a protest against James Prior's 'rolling devolution' initiative. He said it would force his party into 'unremitting opposition' to the Government in Parliament.

ROSSI, SIR HUGH ALEXIS LOUIS. Minister of State, NI Office, 1979–81. b. 21 June 1927. LL.B. (London). Solicitor. Knight of Holy Sepulchre, 1966. Conservative MP for Haringey, Hornsey, 1966–74. Government Whip, 1970–2. Europe Whip, 1971–3. Lord Commissioner of Treasury, 1972–4. Parliamentary Under-Secretary, Department of Environment, 1974. Deputy leader, UK delegation to Council of Europe, 1972–3. Opposition spokesman on housing and land, 1974–9. Responsible at NI Office for Finance and Manpower Services. On leaving the NI Office, he became Social Security Minister. He was dropped from the government after the June, 1983 election but given knighthood.

ROWNTREE TRUST. The Joseph Rowntree Social Service Trust has contributed substantially to help political parties and pressure groups in NI. Its total grants in 1974 amounted to £70,000. Some £11,000 of this went to the SDLP, including a contribution to the party's election expenses in October 1974. The Alliance Party, NILP and the New Ulster Movement have also been helped, and the Trust assisted the loyalist paramilitaries to finance a conference in Belfast in 1975, and contributed to the expenses of paramilitary delegates attending an Oxford conference on NI in 1974. Some payments have been made to individuals and Merlyn Rees MP, as shadow NI Secretary, got a fellowship to enable him to employ a special adviser.

ROYAL BLACK INSTITUTION. Effectively the senior branch of the Orange Order. Its full title is the Imperial Grand Black Chapter of the British Commonwealth. Like the Orange Order, it has a substantial membership outside NI, including lodges in Great Britain, the USA, Canada, Australia, New Zealand and various African countries. Its headquarters are at Lurgan, Co. Armagh, and its sovereign Grand Master is James Molyneaux MP,

leader of the Off. U. MPs at Westminster. Its main demonstrations are staged on the last Saturday of August each year, when some 30,000 members parade with bands and banners. The 'Blackmen', as they are commonly termed, also sponsor an event on 13 July each year – the 'sham fight' at Scarva, Co. Armagh – when a colourful mock battle is staged between 'King William' and 'King James'. Although there are few political speeches at its demonstrations, it is just as committed as the Orange Order generally to Unionism and defence of Protestantism.

ROYAL ULSTER CONSTABULARY. See Security Section (p. 305).

RUBBER BULLET. See Security Section (p. 315).

S

SANDELSON, NEVILLE DEVONSHIRE. SDP spokesman on NI, 1981-3. b. 27 November 1923. MP for Hayes and Harlington, 1971–83. (Lab., 1971–81; SDP, 1981–3.) Has visited NI for talks with local parties and to attend annual party conferences.

SANDS, ROBERT (BOBBY). Anti-H-Block MP for Fermanagh and S. Tyrone, April-May, 1981. b. Rathcoole, Belfast, 1954; died on hunger strike in Maze prison, 5 May 1981, on 66th day of his fast in support of the demand for political status or the 'five demands' (see H-BLOCKS). He was the

first of ten Republican prisoners to die during the protest. In 1972, Sands' family moved from Rathcoole to Twinbrook, on the fringe of W. Belfast, and are said to have been forced by loyalists to move home. He was sentenced in 1973 to five years' imprisonment on an arms charge, and had special category status in the Maze prison until his release in April, 1976. Soon afterwards, he and three others were found in a car with weapons. In 1977, he was sentenced to 14 years' imprisonment, and alleged that he had been subjected to ill-treatment while being interrogated at Castlereagh. He immediately joined PIRA prisoners protesting against the denial of special category status, and during the 1980 hunger strike became leader of the PIRA prisoners in the H-Blocks. On 1 March 1981 he began his fast 'unto death' in support of political status, and the readiness of some 30,000 voters in Fermanagh and S. Tyrone to give him a majority in the April by-election (see Elections Section) gave a new spur to Republicanism, and the emotions stirred by his death found an echo in many countries. Many politicians and churchmen sought to persuade him to end his fast, among them Monsignor John Magee, Newry-born emissary of Pope John Paul II, who gave Sands a crucifix sent by the Pope. Westminster moved quickly to prevent another hunger-striker being nominated for the by-election following his death.

SANDY ROW. Ultra-loyalist area close to central Belfast, usually linked with the Shankill Road as denoting militant Protestantism. During the 1969 violence, local people put up barricades at the Boyne Bridge to prevent, they said, republicans entering from the nearby Grosvenor Road area. Some bomb damage was caused to pubs and other premises in the main thoroughfare. The area will be altered radically if road development plans are carried out.

SAOR EIRE. This name appeared originally in Dublin in 1931 as the title of a strongly left-wing republican group, which was declared illegal for a time in Southern Ireland. It had some support from the IRA at the time. The name emerged again in the early 1960s as the Saor Eire Action Group, and it was blamed for many bank raids in the Republic in 1966 and 1967. In 1971, a Marxist journal, *Red Mole*, carried what purported to be a statement from Saor Eire strongly criticising Official republican movement. It said that Saor Eire had been formed by former members of the republican movement and the political left. It also said that many so-called left wingers were divesting the republican movement of its revolutionary potential by dismantling and undermining its armed wing. In 1973, there were claims of a threat by its Derry unit to avenge sectarian murders by loyalists. In the same year, there were reports of misappropriation of funds by some of its leaders. In 1975, it was credited with a threat to take action against either the IRSP or the OIRA if those two groups did not cease their feud in Belfast. The group has been regarded by the security forces in NI as a minor element in the violence, and they questioned a claim that it was responsible for killing some members of the security forces in 1972.

SCARMAN TRIBUNAL. The inquiry body which investigated the riots and shootings in the summer of 1969. Mr Justice Scarman presided, and he was assisted by two NI businessmen − William Marshall, Protestant, and George Lavery, a Catholic. It heard 400 witnesses at 170 sittings. It reported in April 1972, that there was no plot to overthrow the NI government or to mount an armed insurrection. The riots were described as communal disturbances arising from a complex political, social and economic situation. It also said that while there was no conspiracy, it would be the height of naiveté to deny that the teenage hooligans who almost invariably threw the first stones were manipulated and encouraged by those seeking to discredit the government. The tribunal found that the RUC was seriously at fault on six occasions. It said there was lack of firm direction in handling the disturbances in Derry during the early evening of 12 August; in the decision to put the USC on riot control in Dungannon and Armagh without disarming them; and in the use of Browning machine guns in Belfast on 14 and 15 August. It described as 'wholly unjustifiable' the firing of a Browning gun into Divis Flats, on the Falls Road, where Patrick Rooney, aged nine, had been shot dead. The RUC were also blamed for failing to prevent Protestant mobs from burning the homes of Catholics in Belfast, and for failure to take any effective action to disperse or protect lives and property in the riot areas on 15 August before the army came in. The tribunal said the RUC did, however, struggle manfully to do their duty in a situation they could not control, and their courage had been beyond praise. The report added: 'Once large-scale communal disturbances occur, they are not susceptible to control by police. Either they must be suppressed by overwhelming force which, save in the last resort, is not acceptable in our society – and

it was not within the control of the NI government – or a political solution must be devised.' The tribunal cleared the RUC of the charge that it was a partisan force co-operating with Protestant mobs to attack Catholics. But it added that the incidents in W. Belfast on 14 August had resulted in a complete loss of confidence by the Catholic community in the police force as it was then constituted. The USC was said to have neither the training nor the equipment for riot duty, and outside Belfast it had shown on several occasions a lack of discipline with firearms. The tribunal found that politicians opposed to the government, and specifically the Rev. Ian Paisley, had not been implicated in the violence, although their speeches had helped to build up tension. It found that the Protestant and Catholic communities had exhibited the same fears, the same sort of self-help, and the same distrust of lawful authority.

SCOTT, NICHOLAS PAUL. Parliamentary Under-Secretary, NI Office, 1981–. b. 1933. Cons. MP for Chelsea, 1974–. MP for Paddington S., 1966–74. Parliamentary Under-Secretary, Employment, 1974. In the NI Office he took charge of security and education, and faced a variety of problems, including controversy over the future of the Catholic teacher training colleges and opposition to school closures. He also announced the merger of the New University of Ulster and the Ulster Polytechnic. He campaigned for greater contacts between the State system of education (mainly Protestant) and the voluntary (largely Catholic).

SEAWRIGHT, GEORGE. DUP Assembly member for N. Belfast, 1982–. Belfast City Council, 1981–. Elected to 1982 Assembly on slogan: 'A Protestant candidate for a Protestant people.'

SHANKILL DEFENCE ASSOCIATION. A loyalist vigilante group formed in the Shankill Road area of Belfast in the violent summer of 1969. It was under the chairmanship of John McKeague, and soon claimed a membership of 1,000. Its members, armed on occasion, were involved in clashes in areas adjoining the Falls Road, and according to the Scarman report, it was 'active in assisting Protestant families to move out of Hooker Street, and there is evidence, which we accept, that it encouraged Catholic families to move out of Protestant streets south of the Ardoyne'. On 2 August 1969 it was claimed by the security forces that SDA members had set up a cordon round the Unity flats complex, occupied by Catholics, and had tried to force their way into the flats after reports that Junior Orangemen had been attacked in the area. Petrol bombs were used in the rioting which followed, and the SDA was particularly critical of the use by the RUC of water cannon. They gave a warning that the people of the Shankill wouldn't have any further confidence in the RUC. And the UCDC, headed by the Rev. Ian Paisley, denied that either the UCDC or the UPV had any connection with the SDA. Many members of the SDA were believed to be members of the USC. And when the Hunt report was published on 10 October 1969, recommending the replacement of the USC by a new part-time force under the army GOC, the SDA called for the resignation of the Chichester-Clark government, and said the time was fast approaching when responsible leaders of the SDA would not be able to restrain the 'backlash of outraged loyalist opinion'. The following night there was serious rioting on the Shankill Road, and the RUC suffered its first casualty when Constable Victor Arbuckle was shot dead. In November 1969 the SDA chairman, John McKeague (see separate entry), was cleared of a charge of conspiracy to cause explosions.

SHANKILL ROAD. The Belfast area which is considered to be the major stronghold of Ulster loyalists. Over the years, it has been a bastion of Unionism, and during the violence Unionism of the more militant varieties. Organisations like the UVF and the UDA have drawn much of their support from the Shankill. In 1969, there were serious riots in the area, and the Peace Line was erected between the Shankill and the adjoining (Catholic) Falls Road to prevent confrontations between hostile crowds. By a strange irony, the first RUC man to be shot dead (Constable Victor Arbuckle) was killed during a riot on the Shankill Road in October 1969, when loyalists demonstrated against the government's acceptance of the Hunt report on the reorganisation of the RUC. The character of the area has been greatly affected by demolition of the older streets and rehousing, and in 1978, the UVF was threatening to prevent further demolition.

SHAW, JOHN GILES DUNKERLEY. Parliamentary Under-Secretary. NI Office, 1979–81. b. 1931. M.A. (Cantab.). President of the Union, 1954. Marketing director, Rowntree Mackintosh Ltd., 1970–4. Conservative MP for Pudsey, February 1974. Responsible at NI Office for the departments of Commerce and Agriculture.

SHILLINGTON, SIR GRAHAM. Chief Constable of the RUC, 1970–3. b. Portadown, Co. Armagh, 1911. When he took charge of the RUC, he had been Deputy Chief Constable for nearly two years, and had been concerned with the reorganisation of the force as a consequence of the Hunt report. Earlier, he had been RUC City Commissioner in Belfast. His appointment as Chief Constable was welcomed by Unionists, but questioned by civil rights supporters. His tenure of office as Chief Constable covered the introduction of internment and the violence which followed direct rule. He had to cope with a high level of sectarian assassinations, and his term of office was marked by close collaboration of RUC and army in joint patrols.

SHORT STRAND. A mainly Catholic enclave in predominantly Protestant E. Belfast. In the early days of the troubles, notably in 1972, there were clashes between Protestants and Catholics, and occasionally serious riots on the fringes of the district, where IRA supporters tended to pursue an independent course.

SILENT TOO LONG. An organisation established in 1981 of relatives of innocent Catholic victims of violence. It claimed that the deaths of 600 such victims had been virtually ignored by the authorities.

SILKIN, SAMUEL CHARLES. Attorney-General for England and NI, 1974–9. b. 6 March 1918. QC and Labour MP for Dulwich, 1964–83. Founder member and chairman of the Society of Labour Lawyers, 1964–71.

SIMPSON, FREDERICK VIVIAN. NILP MP for Oldpark, 1958–72. b. Dublin, 23 August 1903. Draper and footwear merchant in Carrickfergus, where he served in local council, 1947–58. Methodist lay preacher. Died 1977.

SIMPSON, MRS MARY. Off. U. Assembly member for Armagh, 1982–. Craigavon Council, 1977–. Mayor of Craigavon, 1981–2. Hon. Sec., Central Armagh Unionist Association, 1974–.

SIMPSON, DR ROBERT. First Minister of Community Relations, 1969–71, the appointment being part of the reform package arising from the visit of James Callaghan as Home Secretary. On taking office, Dr Simpson resigned from the Masonic and Orange Orders. b. Ballymena, 3 July 1923. M.B. B.Ch., B.A.O.

(QUB). Unionist MP for Mid-Antrim, 1952–72. Has written extensively on travel, holiday and medical topics.

SIX COUNTIES. A term sometimes used to describe Northern Ireland, particularly in Nationalist newspapers.

SMITH, SIR HOWARD FREDERICK TRAITON. Last UK government representative, NI, 1971–2. b. 15 October 1919. He was the last holder of an office which extended from 1969 until the introduction of Direct Rule in March 1972. His main activity was in the crucial period leading up to direct rule, including 'Bloody Sunday' in Londonderry. He arrived in NI from Czechoslovakia, where he had been Ambassador, and he became Ambassador to Moscow in 1976.

SMYTH, CLIFFORD A. DUP Assembly and Convention member for N. Antrim, b. Londonderry, 1944. B.A. (QUB) Chairman, QUB Conservative and Unionist Association, 1971. He was elected to the Assembly in June 1974, after it had already been prorogued, heading the poll in the by-election. In the Convention, he was secretary of the UUUC. In 1977 he returned to the OUP (as a student he had been secretary of the Young Unionist Council) and unsuccessfully contested N. Down in 1979 Westminster election.

SMYTH, HUGH. Independent Unionist Assembly (1973–4) and Convention (1975–6) member for W. Belfast. b. Shankill, Belfast, 1941. Belfast City Council, 1972–. Deputy Lord Mayor, 1983. Heavily involved in political and welfare work in the Shankill area, he was one of the founders of the Loyalist Front, which was active in 1974, and which had the support of the UVF. After the 1974 loyalist strike, he claimed that loyalist leaders had only shown their hand when they were sure that the strike was going to succeed, and that in future the decisions must be taken by the workers. He helped to found the short-lived Volunteer Political Party – political arm of the UVF – and in 1978 he was appointed leader of the Belfast-based Independent Unionist Group which became Progressive Unionist Party in 1979. Unsuccessful candidate in W. Belfast in the 1982 Assembly election.

SMYTH, REV. (WILLIAM) MARTIN. Off. U. MP for S. Belfast, 1982–. Grand Master of the Orange Order in Ireland, 1972–. b. Belfast, 1931. Originally joined junior Orange lodge in Sandy Row area of Belfast, and for 10 years (1972–82) combined his career as a Presbyterian minister (Alexandra church in N. Belfast) with leadership of the Orange Order and the post of vice-president of the Council of the OUP. During that period, he was Imperial Grand Master of the Orange Order as well as head of the Order in Ireland. On his election as MP for S. Belfast in the Feb., 1982 by-election (created by the assassination of his predecessor as MP, the Rev. Robert Bradford), he resigned his church ministry and the post of Imperial

Grand Master of the Orange Order. He also suggested that he should give up the post of Irish Grand Master, but was persuaded by Orange colleagues to remain. He made his first election bid in the Convention election of 1975, and headed the poll in S. Belfast. When the Convention broke up, he incurred some criticism from Unionists for taking part in secret, but unsuccessful talks with the SDLP, represented by John Hume and Paddy Devlin, in an attempt to break the political deadlock. He worked closely with OUP leader James Molyneaux when he became the party's director of information in 1979, and his win in the 1982 by-election in S. Belfast was psychologically important for his party since it seemed to mark a halt to the loss of electoral ground to the DUP. He has voiced his 'dream' that the 26 counties of the Irish Republic might eventually return to the UK. He has also expressed the hope that the Independent Orange Order might unite with the main body of Orangeism. First chairman of 1982 Assembly's health and social services committee.

SOCIAL DEMOCRATIC PARTY. A local forum of the SDP in NI claimed in 1982 that it was the only major national party recruiting members in NI. The forum, which did not have the status of a branch of the party, said the SDP could help to break the rigid mould of politics in the province. One of its founders, Mrs Shirley Williams, took a special interest in NI affairs when she was on Labour's NEC, and sometimes spoke for the Executive on the subject. On a visit to Dublin in April, 1982, she described the response of the SDLP and the Republic's Government to the Prior initiative as 'disappointing.' In Parliament, the SDP gave general support to the 'rolling devolution' initiative although it had not at that time formulated a detailed NI policy. In the 1983 election campaign, Dr David Owen protested that NI had been 'put on the back-burner of British politics.'

SOCIAL DEMOCRATIC AND LABOUR PARTY. The party which speaks for the majority of Catholics in Northern Ireland. Founded on 21 August 1970, it absorbed most of the supporters of the old Nationalist Party, National Democratic Party and Republican Labour Party, and served to weaken the appeal of the NILP. It is a member of the Socialist International and the Confederation of Socialist Parties of the European Community. The party was lauched by seven Stormont politicians – Gerry Fitt MP, then Republican Labour, who became party leader; three Independent MPs, who had been prominent in the civil rights campaign – John Hume, Ivan Cooper and Paddy O'Hanlon – Austin Currie, a Nationalist MP; Paddy Devlin, NILP MP; and Paddy Wilson, Republican Labour Senator, who was to become a murder victim. It was put forward as a radical, left-of-centre party, which would seek civil rights for all and just distribution of wealth. It would work to promote friendship and understanding between North and South, with a view to the eventual unity of Ireland, through the consent of the majority of the people, North and South. The SDLP's first major move was to withdraw from Stormont in July 1971. It stated that it was withdrawing its consent from the institutions of government. With the introduction of internment without trial in August 1971 it sponsored a civil disobedience campaign, involving the withholding of rents and rates. In the autumn of 1971, it was involved in the Assembly of the Northern Irish People – the unofficial 'Dungiven Parliament'. The imposition of direct rule in 1972, with the suspension of Stormont, gave it the opportunity to suggest new forms of government. In *Towards a New Ireland*, it proposed a form of condominium, with Britain and the Republic exercising joint sovereignty over NI. There would be an Assembly elected by PR, but legislation would have to be approved by two commissioners appointed by the British and Irish governments. The Executive would be elected by the Assembly, also by PR. The party also called for a declaration by Britain in favour of Irish unity, and the setting up of a 'National Senate' by the Assembly and the Dail to plan progress towards a united Ireland. The SDLP opted out of the Darlington conference, organised in September 1972 by Secretary of State William Whitelaw, despite an appeal by Mr Heath. But it took comfort from the government's Green Paper, which urged power-sharing between the communities and an Irish Dimension, and it supported the White Paper

which followed. Its Assembly election manifesto, *A New North, a New Ireland*, stressed partnership government and a cross-border Council of Ireland, which could encourage unity within the EEC context. In the Assembly election, the SDLP got nineteen of the seventy-eight seats, and 22.1 per cent of first-preference votes. It had four seats in the 1974 power-sharing Executive, including that of Deputy Chief Executive, held by Gerry Fitt. The collapse of the Executive as a result of the loyalist strike was a serious blow to the party. It angrily blamed the British government for failing to tackle the paramilitary groups backing the stoppage. In its Convention manifesto, *Speak with Strength,* it stuck to the main points of its policy, with perhaps a shade less emphasis on the Irish dimension. It secured 23.7 per cent of first-preference votes but got only seventeen seats, two fewer than in the Assembly. The loyalist majority in the Convention showed no disposition to accept power-sharing other than in the framework of departmental committees. And since the UUUC rejected William Craig's plan for an emergency voluntary coalition, the SDLP was never called upon to declare its attitude to a scheme which fell short of full power-sharing and excluded a Council of Ireland. After the Convention was wound up, the party's deputy leader, John Hume, and Paddy Devlin had private exploratory talks with the Rev. Martin Smyth and Austin Ardill of the Official Unionists, but the exchanges were unproductive. With renewed direct rule, the SDLP became unhappy at what it saw as lack of effort by the British government to deal with 'loyalist intransigence'. It also saw evidence of a trend towards integration, with Westminster support for five extra NI MPs. In a policy statement, *Facing Reality*, endorsed at its 1977 conference, it urged an 'agreed Ireland – the essential unity of whose people would have evolved in agreement over the years, whose institutions of government would reflect both its unity and diversity, and whose people would live in a harmonious relationship with Britain'. Many Unionists regarded the statement as more angled towards a united Ireland than previous statements, but this was denied by party spokesmen. They also rejected the claim of Paddy Devlin that there was a move away from socialism, and Mr Devlin was expelled in the autumn of 1977. In 1978, the three major Dublin parties indicated that they would respond to a plea by John Hume that they should spell out precisely their ideas for Irish unity. In local government elections, the party has established a firm base. In the 1977 district council elections, it won 113 seats (20.6 per cent of first-preference votes) as compared with eighty-three seats in 1973. At its 1978 conference the party renewed its call for the British and Irish governments and both sides of the NI community to get together to work out a settlement, but its motion also referred to eventual British withdrawal as 'desirable and inevitable' and this point was seized on by Unionist critics. In the 1979 Westminster election, the party retained W.

Belfast, but did not come close to winning any other seat. Its Chief Whip, Austin Currie, resigned to fight, unsuccessfully, Fermanagh and S. Tyrone as Independent SDLP. In the 1979 European election, the party's deputy leader, John Hume, achieved a record vote for the party – nearly 25 per cent – in taking one of the three NI seats in the European parliament. The announcement of a Constitutional Conference by Secretary of State Humphrey Atkins in November, 1979, created a crisis for the party. The SDLP regarded the agenda as far too limited to produce a political settlement. Gerry Fitt immediately denounced its attitude and resigned from the party, claiming that it was losing its Socialism and becoming 'green Nationalist.' John Hume rejected the charge and succeeded Fitt as party leader. In the end, the SDLP did join the Stormont conference, after persuading the Secretary of State to set up a parallel meeting in which cross-border relations, security and the economy could be discussed. In the main conference, the party proposed a power-sharing administration in which places would be allocated in proportion to party strength. In the parallel conference it attacked Government policy, and when the main conference failed to produce agreement, it turned down a further Government idea of a 50-member Advisory Council. In the H-Block hunger strike, it called for concessions short of political status, but its proposals were rejected by the Government. During the hunger strike, it suffered some internal strains as a

215

result of its decision to stay out of the Fermanagh and S. Tyrone by-elections, and the Maze protest also hit its expectations in the 1981 council elections. Although it lost only a few council seats, its share of the poll dropped 3 per cent to 17.5 per cent. In 1982, the party came out strongly against the 'rolling devolution' plan, which it attacked as 'unworkable,' and it was firmly supported in this view by the Republic's Taoiseach, Charles Haughey, while the Fine Gael leader, Dr Fitzgerald, also expressed strong reservations about the British scheme. The SDLP went into the election, urging a 'Council for a New Ireland' to enable politicians from NI and the Republic to get together to discuss the implications of Irish unity. It also decided not to attend the Assembly. For the first time, it had to face competition from Provisional Sinn Fein candidates in strongly Nationalist areas, and in consequence its total of 14 Assembly seats was down on both the 1973 Assembly and the 1975 Convention. With just under 19 per cent of first preferences, its share of the vote was also down on previous Stormont elections, although an improvement on the 1981 council contests. It also lost one of its Assembly seats in Armagh when its deputy leader, Seamus Mallon, was unseated because of his membership of the Republic's Senate. At its 1983 conference, the party reaffirmed its opposition to the Assembly, and backed Mr Hume's call for it to meet the PSF challenge 'head on' and contest all 17 seats at the Westminster election. It implemented this decision and

fought on a platform of support for the Forum for a New Ireland (see separate entry). In the event, the 1983 election saw the party maintain its vote numerically in face of the PSF challenge in fourteen seats. But because of the larger poll and PSF competition, its percentage vote dropped to 17.9 and it secured only one seat, Foyle, won by John Hume.

SOCIALIST LABOUR PARTY. The Dublin-based party set up in November 1977, to promote the ideals of James Connolly. By early 1978, it had set up branches in Belfast and Londonderry. It grew out of the general election campaigns of Dr Noel Browne and Matt Merrigan in 1977.

SOLEY, CLIVE STAFFORD. Labour front-bench spokesman on NI, 1981–. B.A. (hons.) (Strathclyde); Dip., applied social services (Southampton). MP for Hammersmith W., 1979–. In January, 1983, he said that an all-Ireland economic council would be among measures which would be considered by a future Labour Government. He also suggested an all-Ireland court and police force to strengthen cross-border security.

SOUTH ARMAGH REPUBLICAN ACTION FORCE. An organisation which claimed many murders in S. Armagh, particularly in 1975. Regarded by the security forces as a 'flag of convenience' for some local PIRA units.

SPEAKER'S CONFERENCE. Conference headed by the

Speaker of the Commons, George Thomas MP, which reported in February 1978, that NI should have seventeen MPs at Westminster instead of twelve. It also suggested that the NI Boundary Commission should be free to vary this figure by one either way to facilitate drawing of boundaries. The conference represented all the Westminster parties, and included three NI MPs – Enoch Powell, James Molyneaux (Official Unionists) and Gerry Fitt (SDLP), who was alone in standing out against any increased representation. The NI Boundary Commission decided on seventeen seats, and the change took effect in the 1983 election.

SPECIAL AIR SERVICES. See Security Section (p. 310).

SPECIAL CATEGORY. The special status accorded to prisoners who were members of paramilitary organisations, as a result of a decision by William Whitelaw, Secretary of State, in June 1972, after a prolonged hunger strike by prisoners in Belfast prison. The privileges applied to prisoners sentenced to more than nine months imprisonment for offences related to the civil disturbances. Because of the lack of cell accommodation they were housed in compounds. They were not required to work, could wear their own clothes, and were allowed extra visits and food parcels. By 31 December 1974, the number of prisoners enjoying special category, or political status, had risen to 1,116, including fifty-one women. At that time there were 545 male special category

prisoners at the Maze Prison; 502 at Magilligan, Co. Derry, and eighteen in Belfast. The women were in Armagh prison. The prisoners were from both wings of the IRA and the various loyalist paramilitary groups, and the paramilitary organisations ran a prisoner-of-war type regime in the compounds, some of which had ninety prisoners each. The Gardiner committee, in 1975, came out against special category status. It said it meant virtually the loss of disciplinary control by the prison authorities. Merlyn Rees, as Secretary of State, announced the phasing out of special category as from 1 March 1976. This meant that no one convicted of an offence committed after that date was admitted to special category status and in 1980, Secretary of State Humphrey Atkins stopped all new admissions to special category. At the end of 1976, the total of special category prisoners was more than 1,500; by mid-1978 it had dropped to about 800. Prisoners who would normally have been placed in compounds were now put in cells, and eight new blocks, each with 100 cells, were built at the Maze prison. They became known as H-Blocks because of the layout, and were linked to recreational facilities, as well as special workshops and vocational training accommodation. But republican prisoners immediately made it clear they would refuse to co-operate with the removal of special status. They refused to wear prison clothing, and simply covered themselves with a blanket; hence the description of the protest as 'on the blanket'. With the British gov-

NORTHERN IRELAND – A POLITICAL DIRECTORY, 1968–83

ernment refusing to make any concessions to the protesters, the prisoners involved – they now numbered more than 300 – began to intensify their protest in March 1978. They refused to wash or use the toilets, and smashed up the furniture in their cells. This 'dirty protest' continued, with one interruption, until March, 1981, when it was dropped so as to focus attention on Bobby Sands' hunger strike. At the beginning of 1983, 230 prisoners at the Maze were still enjoying special category, and living in compounds. There were 105 in the PIRA-INLA compound, 12 OIRA, 67 UVF, and 46 UDA. See H-BLOCKS.

SPEERS, JAMES ALEXANDER (JIM). Off. U. Assembly member for Armagh, April, 1983–. b. 1946. Local official of Ulster Farmers' Union. Armagh Council, 1977–. Secretary, Mid and South Armagh Unionist Association, 1970–. Stood unsuccessfully in 1982 Assembly election in Armagh, but returned in April, 1983 by-election following disqualification of Seamus Mallon (SDLP).

SPENCE, AUGUSTUS ('GUSTY'). Best-known figure in the revived UVF, the illegal loyalist paramilitary group. b. Belfast, 1933. Like many UVF men, he had served in the army – with the Royal Ulster Rifles in Germany and later in Cyprus during the EOKA campaign. He was sentenced to life imprisonment in 1966 for shooting a young Catholic barman at a public house in Malvern Street in the Shankill Road area of Belfast. Soon after-

wards, the UVF was proscribed. He and his friends always insisted that he was innocent of the crime. On several occasions, he went on hunger strike to support his claim, and in 1972, when he was given parole to attend his daughter's wedding, UVF members 'kidnapped' him to draw attention to his case. Four months later, he was recaptured, but his friends said he had given himself up because of his heart condition. Among militant loyalists on the Shankill Road, he remained a local hero. Tea towels were produced with his portrait and facsimile. £5 notes were printed on which the Queen's head was replaced by Spence's. 'His only crime was loyalty,' was the slogan used by those who campaigned for his release. In 1977, as UVF commander inside the Maze Prison, he issued a message supporting reconciliation and attacking violence, which he said, could now be counter-productive. He believed that the loyalists had achieved their aim of self-determination. He was also reported to be learning Irish, and his general attitude was not welcomed by all UVF prisoners. In March, 1978, he resigned as UVF commander in the prison. A spokesman outside insisted that he had resigned for health reasons only.

STALLARD, LORD. Chairman of the Labour Party's backbench NI committee at Westminster, 1979–83. MP for Camden, St Pancras N., 1974–83. MP for St Pancras N., 1970–4. Minister of State (Housing), 1974–6. Government Whip, 1976–9.

STANDING ADVISORY COMMISSION ON HUMAN RIGHTS. An official body set up under the Constitution Act of 1973 to monitor the effectiveness of laws against discrimination on the grounds of religion or politics. The Commission has taken a highly independent line. In May, 1979, it recommended the Secretary of State to drop the power to intern without trial, and the provision was abandoned the following year. It has prompted widespread discussion on a possible Bill of Rights, and while it basically favours such a measure for the whole UK, it said in its 1980-1 report that there might be circumstances which would justify a Bill for NI alone. Earlier, it urged that the laws on divorce and homosexuality should be brought into line with those in Great Britain. The divorce reform took effect in 1979, but local opposition to dropping the ban on male homosexuality delayed this reform. The Callaghan Government failed to press on with an Order on reform, and despite the commitment by the Conservative administration to implement the finding of the European Court of Human Rights that the existing law was in breach of the European Convention, the change did not take effect until 1982. In 1981, the Commission was strongly critical of the change in electoral law passed in the wake of the election of hunger striker Bobby Sands as an MP and which prevented a convicted prisoner being nominated. The Commission said it was an infringement of the citizen's right to choose.

STORMONT. The seat of government in NI, on a commanding site about five miles from Belfast city centre. Comprises Parliament Buildings, Stormont Castle (Secretary of State's office), and Stormont House (residence of Speaker of NI Commons, but provided residential accommodation for British Ministers under Direct Rule). Parliament Buildings were designed by Sir Arnold Thornley in Greek classical style, and with exterior faced in Portland stone above a plinth of unpolished granite from the Mountains of Mourne. The building is 365 feet long, 164 feet wide, and rises to 92 feet.

STOWE, SIR KENNETH RONALD. Permanent Secretary, NI Office, October, 1979-81. b. 17 July 1927. MA (Oxon). Was principal private secretary to the Prime Minister, 1973-9, and in recognition of his work in arranging the Prime Minister's weekly audience with the Queen, he was made a Commander of the Victorian Order in 1979. During his earlier civil service career, he was seconded to the UN Secretariat in New York in 1958.

STRABANE. The Co. Tyrone border town often cited as an example of underdevelopment in W. Ulster. Its rate of unemployment has nearly always exceeded 25 per cent, and at the end of 1982 male unemployment was approaching 50 per cent. The town has suffered heavily from violence, and throughout the troubles there have been frequent allegations that PIRA has been able to operate from adjoining areas of Co. Donegal in the Republic. In the early 1980s there were suggestions that INLA also had bases in Donegal. In late 1982, there were many seizures of arms and explosives by Gardai in N. Donegal, some of them close to Strabane. The shooting dead of Unionist Senator Jack Barnhill by OIRA here in 1971 was one of the earliest political assassinations. In the early days of the civil rights campaign there were many rallies in the town. At one of these meetings in June, 1969, the differing approaches of political speakers underlined the difficulty of keeping the movement together as the reforms developed.

STRONGE, JAMES. Unionist, politician. b. 1933. Shot dead along with his father, Sir Norman Stronge, 86, ex-Speaker of the Stormont Commons, by PIRA, in Jan. 1981. They were killed at their home, Tynan Abbey, close to the border, and the house was destroyed by explosives which set it on fire. The PIRA admission described them as 'symbols of hated Unionism' and said the killings were a reprisal for Loyalist assassinations of Nationalist people. In the 1969 general election, James Stronge succeeded his father in the seat which Sir Norman had held for 31 years, and where he had been opposed only once. Mr Stronge was firmly against the Sunningdale agreement, which he described as 'a great act of political appeasement,' and he withdrew support from Brian Faulkner after Mr Faulkner had resigned the Unionist party leadership when he was defeated within the party on the Sunningdale terms.

SUNNINGDALE CONFERENCE. The conference between the British and Irish Governments and the three parties involved in the NI Executive held at the Sunningdale (Berks) Civil Service College, 6–9 December 1973. Agreement to set up the power-sharing Executive made up of the Unionists led by Brian Faulkner, the SDLP and the Alliance Party had been reached at talks at Stormont on 21 November 1973. The Sunningdale conference was intended to establish the political framework in which the new government would operate. A lengthy communique was issued after the talks, which usually extended late into the night, but the proposed formal conference to sign the agreement was never held, for in May 1974, the Executive collapsed in face of the UWC loyalist strike. The main points of the Sunningdale agreement may be summarised as follows:

1 The government of the Republic and the SDLP upheld their aspiration for a united Ireland, but only by consent. The Unionist and Alliance parties voiced the desire of the majority in NI to remain part of the UK.

2 The Irish government fully accepted and solemnly declared that there could be no change in the status of NI until a majority of the people of NI desired a change in that status.

3 The British government solemnly declared that it was, and would remain, their policy to support the wishes of the majority of the people of NI. The present sta-

tus of NI is that it is part of the UK. If in the future the majority of the people of NI should indicate a wish to become part of a United Ireland, the British government would support that wish.

4 Declarations to this effect by both governments would be registered at the United Nations.

5 A Council of Ireland would be set up, limited to representatives from both parts of Ireland, but with 'appropriate safeguards' for the British government's financial and other interests. The Council of Ministers, which must make decisions by unanimous vote, would have seven Ministers from either side, and there would also be a Consultative Assembly with an advisory role. The Assembly would have sixty members – thirty from the Dail and thirty from the NI Assembly. They would be elected by the members of each parliament, on PR by single-transferable vote. The Council would have a Secretary-General, and its own headquarters.

6 The Council was to have a wide range of functions, including the study of the impact of EEC membership, development of resources, agriculture and otherwise, co-operative ventures in the field of trade and industry, electricity generation, tourism, roads and transport, public health advisory services, sport, culture and the arts.

7 It was agreed by all parties that persons committing crimes of violence, however motivated, in any part of Ireland should be brought to trial, irrespective of the part of Ireland in which they were located. The conference discussed various approaches, including extradition, the creation of a common law enforcement area in which an all-Ireland court would have jurisdiction, and the extension of the jurisdiction of domestic courts so as to enable them to try offences committed outside the jurisdiction. Because of the legal complexity of the problems involved, it was agreed that the British and Irish governments should set up a Joint Law Commission to examine the various proposals. (In the event, this was the only point in the Sunningdale agreement which was jointly implemented. The Joint Law Commission's report led to reciprocal legislation, which permitted a person accused of a scheduled terrorist offence to be brought to trial on whichever side of the border he is arrested).

8 In the field of human rights, the Council of Ireland would consider what further legislation was needed.

9 On law and order and policing, it was broadly accepted that the two parts of Ireland were to a considerable extent interdependent, and that the problems of political violence and identification with the police service could not be solved without taking account of that fact.

10 Accordingly, the British government stated that, as soon as the security problems were resolved and the new institutions were seen to be working effectively, they would wish to discuss the devolution of responsibility for normal policing, and how this might be achieved, with the NI Executive and the police. The Irish Government agreed to set up a police authority and together with the NI

police authority, would consult with the Council of Ministers on appointments. The Secretary of State for NI undertook to set up an all-party committee of the Assembly to examine how best to introduce effective policing throughout NI.

11 The conference took note of the re-affirmation by the British government of its intention to bring detention without trial to an end as soon as the security situation permitted. The Prime Minister, Mr Heath, presided at the Sunningdale conference, travelling back and forth by helicopter to Chequers, his country home, where the Italian Prime Minister was his week-end guest. The Council of Ireland and policing were the crunch issues, and there is much evidence that Mr Faulkner's team were divided on the Council, and that strong pressure was brought to bear by Mr Heath to get quick agreement. The NI Secretary of State, Francis Pym, also attended, but since he had

only recently taken over at Stormont, his predecessor, William Whitelaw, exercised a bigger influence. The Irish team was headed by the Taoiseach, Liam Cosgrave, while the SDLP delegates were led by Gerry Fitt and the Alliance Party members by Oliver Napier. The loyalists opposed to the Sunningdale exercise – that is, the Unionists led by Harry West, the Rev. Ian Paisley and William Craig – were not invited to the talks. After Mr Paisley and Mr Craig had protested at this, they were invited to one session, but they rejected this as being inadequate. When the communiqué appeared they sharply attacked it, and in early January 1978, Mr Faulkner lost his battle to 'sell' Sunningdale to the Unionist Council, and Mr West took over as party leader. In Dublin, the Fianna Fail leader, Jack Lynch, gave the agreement a cautious welcome and hoped the Council of Ireland would turn out to have real powers.

T

TARA. A secret loyalist organisation which began as an anti-Catholic, anti-Communist pressure group in the mid-1960s, but which took on a paramilitary character with the outbreak of violence in 1969. It described itself as 'the hard core of Protestant resistance, and in a statement issued in August, 1971, it urged loyalists to organise themselves into platoons of twenty under the command of someone capable of acting as a sergeant. It said that every effort

must be made to arm these platoons with 'whatever weapons are available.' Its membership was drawn mainly from Orange ranks, and it disclaimed any connection with any other political or paramilitary group. It also said that the Roman Catholic Church should be declared illegal, and all its schools closed. Roy Garland, who was deputy commander of TARA, in an article in the *Irish Times* named its commander as William McGrath, who was jailed in 1981 for sexual offences against boys in his care at Kincora boys' home in East Belfast.

TARTAN GANGS. Gangs of Protestant youths who often wore tartan scarves in memory of the three young soldiers of the Royal Highland Fusiliers who were shot dead in Belfast on 10 March 1971. (Both the OIRA and PIRA denied responsibility for the murders). The tartan gangs were largely based in Protestant estates in the Belfast area. The slogan 'Tartan Rule OK' became common in 1971 and 1972, and they were active during the loyalist strike in 1974, when they were frequently accused of intimidation of shopkeepers and workers who wanted to stay at work. They co-operated with the UDA in the manning of barricades in loyalist areas. From time to time, they were involved in riots and in damage to Catholic-owned premises.

TAYLOR, JOHN DAVID. Off. U. MEP for NI, June 1979–. MP for Strangford, 1983. Assembly member for N. Down, 1982–. Minister of State, Home Affairs, 1970–2. b. Armagh, 24 December 1937. B.Sc (QUB). Joined Young Unionist movement at QUB and was youngest Stormont Unionist MP when returned for S. Tyrone in 1965. He was Parliamentary Secretary at Home Affairs, 1969–70. He was one of twelve Unionist MPs who, in February 1969, signed a statement saying that only a change of leadership from Terence O'Neill could unite the party. At Home Affairs, he was sometimes critical of the British government's approach to security and he was boycotted for a brief period by the SDLP when he was appointed to the Cabinet in August 1970. In 1972, the OIRA tried to assassinate him in Armagh City. In a hail of machine-gun bullets his jawbone was shattered, and he had to have extensive plastic surgery. As Assembly member for Fermanagh-S. Tyrone, 1973–4, he was a strong opponent of the Sunningdale agreement. At the meeting of the Ulster Unionist Council in January 1974, he moved the motion criticising the agreement and the plan for a cross-border Council of Ireland. The motion was carried and Brian Faulkner resigned as Unionist Party leader. On several occasions between 1972 and 1974, he mentioned the possibility of negotiated independence for NI, stressing that this was very different from UDI. In April 1974, he said that, apart from integration, this might be the only option open to loyalists. A prominent Orangeman, he told the 12 July demonstration in Belfast in 1974 that a new Home Guard should be set up, 'with or without London government legislation'. He was returned to the Convention in 1975 from N. Down, and after its collapse in 1976, he became Off. U. spokesman on the EEC. In the European election in June 1979, he was returned as one of the three MEPs from NI, but because of the poor showing of the OUP in the election, he had to wait until the sixth count, when he benefited from the lower preferences of the OUP leader, Harry West, who had been eliminated. He campaigned on the line that local issues should not be pursued in the European Assembly, and that there must be extensive re-negotiation of the EEC to help areas like NI. In the European Parliament, he joined British Conservatives in the European Democratic group, and as a member of the Parliament's regional committee urged greater EEC aid for NI. He also opposed discussion in the Parliament of constitutional and security issues affecting NI. In 1981, he urged his party to be 'more positive' about devolution, and when the OUP boycotted economic talks with Secretary of State James Prior, he insisted on attending. In January, 1982, he took part in 'Operation USA', a joint OUP-DUP mission to the US to present the Unionist viewpoint. When the 1982 Stormont Assembly held its initial sitting, he was described as 'father of the House', since he was the longest-serving member of Stormont institutions actually attending.

THATCHER, MRS MARGARET HILDA. British Prime Minister, 1979–. Leader of the Conservative Party, 1975–. b. 13 October 1925. As Conservative leader, she showed some anxiety to rebuild the links between the Conservative Party and the Official Unionists, shattered by the Heath Government's suspension of the NI parliament in 1972. On her third visit to NI as opposition leader in June 1978, she voiced strong support for the UK link. She said it was fashionable to talk of a federal Ireland, but it was a fashion her party did not intend to follow. She also expressed Conservative support for the restoration of a top tier of local gov-

ernment – one of the demands of Official Unionists. Her attitude was criticised by the SDLP and the British Liberals. The promise of a regional council or councils was contained in the Conservative manifesto in 1979, but it was conditional on a failure to achieve devolved government. Mrs Thatcher acknowledged in her first Commons speech as Prime Minister that political progress in NI would not be easy, and she indicated a tough security policy in the province and ruled out any amnesty for convicted terrorists. The Official Unionist MPs, or the majority of them, helped Mrs Thatcher bring down the Labour government but they made it clear during the election that they would maintain their neutral stance. After the killing of 18 soldiers and the murder of Earl Mountbatten in August 1979, she made a one-day trip to NI to see the security situation for herself. On a seven-hour visit, she became the first Prime Minister to visit S. Armagh and Crossmaglen during a rapid border tour. Soon afterwards, she met Taoiseach Jack Lynch in London to urge closer cross-border security co-operation. In Anglo-Irish relations, her December, 1980, meeting in Dublin with Charles Haughey, the Fianna Fail Taoiseach, was regarded as a landmark, since it promised a review 'of the totality of relations between the two countries'. It was also the most powerful British Government delegation ever to have visited Dublin, for she was accompanied by the Foreign Secretary, Lord Carrington; Chancellor of the Exchequer, Sir

Geoffrey Howe, and NI Secretary Humphrey Atkins. Predictably, it drew fierce opposition from Unionists and heartened Nationalists, despite her claim that the summit held no constitutional threat to NI. At a private meeting at Westminster, the Rev. Ian Paisley accused her of 'undermining the NI constitutional guarantee, but she denied that she was doing anything of the sort and said she was 'dismayed' by the accusation. She has rejected suggestions from Unionists that the setting up of the British-Irish Intergovernment Council (see separate entry) was in any sense a 'sell-out', and has stressed the importance of friendship with the Republic, as well as security and economic co-operation. She agreed with Dr Garret Fitzgerald as Taoiseach in November, 1981, that the two Governments should pursue the idea of an Advisory Council and Parliamentary tier of the BIIC. She had a deteriorating relationship, however, with Mr Haughey, and was particularly angered by his opposition during the Falklands crisis to anti-Argentina sanctions. And she included Enoch Powell, MP, in Privy Council briefings on the Falklands, although he had several times alleged that the Foreign Office was intriguing against NI's position. She also kept lines open to OUP leader James Molyneaux (appointed PC, 1983). Her basic Unionism was underlined by her declaration in July, 1982, that 'no committment exists for H.M. Government to consult the Irish Government on matters affecting Northern Ireland.' She said that had always

been her Government's position, but in Dublin the Fianna Fail Government said it was difficult to find any justification for Mrs Thatcher's claim. In the H-Block hunger strike, she stood out against any major concessions, and was accused by those sympathetic to the protest of being the real obstacle to a settlement. She certainly reflected Unionist attitudes during the crisis and angered the SDLP, whose leader, John Hume, had a tense meeting with her at the height of the dispute. Her relationship with NI Secretary James Prior was uneasy at the time of his appointment in September, 1981. He was among the Cabinet 'Wets' in his doubts about Government economic policy, and she insisted on moving him from Employment to the NI Office – a move which it had seemed initially he might oppose to the point of resignation. When Mr Prior brought forward his 'rolling devolution' initiative, Whitehall sources suggested that she was distancing herself from the plan. It was not until the Assembly election stage that she said the scheme would have to go ahead.

THIRD FORCE. A DUP-sponsored vigilante organisation set up towards the end of 1981. It made an appearance at several rallies addressed by the Rev. Ian Paisley, and it was claimed that its existence had reduced the number of murders of Protestants in border areas. It was organised on a county basis, and a strength of 15,000 to 20,000 was mentioned. It occasionally set up road checks, but around March, 1982, adopted a lower profile, although it was claimed that it was still active in offering protection to loyalists living in isolated areas. The launching of the organisation was accompanied by warnings from the authorities that private armies would not be tolerated, and sharp criticism from Nationalists. See REV. IAN PAISLEY.

THOMPSON, FRANCIS HENRY ESMOND. Off. U. Convention member for Mid-Ulster, 1975–6. b. Maghera, Co. Derry, 1929. OUP Executive 1971–. Ex-Royal Navy, Ex-UDR.

THOMPSON, ROY. DUP Assembly member for S. Antrim, 1982–. b. 1946. Founder member, DUP, and serves on party executive. Antrim Council, 1981.

THOMPSON, WILLIAM JOHN. Off. U. Assembly member for Mid-Ulster, 1982–. Also represented the constituency in 1973–4 Assembly and 1975–6 Convention. b. 1939. Returned in 1973 as anti-White Paper Unionist. Member of OUP committee which drew up party's Convention manifesto. Resigned in January, 1983, from OUP's Assembly party as a protest against its refusal to join Assembly committees, but remained party member. Secretary, Mid and W. Tyrone Unionist Association, 1972–. Methodist lay preacher.

TIGER BAY. A militant Protestant area adjoining N. Queen Street in N. Belfast which has tended to erupt violently when Unionist interests are thought to be threatened.

TRIMBLE, WILLIAM DAVID. VUPP Convention member for S. Belfast, 1975–6. b. 1944. Unsuccessfully contested N. Down in Assembly election, 1973. He was assistant dean of the Faculty of Law at QUB when he was elected to the Convention, and in the early stages of the Convention took a key role in drafting UUUC proposals. In the split in the Vanguard Unionist Party over the plan put forward by William Craig for a voluntary coalition including the SDLP, he supported Mr Craig and then became deputy leader of VUPP. When the VUPP abandoned its party political role in February 1978, he joined the OUP and continued to press the case for devolved government.

TROOPS OUT MOVEMENT. A group, which operates from a N. London office, and campaigns for the immediate withdrawal of British troops from NI. Now termed the United Troops Out Movement, it has been active since the end of 1969. It organises conferences on the issue, and occasionally sends deputations to NI, which include leading leftist figures in trade unions and trade councils. It has had the support of a small number of Labour MPs, including Joan Maynard and Tom Litterick. One of its regular meetings is held for delegates to the British Labour Party conference. It has particularly attacked tough anti-terrorist laws, the use of undercover soldiers in NI, and the Peace Movement.

TURNLY, JOHN. IIP councillor, who was shot dead by the UFF in June, 1980. He had been

SDLP Convention member for N. Antrim, 1975–6, and joined the newly-established IIP in 1977, after a policy disagreement with SDLP. b. Ballycastle, Co. Antrim, 1935. A company director who had spent some years in Japan, and a Protestant, he was sitting in his car with his Japanese wife and their two children, when he was killed. One of three men convicted of the murder claimed that he had been working for the SAS. Larne Council, 1973–80. Unsuccessfully contested N. Antrim in 1974 Assembly by-election and 1979 Westminster election.

TUZO, GENERAL SIR HARRY CRAUFURD. Army GOC, NI, 1971–3. b. 1917. Oxford-educated, with a flair for diplomacy, he had a larger political role than any other GOC during the period of violence. He arrived in February 1971, and immediately became involved in the arguments between Stormont and Whitehall which preceded the resignation of Major Chichester-Clark as Prime Minister. In a BBC TV interview in June 1971, he said he did not think a permanent solution could be achieved by military means. He thought that about half the Catholic population in NI had republican aspirations, and of these 25 per cent were prepared to lend passive or active support to the IRA or similar organisations. He was reputed to have agreed to internment without trial only with great reluctance. He once described it as 'distasteful'. But he said the alternatives were to kill IRA men or to bring them before courts where juries could be fixed or witnesses intimi-

dated. He had to cope with the upsurge of violence after the introduction of internment, and following direct rule. With the escalating IRA bombing campaign, he developed considerable undercover army activity against the paramilitaries. These included the Military Reconnaissance Force, which went to the length of setting up a fake laundry service, which was eventually uncovered by the IRA. He was also responsible for the direction of 'Operation Motorman', mounted in the summer of 1972 for the re-occupation of 'no go' areas.

TWOMEY, SEAMUS. Became a leading figure in the PIRA in 1971, when he succeeded Joe Cahill as head of the organisation in Belfast. b. Belfast, 1919. Believed to have joined the IRA originally in the 1940s, but was not active in the 1956 campaign. In August 1969 he rejoined the IRA and was one of the leaders of the republican auxiliaries who were active during loyalist attacks in the Falls Road area. At that time, he was manager of a Falls Road bookmaker's. In 1972, as brigade commander in Belfast, he reluctantly negotiated a brief truce with the British army. Soon afterwards, he was flown to London for the secret talks with the Secretary of State, William Whitelaw MP. Became chief-of-staff of PIRA in March 1973, but after three months as leader he was arrested on the Republic's side of the border, and sentenced to three years' imprisonment for IRA membership. But in October 1973, he made a dramatic helicopter escape from Dublin's Mountjoy prison, together with two other leading republicans, Kevin Mallon and Joe O'Hagan. In 1974, he acted again as chief-of-staff when David O'Connell was arrested, and he attended the Feakle meeting with Protestant churchmen in December 1974. During the ceasefire in 1975, at an Easter ceremony at Milltown cemetery in Belfast to mark the 1916 Easter rising in Dublin, he warned that the PIRA would go back to war if its demands were not met in full. In an interview published in the autumn of 1977, Twomey described himself as chief-of-staff. In December 1977 he was recaptured by the Gardai in Dublin. He was released in January, 1982, and was active in the PSF election campaign in the Republic in February, 1982.

TYRIE, ANDY. Commander of the UDA, 1973–. b. Belfast, 1940. He was in the UVF before becoming a UDA officer on the Shankill Road in Belfast, and then head of the paramilitary organisation. He was prominently associated with the loyalist strike in 1974, and the less successful loyalist stoppage in 1977. A tough man of few words, he was credited initially with taking action to 'clean up' the organisation and restrain its violent fringes, and he has said on several occasions that the UDA must not get into confrontation with the Catholic community. In July, 1974, he led a UDA deputation in talks with the SDLP – a discussion which showed agreement only on opposition to internment. In 1976, he took the UDA out of the ULCCC after claiming that some of its members had been talking to Republicans about independence. But in 1979, the UDA, under his leadership, sponsored the New Ulster Political Research Group, which produced a plan for negotiated independence for NI, and he visited the US with UDA deputation for talks with politicians to promote the policy. Independence was also a central point of policy for the political party, the ULDP, which the UDA launched in 1981. All the indications are that Tyrie has faced a serious problem in reconciling conflicting views within the UDA on what its role should be. In early 1981 he said the UDA might have to cross the border to 'terrorise terrorists', a threat which precipitated fresh demands for the proscription of the organisation. After that speech, the RUC apparently gave greater attention to the UDA, and raided its headquarters in 1981 and 1982. See ULSTER DEFENCE ASSOCIATION.

U

ULSTER. A term frequently applied to Northern Ireland, but is strictly the name of the ancient nine-county province of Ireland, which includes three counties now in the Republic – Monaghan, Cavan and Donegal – in addition to the six NI counties.

ULSTER ARMY COUNCIL. A grouping of loyalist paramilitary organisations which had a vital role in building support for the 1974 loyalist strike. The body was formed in December 1973, and included the UDA, UVF, Ulster Special Constabulary Association, Loyalist Defence Volunteers, Orange Volunteers, and Red Hand Commandos. It said it would work closely with the newly-formed UUUC. When the UUUC politicians held a conference in Portrush in April 1974, it joined the UWC in urging the politicians to call for an end to the power-sharing Executive, a return to direct rule without any power of veto for the Secretary of State; new elections on PR in smaller constituencies; and an end even to discussion of a Council of Ireland. The UAC warned on the eve of the 1974 loyalist strike that 'if Westminster is not prepared to restore democracy, i.e., the will of the people made clear in an election, then the only way it can be restored is by a *coup d'état.*'

ULSTER CITIZEN ARMY. The name cropped up several times in 1974, apparently being the title of a group of dissidents from the UDA and UVF. In February 1974 it put out a statement saying that it would assassinate business executives and army officers if the government succeeded in throwing NI into 'vicious sectarian warfare'. Then in October 1974 it was issuing handbills which alleged that 'power-crazed animals have taken over control of the loyalist paramilitary organisations and have embarked on a programme of wanton slaughter, intimidation,

robbery and extortion'. It said that during the previous month a dozen people had been butchered by psychopaths, acting on the orders of loyalist leaders. It promised to supply the addresses of those involved to the security forces. The UCA was also believed to have operated under the name, 'The Covenanters'.

ULSTER CONSTITUTION DEFENCE COMMITTEE. Set up in 1966 under the chairmanship of Rev. Ian Paisley, and active initially in mounting counter-demonstrations to republican Easter parades and later to coincide with civil rights marches. Closely linked with UPV. In June 1966 Mr Paisley said in a speech in Holywood that the UCDC had absolutely no connection with the UVF, which had just been proscribed. The UCDC was prominent in Mr Paisley's 'O'Neill must go' campaign.

ULSTER DEFENCE ASSO-CIATION. The largest Protestant paramilitary organisation. Started in September 1971 as a co-ordinating body for the great variety of loyalist vigilante groups, many of them calling themselves 'Defence Associations', which had grown up in Protestant areas of Belfast and in estates in adjoining areas, such as Newtownabbey, Dundonald and Lisburn. It adopted the motto, 'Law before Violence', and took on a distinctly working-class image, excluding MPs and clergymen from membership. It is organised on military lines, and at its peak, in 1972, it probably had about 40,000 members. By 1978, this had dropped to between 10,000 and 12,000 – a reduction brought about, according to its spokesmen, not by lack of support, but because of a deliberate policy of limiting membership to a readily controllable size. Although some of its members have been convicted of serious crimes, including murder, its leaders have always publicly deplored such involvement. Its first leader, Charles Harding Smith, was acquitted, together with five other men, of being concerned in dealing in £350,000 worth of arms, including a large number of rifles, in early 1972. Smith claimed that meetings set up in London at the time, and which came to the attention of the Special Branch, were really intended to trap IRA arms dealers. He also said that he had assisted the security forces in NI, and at the trial a letter was read from the Assistant Chief Constable of the RUC, stating that on many occasions Smith had been a pacifier in quarrels between Protestants and Catholics in Belfast. According to police evidence, a two-page official document, listing names and ranks of junior IRA officers, and mentioning Seamus Twomey, Belfast commander of the PIRA, had been found at Smith's Belfast home. In the anti-direct rule protests of 1972, the UDA was closely involved with the Vanguard movement and the LAW, and intermittently with the more violent UVF. Its largest demonstrations took the form of massive parades in Belfast in the summer of 1972. Thousands of UDA men, sometimes masked, and wearing combat jackets with military style caps or bush hats,

marched through the city centre. In July and August 1972 local units set up their own 'no go' areas in some loyalist districts of Belfast as a protest against the existence of 'no go' areas in the Bogside and Creggan areas of Derry. The erection of barricades often entailed the use of concrete mixers, cement blocks and metal spikes. One dispute, on 3 July 1972, over a plan for loyalist barricades between the Springfield (Catholic) and Shankill (Protestant) areas led to about 8,000 uniformed UDA men, many of them carrying iron bars, confronting some 250 troops for an hour and a half while anxious negotiations went on between UDA chiefs and senior officials and army officers. The situation, the ugliest involving Protestants and the security forces since the Shankill Road riots of 1969, was regarded by the UDA as an impressive demonstration of the speed with which they could move a large force of their supporters to a given position. But this incident, and the massive parades, were regarded by Catholic interests as evidence that the British administration was adopting too soft a line towards loyalist militants. Privately, however, the army was talking toughly to the UDA. In the 'no go' row, the UDA held its hand over the Twelfth of July period of 1972 and then its thirteen-man Council had talks with the Secretary of State, Mr Whitelaw. They got the impression that government action was pending against the Derry barricades, and in the event the Bogside and Creggan were opened up in 'Operation Motorman' at the end of July. But in the autumn of 1972, when the UDA mounted street protests against the government's security policy, they were involved in disputes with the army about the circumstances in which some Protestants had been killed. In mid-October after a meeting between the UDA leaders and the army, there was a statement that both sides would try to take the heat out of the situation, and an assurance that all complaints against the army would be investigated by the RUC. In September 1973, Tommy Herron, who had been the UDA's deputy leader until he unsuccessfully fought the Assembly election in E. Belfast, was murdered in mysterious circumstances. His body was found near Lisburn, and he had been shot in the head. There were many rumours that he had been killed by loyalist extremist but this was rejected by the UDA, who said they were satisfied that no Protestant organisation had been involved. Probably the major operation of the UDA was in the loyalist strike of May 1974, which led to the break-up of the power-sharing administration. The UDA was first involved in the 'Ulster Army Council', a small grouping of Protestant paramilitaries and then in the larger Ulster Workers' Council, which organised the strike effort. The UDA commander, Andy Tyrie, was on the UWC Co-ordinating Committee, and the organisation provided much of the muscle-power in terms of mounting road blocks. Critics of the strike alleged that UDA members had been heavily engaged in intimidation of people who wanted to stay at work. In June,

after the fall of the Executive, the UDA said that while it ruled out talks with the PIRA, it was prepared to meet elected representatives, including Provisional Sinn Fein. In the same month, the UDA issued a statement on behalf of the illegal Ulster Freedom Fighters saying that the UFF wanted an end to violence. In July 1974, there was a claim at Winchester Crown Court that the UDA had 6,000 members in Great Britain who would be prepared to go to NI to support the UDA there in the event of a civil war. The claim was made at the trial of nine men who pleaded guilty to the possession of firearms, including sten guns, and who were given two-year jail sentences. In August 1974, after the UDA had resigned from the UWC and the ULCCC, it had a meeting with SDLP representatives. The SDLP spokesmen were Gerry Fitt, John Hume, Paddy Devlin, Ivan Cooper and Hugh Logue. The UDA was represented by Andy Tyrie, Bill Snoddy, Tommy Lyttle, and Ronnie Reid. But while there was united opposition to internment, there was no agreement about the political future. The UDA said the SDLP had been hypocritical, and insisted that it should drop its United Ireland aspiration. Mr Fitt felt that the meeting had shown an intense power struggle within the UDA. In November 1974 a UDA delegation visited Libya, headed by its political adviser, Glen Barr, a Vanguard Assemblyman. The meeting created controversy, since a Provisional Sinn Fein deputation was in Libya at the same time. Both sides denied that there had been any negotiations between them, and a Dublin banker who had arranged the UDA visit said it had been concerned with the development of offshore oil and other resources. But in a personal comment, Mr Barr admitted that the deputation had been seeking possible economic aid for an independent Ulster. During the Constitutional Convention, Mr Barr's support for Vanguard leader, William Craig's idea of a voluntary coalition, including the SDLP, seems to have influenced UDA thinking. Andy Tyrie expressed support for Mr Craig's scheme, and blamed the Rev. Ian Paisley and Harry West for the failure of the Convention, and suggested that they would be responsible for further deaths. If there was to be further fighting, the politicians should do it as well, he said. It was a theme to which he returned at intervals over the next two years. In September 1975, the bodies of two UDA men were found near Whitehead, Co. Antrim. The two, who had disappeared in the previous April, were Hugh McVeigh, aged thirty-six, and David Douglas, aged twenty. Two years later, a number of UVF men were found guilty of the murder. But whatever their reservations about the loyalist politicians, the UDA supported the United Unionist Action Council when it mounted a strike in May 1977, as a protest against government security policy and continued direct rule. The Rev. Ian Paisley and Ernest Baird were the two main politicians involved in the UUAC, and the strike turned out to be half-hearted affair. In early 1978, the UDA warned against retaliation by Protestants when twelve people were burned to death in a Comber, Co. Down restaurant which had been fire-bombed by the PIRA. At the same time, the organisation was indicating that it was turning its attention more to political policy, but it warned in its magazine in July 1978 that it would 'no longer be the willing tool of any aspiring or ready-made politician'. In February 1979, a deputation visited the US for talks with leading politicians and in the following month it was associated with the publication of a plan for an independent NI. It was also urging public pressure to secure the segregation of UDA prisoners from republican prisoners involved in the 'no wash, no toilet' protest at the Maze prison. In June 1979, eleven Scottish UDA men were given heavy prison sentences for furthering the aims of the organisation by criminal means by unlawfully acquiring arms and ammunition. One group of seven were given 164 years between them, and the supreme commander of the UDA in Scotland, James Hamilton, aged forty-four, was sentenced to fifteen years – the heaviest sentence. Four others were sentenced to between seven and twelve years for furthering the aims of the UDA in Paisley and the West of Scotland. The judge, Lord Wylie, spoke of a 'reign of terror' by the UDA commander in Paisley, William Currie, who was sentenced to twelve years' imprisonment. The organisation mentioned the possibility of reviving paramilitary activity after the Mountbatten murder and the Warrenpoint killings, but there was no immediate evidence of such activity. In the early 1980s, the UDA seemed to be beset by uncertainties, with an internal clash between those who argued for more political action and those who regarded it as essentially a Protestant counter-terror organisation. Certainly, republicans continued to insist that its members were implicated in murders, and there were strong indications that it maintained contacts with the UFF. (See separate entry.) The organisation refused to back the Rev. Ian Paisley's 'Day of Action' and 'Third Force' in 1981, and seemed to ridicule the idea of protest marches. But in April and May, 1981, it mounted some local shows of strength, putting some 2,500 men on the Shankill Road, Belfast, in what was termed 'purely defensive mobilisation' and several hundred men on parade in the Fountain area of Londonderry. In February, 1981, Tyrie threatened that UDA men might cross the border to 'terrorise the terrorists'. This statement revived demands from anti-Unionists for the outlawing of the organisation, but proscription was once more rejected by the NIO. But the security forces kept up pressure on the UDA centrally, and its Belfast HQ was raided in May, 1981, and again in April, 1982. On both occasions, some arms and ammunition were found, and in April, 1982, charges were brought against several leading members but were later largely dropped. The court was told during a preliminary hearing that files on judges, police and IRA suspects had been found during the police raids. In 1981,

INLA shot dead a leading UDA man, Billy McCullough, on the Shankill Road in Belfast, in retaliation, it said, for Loyalist murders of Catholics. In the same year, it shot and seriously injured UDA Councillor Sammy Millar at his home in the Shankill area. In August, 1981, the UDA renewed its interest in politics by launching the Ulster Loyalist Democratic Party. (See separate entry.) The Scottish connection was stressed again in February, 1981, when a Scottish member claimed on TV that there were 2,000 UDA members in Scotland. He also said there were Scottish stockpiles of arms and 'safe houses' for Loyalist fugitives, and that arms and ammunition had been smuggled to NI through Larne. In 1980, some UDA prisoners in the Maze briefly adopted the Republican hunger-strike tactic in support of political status – a move which brought some criticism from Unionist politicians. UDA prisoners were also engaged in the campaign for segregation from Republican prisoners which became intense in 1982.

ULSTER DEFENCE REGIMENT. See Security Section (p. 312).

ULSTER DOMINION GROUP. See BRITISH ULSTER DOMINION PARTY.

ULSTER FREEDOM FIGHTERS. Illegal Protestant paramilitary group. Began mid-1973 and apparently a splinter group from the UDA. Between 1973 and 1977 made numerous telephone claims of murders of Catholics (often alleging that their victims had IRA associations) and bomb attacks on Catholic churches, schools and public-houses. The phone calls were often said to be from 'Captain White' or 'Captain Black'. Among such claims were the murders of Fine Gael Senator Billy Fox in Co. Monaghan in March 1974, and of SDLP Senator Paddy Wilson in Belfast in June 1973. The claim in respect of Senator Fox was not, however, taken seriously in the Republic. On 22 June 1974, after a period of intense UFF activity in the Belfast area, the UDA issued a statement saying that the UFF had seen enough of violence and would be happy if, after the Assembly elections, it was discovered that all shades of opinion could work together. But the UFF reserved the 'right' to retaliate if attacks were made on loyalist areas. In July 1977, the UFF in Londonderry claimed to have bombed a Catholic church at Greysteel, Co. Derry, in reprisal, they said, for the burning of Bellaghy Orange Hall. The PIRA has made contradictory claims about the make-up of the UFF. In January 1974, it declared that the UFF was a killer squad of the British army, but in July 1974 it said the body was composed of 'criminals from the Catholic and Protestant communities'. It announced in September, 1979, following the murders of Lord Mountbatten and 18 soldiers that it would 'strike back' at PIRA. A clandestine news conference in Belfast was told that it had been re-organised and re-equipped and was now the most powerful loyalist paramilitary organisation. It also claimed to have drawn up a 'death list' of known Republicans in NI, Great Britain and the Republic. Almost immediately afterwards, it claimed the murder of a 27-year-old married man in N. Belfast. Two men jailed for the murder of IIP councillor John Turnly in Carnlough, Co. Antrim, in June, 1980, were said by the prosecution to be members of the UFF. It was active during the H-Block hunger strike, and is believed to have carried out at least five sectarian murders during 1981. In September, 1981, it referred to another 'death list', this time related to alleged PIRA and INLA informers.

ULSTER INDEPENDENCE ASSOCIATION. A group campaigning for an independent, sovereign NI. Urges an assembly elected by PR list system of up to 100 members, with a consensus government and non-political president. The transfer of responsibility from Westminster would be achieved by negotiation, particularly on interim financial arrangements. It would seek a declaration from the Republic that it respects the sovereignty of an independent, peaceful NI. Claims some Catholic support. The association was active in 1979 in seeking to arrange a Washington peace forum, and it handled invitations on behalf of Congressman Mario Biaggi, chairman of the NI Ad Hoc Committee in Washington. Its chairman, George Allport, a businessman, visited the US in 1977 and 1979 for talks with politicians. One of its deputy leaders was E. Belfast loyalist John

McKeague, shot dead in 1981 by INLA.

ULSTER INDEPENDENCE PARTY. Launched on a small scale in October 1977 with the object of securing 'by democratic means, a sovereign, free and independent Ulster'. Government would be based on proportional power-sharing at all levels, and the party said Protestants and Catholics should join hands in a spirit of friendship. An initial statement said that in May 1976 the Ulster Independence Movement had issued an economic survey and feasibility study. This had been published in the USA in July 1976, by the Ulster Heritage Society, under the title, *Towards an Independent Ulster*. These documents had shown that Ulster, with an export performance much superior to that of either Great Britain or the Irish Republic, could be economically feasible on its own. In January 1978, the UIP said it could not accept the idea of 'interim independence' mentioned as a possibility by the Roman Catholic Primate, Cardinal O'Fiaich, since this would be a contradiction in terms.

ULSTER LIBERAL PARTY. The party, linked with the British Liberal Party, has been at a low ebb in recent years, and the presumption is that many of its supporters moved to the Alliance Party. Miss Sheelagh Murnaghan sat in the former Stormont parliament for QUB. She and the former chairman, Rev. Albert Mc-Elroy, were prominent in the demand for reforms. Two candidates who stood in the Assembly elections in 1973 forfeited their deposits and the party was not represented in the Convention election in 1975. In 1977 and 1978, it organised 'fringe' meetings on NI at the British Liberal assemblines. The party put up a candidate, Jim Murray, a teacher, in the 1979 European election, but he received only 932 first-preference votes (0.1 per cent). In the next few years, its activities seemed to be minimal, although it did sponsor a candidate in S. Belfast in the 1982 Assembly election, who secured 65 votes.

ULSTER LOYALIST ASSOCIATION. A body prominent between 1969 and 1972 in opposing any interference with the NI constitution, and urging stronger security policies, notably against the IRA. Its leading figures were William Craig, the Rev. Martin Smyth and Captain Austin Ardill, and many of its members were also Orangemen. The ULA organised a series of rallies throughout the province and Captain Ardill, speaking as chairman in 1971, called for the severing of diplomatic relations with the Republic and the sealing of the border.

ULSTER LOYALIST CENTRAL CO-ORDINATING COMMITTEE. The organisation set up after the 1974 loyalist strike to act as a forum for loyalist paramilitary organisations. It replaced the Ulster Army Council set up in 1973. The ULCCC originally included the UDA, UVF, Red Hand Commandos, LAW, Vanguard Service Corps, Orange Volunteers, and Down Orange Welfare. In 1976, the UDA and

Down Orange Welfare withdrew after suggestions that some members of the ULCCC were meeting members of the PIRA and talking to a wide range of Catholics about the possibility of an independent NI. Its co-chairman, loyalist John McKeague, was shot dead in his E. Belfast shop in January, 1982. A claim by INLA that it was responsible was generally accepted, although there had been a telephone claim of responsibility, allegedly from the Red Hand Commandos.

ULSTER LOYALIST DEMO-CRATIC PARTY. The UDA-sponsored political party set up in June, 1981, to replace the New Ulster Political Research Group. The NUPRG was founded in January 1978, after discussions between Andy Tyrie, head of UDA, and Glen Barr, former deputy leader of Vanguard, which produced plans for an independent NI in March 1979. They said that negotiated independence was the only basis for a constitutional settlement acceptable to both sections of the community. They proposed that both Britain and the Republic should drop all claims to sovereignty over NI, and that the new state should be neither Pro-testant-dominated nor moving towards a united Ireland, although Britain should pledge financial backing for at least twenty-five years. An Assembly would be elected for four years, but Ministers would be appointed – as in the USA – and neither they, nor the Prime Minister, would sit in the Assembly. The Ministers would be chosen by the elected President, his deputy, and the Prime Minister although they would have to be endorsed by the Assembly, which would deal with legislation. In the June, 1981, council elections, one NUPRG candidate was returned in Belfast (Sammy Millar, who had been seriously injured in an assassina-tion attempt). Then, coincidental with the withdrawal of NUPRG chairman, Glen Barr, from active politics, for health reasons, the ULDP was announced to replace NUPRG. UDA spokesmen denied that the move was intended to counter a recent arms find at the UDA headquarters in E. Belfast. The new party main-tained the independence approach of the NUPRG, but stressed it less in its public utter-ances, and gave more emphasis to a role for the monarchy. Its line seemed to be independence within the Commonwealth and the EEC, which its first chairman, John McMichael, suggested, would be acceptable to many Roman Catholics. The party seemed to take a good deal of encouragement from the support for independence from the *Sunday Times* and ex-Prime Minister James Callaghan. But it found the electoral going hard. It failed in its first bid – a Belfast council by-election in E. Belfast in August, 1981 – and John McMichael got fewer than 600 votes in the S. Belfast by-election in February, 1982. Its two candidates in the 1982 Assembly election (both in N. Belfast) fared badly.

ULSTER PROTESTANT ACTION GROUP. A paramili-tary group active mainly in 1974 which was responsible for the assassination of many Catholics. The security forces believed that it was comprised of dissident members of the UDA. In a statement in October 1974, it said that the assassinations would continue 'until the Provisional IRA are exterminated'. The group apparently adopted the name of an organisation active before the troubles in encouraging the employment of Protestants in industry. The name 'Protestant Action' reappeared in 1981 when there were claims at a clandestine news conference that it would kill 'active Republicans'. In 1982, it claimed the murders of several people, including a Provisional Sinn Fein election worker in Armagh. At that time, there were suggestions that it had some link with the illegal Red Hand Commandos.

ULSTER PROTESTANT VOLUNTEERS. A loyalist paramilitary group associated with the UCDC. It was involved in many counter-demonstrations to civil rights meetings in the period 1968–71. Organised in local divisions, it styled itself 'a united Society of Protestant patriots, pledged by all lawful methods to uphold and maintain the constitution of NI as an integral part of the United Kingdom so long as the UK maintains a Protestant monarchy and the terms of the revolution settlement'. The UPV accompanied most of the Rev. Ian Paisley's parades during the early civil rights period.

ULSTER SERVICE CORPS. A loyalist vigilante group established in 1977, with the support of the United Unionist Action Council. In the spring of 1977, it mounted road blocks from time to time in parts of S. Derry, Armagh and Tyrone, and claimed to have some liaison with members of the RUC and UDR, although this was denied by the authorities. Its activities included observation of alleged IRA 'safe houses'. It claimed to have a province-wide membership of about 500. Some of its members were summoned for obstruction, and a spokesman for the government accused it of wasting the time of the security forces who had to be diverted to deal with it. The SDLP protested strongly that there was evidence of collusion with the UDR to the extent that joint patrols were operated in some areas of Mid-Ulster. Most of its original members are believed to have served with the former Ulster Special Constabulary.

ULSTER SPECIAL CONSTABULARY. See Security Section (pp. 304–5).

ULSTER SPECIAL CONSTABULARY ASSOCIATION. An association bringing together ex-B Specials, who were disbanded officially in 1970, following the adoption by the government of the Hunt Report. The USCA has operated as a pressure group, calling for tougher anti-IRA measures and more local control of security. It has been associated with loyalist paramilitary groups, notably in support of the loyalist strike in 1974. Exact strength uncertain, but probably had backing of 10,000 ex-B Specials in 1970.

ULSTER UNIONIST PARTY.

Popularly styled the Official Unionist Party in recent years, it is the largest political entity in the province. It is substantially the party which provided the government of NI at Stormont from 1921 until March 1972, when direct rule from London was imposed. Up to the late 1960s, when Pro- and Anti-Premier O'Neill factions became sharply differentiated, the party was essentially a coalition embracing a left-to-right spectrum of opinion committed to the maintenance of the link with Britain and the defence of the Northern Ireland parliament. In the face of demands for reform from the civil rights movement, and tensions caused by the violence, it was weakened by a series of breakaway movements: supporters of O'Neill who moved to the Alliance Party or out of active politics; anti-O'Neill people who moved to Vanguard or the DUP; pro-Faulkner members who moved to UPNI. In most of the parliaments from 1921 until 1972, the Unionists held around forty of the fifty-two seats in the NI House of Commons, and they usually held at least ten of the twelve Westminster seats. It was unquestionably a party of government, and many Unionist MPs had never had to fight an election. So the closing down of the old Stormont parliament in 1972 was a severe shock, and one which eventually forced the hard core of the party into combination with smaller Unionist parties. Under the pressure of events, the working-class element in the party became more powerful, and the influence of the 'county families'

was visibly reduced. Key meetings of the party ceased to be held midweek when few average workers were able to attend. An enlarged executive took charge of policy, instead of the former 1,000-strong Unionist Council and 300-member Standing Committee which had held frequent meetings during the O'Neill crisis. And although the party was a branch of the British Conservative Party, entitled to send full voting representatives to party conferences, the action of the Heath government in suspending Stormont strained to breaking point an inter-party link which had existed from the days of the earliest Home Rule controversy in the late nineteenth century. In the 1973 election to the new Assembly, the party was split between those who followed Mr Faulkner's lead and backed the power-sharing policy of Westminster and those who opposed the British government's White Paper. The election resulted in the return of twenty-three candidates supporting the White Paper, and ten who were against. A major crisis for the party developed in January 1974, after Mr Faulkner and his colleagues had joined a power-sharing Executive which included the SDLP and the Alliance Party. The Ulster Unionist Council rejected by 427 to 374 the Sunningdale agreement, which provided the basis for the Executive. This brought about the resignation of Faulkner as party leader, and he was succeeded by Harry West. Soon afterwards, the February 1974 Westminster election gave the anti-Sunningdale Unionists the opportunity to test their support. They chose to join with the DUP and Vanguard in the UUUC. The Unionist Coalition secured eleven out of the twelve seats, and Mr West was returned in Fermanagh-S. Tyrone and led the Coalition at Westminster in adopting a neutral stance at a time when their votes could have kept the Heath government in office. The fact that the Unionist Coalition had got more than 50 per cent of the votes in the province was a severe blow to the three-party Executive. But the new Labour government was just as committed to power-sharing as the Conservatives, and the Executive survived until the loyalist strike, organised by the UWC and backed by the Official Unionists and its partners, effectively brought life to a standstill in May 1974. The Coalition continued into the elections for the Constitutional Convention in 1975, but the fragmentation of Unionism had its effects. The Official Unionists now obtained 25.8 per cent of the votes, and nineteen seats; they were no longer the predominant party, and if they were still against any partnership with the SDLP, they had to face the fact that they must co-operate with some other parties to achieve anything. The Official Unionists together with the DUP and Vanguard, backed the majority Convention Report which provided for majority Cabinet rule, and argued that opposition influence should be achieved through a system of committees linked to the various Stormont departments. But it did not meet Westminster's criteria for devolved government. In the later stage of the Convention, the

Official Unionists stood out against the move by William Craig to try to get agreement for a voluntary coalition which would include the SDLP for the period of the emergency. And it now formed part of the UUUC which included the DUP and those members (the majority) of Vanguard who disagreed with Mr Craig, and who now made up the UUUM under Ernest Baird, who had been Mr Craig's deputy in Vanguard. After the break-up of the Convention in 1976, two Official Unionists (the Rev. Martin Smyth and Captain Austin Ardill) became involved in private, but unsuccessful, talks with John Hume and Paddy Devlin of the SDLP. The secrecy surrounding these talks gave rise to friction between the party and the Rev. Ian Paisley and Ernest Baird. This gap was widened in 1977 when the Official Unionists stood aside from the Action Council which organised the loyalist strike – a largely abortive stoppage – in May 1977 against direct rule and in support of a tougher security policy. The Official Unionists also refused to support a parallel operation – an unofficial vigilante group known as the Ulster Service Corps, which appeared briefly in some areas during 1977. Again, Official Unionists declined to have any UUUC endorsement of their candidates in the May 1977 district council elections. In that election, Official Unionists had 29.6 per cent of the first-preference votes and 33.8 per cent of the seats (178). In June 1977, the Official Unionists accepted 'the de facto collapse of the UUUC'. The party was now set upon a more independent course, and the Parliamentary Unionist Coalition at Westminster also ended. Six Official Unionist MPs, under the leadership of James Molyneaux, became a separate group, and William Craig joined them in 1978. Since October 1974 Enoch Powell in S. Down had been an Off. U. MP and his aversion to the Conservatives was obviously a factor in securing Labour government support for a Speaker's Conference to examine the long-standing demand of Unionists for extra seats for NI at Westminster. This all-party conference reported in 1978 in favour of five extra NI seats, with discretion to the Boundary Commission to have one more or one fewer. But the Conservatives, also with an eye to Unionist votes at Westminster strongly backed the Official Unionist call for the introduction of regional councils in NI as a way of filling the administrative gap created by the absence of any Stormont Assembly. In 1978, the Official Unionists turned down a plea by the DUP for some sort of agreement on the allocation of candidates in the coming Westminster elections. Party leader Harry West pointed out to the Rev. Ian Paisley that the party's constitution prevented it giving any directions to local associations on the choice of candidates. Although the OUP retains its long-standing association with the Orange Order, its importance has declined in recent years with the divisions in Unionism. In the 1979 European election, one of its two candidates, John Taylor, was successful on the sixth count, but party leader Harry West was eli-

minated. The party's overall performance was not impressive. The combined total of first preferences for the party was 21.8 per cent compared with 29.8 per cent for DUP leader, the Rev. Ian Paisley, and 24.5 per cent for SDLP candidate John Hume. Mr West conceded that perhaps 100,000 party supporters had refused to back the party line of calling for extensive re-negotiation of the EEC as distinct from the outright opposition of Mr Paisley. The result led directly to the resignation of Harry West as party leader in July 1979. The parliamentary leader, James Molyneaux, succeeded him. But the hopes of Official Unionists that the Thatcher Government would prove helpful to their aims were soon disappointed. The party's annual report regretted that the Prime Minister 'has followed, not her own instincts, but those of Lord Carrington and the Foreign Office.' There was some surprise, however, that the OUP decided to boycott the Stormont Constitutional Conference announced by Secretary of State Humphrey Atkins in November, 1979. Mr Molyneaux called it 'a time-wasting exercise and window-dressing.' But although the party stayed away from the discussions, it sent proposals for majority government to the Prime Minister. When the failure of the Constitutional Conference was followed by a plan for a 50-member Advisory Council, this, too, was turned down by the party. The OUP was also highly suspicious of the London-Dublin contacts, and especially the December, 1980 summit in Dublin at which Mrs Thatcher and Charles Haughey initiated a review of 'the totality of relations between the two countries'. Although the Prime Minister repeated on every possible occasion the constitutional pledge on NI, many OUP people, and notably Enoch Powell, saw a Foreign Office conspiratorial approach in every Anglo-Irish gesture. OUP-DUP rivalry was renewed in the 1981 council elections, and again the OUP fell behind the DUP, if only marginally, in terms of votes, although it maintained its superiority in seats. The OUP also became quickly antagoistic towards Mr Atkins' successor, James Prior. After the murder of the party's S. Belfast MP, the Rev. Robert Bradford, in November, 1981, its anger was directed at the Government's security policy. It joined in the Loyalist 'day of action' on 23 November, when rallies and meetings were sponsored by both the OUP and DUP to demand a more aggressive approach to security by the authorities. It also co-operated for a time with the DUP in the adjournment of Loyalist-controlled councils as part of the security protest. The OUP tended, however, to distance itself from the DUP, and rejected the DUP suggestion that a united Unionist candidate should be run in the S. Belfast by-election in February, 1982, and it had the satisfaction of seeing its candidate, the Rev. Martin Smyth, win easily, with the DUP in third place. Mr Prior's 'rolling devolution' initiative in 1982 found the OUP slightly divided, but most opinion went along with the leadership in regarding the Assembly as a revival of power-sharing and Sunningdale and as an institution which could fit in with Government plans for a parliamentary tier of the British-Irish Intergovernment Council. Since the DUP was welcoming the scrutiny powers of the proposed Assembly, many OUP members saw the possibility of outflanking the Rev. Ian Paisley in the Assembly elections. OUP MPs, for the most part, were active in opposing the legislation for the Assembly and they co-operated, to some extent, with right-wing Conservatives who mounted a filibuster on the committee stage. They also propagated the view that Mrs Thatcher was by no means wholeheartedly behind the Prior plan. When the Falklands crisis broke, the OUP MPs threw themselves enthusiastically behind the Prime Minister's strong response, and even drew parallels with the Irish Republic's claims over NI. They were aided in this by the Republic's opposition to sanctions against Argentina, and Mrs Thatcher pointedly included Enoch Powell in her Privy Council briefings on the situation. Mr Prior warned against making comparisons between the Falklands and the NI situation. In the end, the OUP had to face the fact that Mr Prior had got his Assembly measure through virtually unscathed, but they did recover their lead in the popular vote in the Assembly elections and got 26 seats to the DUP's 21. In the 1983 Westminster election, the party went a small way with the Rev. Ian Paisley's bid to secure an electoral pact. It reached an arrangement on three seats whereas the DUP leader wanted to cover six. The

1983 Westminster election represented the party's best showing since before direct rule. It took 34 per cent of the votes and eleven of the seventeen seats. It thus pulled 14 per cent ahead of DUP which got three seats and 20 per cent of the vote. There was, however, a 'limited understanding' between the two parties. This meant that DUP did not contest Newry-Armagh and Fermanagh and S. Tyrone while OUP stood down in Foyle.

ULSTER VANGUARD. A pressure group within Unionism, led by William Craig, and launched at the beginning of 1972, when the possibility of direct rule from Westminster began to be discussed seriously. Its purpose was to provide an umbrella organisation for loyalists in a bid to overcome the weaknesses of their party divisions. It had strong support from loyalist paramilitary groups. The deputy leaders, at the start, were the Rev. Martin Smyth and Captain Austin Ardill. Vanguard organised rallies, to which Craig travelled frequently in an open car with a motor cycle escort provided by the Vanguard Service Corps, a paramilitary group directly linked with the organisation. A rally in Ormeau Park, Belfast, in March 1972 attracted about 60,000 people, and it mounted a forty-eight-hour strike by its supporters against direct rule. William Craig's remark at the Ormeau Park rally that 'if the politicians fail, it will be our duty to liquidate the enemy', brought angry protests from his critics that Vanguard was a fascist movement. Mr Craig denied that it was neo-Nazi. He said that any paramilitary appearance was due simply to the symbolic gesture of men of different political affiliations standing together shoulder to shoulder. Vanguard turned out in strength for a demonstration at Parliament Buildings on 28 March 1972, to protest against the introduction of direct rule. It was the last sitting day of the old Stormont parliament, and Craig appeared on the balcony of Parliament Buildings alongside the Prime Minister, Brian Faulkner, and several Cabinet Ministers. But the unity was more apparent than real on that occasion, and Faulkner made it clear later that he was embarrassed by the link-up with Vanguard. In May 1972, Vanguard shed some support among Official Unionists with a policy statement entitled, 'Ulster – a Nation'. It said that NI might, if reluctantly, have to go it alone. More immediately, it called for re-negotiation of the relationship with Westminster to ensure local control of security in view of the unilateral application of direct rule. In 1973, the setting up of the Vanguard Unionist Progressive Party meant the disappearance of Vanguard as an umbrella group. But Ulster Vanguard re-emerged in February 1978, when VUPP was wound up as a political party. Craig, who had now rejoined the OUP, remained at its head, and David Trimble, the deputy leader of VUPP, was appointed his deputy. See VANGUARD UNIONIST PROGRESSIVE PARTY.

ULSTER VOLUNTEER FORCE. Illegal Protestant paramilitary force, sometimes described as the 'secret Protestant army'. In 1966, it revived the title applied to the Unionist-Protestant force established in 1912 to fight Irish Home Rule. Known sometimes as 'Carson's Army', after Lord Carson, the original UVF organised the training of volunteers as well as gun-running to Ulster. When war broke out in 1914, and Home Rule was set aside for the moment, its members very largely became the 36th (Ulster) Division in the British Army, which suffered severe losses at the Battle of the Somme in July 1916. The new UVF of the 1960s was completely opposed to the liberal Unionist regime of Capt. Terence O'Neill. It first attracted attention in May 1966, when a statement over the name 'Capt. Wm. Johnston' threatened war against the IRA, and said that it was the UVF's intention to kill IRA men mercilessly. Six days later, a man named John Scullion was fatally stabbed on the Falls Road in Belfast. On 26 June, an eighteen-year-old Catholic barman, Peter Ward, was shot dead as he left a bar in the Protestant Shankill Road area of the city. Augustus (Gusty) Spence, the best-known UVF leader, was sentenced to life imprisonment for this murder. Prime Minister O'Neill announced in parliament that the UVF was to be declared illegal. He said that 'this evil thing in our midst' had misappropriated the name UVF and would now take its proper place alongside the IRA in the schedule of illegal bodies. He also branded it as 'a dangerous conspiracy'. The Prime Minister claimed that the

Rev. Ian Paisley had links with the UVF and that he had voiced support for it in speeches, but Mr Paisley and his newspaper angrily denied that he had been associated with the organisation or had advocated violence. The UVF, now organising underground on military lines, and apparently attracting mainly ex-soldiers, is thought to have attained a strength of about 1,500 by 1972. In that year – the year in which direct rule from Westminster was imposed – it was heavily involved in the assassination of Catholics. It also claimed to be well armed with a variety of weapons, including Browning, Bren, Sterling and Thompson guns. In October 1972, it admitted to a raid on a military arsenal in Lurgan, Co. Armagh. Its main centres of strength at that time were the Shankill area of Belfast, E. Antrim and Co. Armagh. In July 1972, 'Gusty' Spence, then described as second-in-command, vanished while on two days' parole from Belfast Prison. He was said to have been held by his UVF comrades in a bid to force a new trial for Spence, but a few months later he was recaptured and went to the Maze Prison to preside over the compound where UVF prisoners who had special-category status were held. In April 1974 Secretary of State Merlyn Rees removed the proscription on the UVF to encourage it to turn to political activity. But on 3 October 1975 the UVF admitted that it had been responsible for most of the violence of the previous day in which twelve people died and about forty were injured, most of them Catholics. In declaring the organisation illegal again, Mr Rees said that the UVF had shown that it was still wedded to violence, including the murder of innocent citizens. In reply, the UVF threatened further 'anti-IRA action' and expressed its 'utter disgust' at what it said was the failure of the military and civil authorities to act effectively against the IRA. Shortly before it was banned, leading members of the UVF met government officials and put a series of demands to the government. These were, apparently, that the IRSP should be declared illegal and that the incident centres set up to monitor the IRA ceasefire should be closed. However, these talks were unproductive. In fact, the security forces were already poised to swoop on the homes of UVF suspects in Belfast and E. Antrim. On 5 October, 1,000 troops and police were involved in the operation, which had been planned since a day in the previous August when a twenty-seven-year-old UVF officer ran to a police station in Carrickfergus to report that a UVF court-martial was under way in the Royal British Legion Hall in the town. He feared that he was going to be tried and shot by the UVF, and his information on the organisation proved to be the link the security forces needed to break up a strong UVF unit in that area. In March 1977, after a £2m trial, the most costly in NI's criminal history, twenty-six UVF men were given a total of 700 years' imprisonment, including eight life sentences. There were fifty-five charges against the men, including four murders. One was the murder of a UVF man and two

others murders of UDA men, Hugh McVeigh and David Douglas, whose bodies were found in a shallow grave in Co. Antrim five months after they disappeared. About the same time, ten men from the Ballyclare, Co. Antrim, unit were sentenced for a variety of terrorist offences, and it is known that units in Bangor, Co. Down, and Coleraine also found difficulty in surviving arrests in early 1977. The UVF probably maintains a small but ruthless organisation in Belfast, and it has a welfare secion which looks after assistance for prisoners and their families. In June 1977, there were confused reports about a ceasefire, which seemed to confirm the belief that the UVF was somewhat divided in its leadership. In June 1979, nine Scottish UVF members were sentenced to between twelve and eighteen years' imprisonment for plotting to further the aims of the UVF. Four of the men were also convicted of bombing two Glasgow pubs and the judge, Lord Ross, described the gang as 'wicked, brutal and senseless'. He also urged that the organisation should be declared illegal in Scotland. The convictions were believed to have broken up a sixty-strong UVF unit in Glasgow which had been engaged in supplying explosives to the UVF in NI. In the early 1980s, the UVF suffered from informers both in Belfast and in Co. Armagh. Eighteen of 20 men arrested in Co. Armagh in 1982 on the evidence of ex-UVF informer Clifford McKeown pleaded guilty to a variety of terrorist offences, some of which indicated that the organisation was then involved in sectarian murder attempts. In the Shankill area in the same year, police raids broke up a UVF group and uncovered firearms, including a home-made machine-gun, and ammunition, and seven UVF men from Larne got a total of 89 years' imprisonment on charges such as armed robbery and having guns and bombs. There were reports about the same time of internal differences in the organisation, notably in Belfast. In 1982, the UVF reacted angrily to a comment by the Chief Constable that weapons favoured by PIRA had been found in the possession of loyalists. 'Is he not aware,' it asked, 'that the black market on which these weapons are purchased is not interested in the politics of Northern Ireland, but only in the cash and business which our conflict brings?' The same statement described the UVF as 'political soldiers with the spirit of 1912.' The organisation suffered a severe blow in April, 1983, when one of its battalion commanders, Joseph Bennett, turned 'supergrass' and gave evidence which resulted in the conviction of 14 leading members, two of whom were sentenced to life imprisonment. Those convicted included John Graham, described as 'brigadier-general.' Bennett was given immunity in respect of two murders and other offences. In the summer of 1983 there were more arrests arising from the activities of informers.

ULSTER WORKERS' COUNCIL.

The body which organised and ran the loyalist strike in May 1974, which led to the collapse of the power-sharing administration. By the cutting of power supplies and extensive backing from Protestant paramilitary groups, it halted industrial and other activity, and the chaotic situation which had developed after fourteen days caused Unionist members to resign from the Executive and so render it ineffective. The UWC operated through a Co-ordinating Committee, headed by Vanguard Assemblyman Glen Barr. It included three leading politicians – Harry West (Official Unionist); Rev. Ian Paisley (DUP); and William Craig (Vanguard). Among the paramilitary representatives were Andy Tyrie (UDA), Colonel Brush (Down Orange Welfare), Ken Gibson and Bill Hannigan (UVF political spokesmen), George Green (USC Association) and Bob Marno (Orange Volunteers). Its best-known spokesmen during the stoppage were Jim Smyth and Harry Murray, and other members were Billy Kelly (power workers), Hugh Petrie and Tom Beattie. The UWC was again active in the 1977 loyalist strike – a more limited affair – which had been backed by the United Unionist Action Council. But failure to halt electricity supplies in 1977 reduced its effectiveness. And in 1977, the Official Unionists and Vanguard were opposed to the strike, although it was supported by the Rev. Ian Paisley and Ernest Baird, now leading the UUUP. In February 1981, its former chairman Harry Murray, announced that the UWC was being re-formed to campaign for jobs and to promote the unity of workers. He said it would not have paramilitary links.

UNIONIST PARTY OF NORTHERN IRELAND.

Formed by those ex-members of the OUP who continued to support Brian Faulkner after the Sunningdale proposals had been rejected by the OUP, and Mr Faulkner had resigned as party leader. Initially those who had rallied round Mr Faulkner simply adopted the description 'Unionist Pro-Assembly', and six candidates employing this label unsuccessfully contested the February 1974 Westminster election. UPNI was formally launched in September 1974, four months after the collapse of the Executive, and Mr Faulkner boldly expressed the view that it could become the 'mainstream' Unionist Party. But two of its nominees failed to get elected in the October 1974 Westminster election. In the Constitutional Convention, UPNI continued its support for power-sharing, and stressed the need for a strong regional government, with a maintenance of the UK link. But it dropped the idea of a Council of Ireland, which it held to be counter-productive in developing social and economic co-operation between NI and the Irish Republic. Its total of first-preference votes in the election was 50,891 (7.7 per cent of the total) and it got five seats out of the seventy-eight. In 1976, after the failure of the Convention, Brian Faulkner (later Lord Faulkner) withdrew from the leadership of the party, and from active politics, and he died in a hunting accident in 1977. He was succeeded by Mrs Anne Dickson. In the 1977 district council elections, the party fought on a narrow front, and

secured 13,691 first-preference votes (2.4 per cent of the total) and took six seats out of the 526. The party's viewpoint was represented in the House of Lords by Lord Brookeborough and Lord Moyola, and it continued to enjoy the support of several other former members of Unionist governments, including Sir John Andrews. In 1978, there were some rumours of a possible link-up with the OUP, but the party continued to differ with the OUP on the power-sharing issue, and seemed to be determined to maintain its independent stance. In the 1979 Westminster election, it ran three candidates in Belfast, but its total vote was only 8,021 (1.2 per cent of the total vote) and all three candidates lost their deposits. In the 1979 European election, it fared no better. Its candidate, consultant engineer Eddie Cummings, had 0.6 per cent of first-preference votes and lost his deposit. Because of its poor showing in the 1981 council elections, when it shared seven seats in a temporary coalition with UPUP, the party decided to wind up its organisation.

UNITED LABOUR PARTY.

A party launched in 1978, with the declared aim of trying to establish a government in NI based on democratic socialism. Paddy Devlin, formerly of the SDLP, was one of the founders. Its draft constitution urged co-operation with other Labour movements throughout the British Isles. It also stated that the constitutional position of NI should only be changed if that would further political accommodation and have majority support from the electors. Mr Devlin got just over 6,000 first preference votes when he ran unsuccessfully as ULP candidate in the 1979 European election, and its nominee in the S. Belfast by-election for Westminster in 1982 secured 303 votes.

UNITED ULSTER UNIONIST COUNCIL. Sometimes called the Unionist Coalition, it was set up in January 1974 to fight the Sunningdale agreement, which it saw as a step to a United Ireland. It followed on the split in the Unionist Party, which elected Harry West as leader in succession to Brian Faulkner, who had become Chief Minister in the power-sharing Executive. The UUUC comprised the Official Unionists headed by Mr West, the Democratic Unionist Party, led by the Rev. Ian Paisley, and the Vanguard Unionists, headed by William Craig. The group won eleven of the twelve NI seats in the February 1974 Westminster election. After the election, these MPs formed a Unionist Parliamentary Coalition led by Mr West and James Molyneaux MP succeeded Mr West when the latter lost his Fermanagh-S. Tyrone seat in October 1974. The support of the UUUC for the UWC strike in May 1974 was an important element in the success of the stoppage. It continued to operate in the Convention election in 1975 and in the Convention it carried through the majority report which failed, however, to get backing from other parties. Mr Craig's support for the idea of a voluntary

coalition, embracing the SDLP for an emergency period, led to a split in Vanguard, the majority of whose Convention members remained loyal to the UUUC when Mr Craig was expelled from the Unionist Coalition. In early 1977 the UUUC, now made up of the Official Unionists, DUP and the UUUM headed by Ernest Baird (the UUUM included the majority section of Vanguard which had refused to follow Mr Craig) began to show signs of serious internal strain. This was aggravated by the formation by the UUUC steering committee of United Unionist Action Council which eventually took in paramilitary groups and mounted the abortive 'loyalist strike' in May 1977. The Official Unionists condemned this venture, and the UUUC effectively collapsed. The Parliamentary Coalition at Westminster also broke up at the time of the May stoppage, since two of its MPs, the Rev. Ian Paisley and John Dunlop, supported the stoppage. But the UUUC experiment at Westminster had important political implications. It marked the real break between the Conservative Party and Ulster Unionists in parliament, and the close balance in the Commons in 1977 gave the Unionist MPs the influence to secure Labour government support for a Speaker's Conference to consider extra NI seats at Westminster – a longstanding demand of all shades of Unionism and a move hitherto opposed by Labour – and the NI Boundary Commission recommended 17 seats. The change took effect in the 1983 election and very much benefited the OUP.

UNITED ULSTER UNIONIST MOVEMENT. See UNITED ULSTER UNIONIST PARTY and VANGUARD UNIONIST PROGRESSIVE PARTY.

UNITED ULSTER UNION-IST PARTY. The party led by Ernest Baird which emerged to fight the district council elections in May 1977. It was based on the UUUM – the breakaway movement from the Vanguard Party during the Constitutional Convention. UUUM was made up of the former Vanguard Convention members who were opposed to William Craig's idea of a voluntary coalition. Initially, UUUM campaigned for the creation of a single, united Unionist party. When this appeared unattainable, Baird announced that the UUUM would become a political party as UUUP. In the 1977 council elections, it got 3.2 per cent of first-preference votes and twelve seats. In the 1979 Westminster election it retained Mid-Ulster, where the sitting MP, John Dunlop, was not opposed by the Official Unionists. Ernest Baird was unsuccessful in Fermanagh-S. Tyrone. The party share of the vote in the election was 5.6 per cent (two seats contested). In the 1982 Assembly election, it ran 12 candidates, but none was returned, and its share of the total vote was 1.8 per cent. The candidates included party leader Ernest Baird, deputy leader Reg Empey and John Dunlop, MP. The party did not contest the 1983 Westminster election, and there were doubts at that time about its future.

UNITED UNIONIST ACTION COUNCIL. The body which organised vigilante patrols, known as the Ulster Service Corps, in the spring of 1977. It also promoted the loyalist strike in May, 1977, against direct rule and in favour of tougher security measures – a stoppage which drew much less support than the UWC strike of 1974. The UUAC included the Rev. Ian Paisley and Ernest Baird, and its chairman was former Unionist MP, Joseph Burns. It included representatives of the UWC, UDA, Orange Volunteers and Down Orange Welfare. The UUAC was technically a sub-committee of the steering com-mittee of the UUUC. It was not, however, supported by the OUP or the VUPP, and, unlike the organisers of the 1974 stoppage, failed to get the backing of the power workers.

UNITY MOVEMENT. An anti-Unionist group launched in April 1973. Its main personality was Frank McManus, then MP for Fermanagh and S. Tyrone. In May 1973, it issued a manifesto calling for an amnesty for all poli-tical prisoners, disbandment of the RUC, the setting up of a new police force, and repeal of all 'offensive and repressive' legisla-tion. In the February 1974 West-minster election, McManus lost his seat and another Unity candi-date in Armagh polled very few votes. In 1977, McManus was one of the founders of the Irish Inde-pendence Party.

V

VANGUARD SERVICE CORPS. The paramilitary organisation linked with Ulster Vanguard in its early years. When Ulster Vanguard became the Ulster Vanguard Progressive Party in 1973, the VSC took the title, 'Ulster Volunteer Service Corps.' Its main purpose was to provide an escort for Vanguard speakers.

VANGUARD UNIONIST PROGRESSIVE PARTY. A political party which developed out of the Vanguard Movement, led by William Craig. It was established as a party in March 1973, and mainly comprised ex-members of the Unionist Party disenchanted with the policies of recent leaders, Terence O'Neill, James Chichester-Clark and Brian Faulkner. In the Assembly election of 1973, it secured seven seats and 10.5 per cent of the total vote, and in the Convention election of 1975 (as part of the UUUC) it doubled its representation to fourteen seats, although its share of the total vote had increased only to 12.7 per cent. This indicated the shrewdness with which the UUUC had distributed its candidates. VUPP reflected the strong opposition to direct rule of the Vanguard movement from which it sprang. It also opposed the British government's White Paper on which the Assembly was based, and it pressed for tough measures against the IRA. In the Convention, it was seriously split over Mr Craig's support for the idea of voluntary coalition with the SDLP. Apart from Mr Craig himself and two other members, David Trimble and Glen Barr, the rest of the party broke away under the leadership of Ernest Baird, deputy leader, to form the UUUM, which in 1977 became the UUUP. The VUPP did not contest the 1977 district council elections as an entity and in February 1978, it ceased to be a political party, and reverted to its former status of the Vanguard Movement. Mr Craig, then MP for E. Belfast, moved to the OUP. The VUPP's other MP elected in 1977, John Dunlop in Mid-Ulster, had already joined the UUUP. In 1982, Mr Craig, clearly disillusioned with the OUP, stood as Vanguard Unionist in E. Belfast, but got only 2,200 first-preference votes. See ULSTER VANGUARD.

VAN STRAUBENZEE, WILLIAM RADCLIFFE. Minister of State, NI Office, 1972–4. b. 27 January 1924. Conservative MP for Wokingham, 1959–. Church (of England) Commissioner, 1967–. Known as 'the Bishop' in Westminster circles, he presided as NI Minister of State over a committee which drew up proposals to counter religious and political discrimination in jobs, and which led eventually to the setting up of the Fair Employment Agency.

VITTY, DENNY. DUP Assembly member for E. Belfast, 1982–. b. 1950. Castlereagh Council, 1977–. Chairman, DUP's E. Belfast Association.

VOLUNTEER POLITICAL PARTY. Political wing of the Protestant para-military organisation, the UVF, it emerged briefly in September 1974. Its chairman, Ken Gibson, contested the October 1974 Westminster election in W. Belfast. He had some support from the UDA in the area, but polled only 2,690 votes. The VPP supported the link with Britain, and said either a united Ireland or UDI would mean a cut in social security benefits and higher taxes.

W

WARRENPOINT. South Co. Down port and seaside resort, near which eighteen soldiers died on 27 August, 1979, in two PIRA explosions. It was the largest death-toll in any incident up to that date. The ambush came only a few hours after Lord Mountbatten had been killed when his boat was blown up by PIRA off the Co. Sligo coast in the Republic.

WELLS, JAMES HENRY. DUP. Assembly member for S. Down, 1982–. b. 1957. Honours graduate, geography (QUB). Lisburn Council, 1981–.

WEST, HENRY WILLIAM (HARRY). Leader of the OUP, 1974–9. b. Enniskillen, 27 March 1917. Large-scale farmer in Co. Fermanagh, High Sheriff, Fermanagh, 1954. President, Ulster Farmers' Union, 1955–6. Unionist MP for Enniskillen, 1954–72. Parliamentary Secretary, Ministry of Agriculture, 1958. Minister of Agriculture, 1960–6 and 1971–2. MP for Fermanagh-S. Tyrone, 1974, and leader of United Unionist Parliamentary Coalition at Westminster, 1974. Elected from Fermanagh-S. Tyrone to Assembly, 1973–4 and Constitutional Convention, 1975–6. During the 1968–71 period, he led the West Ulster Unionist Council and strongly criticised reforms which he saw as weakening Unionism and the position of the NI government. In particular, he opposed local government changes and the setting up of a central housing authority. He also resisted the idea of an unarmed police force, and the abolition of the USC. But he resigned from the West Ulster Unionist Council in June 1971, and accepted Brian Faulkner's invitation to return as Minister of Agriculture. He was not, however, prepared to follow Mr Faulkner on the issue of power-sharing government and the Sunningdale agreement, and in January 1974 he was elected to succeed Mr Faulkner as OUP leader, when the Ulster Unionist Council rejected the Sunningdale package. He aligned the OUP with the DUP and Vanguard in the UUUC and he gained the Fermanagh-S. Tyrone seat as official UUUC candidate in the February 1974 election. He lost it again in October 1974 when anti-Unionists combined to support Frank Maguire, Independent. In the Assembly, he led his party in opposition to the three-party Executive, although he dissociated his supporters from rowdy scenes in and around the Assembly chamber. He backed the UWC strike in May 1974 which led to the fall of the Executive. In the Constitutional Convention, he continued to resist the idea of power-sharing at Cabinet level, although he always insisted that his attitude was not anti-Catholic, but only directed to refusing co-operation in government with those who sought a united Ireland. In early 1977, he gradually drifted apart from the Rev. Ian Paisley and Ernest Baird, the other two leaders of the UUUC. The differences centred on a Unionist Action Council which mounted a strike in May 1977 against direct rule and in favour of a much tougher security policy. Mr West and his party refused to back the strike, which got only limited support from loyalists, and the result was to confirm the break-up of the UUUC. Between 1977 and 1979, he was engaged in many discussions with Secretary of State Roy Mason on the possibility of some form of interim devolution, but the talks were unproductive. In the European Assembly election in June 1979, he secured just under 57,000 first-preference votes, which inevitably led to comparisons with the Rev. Ian Paisley's 170,000 and he was eliminated on the fourth count. The result led to speculation about his future as party leader, but OUP chiefs argued that there were special circumstances in the election, and that he was not at fault. He claimed himself that some 100,000 OUP voters had just refused to turn out because of their doubts about the Common Market. But he immediately tendered his resignation as party leader, and on 2 July – within four weeks of the election – he confirmed this and was succeeded by James Molyneaux MP. He lost to hunger striker Bobby Sands in the April, 1981, Westminster by-election in Fermanagh and S. Tyrone.

WEST ULSTER UNIONIST COUNCIL. A large pressure group within the OUP, active between 1969 and 1971 in defending traditional Unionism. It opposed reforms such as the reduction of the powers of local authorities and the setting up of a central housing authority. It also demanded tougher security policies. It was spearheaded by Fermanagh Unionist Association, and although the bulk of its membership was made up of Unionist Associations in W. Ulster, it also had the support of several constituency associations in Belfast and E. Ulster. It was frequently attacked by liberal Unionists as a divisive force, but Harry West MP, who led it for most of the time, insisted that it spoke for the majority of grassroots Unionists. He resigned from the Council in 1971, when he became Minister of Agriculture in the Faulkner government.

WHITELAW, VISCOUNT WILLIAM STEPHEN IAN. First Secretary of State of NI, March 1972–Nov. 1973. b. 28 June 1918. Golfing blue, Cambridge University, 1936–9. Took up farming on Cumberland estate after resigning army commission, 1947. Conservative MP for Penrith and the Border, 1955–83. Chief Conservative Whip, 1964–70. Lord President of the Council and Leader of the Commons, 1970–2. Employment Secretary, 1973–4. Chairman Conservative Party, 1974–5. Deputy leader of Conservative Party, 1975–9 and spokesman on Home Affairs, 1975–9. Deputy Prime minister and Home Secretary, 1979–83. Lord President of Council and Leader of Lords, 1983–. On taking over at Stormont in 1972, the genial Mr Whitelaw had to face a double threat – the wrath of loyalists deprived of a local parliament and government and a big effort by the PIRA, so that the overall result was a year with 467 violent deaths. In a bid to keep a brief IRA ceasefire going, he tried a controversial initiative in early July 1972. He met IRA leaders secretly in London, but the Provisionals' terms were too sweeping to be acceptable to the British government. The Secretary of State reported to MPs that the IRA wanted:

(1) a public declaration that the Irish people as a whole should decide the future of Ireland.

(2) the withdrawal of all British troops from Irish soil by 1 January 1975.

(3) Pending the withdrawal, all troops should be withdrawn immediately from 'sensitive areas'.

(4) a general amnesty for all political prisoners, internees and persons on the wanted list.

Mr Whitelaw also said the Provisionals had expressed regret that internment had not been halted in response to their ceasefire, which had been ended after a fortnight, following a single dispute about housing in W. Belfast which, Mr Whitelaw claimed, could easily have been resolved peacefully. The thinking behind the meeting with the IRA, according to the Minister of State at the time, David Howell (*The Times*, 10 February 1975) was that the government wanted to show that everything had been tried, including truce and meeting, so that the IRA would be seen to be concerned only with violence. About the same time, Mr Whitelaw made what he later admitted to parliament was a mistake – he agreed to special privileges for convicted terrorists who belonged to the political paramilitary groups. This 'special category' system began following a hunger strike in Belfast prison during which one IRA leader, Billy McKee, was close to death. But after 'Bloody Friday', in Belfast – 21 July 1972 – when ten civilians and three soldiers died in the city, Mr Whitelaw ordered the takeover of the 'no-go' areas. These were the areas, mainly in W. Belfast and in Londonderry's Bogside, where there was little control by the security forces. On 31 July 1972, the army moved into the areas in strength in 'Operation Motorman', and while two people were killed by troops in Derry, there was little resistance generally. But despite the continuance of violence, both from the IRA and loyalist groups, he tried to move the emphasis to political progress, and organised a conference of local political parties at Darlington in September 1972. Too few parties accepted to make the exercise worthwhile. Nonetheless, at the end of October 1972, he produced a discussion paper (a 'green paper' in British parliamentary terms, but the phrase was officially avoided) which pointed to the need to recognise both the British and Irish dimensions in the NI situation. In March 1973 this was translated into a White Paper which set out the government's plans for new-style devolved government. It proposed a seventy-eight member Assembly elected by PR, and power-sharing between the parties as an alternative to majority government. Unionists were sharply divided on the document, but SDLP and Alliance gave it a general welcome. Whitelaw began the most severe test of his diplomacy on 5 October 1973 (that is, precisely five years after the violent scenes in Derry's Duke Street) when he met the delegations from three parties at Stormont Castle. The Unionists were led by Brian Faulkner, the SDLP by Gerry Fitt, and Alliance by Oliver Napier. The talks were patiently piloted by Mr Whitelaw over seven weeks, and often they came close to breakdown. But, finally, on 21 November 1973, a formula was agreed for a three-party Executive (in effect, a coalition). But the final seal on strategy had to be left to a conference at Sunningdale in Berkshire, in early December, attended by Mr Heath as Prime Minister and by Irish Ministers, headed by the Taoiseach, Mr Cosgrave. Immediately before the conference, Mr Whitelaw moved to the Deparment of Employment, and he was succeeded by Francis Pym as NI Secretary. In the event, he was called to Sunningdale by Mr Heath when discussions there became particularly critical. As Conservative deputy leader, he resisted pressures from within the party to depart from the broadly bi-partisan approach to NI which had been established in 1969. As Home Secretary and Deputy Premier in the Thatcher Government, he was a member of the Cabinet committee considering efforts to restore devolution to the province. In 1981, he announced an inquiry by Lord Jellicoe into the operation of the Prevention of Terrorism Act. He caused some surprise when he hinted at the 1982 Conservative conference that citizens of the Irish Republic living in Great Britain might lose their voting rights. In December, 1982, he banned two PSF Assembly members, Gerry Adams and Danny Morrison, from entering GB because of their alleged links with terrorism. One of his last acts as Home Secretary in June, 1983, was to remove the ban on Adams, once he had been elected in W. Belfast.

WHITTEN, HERBERT. Off. U. member of NI Assembly, 1973–4, and Convention, 1975–6, elected from Armagh, b. Portadown, Co. Armagh, 1909; died Dec., 1981. He was one of three Off. U. members of the Assembly who voted against a vote of confidence in the power-sharing Executive in February 1974. Prominent in Orange Order in Co. Armagh. Stormont MP for Central Armagh, 1969–72. Portadown Borough Council, 1968–72, Craigavon District Council, 1973–81. (Mayor, 1968–9.)

WIDGERY REPORT. See 'BLOODY SUNDAY'.

WILLIAMS, BETTY. One of the three founders of the Peace People in 1976. Awarded Nobel Peace Prize, 1976, b. Belfast, 1943. A housewife from Andersonstown, one of Belfast's republican strongholds, she witnessed the tragedy (that is, the accident in which the three Maguire children were killed) which inspired her, together with Mairead Corrigan and Ciaran McKeown, to launch the Peace Movement. She has travelled abroad extensively to talk about the movement. In 1980 she stepped down from the Peace People executive, although continuing to campaign for it. Before leaving NI to live in the US in October, 1982, she spoke of her inability to secure employment in NI. She said she had had 200 job refusals in 18 months. In December, 1982, she married an American businessman, Jim Perkins, in Florida.

WILSON, GERARD PADDY. SDLP Senator who was stabbed to death at a lonely quarry on the Upper Hightown Road, in N. Belfast, on 26 June 1973. b. 1933. A woman friend, to whom he had given a lift in his car, was murdered at the same time. The murders were claimed by the Ulster Freedom Fighters as part of a campaign to secure the release of their members from detention. Senator Wilson had been elected to the Senate in 1968 as Rep. Lab. but left that party in 1970 when he was one of the founders of the SDLP. He was also a Belfast City Councillor. At the time of his death he had been acting as election agent to Gerry Fitt MP for the Assembly elections, for which polling took place only two days after his death. He had always refused to carry a gun for his own protection.

WILSON, HUGH. Alliance Assembly (1973–4) and Convention (1975–6) member for N. Antrim. b. Ballyclare, Co. Antrim, 1905. M.B. B.Ch., B.A.O. (QUB). Consultant surgeon (F.R.C.S.). Narrowly defeated in Larne by William Craig in the 1969 Stormont general election. Founder member of the Alliance Party. Unsuccessfully contested N. Antrim seat (held by the Rev. Ian Paisley) in Westminster election, October 1974.

WILSON, SIR JAMES HAROLD. Labour Prime Minister, 1964–70 and 1974–6. b. 11 March 1916. Harold Wilson's career touched NI at many points. As a young civil servant, he toyed with the idea of seeking the post of economic adviser to the NI government. As Labour Party leader (1963–6), he was highly conscious of the importance of the Irish vote in Britain. He often remarked that he had reminded successive Prime Ministers of the Irish Republic that he had more Irish people in his Huyton (Liverpool) constituency than they had in theirs. As Prime Minister at the start of the civil rights campaign in 1968, he and Home Secretary James Callaghan had to deal with the crisis produced by the demands for reform, and later, in 1969, with the serious violence in Belfast, Londonderry and other towns. Harold Wilson had, apparently, already made up his mind to send troops to NI when the appeal for them came from Stormont in August 1969. And he personally handled the critical talks with NI Ministers which set the stage for reforms – social, political and in the reorganisation of the RUC and disbandment of the 'B' Specials. His most comprehensive statement of his personal views was in a speech as opposition leader in the Commons in November 1971. He urged more attention to the aspiration of a united Ireland, while stressing that it could come only with the agreement of people in NI. But he said the dream must be there. 'If men of moderation have nothing to hope for, men of violence will have something to shoot for.' So he suggested talks between the Westminster, Dublin and Stormont parliaments which could lead to a Constitutional Commission which would work out arrangements for a united Ireland, which could become effective fifteen years after agreement had been reached, provided that political violence had ceased. He also urged the participation of Ulster Catholics at all levels of government, and the removal of all security powers from Stormont and their transfer to London. His approach was condemned by Unionists and by some members of the NILP, but given a cautious welcome by Catholic politicians. Wilson had never been enthusiastic about direct rule, but he backed the decision of the Heath government to impose it in 1972. In 1974, he returned to power to face the challenge of the loyalist strike, and was attacked both by loyalists and by the SDLP. The Unionists resented fiercely his speech on 25 May 1974, in which he condemned the strike organisers as people 'purporting to act as though they were an elected government, spending their lives sponging on Westminster...' The SDLP said he had failed to act toughly enough to smash the strike. In 1975, he travelled to Stormont to announce the date of the Convention election, and he saw the Convention fail before he left office in 1976. Life Peer, 1983.

WINDLESHAM, LORD. Minister of State, NI Office, 1972–3. b. 28 January 1932. Lord Windlesham, a Roman Catholic, was deputy to William Whitelaw MP when he took over as Secretary of State, NI, in March 1972. Has strong Irish links, since his ancestor, Richard Hennessy (1720–1800), b. Co. Cork, went to Cognac, France, in 1765, and founded the firm of Hennessy. At the NI Office, Lord Windlesham was spokesman in the House of Lords, and his responsibilities included community relations, Home Affairs and Development. In 1973, he became government leader in the Lords, and Conservative leader there when Labour came to power in 1974.

WOMEN TOGETHER. A peace movement launched in November 1970, which brought together women from Protestant and Catholic areas in mixed groups to campaign against violence. The group was strongly criticised by Provisional Sinn Fein, some of whose supporters disrupted WT meetings. Monica Patterson who was chairman of the movement from 1970 to 1973, says that it quickly achieved the position where it was listened to by the army chiefs, the Secretary of State and even Prime Minister Harold Wilson. She said that if it vouched for the innocence of youths who had been 'lifted', they were released. 'We were out on the streets', she wrote in 1978, 'stopping rowdyism between gangs of youths ... stopping armed youths engaged in vandalism of property, sweeping the streets and having burned-out vehicles removed ... supporting the victims of intimidation ...'

WOODFIELD, SIR PHILIP JOHN. Permanent Secretary, NI Office, 1981–3. b. 30 Aug. 1923. His arrival as head of the official side of the NI Office almost coincided with James Prior's appointment as Secretary of State, and he brought to the post very diverse political experience, including a spell in the early 1970s as deputy secretary at Stormont. He joined the Home Office in 1950 and served there for three different periods, and from 1961 to 1965 he was at 10 Downing Street, as private secretary to three Prime Ministers – Macmillan, Douglas-Home, and Wilson. He was also with the Federal Government of Nigeria from 1955 to 1957, and in 1966 was secretary to Lord Mountbatten's committee of inquiry into prison conditions.

WORKERS' PARTY, THE. A Republican party with a strong Socialist content operating in both NI and the Republic. Up to 1982,

it was known as Official Sinn Fein in the Republic and Republican Clubs in NI. In 1982, its three Dail TDs supported Charles Haughey as Taoiseach and enabled him to form a minority government. Its change of name was clearly designed to dissociate itself from paramilitarism, since with the split in the Republican movement in 1970, Official Sinn Fein and the Republican Clubs were the political counterpart of the OIRA. As Republican Clubs, the organisation was declared illegal in NI in March 1967, by William Craig as Minister of Home Affairs. He made an order prohibiting it under the Special Powers Act. On an appeal to the House of Lords, a majority of Law Lords (three to two) upheld Mr Craig's decision. In April 1973 – that is, a year after the OIRA had begun its ceasefire – the proscription was removed. It was a move by the British government to try to bring more militant elements into the political process. By that time, the Republican Clubs had become more Marxist, in line with the general trend in Official Sinn Fein. In the Assembly election in 1973, they opposed the British government's White Paper and urged an all-Ireland socialist republic. They put up ten candidates, but emphasised that, if elected, they would only take their seats when internment ended, and emergency powers were dropped. But none of their nominees were returned, and the party's total first-preference vote was 13,064 (1.8 per cent of the total). They adopted a very similar approach in the Convention elections, but again, their seventeen candidates were all unsuccessful.

The party tally was 14,515 first-preferences votes (2.2 per cent of the total). In the District Council elections in May 1977 they got six seats out of the 556, with 14,277 first preference votes (2.6 per cent of the total). But in the 1981 council elections they lost three of their six seats, and had only 1.8 per cent of first-preferences. In the 1982 Assembly election, the party improved its showing in terms of the overall vote, with 2.7 per cent of first-preferences, but failed to secure any representation. It also contests Westminster elections, but has not so far achieved a significant vote.

WRIGHT, SIR JOHN OLIVER. First UK government representative in NI, August 1969–March 1970. b. 6 March 1921. A senior diplomat, he was sent to NI in a 'watch-dog' role for the Prime Minister, Harold Wilson. He was engaged in the delicate negotiations about the removal of the barricades in Belfast's Falls Road in 1969, and in monitoring the NI government's reform programme. He established a pattern of meeting politicians on all sides. On leaving NI, he said that Britain had tended to neglect the province in the past, and NI had tended willingly to run its own affairs, and this had been wrong for both sides of the equation. British Ambassador to W. Germany, 1975–81. With increased Irish-American activity, his appointment as ambassador to Washington in 1982 was seen by NI Office as timely.

Y

YOUNG, SIR ARTHUR EDWIN. Chief Constable. RUC, 1969–70. b. 1908, died January 1979. Sir Arthur interrupted his career as City of London Police Commissioner to take over control of the RUC during the crucial period of reorganisation of the RUC arising from the Hunt report. He did so at the personal request of the Prime Minister, Harold Wilson, who saw Sir Arthur's experience of terrorism in Malaya and elsewhere as valuable in restoring the morale of the force, which had been shaken by the violence of the summer of 1969. In carrying out the policy of civilianising the RUC he angered many Unionists, some of whom dubbed him 'Mr Softly, Softly'.

YOUNG CITIZENS VOLUNTEER FORCE. A Protestant extremist youth group active mainly in 1974 and 1975. An RUC detective told a court in February 1975, that it had been formed for the sole purpose of killing Catholics. In the summer of 1974, there were reports that it was involved in the petrol-bombing of Catholic homes. Probably not a sizeable organisation.

YOUNG MILITANTS. A loyalist paramilitary group first mentioned in 1972, when it was assumed to be a breakaway from the UDA. But this was denied by the UDA. It has claimed several explosions in NI and the Republic.

Election Results, 1968–83

1968 Stormont By-elections

Lisnaskea

	% poll 81.0
Brooke, J. (U.)	4,428
Patterson, F. (Ind. U.)	3,270
Wynne, J. (Lib.)	1,102
March 1968 U. maj.	1,158

Derry City

	% poll 68.8
Anderson, A. W. (U.)	9,122
Wilcox, Mrs J. (NILP)	3,944
May 1968 U. maj.	5,178

South Antrim

	% poll 49.6
Ferguson, R. (U.)	16,288
Coulthard, J. (NILP)	2,848
November 1968 U. maj.	13,440

1969 Stormont General Election

The Stormont General election on 24 Feb. 1969 was dubbed by the Prime Minister, Captain Terence O'Neill, the 'crossroads election'. He insisted that it was the last chance for Ulster people to vote for sensible, reformist policies which would enable NI to have the respect of Westminster, and which would assure its continued membership of the United Kingdom. At the same time, civil rights supporters were suspicious of the will, or the ability, of the Premier to deliver reforms. And, within Unionism, he was assailed by many who suggested he was selling out to those who wanted a united Ireland. So the election battle took on a wholly new character – there were Unofficial Unionists who supported O'Neill against Official Unionists who opposed him. There were Independents who represented the broad civil rights platform, and People's Democracy candidates who spoke for the more revolutionary wing. The Prime Minister had been strongly criticised for attacking Official Unionists who did not share his view. But the Premier replied that he couldn't support those who equivocated or hedged, and who didn't back vital parts of the Unionist manifesto. He was under fire from the former Prime Minister, Lord Brookeborough, and from his ex-ministerial colleague, Brian Faulkner, who had resigned from the government the previous month. The overall result of the election posed no problem for Unionists, who slightly improved their position. Of the thirty-nine

Unionist MPs, twenty-four were Official (pro-O'Neill) and three Unofficial (pro-O'Neill) while ten were Official (anti-O'Neill) and two Official, but unclear in their attitude to the Premier. But the divisions at the grassroots of Unionism were serious, and tensions were building up steadily with civil rights marches and loyalist counter-demonstrations. And although Captain O'Neill declared after the election that he would stay on and fight, he resigned two months later.

Overall result, with previous party strengths in parentheses

Unionist	39	(37)
Nationalist	6	(9)
Independent	3	(0)
NILP	2	(2)
Rep. Lab.	2	(2)
Liberal	0	(1)
Nat. Dem.	0	(1)
	52	(52)

*Indicates outgoing MP.

Belfast – Ballynafeigh

Elec. 14,572	% poll 64.0
*Neill, I. (U.)	6,523
Holmes, E. (NILP)	2,675
No change	U. maj. 3,848

Belfast – Bloomfield

Elec. 21,142	% poll 70.4
*Scott, W. (U.)	9,084
Spence, W. (Prot. U.)	3,568
Caldwell, W. (NILP)	2,196
No change	U. maj. 5,516

Belfast – Central

Elec. 6,384	% poll 58.3
Kennedy, P. (Rep. Lab.)	2,032
*Brennan, J. (Nat. Dem.)	1,538
Rep. Lab. gain	Rep. Lab. maj. 494

Belfast – Clifton

Elec. 16,196	% poll 74.5
Hall-Thompson, L. (Unoff. U.)	6,066
*Morgan, W. (U.)	3,215
Thompson, N. (NILP)	1,681
McKeown, M. (Nat. Dem.)	1,079
Unoff. U. gain Unoff. U. maj.	2,851

Belfast – Cromac

Elec. 13,542	% poll 61.5
*Kennedy, W. (U.)	6,320
Barkley, J. (NILP)	1,134
Wiegleb, E. (P.D.)	752
No change	U. maj. 5,186

Belfast – Dock

Elec. 7,212	% poll 73.0
*Fitt, G. (Rep. Lab.)	3,274
Smith, H. (U.)	1,936
No change	Rep. Lab. maj. 1,338

Belfast – Duncairn

Elec. 18,415	% poll 66.0
*Fitzsimmons, W. (U.)	7,435
Porter, N. (Unoff. U.)	4,321
No change	U. maj. 3,114

Belfast – Falls

Elec. 19,802	% poll 60.5
Devlin, P. (NILP)	6,275
*Diamond, H. (Rep. Lab.)	5,549
NILP gain	Lab. maj. 726

Belfast – Oldpark

Elec. 17,817	% poll 69.0
*Simpson, V. (NILP)	6,779
Cairns, J. (U.)	5,224
No change	Lab. maj. 1,555

Belfast – Pottinger

Elec. 8,328	% poll 68.5
Cardwell, J. (U.)	2,902
McBirney, M. (NILP)	2,744
U. gain	U. maj. 158

Belfast – Shankill

Elec. 18,186	% poll 72.0
*Boal, D. (U.)	6,384
Walsh, H. (Unoff. U.)	4,545
Overend, D. (NILP)	1,997
No change	U. maj. 1,839

Belfast – St. Anne's

Elec. 19,041	% poll 71.0
*Laird, Dr N. (U.)	7,126
McKee, Sir C. (Unoff. U.)	4,183
Murphy, J. (Nat. Dem.)	2,136
No change	U. maj. 2,943

Belfast – Victoria

Elec. 19,504	% poll 76.0
*Bradford, R. (U.)	9,249
Coulthard, J. (NILP)	2,972
Bunting, R. (Prot. U.)	2,489
No change	U. maj. 6,277

Belfast – Willowfield

Elec. 12,427	% poll 68.9
*Caldwell, T. (Unoff. U.)	4,613
Hinds, W. (U.)	2,134
Boyd, B. (NILP)	1,747
Unoff. U. gain Unoff. U. maj.	2,479

Belfast – Windsor

*Kirk, H. V. (U.)	unopposed

Belfast – Woodvale

Elec. 19,984	% poll 72.2
*McQuade, J. (U.)	7,299
Boyd, W. R. (NILP)	3,878
Bell, L. (Unoff. U.)	3,231
No change	U. maj. 3,421

Bannside

Elec. 20,635	% poll 78.7
*O'Neill, Capt. T. (U.)	7,745
Paisley, Rev. I. (Prot. U.)	6,331
Farrell, M. (PD)	2,310
No change	U. maj. 1,414

Carrick

Elec. 22,905	% poll 64.3
Dickson, Mrs A. (U.)	9,529
Craig, J. (Unoff. U.)	5,246
No change	U. maj. 4,283

Larkfield

Elec. 20,774	% poll 68.3
McIvor, B. (U.)	8,501
Sherry, T. (Nat. Dem.)	2,386
Magee, T. (NILP)	1,714
O'Hare, G. (Rep. Lab.)	1,591
New seat	U. maj. 6,115

Larne

Elec. 20,728	% poll 79.5
*Craig, W. (U.)	8,550
Wilson, H. (Unoff. U.)	7,897
No change	U. maj. 653

Antrim *Minford, N. (U.) unopposed

Mid-Antrim

Elec. 21,992	% poll 58.8
*Simpson, Dr R. (U.)	10,249
Galbraith, R. H. (NILP)	2,124
No change	U. maj. 8,125

Newtownabbey

Elec. 22,151	% poll 54.3
Baillie, R. (U.)	9,852
McDowell, J. W. (NILP)	3,410
New seat	U. maj. 6,442

North Antrim

Elec. 19,611	% poll 63.0
*O'Neill, P. (U.)	9,142
Wylie, Rev. J. W. (Prot. U.)	3,241
No change	U. maj. 5,901

South Antrim

Elec. 24,693	% poll 64.7
*Ferguson, R. (U.)	10,761
Beattie, Rev. W. (Prot. U.)	5,362
No change	U. maj. 5,399

Ards *Long, Capt. W. (U.) unopposed

Bangor

Elec. 20,886	% poll 61.8
McConnell, R. D. (Unoff. U.)	7,714
Campbell, R. (U.)	5,190
New seat	Unoff. U. maj. 2,524

East Down

Elec. 18,230	% poll 86.0
*Faulkner, B. (U.)	8,136
McGrady, E. (Nat. Dem.)	6,427
Lt-Col. D. Rowan-Hamilton (Unoff. U.)	1,248
No change	U. Maj. 1,709

Iveagh

Elec. 16,172	% poll 70.0
*McGowan, S. (U.)	6,869
Poots, C. (Prot. U.)	4,365
No change	U. maj. 2,504

Lagan Valley

*Porter, R. QC (U.) unopposed

Mid-Down

Kelly, B. QC (U.) unopposed

Mourne

Elec. 16,272	% poll 81.0
*O'Reilly, J. (Nat.)	7,335
Newell, C. (U.)	5,960
No change	Nat. maj. 1,375

North Down

Elec. 18,408	% poll 57.0
*Babington, Robert (U.)	9,013
Murnaghan, Miss S. (Lib.)	1,567
No change	U. maj. 7,446

South Down

Elec. 17,486	% poll 56.0
*Keogh, M. (Nat.)	4,830
Woods, P. (PD)	4,610
No change	Nat. maj. 220

West Down

Elec. 16,584	% poll 70.7
*Dobson, J. (U.)	7,608
Buller, A. W. (Unoff. U.)	5,219
No change	U. maj. 2,389

Central Armagh

*Whitten, H. (U.)	unopposed

Mid-Armagh

Elec. 15,901	% poll 80.8
Stronge, J. (U.)	6,932
Toman, C. (PD)	3,551
Magowan, I. (Unoff. U.)	2,321
No change	U. maj. 3,381

North Armagh

Elec. 20,652	% poll 72.0
Mitchell, R. J. (U.)	9,087
Kennedy, A. (Nat. Dem.)	5,847
No change	U. maj. 3,240

South Armagh

Elec. 18,140	% poll 71.0
O'Hanlon, P. (Ind.)	6,442
*Richardson, E. (Nat.)	4,332
Byrne, P. (NILP)	1,794
Ind. gain	Ind. maj. 2,110

City of Derry

Elec. 19,344	% poll 81.5
*Anderson, A. (U.)	6,480
Wilton, C. (Lib.)	5,770
Campbell, P. (Unoff. U.)	4,181
No change	U. maj. 710

Foyle

Elec. 19,875	% poll 84.0
Hume, J. (Ind.)	8,920
*McAteer, E. (Nat.)	5,267
McCann, E. (NILP)	1,993
Ind. gain	Ind. maj. 3,653

Mid-Derry

Elec. 16,411	% poll 82.0
Cooper, I. (Ind.)	6,056
Shields, R. (U.)	4,438
*Gormley, P. (Nat.)	2,229
O'Kane, J. (Rep. Lab.)	709
Ind. gain	Ind. maj. 1,618

North Derry

Elec. 24,457	% poll 76.6
*Burns, J. (U.)	9,364
Barr, J. (Unoff. U.)	9,249
No change	U. maj. 115

South Derry

Elec. 18,393	% poll 83.5
*Chichester-Clark, Maj. J. (U.)	9,195
Devlin, Miss B. (PD)	5,812
No change	U. maj. 3,383

East Tyrone

Elec. 17,432	% poll 89.9
*Currie, A. (Nat.)	9,065
Curran, E. (U.)	6,501
No change	Nat. maj. 2,564

Mid-Tyrone

Elec. 11,779	% poll 69.4
*Gormley, T. (Nat.)	5,149
McDonald, P. (Ind.)	2,992
No change	Nat. maj. 2,157

North Tyrone

Elec. 18,024	% poll 85.5
Fyffe, W. (U.)	8,290
McLaughlin, D. (Nat. Dem.)	6,596
O'Kane, L. (Ind.)	559
No change	U. maj. 1,694

South Tyrone

Elec. 17,132	% poll 83.6
*Taylor, J. (U.)	7,683
Eakins, Rev. G. (Unoff. U.)	6,533
No change	U. maj. 1,150

West Tyrone

*O'Connor, R. (Nat.)	unopposed

Enniskillen

Elec. 11,695	% poll 87.0
*West, H. (U.)	4,891
Egan, B. (PD)	2,784
Archdale, D. (Unoff. U.)	2,418
No change	U. maj. 2,107

Lisnaskea

Elec. 10,506	% poll 88.0
*Brooke, Capt. J. (U.)	4,794
Henderson, Maj. J. (Unoff. U.)	2,702
Carey, M. (PD)	1,726
No change	U. maj. 2,092

South Fermanagh

Elec. 8,322	% poll 74.9
*Carron, J. (Nat.)	4,108
Cosgrove, P. (PD)	2,100
No change	Nat. maj. 2,008

1969 Westminster By-election

In the by-election caused by the death of George Forrest, the Unionist MP for Mid-Ulster, his wife, Anna, the Unionist candidate, was defeated by Bernadette Devlin, Unity, in a hard-fought contest.

Mid-Ulster

	% poll 91.5
Devlin, Miss B. (Unity)	33,648
Forrest, Mrs A. (U.)	29,437
April 1969	Unity maj. 4,211

1970 Stormont By-elections

The two by-elections which took place on 16 April 1970 were probably the most vital in the history of the Stormont House of Commons. They were at Bannside, vacated by the former Prime Minister, Captain Terence O'Neill, and at S. Antrim, left vacant by the resignation of one of his leading supporters, Richard Ferguson, a young barrister. First, they were a test of Unionist feeling on the reforms carried through by the Chichester-Clark government. Second, they were a measure of the support for Mr Paisley, since he was standing in Bannside and the deputy leader of his Protestant Unionist Party, the Rev. William Beattie, in S. Antrim. In the event, the government suffered a shattering defeat, losing both seats.

Bannside

Paisley, Rev. I (Prot. U.)	7,981
Minford, Dr. B. (U.)	6,778
McHugh, P. (NILP)	3,514
Prot. U. maj.	1,203

South Antrim

Beattie, Rev. W. (Prot. U.)	7,137
Morgan, W. (U.)	6,179
Corkey, D. (Ind.)	5,212
Whitby, A. (NILP)	1,773
Prot. U. maj.	958

1970 Westminster General Election

The main local feature of the June 1970 Westminster General Election was that, for the first time, Official Unionists secured only eight of the twelve seats. The Rev. Ian Paisley gained N. Antrim and Frank McManus, Unity, Fermanagh and S. Tyrone, while Gerry Fitt held W. Belfast, and Bernadette Devlin held Mid-Ulster. In UK terms, the big change was that James Callaghan was no longer master-minding the reforms from London, since the Conservatives had returned to power and Reginald Maudling had replaced Callaghan at the Home Office.

Overall Figures

Party	Votes cast	% of total poll
Unionists	422,036	54.1
NILP	98,464	12.6
Unity	76,204	9.7
Independent (B. Devlin)	37,739	4.8
Prot. U.	35,303	4.5
Rep. Lab.	30,649	3.9
Nat.	27,006	3.4
Liberals	12,005	1.5
Nat. Dem.	10,343	1.3
Others	29,004	3.7
Total valid votes	778,753	99.5
Spoiled votes	440	0.5
Total votes polled	779,193	100.0

*Indicates outgoing MP.

West Belfast

Elec. 69, 245	% poll 84.0
*Fitt, G. (Rep. Lab.)	30,649
McRoberts, B. (U.)	27,451
No change	Rep. Lab. maj. 3,198

East Belfast

Elec. 59,524	% poll 76.0
*McMaster, S. R. (U.)	26,778
Bleakley, D. W. (NILP)	18,529
No change	U. maj. 8,249

North Belfast

Elec. 75,740	% poll 78.0
*Mills, S. (U.)	28,668
Sharkey, J. (NILP)	18,894
Beattie, Rev. W. (Prot. U.)	11,173
McKeague, J. D. (Ind.)	441
No change	U. maj. 9,774

South Belfast

Elec. 57,112	% poll 68.0
*Pounder, R. (U.)	27,523
Coulthard, J. (NILP)	11,567
No change	U. maj. 15,956

South Antrim

Elec. 144,743	% poll 67.0
Molyneaux, J. (U.)	59,589
Johnston, R. (NILP)	19,971
Caldwell, H. (Ind. U,)	10,938
MacAllister, J. (Nat. Dem.)	6,037
Smith, A. M. (Lib.)	913
No change	U. maj. 39,618

North Antrim

Elec. 80,510	% poll 73.0
Paisley, Rev. I. (Prot. U.)	24,130
*Clark, H. M. (U.)	21,451
McHugh, P. (NILP)	6,476
McDonnell, A. (Nat. Dem.)	4,312
Moore, G. (Lib.)	2,269
Prot. U. gain.	Prot. U. maj. 2,679

Armagh

Elec. 86,846	% poll 78.0
*Maginnis, J. (U.)	37,667
Lewis, H. (Unity)	21,696
Holmes, E. (NILP)	8,781
No change	U. maj. 15,971

North Down

Elec. 121,284	% poll 66.0
Kilfedder, J. (U.)	55,679
Young, K. (NILP)	14,246
Nixon, R. (Ind. U)	6,408
McGladdery, J. R. (Ind.)	3,321
Simmons-Gooding, H. (Lib.)	1,076
No change U. maj. (largest in UK)	41,433

South Down

Elec. 87,384	% poll 73.0
*Orr, L. P. S. (U.)	34,894
Golding, H. (Unity)	21,676
Quinn, J. G. (Lib.)	7,747
No change	U. maj. 13,218

Londonderry

Elec. 90,800	% poll 81.0

*Chichester-Clark, R. (U.)	39,141
McAteer, E. (Nat.)	27,006
McCann, E. (Unoff. Lab.)	7,565
No change	U.maj. 12,135

Mid-Ulster

Elec. 78,473	% poll 90.0

*Devlin, B. (Ind.)	37,739
Thornton, W. N. J. (U.)	31,810
Cunningham, M. (Ind. Unity)	771
O'Neill, P. (National Socialist)	198
No change	Ind. maj. 5,929

Fermanagh and South Tyrone

Elec. 70,641	% poll 92.0

McManus, F. (Unity)	32,832
*Hamilton, Lord (U.)	31,390
Unity gain	Unity maj. 1,442

1973 District Council Elections

In the first election for the twenty-six new district councils, held on 30 May 1973, proportional representation was used in NI for the first time since the 1920s. Parties tended to regard the contest as a trial run for the coming Assembly election. Unionist and loyalist candidates secured more than 300 of the 526 seats. Official Unionists and Unionists, adopted almost exclusively by OUP associations, got control of twelve councils, with 216 seats. The DUP won twenty-one seats, and a variety of other loyalists had about sixty in all. The SDLP took eighty-three seats, and were the largest party in three councils, while Alliance took sixty-three seats and Republican Clubs seven.

Results

Antrim: Off. U. 8; All. 2; Ind. 2; Un. 1; DUP 1; VUPP 1.

Ards: Off. U. 11; All. 2; SDLP 1; NILP 1; VUPP 1.

Armagh: Off. U. 10; SDLP 5; DUP 2; U. 1; All. 1; Ind. 1.

Ballymena: Off. U. 9; DUP 5; VUPP 1; All. 1; Ind. 2; Non-Party 3.

Ballymoney: Non-Party 5; Off. U. 4; U. 2; SDLP 2; DUP 1; All. 1; Ind. 1.

Banbridge: U. 10; Ind. 3; SDLP 1; Off. U. 1.

Belfast: U. 25; All. 8; SDLP 7; DUP 2; Rep. C. 2; NILP 2; Ind. U. 2; Utd. Loy. 2; VUPP 1.

Carrick: Off. U. 5; Utd. Loy. 5; All. 3; Loy. 1; Non-Party 1.

Castlereagh: Off. U. 5; U. 5; All. 5; Utd. Loy. 2; Loy. Coal. 1; Ind. 1.

Coleraine: Off. U. 12; All. 3; U. 1; Ind. U. 1; SDLP 1; Ind. 1; Non-Party 1.

Cookstown: Off. U. 7; SDLP 3; Loy. Coal. 1; U. 1; Rep. C. 1; Ind. 1; Non-Party 1.

Craigavon: Off. U. 7; All. 4; Dup 3; U. 3; Loy. Coal. 3; VUPP 2; SDLP 2; Ind. 1.

Down: U. 8; SDLP 8; All. 2; VUPP 1; Ind. 1.

Dungannon: U. 11; SDLP 5; Unity 2; Rep. 2.

Fermanagh: Off. U. 4; U. 4; SDLP 4; Unity 4; U. Unity 1; Ind. U. 1; Ind. 1; Non-Party 1.

Larne: Loy. 8; All. 3; Ind. 2; Off. U. 1; Non-Party 1.

Limavady: Utd. U. 8; SDLP 4; All. 2; Ind. 1.

Lisburn: Off. U. 14; DUP 4; All. 3; VUPP 1; SDLP 1.

Londonderry: SDLP 10; Utd. Loy. 9; All. 4; Nat. 3; Rep. C. 1.
Magherafelt: SDLP 6; U. 3; Off. U. 2; VUPP 1; Utd. Loy. 1; Rep. C. 1; Ind. 1.
Moyle: Ind. 5; Off. U. 4; Non-Party 4; SDLP 2; U. 1.
Newry and Mourne: SDLP 13; Non-Party 6; All. 4; U. 3; Ind. 2; Rep. C. 2.
Newtownabbey: Off. U. 9; U. 3; DUP: 3; All. 3; Utd. Loy. 1; Loy. 1; NILP 1.
North Down: Off. U. 7; All. 7; Loy. 4; U. 2.
Omagh: U. 6; SDLP 4; All. 3; Community 3; U. Unity 2; Off. Rep. 1; Nat. 1.
Strabane: U. 6; SDLP 4; All. 2; Ind. 2; Utd. Loy. 1.

1973 Assembly Election

The Assembly of seventy-eight members was elected by PR (single transferable vote) on 28 June 1973. Because of the divisions in Unionism the party labels were not always an accurate guide to the attitude of candidates to the British Government's White Paper which envisaged a partnership government. For example, several Official Unionists were against the scheme and the policy of the party leader, Brian Faulkner. So the anti-White Paper Unionists were split between ten official candidates, the Vanguard Unionist Loyalist Coalition (led by William Craig), the Democratic Unionist Loyalist Coalition (led by Rev. Ian Paisley) and three members of the West Belfast Loyalist Coalition. The Alliance and Northern Ireland Labour Parties did less well than they expected, and for the first time in the history of Northern Ireland no Nationalist was elected. The SDLP, with nineteen seats, established itself as the second party.

Seats and Votes

Party	Seats	Votes	% Total votes
Official Unionists	24	211,362	29.3
Unionists	8	61,183	8.5
DULC	8	78,228	10.8
VULC	7	75,759	10.5
WBLC	3	16,869	2.3
Other Loyalist	0	3,734	0.5
SDLP	19	159,773	22.1
Alliance	8	66,541	9.2
NILP	1	18,675	2.6
Rep. C.	0	13,064	1.8
Nationalist	0	8,270	1.2
Rep. Lab.	0	1,750	0.2
Liberal	0	811	0.1
Communist	0	123	–
Independents	0	6,099	0.9
	78	722,241	100.0

West Belfast

Elec. 70,791   % poll 62.5

6 elected: (Quota 5,911)		1st pref.
Count 1	Laird, J. D. (U.)	11,479
Count 1	Devlin, P. J. (SDLP)	7,743
Count 3	Smyth, H. (Ind. U.)	3,625
Count 9	Coulter, R. J. (U.)	1,765
Count 12	Cooper, R. G. (All.)	3,160
Count 12	Gillespie, D. E. (SDLP)	1,940

East Belfast

Elec. 80,421   % poll 71.7

6 elected: (Quota 8,113)		1st pref.
Count 1	Bradford, R. H. (Off. U.)	13,187
Count 13	Cardwell, J. (Off. U.)	5,001
Count 16	Paisley, E. (DULC)	5,518
Count 18	Napier, O. J. (All.)	4,941
Count 18	Bleakley, D. W. (NILP)	4,425
Count 18	Agnew, N. (Off. U.)	3,615

North Belfast

Elec. 75,768   % poll 68.7

6 elected: (Quota 7,255)		1st pref.
Count 1	Fitt, G. (SDLP)	8,264
Count 11	McQuade, J. (DULC)	5,148
Count 14	Hall-Thompson, L. (Off. U)	5,694
Count 15	Morgan, W. J. (Off. U.)	5,190
Count 15	Millar, F. (U.)	4,187
Count 15	Ferguson, J. (All.)	1,958

South Belfast

Elec. 75,990   % poll 70.6

6 elected: (Quota 7,532)		1st pref.
Count 11	McIvor, W. B. (Off. U.)	6,930
Count 12	Glass, J. B. C. (All.)	5,148
Count 14	Burns, T. E. (DULC)	4,640
Count 15	Elder, N. (Off. U.)	4,807
Count 15	Kirk, H. V. (Off. U.)	5,426
Count 16	Magee, R. A. E. (Off. U.)	3,656

South Antrim

	Elec. 114,240	% poll 66.9
8 elected: (Quota 8,338)		1st pref.
Count 1	Beattie, W. J. (DULC)	10,126
Count 1	Dickson, A. L. (Off. U.)	9,033
Count 9	McCloskey, E. V. (SDLP)	7,899
Count 13	Crothers, D. S. F. (All.)	5,975
Count 17	Minford, N. O. (Off. U.)	5,289
Count 18	Ardill, R. A. (Off. U.)	5,234
Count 18	Lindsay, K. (VULC)	3,055
Count 18	McLachlan, P. (Off. U.)	3,983

North Antrim

	Elec. 99,635	% poll 72.5
7 elected: (Quota 8,907)		1st pref.
Count 1	Paisley, Rev. I. R. K. (DULC)	14,533
Count 1	Baxter, J. L. (Off. U.)	9,009
Count 2	Craig, W. (VULC)	8,538
Count 12	O'Hagan, J. J. (SDLP)	6,204
Count 15	McCarthy, D. (Off. U.)	5,125
Count 15	Wilson, J. (All.)	2,876
Count 15	Craig, J. (DULC)	3,871

Armagh

	Elec. 89,056	% poll 71.1
7 elected: (Quota 7,676)		1st pref.
Count 1	O'Hanlon, P. M. (SDLP)	8,219
Count 1	Mallon, S. F. (SDLP)	7,995
Count 7	Whitten, H. (Off. U.)	6,891
Count 8	Carson, T. D. (VULC)	6,866
Count 10	Stronge, J. M. (Off. U.)	4,355
Count 12	News, H. (SDLP)	4,731
Count 12	Hutchinson, D. (DULC)	4,552

North Down

	Elec. 89,682	% poll 69.4
7 elected: (Quota 7,682)		1st pref.
Count 1	Kilfedder, J. A. (Off. U.)	20,684
Count 2	Brooke, J. (Off. U.)	6,160
Count 12	Poots, C. B. (DULC)	4,364
Count 13	Lord Dunleath (All.)	4,482
Count 13	Campbell, R. W. (Off. U.)	3,760
Count 13	Brownlow, W. S. (Off. U.)	2,620
Count 13	McConnell, R. D. (All.)	3,271

South Down

	Elec. 89,324	% poll 73.2
7 elected: (Quota 8,005)		1st pref.
Count 1	Faulkner, A. B. D. (Off. U.)	16,287
Count 7	McGrady, E. R. (SDLP)	7,870
Count 12	Broadhurst, R. J. C. (Off. U.)	1,515
Count 14	Feely, F. (SDLP)	6,857
Count 15	O'Donoghue, P. (SDLP)	4,322
Count 17	Harvey, C. (VULC)	5,006
Count 17	Heslip, J. (U.)	3,838

Londonderry

	Elec. 89,849	% poll 75.9
7 elected: (Quota 8,308)		1st pref.
Count 1	Hume, J. (SDLP)	12,596
Count 1	Morrell, L. J. (U.)	9,685
Count 2	Logue, H. A. (SDLP)	7,230
Count 3	Douglas, W. A. B. (U.)	8,245
Count 9	Barr, G. (VULC)	6,511
Count 11	Canavan, M. W. E. (SDLP)	3,647
Count 11	Conn, S. E. (U.)	6,550

Mid-Ulster

	Elec. 79,331	% poll 82.4
6 elected: (Quota 9,145)		1st pref.
Count 1	Cooper, I. A. (SDLP)	12,614
Count 1	Pollock, T. D. (Off. U.)	9,557
Count 10	Duffy, P. A. (SDLP)	4,437
Count 11	Dunlop, J. (VULC)	7,082
Count 11	Thompson, W. J. (U.)	5,352
Count 13	Larkin, A. J. (SDLP)	4,045

Fermanagh and South Tyrone

	Elec. 68,733	% poll 84.6
5 elected: (Quota 9,448)		1st pref.
Count 1	Currie, J. A. (SDLP)	11,016
Count 4	Baird, E. A. (VULC)	8,456
Count 7	Taylor, J. D. (U.)	8,410
Count 7	Daly, T. A. (SDLP)	7,511
Count 7	West, H. W. (U.)	8,198

February 1974 Westminster General Election

This election, held on 28 February, proved to have enormous political repercussions. The NI power-sharing Executive had been in office only since the start of the year and the UUUC campaign was directed both against the principle of partnership with the SDLP and the idea of a Council of Ireland as envisaged in the Sunningdale agreement. The three Executive parties – Brian Faulkner's Unionists, the SDLP and the Alliance Party – were seriously embarrassed at having to defend a system that had barely got off the ground. And to maximise its effort, the UUUC had a single candidate in each constituency, and it adopted what proved to be a telling slogan, 'Dublin is just a Sunningdale away'. The UUUC got eleven of the twelve seats, with Gerry Fitt, Deputy Chief Executive, retaining his W. Belfast seat for the SDLP. The UUUC, having secured more than half the total votes cast, claimed that the result was a vote of no confidence in the new administration.

Overall Figures

Party	Votes cast	% of total poll
UUUC	366,703	50.8
Pro-Assembly U.	94,301	13.1
SDLP	160,437	22.2
Alliance	22,660	3.1
NILP	15,483	2.1
Republican Clubs	12,106	1.7
Others (Ind. Lab., Unity) and Inds.)	45,936	6.4
Total valid votes	717,626	99.4
Spoiled votes	4,656	0.6
Total votes polled	722,282	100.0

*Indicates outgoing MP.

West Belfast

Elec. 65,656	% poll 73.0
*Fitt, G. (SDLP)	19,554
McQuade, J. (DUP-UUUC)	17,374
Price, A. (Ind.)	5,662
Brady, J. (Rep. C.)	3,088
Boyd, W. R. (NILP)	1,989
No change	SDLP maj. 2,180

East Belfast

Elec. 78,818	% poll 73.1
Craig, W. (VUPP-UUUC)	27,817
*McMaster, S. R. (U. Pro-A.)	20,077
Bleakley, D. W. (NILP)	8,122
Gillespie, D. E. (SDLP)	1,502
UUUC gain	UUUC maj. 7,740

North Belfast

Elec. 71,083	% poll 69.9
Carson, J. (U–UUUC)	21,531
Smyth, D. W. (U. Pro-A.)	12,755
Donnelly, T. (SDLP)	12,003
Scott, A. (NILP)	2,917
No change	UUUC maj. 8,776

South Belfast

Elec. 74,542	% poll 69.8
Bradford, R. J. (VUPP–UUUC)	22,083
*Pounder, R. J. (U. Pro-A.)	18,085
Cook, D. S. (All.)	5,118
Caraher, J. B. (SDLP)	4,149
Holmes, J. E. (NILP)	2,455
UUUC gain	UUUC maj. 3,998

South Antrim

Elec. 116,710	% poll 61.5
*Molyneaux, J. H. (U–UUUC)	48,203
Kinahan, C. H. G. (All.)	12,559
Rowan, P. J. (SDLP)	8,769
Kidd, R. J. (Ind.)	1,801
No change	UUUC maj. 35,644

North Antrim

Elec. 102,983	% poll 63.4
*Paisley, Rev. I. R. K. (DUP–UUUC)	41,282
Utley, T. E. (U. Pro-A.)	13,651
McAlister, M. (SDLP)	10,056
No change	UUUC maj. 27,631

Armagh

Elec. 90,262	% poll 67.7
McCusker, J. H. (U–UUUC)	33,194
O'Hanlon, P. M. (SDLP)	18,090
Glendenning, R. J. (All.)	4,983
Moore, T. O. (Rep. C.)	4,129
Lewis, H. (Unity)	1,364
No change	UUUC maj. 15,104

North Down

Elec. 92,800	% poll 67.6
*Kilfedder, J. A. (U–UUUC)	38,169
Bradford, R. H. (U. Pro-A.)	21,943
Curran, D. (SDLP)	2,376
No change	UUUC maj. 16,226

South Down

Elec. 90,613	% poll 66.6
*Orr, L. P. S. (U.–UUUC)	31,088
Hollywood, S. (SDLP)	25,486
Golding, H. (Rep. C.)	3,046
No change	UUUC maj. 5,602

Londonderry

Elec. 92,192	% poll 69.2
Ross, W. (U–UUUC)	33,060
Logue, H. A. (SDLP)	23,670
Montgomery, M. J. (Rep. C.)	2,530
Foster, R. J. (Lab. and TU)	846
No change	UUUC maj. 9,390

Mid-Ulster

Elec. 80,982	% poll 82.7
Dunlop, J. (VUPP-UUUC)	26,044
Cooper, I. A. (SDLP)	19,372
*McAliskey, B. (Ind. Soc.)	16,672
Thornton, W. N. J. (U. Pro-A.)	4,633

UUUC gain   UUUC maj. 6,672

Fermanagh and South Tyrone

Elec. 70,615	% poll 87.6
West, W. H. (U-UUUC)	26,858
*McManus, F. J. (Unity)	16,229
Haughey, P. D. (SDLP)	15,410
Browne, H. I. (U. Pro-A.)	3,157

UUUC gain   UUUC maj. 10,629

October 1974 Westminster General Election

The Westminster election of 10 October brought only one change of party strength. The Official Unionist leader, Harry West, lost his Fermanagh-South Tyrone seat to Independent Frank Maguire, who had stood as an agreed anti-Unionist nominee. In a sense, the contest was a test of the standing of the UUUC after its successful campaign against the power-sharing Executive, and also of the more independent line adopted by Unionists at Westminster. After the election, Mr West was succeeded as UUUC Parliamentary leader by James Molyneaux, and Enoch Powell was returned in South Down to provide valuable parliamentary expertise for the UUUC. Gerry Fitt, for the SDLP, stressed partnership in government, and Brian Faulkner's newly-established

UPNI made its first election bid, and one which proved disappointing for it. Alliance ran five candidates, but found that its call for an end to violence as the first priority did not make sufficient impact.

Overall Figures

Party	Votes cast	% of total poll
UUUC	407,778	57.4
UPNI	20,454	2.9
SDLP	154,193	21.7
Alliance	44,644	6.3
Rep. C.	21,633	3.1
NILP	11,539	1.6
Others	41,853	5.9
Total valid votes	702,094	98.9
Spoiled votes	7,805	1.1
Total votes polled	709,899	100.0

*Indicates outgoing MP

West Belfast

Elec. 66,278	% poll 68.0
*Fitt, G. (SDLP)	21,821
McQuade, J. (DUP-UUUC)	16,265
O'Kane, K. (Rep. C.)	3,547
Gibson, S. McK. (VPP)	2,690
Kerins, P. (Comm.)	203

No change   SDLP maj. 5,556

East Belfast

Elec. 79,629	% poll 67.4
*Craig, W. (VUPP-UUUC)	31,594
McLachlan, P. (UPNI)	14,417
Bleakley, D. (NILP)	7,415

No change   UUUC maj. 17,177

North Belfast

Elec. 71,774	% poll 66.6

*Carson, J. (U-UUUC)	29,622
Donnelly, T. (SDLP)	11,400
Ferguson, J. (All.)	3,807
Boyd, W. (NILP)	2,481

No change   UUUC maj. 18,222

South Belfast

Elec. 75,147	% poll 67.9

*Bradford, R. J. (VUPP-UUUC)	30,116
Glass, B. (All.)	11,715
McMaster, S. (Ind. U.)	4,982
Carraher, B. (SDLP)	2,390
Holmes, E. (NILP)	1,643

No change   UUUC maj. 18,401

South Antrim

Elec. 118,483	% poll 58.0

*Molyneaux, J. (U-UUUC)	48,892
Kinahan, C. (All.)	10,460
Rowan, P. (SDLP)	9,061

No change   UUUC maj. 38,432

North Antrim

Elec. 103,763	% poll 57.7

*Paisley, Rev. I. R. K. (DUP-UUUC)	43,186
Wilson, H. (All.)	8,689
McAlister, M. (SDLP)	7,616

No change   UUUC maj. 34,497

Armagh

Elec. 91,085	% poll 69.5

*McCusker, H. (U-UUUC)	37,518
Mallon, S. (SDLP)	19,855
McGurran, M. (Rep. C.)	5,138

No change   UUUC maj. 17,663

North Down

Elec. 93,641	% poll 61.2

*Kilfedder, J. A. (U-UUUC)	40,996
Jones, K. (All.)	9,973
Brownlow, W. (UPNI)	6,037

No change   UUUC maj. 31,023

South Down

Elec. 91,792	% poll 70.0

Powell, E. (U-UUUC)	33,614
Hollywood, S. (SDLP)	30,047
O'Hanlon, G. (Rep. C.)	2,327
Vipond, D. (Comm.)	152

No change   UUUC maj. 3,567

Londonderry

Elec. 93,207	% poll 71.3

*Ross, W. (U-UUUC)	35,138
Hume, J. (SDLP)	26,118
Montgomery, M. J. (Rep. C.)	2,530
Foster, R. (Lab.-TU)	846

No change   UUUC maj. 9,020

Mid-Ulster

Elec. 82,718	% poll 79.2

*Dunlop, J. (VUPP-UUUC)	
	30,552
Cooper, I. (SDLP)	25,885
Donnelly, F. (Rep. C.)	8,091

No change	UUUC maj. 4,667

Fermanagh and South Tyrone

Elec. 71,343	% poll 88.7

Maguire, F. (Ind.)	32,795
*West, H. W. (U-UUUC)	30,285
Evans, A. J. (Comm.)	185

Ind. gain	Ind. maj. 2,510

1975 Convention Election

The election for the Constitutional Convention, like the Assembly contest, was conducted on PR (STV) for seventy-eight seats based on the twelve Westminster constituencies. It was held on 1 May 1975. Because it was not a parliamentary election, but simply the return of delegates to an elected conference, the clash was purely on the basis of what type of constitution would have the widest acceptance in the NI community and would be approved by Westminster. The UUUC, embracing the Official Unionists, DUP and VUPP, were firmly committed to having 'British parliamentary standards' – that is, majority rule on the Westminster model – whereas the parties representing the former power-sharing Executive – that is, SDLP, Alliance and UPNI – urged partnership government of the type which they felt had not had a fair trial in the Assembly. The UUUC, with a special steering committee, worked with great skill to deploy their candidates in order to secure the maximum advantage from PR. In the event 165 candidates contested the seventy-eight seats – fifty-four fewer than in the Assembly election. The total turnout was 65.8 per cent as compared with 72.3 per cent in the Assembly election, indicating perhaps a little election weariness, since this was the seventh poll in NI in little more than two years.

Seats and votes

Party	Seats	Votes	% of total poll	
UUUC:				
Official Unionists	19	169,797	25.8	
DUP	12	97,073	14.8	54.8
VUPP	14	83,507	12.7	
Other Loyalists	2	10,140	1.5	
SDLP	17	156,049	23.7	
Alliance	8	64,657	9.8	
UPNI	5	50,891	7.7	
Rep. C.	0	14,515	2.2	
NILP	1	9,102	1.4	
Ind.	0	2,052	0.3	
Communist	0	378	0.1	
	78	658,161	100.0	

West Belfast	Elec. 63,689	% poll 58.7
6 elected: (Quota 5,103)		1st pref.
Count 1	Laird, J. (U-UUUC)	8,433
Count 1	Devlin, P. (SDLP)	6,267
Count 6	Coulter, J. (U-UUUC)	2,325
Count 8	Cooper, R. (All.)	3,293
Count 8	Hendron, J. (SDLP)	2,840
Count 8	Smyth, H. (Ind. Loy.)	2,644

East Belfast	Elec. 78,340	% poll 65.3
6 elected: (Quota 7,166)		1st pref.
Count 1	Craig, W. (VUP-UUUC)	11,958
Count 6	Napier, O. (All.)	6,341
Count 8	Empey, R. (VUP-UUUC)	4,657
Count 11	Cardwell, J. (UPNI)	3,039
Count 11	Paisley, E. (DUP-UUUC)	3,606
Count 11	Bleakley, D. (NILP)	3,998

North Belfast	Elec. 70,673	% poll 63.3
6 elected: (Quota 6,230)		1st pref.
Count 1	Fitt, G. (SDLP)	6,454
Count 1	Bell, W. (U-UUUC)	6,268
Count 7	Millar, F. (Ind.-UUUC)	5,687
Count 8	Morgan, W. (U-UUUC)	5,558
Count 10	Hall-Thompson, L. (UPNI)	3,577
Count 10	Annon, W. T. (DUP-UUUC)	4,132

South Belfast	Elec. 73,324	% poll 66.3
6 elected: (Quota 6,831)		1st pref.
Count 1	Smyth, Rev. M. (U-UUUC)	15,061
Count 1	Glass, B. (All.)	7,961
Count 2	Burchill, J. (U-UUUC)	4,230
Count 8	Hendron, J. (All.)	2,499
Count 9	Trimble, D. (VUP-UUUC)	2,429
Count 11	Burns, T. (DUP-UUUC)	2,529

South Antrim

	Elec. 119,723	% poll 58.6
8 elected: (Quota 7,646)		1st pref.
Count 1	Beattie, W. (DUP-UUUC)	11,834
Count 1	Ardill, A. (U-UUUC)	10,895
Count 4	McCloskey, V. (SDLP)	6,756
Count 8	Kinahan, C. (All.)	5,294
Count 9	Dickson, A. (UPNI)	5,723
Count 11	Dunlop, S. (DUP-UUUC)	2,461
Count 11	Lindsay, K. (VUP-UUUC)	4,529
Count 12	Morrisson, G. (VUP-UUUC)	2,943

North Antrim

	Elec. 103,469	% poll 61.0
7 elected: (Quota 7,778)		1st pref.
Count 1	Paisley, Rev. I. (DUP-UUUC)	19,335
Count 2	McFaul, K. (DUP-UUUC)	7,658
Count 2	Smyth, C. (DUP-UUUC)	5,806
Count 9	Wilson, H. (All.)	4,601
Count 10	Turnly, J. (SDLP)	4,888
Count 12	Wright, W. (VUP-UUUC)	2,761
Count 12	Allen, D. (VUP-UUUC)	2,268

Armagh

	Elec. 90,640	% poll 67.7
7 elected: (Quota 7,424)		1st pref.
Count 1	Mallon, S. (SDLP)	8,999
Count 1	Armstrong, M. (U-UUUC)	8,802
Count 1	Mutchinson, D. (DUP-UUUC)	7,746
Count 9	Whitten, H. (U-UUUC)	4,843
Count 9	Carson, T. D. (VUP-UUUC)	5,974
Count 9	Black, A. (VUP-UUUC)	5,435
Count 9	News, H. (SDLP)	3,303

North Down

	Elec. 93,884	% poll 62.6
7 elected: (Quota, 7,223)		1st pref.
Count 1	Kilfedder, J. (U-UUUC)	21,693
Count 1	Taylor, J. (U-UUUC)	7,238
Count 3	Green, G. (VUP-UUUC)	4,408
Count 6	Poots, C. (DUP-UUUC)	2,962
Count 7	Dunleath, Lord (All.)	4,616
Count 8	McConnell, R. (All.)	3,099
Count 8	Brookeborough, Lord (UPNI)	3,555

South Down

Elec. 89,912   % poll 68.9

7 elected: (Quota 7,594)   1st pref.

Count 1	Feely, F. (SDLP)	9,730
Count 1	Harvey, C. (VUP-UUUC)	8,843
Count 2	McGrady, E. (SDLP)	7,257
Count 4	O'Donoghue, P. (SDLP)	6,657
Count 9	Faulkner, B. (UPNI)	6,035
Count 9	Brush, E. (U-UUUC)	6,293
Count 9	Heslip, H. (U-UUUC)	6,380

Londonderry

Elec. 92,003   % poll 69.8

7 elected: (Quota 7,801)   1st pref.

Count 1	Hume, J. (SDLP)	11,941
Count 1	Conn, S. (U-UUUC)	8,789
Count 1	Barr, G. (VUP-UUUC)	7,883
Count 4	Logue, H. (SDLP)	6,661
Count 5	Douglas, W. (U-UUUC)	4,999
Count 6	Canavan, M. (SDLP)	4,600
Count 12	McClure, J. (DUP-UUUC)	3,436

Mid-Ulster

Elec. 80,806   % poll 69.8

6 elected: (Quota 7,801)   1st pref.

Count 1	Thompson, W. (U-UUUC)	9,342
Count 1	Cooper, I. (SDLP)	9,073
Count 1	Reid, R. (DUP-UUUC)	8,250
Count 10	Duffy, P. (SDLP)	4,130
Count 11	Thompson, E. (U-UUUC)	4,292
Count 11	Overend, R. (VUP-UUUC)	5,573

Fermanagh and South Tyrone

Elec. 70,344   % poll 78.4

5 elected: (Quota 8,843)   1st pref.

Count 1	West, H. (U-UUUC)	12,922
Count 1	Currie, A. (SDLP)	9,984
Count 3	Baird, E. (VUP-UUUC)	8,067
Count 7	Daly, T. (SDLP)	7,145
Count 9	McKay, J. (U-UUUC)	3,194

1977 District Council Elections
The main feature of this second election for the twenty-six district councils, held on 18 May 1977, was the tendency for support to concentrate on four main parties – Official Unionist, SDLP, Alliance and DUP. The Official Unionists secured 29.6 per cent of the total vote and 178 seats; SDLP, 20.6 per cent and 113 seats; Alliance, 14.4 per cent and seventy seats; DUP, 12.7 per cent and seventy-four seats. The minor parties were well behind; UUUP, 3.2 per cent (twelve seats); Rep. Clubs, 2.6 per cent (six seats); UPNI, 2.4 per cent (six seats); Unity, 1.5 per cent (six seats); VUPP, 1.5 per cent (five seats); and NILP, 0.8 per cent (one seat).

Results
Antrim: Off. U. 8; DUP 3; All. 2; Ind. 2.
Ards: Off. U. 6; DUP 3; All. 5; Ind. 1; NILP 1; SDLP 1.
Armagh: Off. U. 9; SDLP 7; DUP 2; UUUP 1; Ind. 1.
Ballymena: DUP 11; Off. U. 3; Ind. 5; Ind. U. 1; All. 1.
Ballymoney: Off. U. 5; SDLP 3; DUP 3; Ind. 4; All. 1.
Banbridge: Off. U. 8; DUP 3; SDLP 2; Ind. U. 1; Ind. 1.
Belfast: Off. U. 16; All. 13; SDLP 8; DUP 7; Rep. C. 3; UPNI 2; Ind. U. 1; Community Association 1.
Carrick: Off. U. 5; All. 5; DUP 3; UPNI 1; Utd. Loy. 1.
Castlereagh: Off. U. 7; All. 7; DUP 4; Ind. 1.
Coleraine: Off. U. 11; DUP 2; SDLP 2; Ind. 3; All. 1; Ind. U. 1.
Cookstown: Off. U. 4; SDLP 5; UUUC 2; DUP 1; UUUP 1; Ind. 2.
Craigavon: Off. U. 10; SDLP 6; All. 3; DUP 4; Rep. C. 1; UUUP 1.
Down: Off. U. 7; SDLP 10; All. 3.
Dungannon: Off. U. 8; SDLP 6; DUP 2; Ind. 4.
Fermanagh: Off. U. 6; SDLP 7; UUUP 3; Unity 2; Ind. 2.
Larne: Off. U. 1; DUP 3; All. 4; SDLP 1; VUPP 3; UUUC 1; Ind. 2.
Limavady: Off. U. 6; SDLP 6; DUP 2; Ind. 1.
Lisburn: Off. U. 10; DUP 6; All. 3; SDLP 1; VUPP 1; UUUP 1; Ind. 1.
Londonderry: SDLP 13; Off. U. 6; Derry Nat. 4; DUP 2; All. 2.
Magherafelt: SDLP 5; Off. U. 4; DUP 2; UUUP 2; Rep. C. 1; Ind. 1.
Moyle: Ind. 6; Off. U. 5; SDLP 3; DUP 2.
Newry and Mourne: SDLP 15; Off. U. 7; All. 3; Ind. 4; DUP 1.
Newtownabbey: Off. U. 8; All. 6; DUP 4; UPNI 1; Loy. 1; Newtownabbey Lab. Party 1.
North Down: Off. U. 8; All. 7; VUPP 2; DUP 1; UPNI 1; UUUP 1.
Omagh: Off. U. 8 SDLP 6; All. 3; Ind. 1; Community 1; Rep. C. 1.
Strabane: Off. U. 5; SDLP 5; Ind. 3; DUP 2.

May 1979 Westminster General Election
The 3 May, 1979 Westminster election found Unionists, anti-Unionists and Centre parties all split, and three seats, E. Belfast, N. Belfast and N. Down changed hands. The first two were gained from the Official Unionists by the DUP, each by a narrow majority. In N. Down, although there was no change of MP, James Kilfedder's victory in face of opposition from the OUP, from which he had just resigned, was in effect an Ind. Unionist gain.

Overall Figures

Party	Votes cast	% of total poll
Official Unionists	254,578	36.2
SDLP	126,325	18.0
Alliance	82,892	11.8
DUP	70,975	10.1
UUUP	39,856	5.6
IIP	23,086	3.3
Rep. C.	12,100	1.7
UPNI	8,021	1.1
NILP	4,411	0.6
Others	73,643	10.5
Total valid votes	695,887	98.9
Spoiled votes	7,512	1.1
Total votes polled	703,399	100.0

*Indicates outgoing MP.

Armagh

Elec. 93,097 % poll 70.9

*McClusker, H. (Off. U.)	31,668
Mallon, S. (SDLP)	23,545
Calvert, D. (DUP)	5,634
Moore, T. (Rep. C.)	2,310
Ramsay, W. (All.)	2,074

No change   Off. U. maj. 8,123

North Antrim

Elec. 102,224 % poll 62.6

*Paisley, Rev. I. (DUP)	33,941
Burchill, J. (Off. U.)	15,398
Wilson, H. (All.)	7,797
Farren, S. (SDLP)	4,867
Turnly, J. (IIP)	3,689

No change   DUP maj. 18,543

South Antrim

Elec. 126,493 % poll 58.8

*Molyneaux, J. (Off. U.)	50,782
Kinahan, C. (All.)	11,914
Rowan, P. (SDLP)	7,432
Kidd, R. (Utd. Lab. Party)	1,895
Smyth, K. (Rep. C.)	1,615

No change   Off. U. maj. 38,868

East Belfast

Elec. 75,496 % poll 67.6

Robinson, P. (DUP)	15,994
*Craig, W. (Off. U.)	15,930
Napier, O. (All.)	15,066
Agnew, N. (UPNI)	2,017
Chambers, G. (NILP)	1,982

DUP gain   DUP maj. 64

North Belfast

Elec. 65,099 % poll 66.0

McQuade, J. (DUP)	11,690
Walker, C. (Off. U.)	10,695
O'Hare, P. (SDLP)	7,823
Dickson, Mrs A. (UPNI)	4,220
Cushnahan, J. (All.)	4,120
Lynch, S. (Rep. C.)	1,907
Carr, A. (NILP)	1,889

DUP gain   DUP maj. 995

South Belfast

Elec. 88,946 % poll 68.0

*Bradford, Rev. R. (Off. U.)	28,875
Glass, B. (All.)	11,745
McDonnell, A. (SDLP)	3,694
Brennan, V. (UPNI)	1,784
Dudgeon, J. (Lab. Integrationist)	692

No change   Off. U. maj. 17,130

West Belfast

Elec. 58,915	% poll 60.4
*Fitt, G. (SDLP)	16,480
Passmore, T. (Off. U.)	8,245
Dickson, W. (DUP)	3,716
Brennan, B. (Rep. C.)	2,284
Cousins, J. (All.)	2,024
Peters, D. (NILP)	540
(Spoiled votes, 2,283)	
No change	SDLP maj. 8,235

North Down

Elec. 99,889	% poll 62.4
*Kilfedder, J. (Ind. U.)	36,989
Jones, K. (All.)	13,364
Smyth, C. (Off. U.)	11,728
Ind. U. gain	Ind. U. maj. 23,625

South Down

Elec. 89,597	% poll 72.0
*Powell, E. (Off. U.)	32,254
McGrady, E. (SDLP)	24,033
Forde, P. (All.)	4,407
Markey, J. (IIP)	1,853
O'Hagan, D. (Rep. C.)	1,682
Rice, S. (Ind.)	216
Courtney, P. (Reform)	31
No change	Off. U. maj. 8,221

Fermanagh–South Tyrone

Elec. 71,541	% poll 88.9
*Maguire, F. (Ind.)	22,398
Ferguson, R. (Off. U.)	17,411
Currie, A. (Ind. SDLP)	10,785
Baird, E. (UUUP)	10,607
Acheson, P. (All.)	1,070
No change	Ind. maj. 4,987

Londonderry

Elec. 94,800	% poll 67.6
*Ross, W. (Off. U.)	31,592
Logue, H. (SDLP)	19,185
Barr, A. (All.)	5,830
McAteer, F. (IIP)	5,489
Melough, E. (Rep. C.)	888
Webster, B. (Derry Lab.)	639
No change	Off. U. maj. 12,407

Mid-Ulster

Elec. 81,499	% poll 80.9
*Dunlop, J. (UUUP)	29,249
Duffy, P. (SDLP)	19,266
Fahy, P. (IIP)	12,055
Lagan, A. (All.)	3,481
Donnelly, F. (Rep. C.)	1,414
No change	UUUP maj. 9,983

1979 European Parliament Election

Polling: 7 June 1979

The election resulted in the three NI seats being filled by the Rev. Ian Paisley MP, leader of the DUP, John Hume, deputy leader of the SDLP, and John Taylor, EEC spokesman of the Official Unionists. Mr Paisley's easy victory on the first count, and Mr Hume's record SDLP poll, with the two official Unionists – party leader Harry West and Mr Taylor – well behind in first preferences, was regarded as something of a watershed in local politics. The Alliance Party, too, lost ground seriously by comparison with the 1979 Westminster election. The DUP campaign was characterised by Mr Paisley's condemnation of the EEC, and his repeated declarations that he would seek to counter Roman Catholic influence at Strasbourg. And he insisted that his vote meant that he must be regarded as speaking for the NI majority. The Official Unionists, while accepting the UK's commitment to EEC membership, called for major changes to meet NI conditions. They claimed that the result showed that many of their supporters, being opposed to the Common Market, had deserted to Mr Paisley. Both the SDLP and Alliance took a strong pro-European line, but urged more effort to meet regional needs. Mr Hume, as a candidate of the European Socialist group, accepted the Socialist manifesto, with its commitment to deal energetically with unemployment. He also argued that the new European Assembly would have a healing effect locally, since MEPs from both NI and the Republic would be likely to find themselves on the same side in European politics. The election took place in the single NI constituency, with voting by PR (single transferable vote), and the outcome was in accordance with the intention of the European summit meeting which had allocated a third seat to NI in the hope that this would ensure representation of both communities. The turn-out of nearly 57 per cent reflected a higher level of interest than in Great Britain.

Note. The method of determining the number of votes transferred from one candidate to another under the PR system can vary, according to usage in different countries. In NI, the method employed in this election allowed for the calculation of transfers to be determined to two decimal places. This differs from the system which obtains in the Republic, where only whole numbers of votes are transferred.

Details of the count

3 seats

Electorate	1,029,490	Percentage poll	56.92
Valid votes	572,239	Quota	143,060
Spoiled votes	13,774	Votes unaccounted for	47

First Count

Paisley, I. (DUP)	170,688 (29.8%)
Hume, J. (SDLP)	140,622 (24.6%)
Taylor, J. (Official Unionist)	68,185 (11.9%)
West, H. (Official Unionist)	56,984 (9.9%)
Napier, O. (Alliance)	39,026 (6.8%)
Kilfedder, J. (Ulster Unionist)	38,198 (6.7%)
Devlin-McAliskey, B. (Independent)	33,969 (5.9%)
Bleakley, D. (Utd. Community)	9,383 (1.6%)
Devlin, P. (Utd. Labour)	6,122 (1.1%)
Cummings, E. (UPNI)	3,712 (0.6%)
Brennan, B. (Republican Clubs)	3,258 (0.6%)
Donnelly, F. (Republican Clubs)	1,160 (0.2%)
Murray, J. (Liberal)	932 (0.1%)

Paisley elected. His surplus votes were distributed.

Second Count

Hume	+54.56	140,676.56
Taylor	+9,043.68	77,228.68
West	+4,179.04	61,163.04
Napier	+378.08	39,404.08
Kilfedder	+12,424.32	50,622.32
Devlin-McAliskey	+6.72	33,975.72
Bleakley	+217.76	9,600.76
Devlin	+24.80	6,146.80
Cummings	+124.96	3,836.96
Brennan	+5.44	3,263.44
Donnelly	+4.00	1,164.00
Murray	+16.00	948.00

Bleakley, Brennan, Cummings, P. Devlin, Donnelly and Murray eliminated, all with lost deposits. Their votes were distributed.

Third Count

Hume	+5,396.00	146,072.56
Taylor	+2,979.28	80,207.96
West	+789.12	61,952.16
Kilfedder	+3,363.84	53,986.16
Napier	+6,298.88	45,702.96
Devlin-McAliskey	+2,129.72	36,105.44

Hume elected. Devlin-McAliskey eliminated.

Fourth Count

Taylor	+197.96	80,405.92
West	+187.96	62,140.12
Kilfedder	+637.72	54,623.88
Napier	+5,560.80	51,263.76

Napier eliminated.

Fifth Count

Taylor	+16,001.44	96,407.36
Kilfedder	+14,760.08	69,383.96
West	+3,775.52	65,915.64

West eliminated.

Sixth Count

Taylor	+57,059.00	153,466.36
Kilfedder	+3,174.00	72,557.96

Taylor elected

1981 District Council Elections

Polling: 20 May 1981.

The elections were marked by a highly polarised atmosphere, largely due to the H-Block hunger strike, and the results showed a decline in support for centre parties. The DUP took most satisfaction from the outcome, since it succeeded in replacing the official unionists as the party with the largest popular vote, but its lead was so slender (0.1%) that it left the OUP the strongest party in terms of seats. But the DUP more than doubled its share of the first-preference votes as compared with 1977 – 26.6% against 12.7% and its total of seats increased by 68 to 142. The ONP, however, got 151 seats compared with 178 in the 1977 election; that is, it lost 5 per cent of the total seats although its share of the vote dropped by only three per cent. The OUP first-preferences reached 26.5% against 29.6% four years earlier. The Alliance Party fared worst, since its vote dropped from 14.4% to 8.9%, and it now held 38 seats instead of 70. The SDLP also lost ground, although much less dramatically. Its percentage poll was 17.5 as compared with 20.5 in 1977, although because of the larger turnout it dropped fewer than 2,000 votes overall. Its seats tally fell from 113 to 104 in face of increased competition from a variety of Republicans and Nationalists, but most notably from the Irish Independence Party. The IIP, which came into being soon after the 1977 elections, took 3.9% of the votes and picked up 21 seats. The smaller parties found the going hard. A combination of UPUP and UPNI got 7 seats and 1.9% of votes WPRC halved its representation with 3 seats and 1.8% votes; IRSP and PD got 2 seats each, and the NILP held its single seat.

Council make-up:

Belfast: Off. U., 13; DUP, 15; SDLP, 6; All., 7., others 10.

Antrim: Off. U., 7; DUP, 4; SDLP, 2; All., 1; IIP, 1.

Ards: Off. U., 3; DUP, 7; SDLP, 1; All., 3; others, 3.

Armagh: Off. U., 8; DUP, 3; SDLP, 7; others, 2.

Ballymena: Off. U., 5; DUP, 13; others, 3.

Ballymoney: Off. U., 3; DUP, 7; SDLP, 2; All., 1; others, 3.

Banbridge: Off. U., 8; DUP, 4; SDLP, 2; others, 1.

Carrickfergus: Off. U., 3; DUP, 7; All., 3; others, 2.

Castlereagh: Off. U., 5; DUP, 9; All., 4; others, 1.

Coleraine: Off. U., 8; DUP, 6; SDLP, 2; All., 1; others, 3.

Cookstown: Off. U., 4; DUP, 3; SDLP, 5; others, 3.

Craigavon: Off. U., 9; DUP, 7; SDLP, 5; All., 1; WPRC, 2; others, 1.

Down: Off. U., 6; DUP, 3; SDLP, 8; All., 1; WPRC, 1; others, 1.

Dungannon: Off. U., 8; DUP, 3; SDLP, 3; IIP, 1; others 5.

Fermanagh: Off. U., 8; DUP, 2; SDLP, 4; IIP, 4; others, 2.

Larne: Off. U., 4; DUP, 6; All, 3; others, 2.

Limavady: Off. U., 6; DUP, 2; SDLP, 5; IIP, 1; others 1.

Lisburn: Off. U., 8; DUP, 10; SDLP, 2; All., 2; others 1.

Londonderry: Off. U., 4; DUP, 5; SDLP, 14; IIP, 4.

Magherafelt: Off. U., 1; DUP, 4; SDLP, 6; IIP, 1; others 3.

Moyle: Off. U., 4; DUP, 2; SDLP, 5; others, 5.

Newry and Mourne: Off. U., 6; DUP, 2; SDLP, 16; IIP, 4; others, 2.

Newtownabbey: Off. U., 9; DUP, 5; All., 3; others 4.

North Down: Off. U., 4; DUP, 5; All., 6; others, 5.

Omagh: Off. U., 4; DUP, 4; SDLP, 5; All., 2; IIP, 5.

Strabane: Off. U., 3; DUP, 4; SDLP, 4; others, 4.

Westminster By-elections, 1981

Fermanagh & South Tyrone; polling 9 April 1981. The by-election, created by the death of Frank Maguire (Ind.), aroused world-wide interest, since it resolved itself into a straight fight between Bobby Sands, leader of the H-Block hunger strikers, and Harry West (Off. U.), who had held the seat briefly in 1974. Sands had been on hunger strike since 1 March and was said to have lost about two stones in weight by polling day. His campaign from his Maze prison cell stimulated widespread media attention, and in the end provoked an astonishing unity among all shades of Nationalists. Failure to fight the seat created angry dissension within the SDLP. The British authorities made it clear that Sands' narrow victory would not weaken their opposition to H-Block demands, but the result was a powerful boost to the hunger strike campaign:

SANDS, Bobby (anti H-Block/
Armagh Political
    Prisoner)   30,492
WEST, Harry (Off. U)   29,046
      Anti-H-Block maj. 1,446

% Poll, 86.8; spoiled votes, 3,280.

Fermanagh and South Tyrone.

Polling: August 20, 1981. In this second by-election in the constituency in five months, to fill the vacancy created by the death of hunger striker Bobby Sands, his election agent, Owen Carron was successful in a six-cornered contest. With the hunger strike still going on, and the previous by-election result having failed to move the British Government, there was some surprise that Carron, an ordinary member of Provisional Sinn Fein, got 786 votes more than Sands, despite the split in the anti-Unionist vote. The Official Unionist vote, with a new candidate in Ken Maginess, a Dungannon councillor, was virtually the same as in the April contest.

OWEN CARRON (anti-H-Block
Proxy Political Prisoner)   31,278
Ken Maginess (Off. U.)   29.048
Seamus Close (All.)   1,930
Tom Moore (WPRC)   1,132
Martin Green (Peace Lover) 249
Simon Hall-Raleigh
  (General Amnesty)   90

No change
        Anti-H-Block maj. 2,230
Poll: 88.2%   Spoiled votes: 804.

Westminster By-election, 1982

South Belfast – Polling February 4, 1982. The by-election, to fill the vacancy arising from the murder of Off. U. MP, the Rev. Robert Bradford, developed into a bitter struggle between the Official Unionists and the DUP, who were particularly angry at the refusal of the 'Officials' to consider the idea of a United Unionist candidate. The DUP selected a strong contender in the Rev. William McCrea, of Magherafelt, a well-known Gospel singer. But in an eight-cornered contest, the Off. U. nominee, the Rev. Martin Smyth, head of the Orange Order, had a more than 5,000 lead over Alliance candidate David Cook, and the DUP candidate was in third place.

Smyth, Rev. M. (Off. U.)	17,123
Cook, D. (All.)	11,726
McCrea, Rev. W. (DUP)	9,818
McDonnell, A. (SDLP)	3,839
McMichael, J. (ULDP)	576
Caul, Brian (Utd. Lab.)	303
Narain, Dr. J. (One Human Family)	137
Hall-Raleigh, S. (Peace State)	12

Off. U. maj. 5,397
% poll: 66.2 spoiled votes, 312

1982 Assembly Election Polling: 20 October. The 'rolling devolution' election was notable for two things – the achievement of Provisional Sinn Fein, in its first Stormont election, of taking five of the 78 seats with more than 10 per cent of the first-preference votes, and the re-emergence of the Official Unionist Party as the largest group, with 26 seats. The PSF showed an advance of 2.5 per cent over the aggregate pro-H-Block vote in the 1981 council elections, and its share of the popular vote arguably understated its strength since it contested only seven of the 12 consti-

tuencies. It was also unlucky in that it might have expected to get two more seats on the basis of its voting strength. The PSF gains led to SDLP losses, and the total of SDLP seats, at 14, was five down on the 1973 Assembly and three down on the 1975 Convention, although it made a small recovery in terms of first-preferences as against the 1981 council elections. Both SDLP and PSF fought on an abstentionist policy. PSF called simply for British withdrawal, and the SDLP argued that the Assembly was 'unworkable' since Unionists continued to reject power-sharing and the Government had failed to promise a strong enough Irish dimension. On the Unionist side, the DUP had hoped to repeat its 1981 council performance of a slight lead in votes over the OUP, but in the event OUP had a 7 per cent margin over the DUP in first-preferences. Both the OUP and the DUP pledged themselves to seek to persuade the Government to concede majority rule, but the DUP was more enthusiastic than the OUP about the interim scrutiny powers given to the Assembly. With almost the same percentage of first-preferences as in the 1973 Assembly election, Alliance profited from late transfers to give it ten seats – two more than it held in 1973 and in the 1975 Convention. The smaller parties and Independents fared badly, for the most part.

Seats and votes

Electorate: 1,048,807			Turn-out, 61.7%
Party	Seats	1st pref Votes	% total poll
OUP	26	188,277	29.7
DUP	21	145,528	23.0
SDLP	14	118,891	18.8
PSF	5	64,191	10.1
Alliance	10	58,851	9.3
WP	—	17,216	2.7
UPUP	1	14,916	2.3
UUUP	—	11,550	1.8
Other U	1	9,502	1.6
Others	—	4,198	0.7
	78	633,120	100.0

West Belfast	Elec. 57,726	% poll 62.5
4 elected: (Quota 6,852)		1st pref.
Count 1	Adams, G. (PSF)	8,740
Count 5	Hendron, J. (SDLP)	5,207
Count 8	Passmore, T. (Off. U.)	4,505
Count 8	Glendinning, W. (All.)	2,733

East Belfast	Elec. 74,273	% poll 54.3
6 elected: (Quota 5,632)		1st pref.
Count 1	Robinson, P. (DUP)	15,319
Count 1	Burchill, J. (Off. U.)	7,345
Count 1	Napier, O. (All.)	6,037
Count 2	Vitty, D. (DUP)	235
Count 10	Dunlop, D. Mrs (Off. U.)	1,696
Count 10	Morrow, A. (All.)	2,966

North Belfast	Elec. 62,391	% poll 59.0
5 elected: (Quota 5,958)		1st pref.
Count 1	Carson, J. (Off. U.)	7,798
Count 11	Seawright, G. (DUP)	4,929
Count 13	Millar, F. (Ind. U.)	2,047
Count 14	O'Hare, P. (SDLP)	3,190
Count 14	Maguire, P. (All.)	2,527

South Belfast	Elec. 66,683	% poll 61.6
5 elected: (Quota 6,245)		1st pref.
Count 1	Rev. Smyth, M. (Off. U.)	13,337
Count 1	Cook, D. (All.)	6,514
Count 4	McCrea, S. (DUP)	4,091
Count 6	Graham, E. (Off. U.)	2,875
Count 6	Kirkpatrick, J. (Off. U.)	1,126

South Antrim	Elec. 131, 734	% poll 52.0
10 elected: (Quota 6,041)		1st pref.
Count 1	Molyneaux, J. (Off. U.)	19,978
Count 1	Beattie, W. (DUP)	7,489
Count 2	Agnew, F. (Off. U.)	3,302
Count 2	Davis, I. (DUP)	5,394
Count 18	Forsythe, C. (Off. U.)	1,612
Count 19	Thompson, R. (DUP)	2,646
Count 22	McDonald, J. (SDLP)	2,071
Count 23	Close, S. (All.)	2,916
Count 23	Mawhinney, G. (All.)	2,660
Count 23	Bell, W. (Off. U.)	979

(This count, involving 26 candidates, is believed to have established a record for the UK and the Republic. It extended over more than 30 hours).

North Antrim	Elec. 104,683	% poll 57.0
8 elected: (Quota 6,512)		1st pref.
Count 1	Rev. Paisley, I. (DUP)	9,231
Count 2	Allister, J. (DUP)	5,835
Count 6	Gaston, J. (Off. U.)	5,856
Count 8	Farren, S. (SDLP)	5,006
Count 9	Neeson, S. (All.)	3,258
Count 10	McKee, J. (DUP)	4,515
Count 10	Beggs, R. (Off. U.)	4,885
Count 11	Cousley, C. (DUP)	4,133

Armagh   Elec. 95,610   % poll 66.9

7 elected:	(Quota 7,739)	1st pref.
Count 1	McCusker, H. (Off. U.)	19,547
Count 1	Mallon, S. (SDLP)	8,528
Count 7	Nicholson, J. (Off. U.)	2,590
Count 9	McAllister, J. (PSF)	5,182
Count 11	Simpson, M. Mrs (Off. U.)	721
Count 13	Calvert, D. (DUP)	2,661
Count 14	News, H. (SDLP)	2,871

North Down   Elec. 103,619   % poll 53.8

8 elected:	(Quota 6,609)	1st pref.
Count 1	Kilfedder, J. (UPUP)	13,958
Count 2	Taylor, J. (Off. U.)	5,852
Count 6	Gibson, S. (SUP)	4,500
Count 8	Cushnahan, J. (All.)	4,416
Count 9	Lord Dunleath (All.)	3,641
Count 10	Pentland, W. (DUP)	3,340
Count 11	McCartney, R. (Off. U.)	3,782
Count 13	Bleakes, W. (Off. U.)	2,692

South Down   Elec. 93,261   % poll 65.6

7 elected:	(Quota 7,382)	1st pref.
Count 1	Feely, F. (SDLP)	7,391
Count 2	McGrady, E. (SDLP)	7,313
Count 6	Brown, W. (Off. U.)	5,220
Count 7	O'Donoghue, P. (SDLP)	5,916
Count 10	McCullough, R. (Off. U.)	5,802
Count 11	Graham, G. (DUP)	4,075
Count 11	Wells, J. (DUP)	3,779

Londonderry   Elec. 100,198   % poll 66.0

7 elected:	(Quota 8,058)	1st pref.
Count 1	Hume, J. (SDLP)	12,282
Count 1	McGuinness, M. (PSF)	8,202
Count 10	McClure, J. (DUP)	6,857
Count 10	Allen, J. (Off. U.)	6,107
Count 11	Douglas, W. (Off. U.)	5,031
Count 13	Logue, H. (SDLP)	4,828
Count 13	Campbell, G. (DUP)	5,305

Mid-Ulster

	Elec. 84,699	% poll 75.5
6 elected: (Quota 8,853)		1st pref.
Count 1	McCrea, W. (DUP)	10,445
Count 6	Haughey, D. (SDLP)	8,413
Count 10	Thompson, W. (Off. U.)	5,546
Count 11	Kane, A. (DUP)	3,981
Count 12	McSorley, M. Mrs (SDLP)	4,169
Count 12	Morrison, D. (PSF)	6,927

Fermanagh and S. Tyrone

	Elec. 73,930	% poll 83.0
5 elected: (Quota 9,864)		1st pref.
Count 1	Carron, O. (PSF)	14,025
Count 1	Maginnis, J. (Off. U.)	10,117
Count 8	Ferguson, R. (Off. U.)	5,877
Count 9	Currie, A. (SDLP)	6,800
Count 10	Foster, I. (DUP)	4,324

Assembly By-election in Armagh.

Polling 20 April 1983

The by-election was created by the unseating by an Election Court of Seamus Mallon (SDLP), on the ground that he was disqualified from Assembly membership as an Irish Senator at the time of the Assembly election in October, 1982. The SDLP called on voters to ignore the by-election. There were 571 spoiled votes.

Armagh

Elec. 95,100	% poll 34.07
Speers, J. (Off. U.)	26,907
French, T. (WP)	4,920
	Off. U. maj. 21,987

JUNE, 1983 Westminster General Election

The 9 June, 1983, Westminster election was fought on the seventeen new seats – five extra as compared with the 1979 election. The main feature of the results was the dominance of the OUP, which took eleven seats and 34 per cent of the poll and going strongly ahead of the DUP, with three seats and a 20 per cent vote. UPUP had one seat. Thus, Unionists had fifteen of the seats, with the other two going to Provisional Sinn Fein (W. Belfast) and SDLP (Foyle). The campaign had been marked by a bitter struggle on both sides of the community, although a very limited accommodation between OUP and DUP meant that there was only one Unionist in three constituencies – Foyle, Newry-Armagh and Fermanagh and S. Tyrone. SDLP rejected any idea of a pact with PSF, and fought all seventeen seats – the only party to do so. Nonetheless, SDLP's share of the vote was down slightly as compared with 1982 Assembly election – to 17.9 per cent, while PSF passed its target vote of 100,000 and achieved a 13.4 per cent poll, about three per cent up on the Assembly election. Main interest was centred in W. Belfast where Gerry Adams of PSF repeated his 1982 Assembly election success and unseated veteran MP Gerry Fitt. Owen Carron of PSF who won the second 1981 by-election in Fermanagh and S. Tyrone was defeated by Ken Maginnis (Off. U.). There was a high turn-out – 72.8 per cent.

Overall Figures

Party	Votes cast	% of total poll
OUP	259,952	34.0
DUP	152,749	20.0
SDLP	137,012	17.9
PSF	102,601	13.4
Alliance	61,275	8.0
UPUP	22,861	3.1
WP	14,650	2.0
Others (7 candidates)	13,725	1.6
Total valid votes	764,825	100.0

Spoiled votes: 4,358

*Indicates outgoing MP

West Belfast

Elec. 59,750   % poll 74.3

Adams, G. (PSF)	16,379
Hendron, J. (SDLP)	10,934
*Fitt, G. (Ind.)	10,326
Passmore, T. (OUP)	2,435
Haffey, G. A. (DUP)	2,399
McMahon, Ms. M. (WP)	1,893

PSF maj. 5,445

East Belfast

Elec. 55,581   % poll 70.0

*Robinson, P. (DUP)	17,631
Burchill, J. (OUP)	9,642
Napier, O. (All.)	9,373
Donaldson, D. (PSF)	682
Tang, Mrs M. (Lab. & TU)	584
Prendiville, P. (SDLP)	519
Cullen, F. (WP)	421
Boyd, H. (Anti-Noise)	59

DUP maj. 7,989

North Belfast

Elec. 61,128	% poll 69.4
Walker, A. C. (OUP)	15,339
Seawright, G. (DUP)	8,260
Feeny, B. (SDLP)	5,944
Austin, J. (PSF)	5,451
Maguire, P. (All.)	3,879
Lynch, S. (WP)	2,412
Gault, W. (Ind. DUP)	1,134

OUP maj. 7,079

South Belfast

Elec. 53,694	% poll 69.6
*Smyth, Rev. M. (OUP)	18,669
Cook, D. (All.)	8,945
McCrea, R. S. (DUP)	4,565
McDonnell, A. (SDLP)	3,216
McKnight, S. (PSF)	1,107
Carr, G. (WP)	856

OUP maj. 9,724

North Antrim

Elec. 63,254	% poll 69.8
*Paisley, Rev. I. (DUP)	23,922
Coulter, Rev. R. (OUP)	10,749
Farren, S. (SDLP)	6,193
McMahon, P. (PSF)	2,860
Samuel, M. H. (Ecol.)	451

DUP maj. 13,173

South Antrim

Elec. 59,321	% poll 65.5
Forsythe, C. (OUP)	17,727
Thompson, R. (DUP)	10,935
Mawhinney, G. (All.)	4,612
Maginness, A. (SDLP)	3,377
Laverty, S. (PSF)	1,629
Smyth, K. (WP)	549

OUP maj. 6,792

East Antrim

Elec. 58,863	% poll 64.9
Beggs, R. (OUP)	14,293
Allister, J. (DUP)	13,926
Neeson, S. (All.)	7,620
O'Cleary, M. (SDLP)	1,047
Cunning, W. (Ind.)	741
Kelly, A. (WP)	581

OUP maj. 367

North Down

Elec. 61,574	% poll 66.2
*Kilfedder, J. (UPUP)	22,861
Cushnahan, J. (All.)	9,015
McCartney, R. (OUP)	8,261
O'Baoill, C. (SDLP)	645

UPUP maj. 13,846

South Down

Elec. 66,968	% poll 76.6
*Powell, J. E. (OUP)	20,693
McGrady, E. (SDLP)	20,145
Fitzsimmons, P. (PSF)	4,074
Harvey, C. (DUP)	3,743
Forde, P. M. D. (All.)	1,823
Magee, Ms. M. (WP)	851

OUP maj. 548

Strangford

Elec. 60,232	% poll 64.9
Taylor, J. (OUP)	19,086
Gibson, S. (DUP)	11,716
Morrow, A. (All.)	6,171
Curry, J. (SDLP)	1,713
Heath, R. (Ind. LAB)	430

OUP maj. 7,370

Lagan Valley

Elec. 60,099	% poll 67.5
*Molyneaux, J. (OUP)	24,017
Beattie, Rev. W. (DUP)	6,801
Close, S. (All.)	4,593
Boomer, C. (SDLP)	2,603
McAuley, R. (PSF)	1,751
Loughlin, G. (WP)	809
	OUP maj. 17,216

Upper Bann

Elec. 60,795	% poll 72.0
*McCusker, H. (OUP)	24,888
McDonald, J. (SDLP)	7,807
Wells, J. (DUP)	4,547
Curran, B. (PSF)	4,110
French, T. (WP)	2,392
	OUP maj. 17,081

Newry and Armagh

Elec. 62,387	% poll 76.0
Nicolson, J. (OUP)	18,988
Mallon, S. (SDLP)	17,434
McAllister, J. (PSF)	9,928
Moore, T. (WP)	1,070
	OUP maj. 1,554

Fermanagh and S. Tyrone

Elec. 67,880	% poll 88.6
Maginnis, K. (OUP)	28,630
Carron, O. (PSF)	20,954
Flanagan, Mrs. R. (SDLP)	9,923
Kettyles, D. (WP)	649
	OUP maj. 7,676

Mid-Ulster

Elec. 63,899	% poll 84.3
McCrea, Rev. R. T. W. (DUP)	16,174
Morrison, D. G. (PSF)	16,096
Haughey, P. D. (SDLP)	12,044
Thompson, W. J. (OUP)	7,066
Lagan, Dr. J. A. (All.)	1,735
Owens, T. A. (WP)	766
	DUP maj. 78

East Londonderry

Elec. 67,365	% poll 76.3
*Ross, W. (OUP)	19,469
McClure, J. (DUP)	12,207
Doherty, A. (SDLP)	9,397
Davey, J. (PSF)	7,073
McGrath, Mrs. M. (All.)	2,401
Donnelly, F. (WP)	819
	OUP maj. 7,262

Foyle

Elec. 67,432	% poll 77.6
Hume, J. (SDLP)	24,071
Campbell, G. (DUP)	15,923
McGuiness, M. (PSF)	10,607
O'Grady, G. (All.)	1,108
Melaugh, E. (WP)	582
	SDLP maj. 8,148

1984 European Parliament Election

Three members to be elected by PR on 14 June 1984.

Seat 1	Won 1979 by Rev. I. Paisley. (DUP)
Seat 2	Won 1979 by J. Hume (SDLP)
Seat 3	Won 1979 by J. Taylor (OUP)

The Systems of Government and A List of Office Holders, 1968-83

Government: Two Systems Fall

There can be few parts of the world where two totally different systems of government have collapsed in the space of little more than two years. But this was the experience of Northern Ireland between 1972 and 1974. From 1921 to March 1972, the province had its own parliament and government within the UK. The system derived from the Government of Ireland Act, 1920, which was designed to set up parliaments in both parts of Ireland, with a Council of Ireland to look after matters of mutual concern, and possibly lead eventually to a united Ireland. Like later political approaches by Westminster it was aimed at reconciling the conflicting desires of Ulster Unionists and Irish Nationalists. It was more Home Rule than Unionists wanted, and less ambitious than that desired by Nationalists. In fact, Southern Ireland opted for independence, and the 1920 Act became operative only in NI. Unionists, who had shown no enthusiasm for devolution, quickly came to see the advantages of a limited self-goverment. Ulster Nationalists refused to co-operate in promoting the new northern state. Events tended to give permanence to partition. The Southern Irish state adopted a more separatist Constitution in 1937, and became a full republic in 1949. At that point, the NI parliament was given the right to veto any attempt to move NI out of the UK. The pre-1972 Stormont parliament was closely modelled on Westminster. The fifty-two-seat Commons, elected by straight vote in single-member constituencies, followed the procedure and ceremonial of its Westminster opposite number, and the twenty-six member Senate (with two ex-officio members in the Mayors of Belfast and Derry, and twenty-four members elected on PR by the Commons) had delaying powers very like those of the House of Lords. But in practice the upper house, with its Unionist majority, rarely opposed anything of substance originating in the Commons. Usually, two out of three MPs were Unionists, and this majority was reflected in the Senate. All the administrations set up between 1921 and 1972 were Unionist controlled. NI continued to send MPs to Westminster – at least twelve, and thirteen when QUB had a seat – although NI matters received little attention in the British parliament. Some British Ministers have regarded the old Stormont system as nearer to dominion status than to simple devolution. Under a long-established convention, it was not possible for an MP at Westminster to raise any issue within the direct responsibility of a Stormont Minister. Thus, while the 1920 Act declared that the power of Westminster in NI was not diminished in any way by local self-government, the reality was somewhat different. Westminster Ministers considered their responsibilities in relation to NI to be limited to issues such as foreign trade, defence, major taxation, customs and excise and the High Court. The Home Secretary had Cabinet responsibility for NI affairs, and he had a few officials engaged part-time in dealing with them, but until the civil rights movement developed few Home Secretaries got beyond rare and brief token trips to the province. So it required considerable ingenuity for an Ulster MP to find a topic on which he could put a question to a Minister. The NI government, normally comprising the Prime Minister and seven or eight full Cabinet Ministers and a few junior Ministers, controlled most domestic affairs and internal law and order. Up to the late 1960s, relations between London and Belfast were generally amicable. Whitehall allowed NI to give more generous financial inducements to new industry than applied in Great Britain, and finances generally were adjusted to NI's advantage. Some local taxes, such as motor duty, entertainment tax and death duties often differed from those in GB. And although NI had been required by the 1920 Act to make an annual 'imperial contribution' to meet items of national expenditure, such as defence, foreign representation and the national debt, it was accepted in London that this must be a declining liability in face of the high costs of social services. NI had contributed about £460m by way of 'imperial contribution' when it was finally abolished under direct rule. The principle of equality of basic social services throughout the UK implied that there could be no variation in major taxes, and NI never exercised a limited power to reduce income tax (see Economy p. 82). The general pattern of the Stormont Budget was settled in discussions between the Finance Minister and Treasury Officials in London, and there was a Joint Exchequer Board to consider any disputed matters. In matters such as social legislation, including divorce, NI very often went its own way. But the continuing split in the NI community was underlined by the impact of the civil rights movement. The long-entrenched Stormont system came under severe pressure, both from anti-Unionists and from Westminster, and increasing violence soon made it a world issue as well. The NI Government did make changes to meet some of the criticism (see Cameron Commission and Reforms pp. 56 and 203) but the serious violence in the summer of 1969 and the increasing alienation of the parliamentary opposition put large question marks over the very existence of Stormont. The need for army support for the police brought a real change in the relationship between Stormont and Whitehall. An army commander took charge of anti-terrorist operations (see The Security System p. 309) and a new post of British government representative was established, so that the British government would have its own watchdog official at Stormont. The failure of internment without trial to halt the PIRA campaign, and the shooting dead by the army of thirteen civilians in Londonderry (see 'Bloody Sunday' p. 45) persuaded the Heath government that all security and law-and-order powers should be transferred to Westminster. Three NI Premiers – O'Neill, Chichester-

Clark, and Faulkner – had tried to restore stability, but in March 1972 the Conservative government suspended the NI parliament. It was an act which pleased anti-Unionists, but horrified even the most moderate of Unionists. The province, for the first time in fifty-one years, was now ruled wholly from London. It got its own Secretary of State, similar to Scotland and Wales, and the first holder of the new office was William Whitelaw, a senior Conservative politician, who was assisted by a small team of junior Ministers. The province was governed under a Temporary Provisions Act, and NI legislation was brought forward by way of Orders in Council, which could not be amended on the floor of the Commons. In a bid to make direct rule more palatable, Whitelaw set up a locally recruited Advisory Commission. But Unionists boycotted it. The late Brian Faulkner (later Lord Faulkner), NI's last Prime Minister, who, with his colleagues had resigned rather than accept the loss of law-and-order powers, said he was against the province being treated 'like a coconut colony'. The other members of the last Stormont Cabinet under the 1920 Act were: Home Affairs, Brian Faulkner and John Taylor (Minister of State); Finance, Herbert Kirk; Health and Social Service, William Fitzsimmons; Development, Roy Bradford; Education, William Long; Agriculture, Harry West; Commerce, Robin Bailie; Leader of Commons, Nat Minford; Leader of Senate, John Andrews; Community Relations, David Bleakley (Mar.-Sept. 1971) and Basil McIvor (Sept. 1971-Mar. 1972). Outside the Cabinet were John Brooke (later Lord Brookeborough), Minister of State in Finance, and G. B. Newe, Minister of State in the Prime Minister's Department. In 1973, the Heath government tried a new political initiative. NI was given a seventy-eight member Assembly, elected by PR, with the object of giving minorities a bigger chance of representation and therefore participation in government. The scheme was embodied in the Northern Ireland Constitution Act of 1973, which also abolished the office of Governor and introduced a periodical referendum to test opinion on NI's constitutional status in relation to the UK and the Republic (*see* Border Poll p. 47). Towards the end of 1973, talks involving the Secretary of State, Unionists – led by Brian Faulkner – the SDLP and Alliance parties brought agreement on the setting up of an Executive involving these parties. The new administration's approach was worked out at a conference in December which was attended by the Executive parties and by British Ministers headed by Heath, and Ministers from the Republic, led by Liam Cosgrave (*see* Sunningdale Conference p. 220). The new Coalition took office on 1 Jan. 1974 after being sworn in by the new Secretary of State, Francis Pym. Its members were: Chief Executive, Brian Faulkner (Unionist); Deputy Chief Executive, Gerard Fitt (SDLP); Legal Minister and head of Office of Law Reform, Oliver Napier (Alliance); Minister of Information, John L. Baxter (Unionist); Minister of Environment, Roy Bradford (Unionist); Minister of Housing, Local Government and Planning, Austin Currie (SDLP); Minister of Health and Social Services, Patrick Devlin (SDLP); Minister of Commerce, John Hume (SDLP); Minister of Finance, Herbert Kirk (Unionist);

Minister of Education, Basil McIvor (Unionist); Minister of Agriculture, Leslie Morrell (Unionist). Ministers outside the Executive were: Community Relations, Ivan Cooper (SDLP); Manpower Services, Robert Cooper, (Alliance); Planning and Co-ordination, Edward McGrady (SDLP); Chief Whip, L. Hall-Thompson (Unionist). The new administration rapidly ran into trouble. While it had a majority in the Assembly, it faced violent opposition from loyalists opposed to power-sharing, and at one sitting demonstrating loyalists were ejected from the Chamber by the police. At the same time, Brian Faulkner was defeated in the Unionist Council, the 1,000 strong main governing body of his party, when he tried to get endorsement of the Sunningdale agreement. Then, in Feb. 1974, a Westminster general election showed a majority for candidates of the three anti-power-sharing Unionist groups united within the UUUC. Finally, a loyalist strike aimed against power-sharing and a Council of Ireland led to the resignation in May of the Unionist members of the Executive, and the collapse of the administration. Direct rule was then resumed under the Labour government, with Merlyn Rees as Secretary of State, and the Assembly was prorogued. Legal authority for continuing direct rule was provided by the Northern Ireland Act of 1974, which made temporary provision for the government of the province by the Secretary of State and his ministerial team, subject to annual renewal. The Labour government moved quickly to try to break the political deadlock and replace the now defunct Assembly. In July 1974, it announced that local political parties were to be given the opportunity to produce a viable constitution. For this purpose, a seventy-eight member Constitutional Convention was elected in 1975, but the project finally failed in 1976. In the aftermath of the Convention, the government sought to widen consultation outside and inside parliament on NI legislation. A new NI Committee of MPs was set up to allow for general debates on local policy, for example on the economy, housing, agriculture etc. And copies of Orders were shown in advance to local parties to enable them to put forward their views. The Labour government (after James Callaghan became Premier) accepted that there was a case for more than twelve NI MPs at Westminster – a long-standing claim of Unionists. The idea of extra representation was endorsed by the Speaker's Conference in 1978. After the failure of the Convention, the British government did not rush into any new initiative. But in Nov. 1977, Roy Mason, as Secretary of State, put forward a tentative five-point plan for discussion by the parties, which amounted to partial devolution:

1 There should be a single Assembly elected by proportional representation.

2 That Assembly should exercise real responsibility over a wide range of functions and have a consultative role in legislation.

3 The arrangements should be temporary and envisage progress to full legislative devolution.

4 Although temporary, they must be durable, which means that

minority interests must be safeguarded and that the Northern Ireland political parties must be prepared to make them work.

5 They must make good administrative sense.

This outline was discussed by the Secretary of State and representatives of the parties at the end of 1977 and beginning of 1978, but the initial exchanges did not suggest any agreement on the plan. At the same time, the Conservative opposition was urging that the first priority should be given to local government reform − a course frequently urged by many Unionists. But the SDLP made it clear that they feared that a reform of councils would lead to Unionist domination, and remarks in parliament by the Secretary of State indicated that he supported this view. With the resumption of direct rule after the collapse of the Convention, some of the departments established for the convenience of the Executive were dropped and others merged. The work of the Department of Community Relations was taken over by the Department of Education, and the Departments of Environment and Housing, Planning and Local Government were merged into a single Environment Department. By 1976, the following departments were in existence:

Agriculture.   Development of agriculture, forestry and fishing industries. Extensive advisory services; agricultural research, education and training. Agent for Whitehall Ministry in economic support for farming and the implementation of EEC Common Agricultural Policy.

Commerce.   Development of commerce and industry; administration of schemes of assistance to industry, including liaison with Local Enterprise Development Unit; energy policy; development of tourism; main harbours, mines and quarries; mineral development; consumer protection; liaison with Office of Fair Trading; registration of companies, etc.; department of industrial and forensic science.

Environment.   Housing, planning, comprehensive development; construction and maintenance of roads and bridges; water supply, sewerage; local government, transport and traffic, including road safety, pollution control, amenity lands, public health, historic buildings, ancient monuments, street lighting, and fire service.

Education.   Primary, secondary and further education, including higher education and adult education; oversight of the five Area Education and Library Boards; teacher training, examinations, youth welfare and youth services, museums, Arts Council and Armagh Observatory. Also involved in promoting sport and recreation, and in formulating and sponsoring policies for the improvement of community relations.

Finance.   Control of spending of Stormont departments; liaison with Treasury and NI Office on financial matters, economic and social planning and research; savings, borrowing and loan advances; charities;

building regulations and liaison with construction industry; ordnance survey, valuation, registration of births, deaths and marriages; registration of deeds and title of land; miscellaneous licensing, including intoxicating liquor, bookmakers and moneylenders; registration of clubs, law reform, public record office, digest of statistics.

Health and Social Services. Social security scheme and all health and personal social services, including hospital and specialist services, family practitioner service, school health, child health, child care and adoption, services for the elderly and handicapped. These services are administered by four Health and Social Services Boards on behalf of the Department.

Manpower Services. Employment service, employment and unemployment statistics, advisory services to companies, sponsorship of 'Enterprise Ulster'; government training centres, integrated workforce units, industrial training boards, management training, training on employers' premises scheme; industrial relations, factory inspectorate, disabled persons, contracts of employment, redundancy payments, wages councils.

Civil Service. Civil Service Whitley Council, conditions of service, salaries, superannuation, personnel management and training, computers, management services, manpower control and inspection; the civil service commission, central secretariat, including departmental information service.

By 1982, the number of Stormont departments had been reduced to six. Civil Service affairs were absorbed into a Finance and Personnel Department, and Commerce and Manpower had been merged into a Department of Economic Development. With the setting up of the D.E.D. in September, 1982, a new Industrial Development Board, linked with the department, took responsibility for attracting outside industrial investment. Under direct rule, the Secretary of State has overall control of the NI Office and the Stormont departments. In practice, he keeps key issues in his own hands and delegates much of the responsibility for the individual departments to his junior ministers. When James Prior took over as Secretary of State in September, 1981, he concentrated personally on political and constitutional matters, security policy and operations, broad economic questions and other major policy issues. The NI Office itself is concerned with matters such as control of the police and criminal law issues, international issues affecting NI, electoral questions; compensation arising from the violence, and emergency planning. Mr Prior initially allocated ministerial responsibility to his team as follows: Lord Gowrie, Minister of State and Deputy Secretary of State – prisons, police, compensation for criminal injuries; Departments of Finance and Civil Service; spokesman on all NI matters in the Lords. Adam Butler, Minister of State, – Departments of Agriculture, Commerce, and Manpower Services. David Mitchell, Parliamentary Under-Secretary – Department of the Environment. Nicholas Scott, Parliamentary Under-Secretary – Department of Education and responsibility for information services. John Patten, Parliamentary Under-Secretary – Department of Health and Social Services and spokesman in Commons for those matters for which Lord Gowrie was responsible. When the D.E.D. was established, Mr Butler took responsibility for that department, and retained charge of agriculture. (For 1983 changes see table on page 303.)

ROLLING DEVOLUTION

James Prior became Secretary of State at a time when the Constitutional Conference established by his predecessor, Humphrey Atkins (*see* separate entry), had demonstrated that there was no basis for agreement among the NI political parties on a system of devolved government for the province. Nonetheless, Mr Prior had put his reputation 'on the line' on getting political progress, and he at first investigated the possibilities of an Assembly together with local ministers nominated by himself, with a separation of administrative and legislative responsibility on the US model. It was a concept which had surfaced vaguely from time to time, but in the end he settled on the idea of 'rolling devolution', a system where an Assembly would start off with only a consultative and scrutiny role. This could later be extended to embrace the devolution of one or more local departments, but this devolution would depend on the achievement in the Assembly of 'cross-community support'. The Secretary of State and his colleagues saw it as an infinitely flexible patterrn, adding some local democracy to direct rule to start with, and allowing for an input from elected politicians. It was also seen by the small group of Cabinet Ministers who settled NI policy as a means of getting more political support for security policy and giving a semblance of stability which might help in the attraction of outside industrial investment at a time when unemployment was running at around 20 per cent. The scheme which eventually emerged in early 1982 was based, as in 1973, on a 78-seat Assembly elected by PR in the twelve Westminster constituencies. (If the plan for 17 NI seats had been approved by Parliament at that time, the Assembly would probably have had 85 seats – seven in each constituency). The Devolution Bill provided that the Assembly could apply to Westminster for devolved powers if 70 per cent, or 55 members, backed the proposal. This weighted majority was intended to guard against Unionists only being in a position to apply. The Bill also provided that the Assembly could discuss local legislation and set up scrutiny committees for each of the six Stormont departments, and an amendment allowed for a non-statutory security committee. Assembly members would get a salary of £8,700, and committee chairmen an extra £2,900. Members of the Assembly could join a Parliamentary tier of the Anglo-Irish Council as individuals. Predictably, the reaction of the parties was mixed. Both the OUP and DUP rejected the weighted majority and 'cross-community support' provisions as a revival of the 1973 'power-sharing,' although the DUP was attracted more so than the OUP to the initial scrutiny powers. To Alliance, it was a last chance for NI to solve its own problems. The SDLP regarded the scheme as 'unworkable' and an 'expensive charade' (views echoed by the Haughey Government in the Republic). Provisional Sinn Fein, contesting a Stormont election for the first time, sought to displace the SDLP as the main voice of Nationalists and win political support for its 'Brits out' approach. The Secretary of State had to face a 'filibuster' in Parliament from about 20 right-wing Conservative MPs, some of whom were opposed to him for national reasons, some of whom argued that the Conservative 1979 manifesto should be implemented since there was no prospect of agreement on devolution (see CONSERVATIVE PARTY), and some of whom were frankly integrationist. But the measure was put through without difficulty after a 'guillotine' motion had been implemented, and with general support from the Opposition parties. Labour's attempt to make the scheme more acceptable to the SDLP led to an amendment to provide that both Lords and Commons would be able to pronounce on 'cross-community support'. The change did not, however, persuade the SDLP that there was any real Irish dimension. Thus, the stage was set for the election on 20 October 1982 (see Elections Section). With both the SDLP and PSF fighting on an abstentionist platform, although differing on the issue of violence, the Government's hopes for the Assembly were distinctly limited. With the SDLP getting 14 seats (three down on the Convention and five fewer than in the 1973 Assembly) and PSF a surprising five seats, a total of 59 members attended the opening session of the Assembly. OUP had 26, the DUP 21, and Alliance 10, with two other Unionists, one of whom, James Kilfedder, MP, was elected Speaker. The Secretary of State accepted an early invitation to address the Assembly and junior ministers appeared at committees, but the OUP were involved in a row about the allocation of committee chairmanships and initially boycotted these bodies. From outside, the SDLP insisted that all its fears had been realised, and it attacked the idea of setting up a security committee in early 1983. SDLP Assembly members found Ministers accessible, despite their abstention, although PSF members were given a ministerial hearing only on strictly constituency matters and Mr Prior made it clear that he would not meet them unless and until they renounced violence. (For BRITISH-IRISH INTERGOVERNMENTAL COUNCIL, see separate entry.)

Office Holders in Northern Ireland, 1968-83

NOTE: this is not an exhaustive list of holders of government offices, but shows only those in charge of specific departments. Broken lines indicate changes in government under the Stormont parliament.

	Home Secretary/Secretary of State	NI Prime Minister/Chief Executive	Finance	Development	Health and Social Services	Commerce	Home Affairs	Agriculture	Education	Community Relations	Dept. began here →
1968	Callaghan	T. O'Neill	Kirk	Fitzsimmons	Morgan	Faulkner	Craig	Chichester-Clark	Long		
1969		– – –		Neill / Long	– – – / Porter		Long / – – – / Porter		Fitzsimmons / P.O'Neill	Ministry began here →	
1970		Chichester-Clark		Faulkner	Fitzsimmons	Bradford	Chichester-Clark &	P.O'Neill	Long	Simpson	
1971	Maudling	– – – Faulkner		Bradford		– – – Bailie	Taylor / Faulkner & Taylor	– – – West		Bleakley / McIvor	
Direct Rule 1972	Whitelaw		Howell	Lord Windlesham	Channon	Howell	Lord Windlesham	Howell	Channon / Van	Lord Windlesham	
1973	Pym			Howell	Van Straubenzee			Mills	Straubenzee / Lord Belstead	Van Straubenzee	
1974 Executive	– – – Rees	Chief Exec. Faulkner Dpty. CE Fitt	Finance Kirk	Housing, Planning and Local Govt. Currie / Environment Bradford	Health & Social Services Devlin / Manpower Services R. Cooper	Commerce Hume	Legal & Law Reform Napier	Agriculture Morrell	Education McIvor	Community Relations I. Cooper	Planning & Co-ordination McGrady

Year	Home Secretary / Secretary of State	NI Prime Minister / Chief Executive	Finance		Environment	Health and Social Services		Manpower	Commerce	Agriculture	Education		Department not continued
1974 Direct Rule Resumed													
1975			Con-cannon	Con-cannon	Moyle	Lord Donaldson	Orme	Orme		Lord Donaldson	Moyle	Lord Donaldson Merged with Education	
1976	Mason				merged Environment	Lord Melchett				Dunn			
1977			Dunn	Carter	Carter		Con-cannon	Con-cannon		Dunn	Lord Melchett		
1978			Pendry					Con-cannon	Con-cannon	Pendry	Pendry		
May 1979/80	Atkins		Rossi		Goodhart	Alison	Rossi	Rossi	Shaw	Shaw	Shaw	Lord Elton	
1981	Prior		Alison / Lord Gowrie		Environment / Mitchell	Health and Social Services / J. Patten			Man-power / Butler	Commerce / Butler	Agriculture / Butler	Education / Scott	
1982					C. Patten					merged as Dept of Econ. Devt. Butler			
1983			Butler		C. Patten	C. Patten					Lord Mansfield		

The Security System

THE CHANGING PATTERNS

The handling of law-and-order issues has been at the heart of the crisis in the province. It figured strongly in the civil rights campaign, and it was the major factor influencing the British government's decision to impose direct rule from London in March 1972. The civil rights movement had a variety of targets in the law and order sphere. It was critical of the Special Powers Act, with its far-reaching provisions relating to searches and internment without trial. In policing, it questioned the attitude of the RUC in its dealings with the Catholic minority, and argued that its organisation made it the tool of the NI government rather than an independent police force. The USC, popularly dubbed the 'B men', was attacked as a loyalist army since it had no Catholic membership. To a lesser extent, there was criticism of the administration of justice, with the suggestion that too many ex-Unionist politicians were appointed to the bench. NI Ministers defended the Special Powers Act as vital to deal with the IRA threat and they pointed to the stringent laws in the Republic to counter subversion. The Special Powers Act continued to be used by the British government to enforce internment up to the autumn of 1972. But the critics of the USC had an easy victory. It was swept away in the context of the reform of the RUC. The USC had been set up in 1920 to counter the IRA, and it was undoubtedly a potent symbol of local law and order for most Unionists. And Unionist leaders were apt to answer critics by pointing out that it had been established originally by the British government, since the Stormont administration had not then been established. But Lord Brookeborough, former NI Premier, very much regarded himself as the 'father' of the B Specials. Tim Pat Coogan, in his book *The IRA*, described the USC as 'the rock on which any mass movement by the IRA in the North has always foundered'. Wallace Clark, historian of the USC, has said in a memorandum published in *Red Hand, The Ulster Colony*, by Constantine Fitzgibbon: 'Historians of the future, if there is any fairness in the world, will give the Ulster Special Constabulary the credit for having one of the most dedicated and effective part-time forces ever raised within the British Commonwealth'. He conceded, however, that some of the leaders of the USC had been at fault in not eradicating 'a few extremists or bad characters'. But the Scarman tribunal had no doubts about the non-acceptability of the USC to the minority community. It was 'totally distrusted by the Catholics', who saw it was 'the strong arm of the Protestant ascendancy'. Scarman added that the B Specials could not show themselves in a Catholic area without heightening tension, and they were neither trained nor equipped for riot control duty. Scarman has recorded the somewhat confused role of the USC in the summer of 1969. In July, the Minister of Home Affairs, Robert Porter QC, authorised their use in riot control, with batons, but without firearms. After protests from the USC, however, he allowed officers and NCOs to carry arms. On 13 Aug. the NI Prime Minister, James Chichester-Clark, indicated in a broadcast that the USC would not be used for riot control, but next day an instruction was issued stating that they should be so used, but equipped, 'where possible', with batons. It was not until 15 Aug. that the USC were expressly ordered to report with their firearms. This was after the call-out which seems to have been mandatory before troops could go on the streets in support of the RUC. In 1969, there were about 10,000 members on the USC's books. A few hundred of these were full-time, and another 300 were mobilised for full-time duty with the RUC in 1969. Scarman made several critical references to the USC. The tribunal found that the force was not effective when used in communal disturbances in Belfast, and that it had shown lack of proper discipline, particularly in the use of firearms, when employed outside Belfast. It held that USC members in Dungiven on 13 July had fired without provocation over the heads of people emerging from a ballroom. In Armagh, there had been no justification for firing into a crowd which had caused a man's death, and in Dungannon firing into another Catholic crowd had been 'reckless and irresponsible'. But the tribunal praised the USC for protecting Catholic-owned pubs in Belfast from Protestant mobs. At a meeting in Downing Street in Aug. 1969 between the British and NI governments, the Prime Minister, Harold Wilson, indicated in a TV interview that the USC would be phased out. But after the discussions, the NI Premier, Major Chichester-Clark, and his colleagues rejected the idea of abolition of the 'Specials'. The issue produced acrimonious debate within Unionism, with right-wing critics of the NI government claiming that the public was not being told the whole truth. The abolition of the USC was recommended in the Hunt report, published in the autumn of 1969, and the force was eventually stood down on 30 April 1970. With the disappearance of the USC, security became the responsibility of three main elements – the RUC, the regular army and the Ulster Defence Regiment, a mainly part-time force which was designed to undertake much of the work of the former 'Specials'.

THE RUC

In the wake of serious riots of the summer of 1969, it was clear that the British government was intent on securing a new-look police force. Thus the Home Secretary, James Callaghan, inspired the mounting of a special committee of inquiry (*see* Hunt Report p. 117). The Cameron committee, in its initial look at the underlying causes of the crisis, had complained of RUC mistakes, and the Scarman tribunal, in its investigation of the bitter disturbances of 1969, recognised the 'fateful split between the Catholic community and the police'. Scarman said the RUC had been as ready to do its duty in face of Protestant as Catholic mobs. 'But it is painfully clear from the evidence adduced before us that by July [1969] the Catholic minority no longer believed that the RUC was impartial and that Catholic and civil rights activists were publicly asserting this lack of confidence'. Thus, while accepting that the RUC had made mistakes, Scarman rejected 'the general case of a partisan force co-operating with Protestant mobs to attack Catholic people'. Scarman held, however, that there had been six occasions during the 1969 troubles when the RUC had been 'seriously at fault'. In brief these were:

12 Aug.	The incursion by members of the RUC Reserve Force into Rossville Street, Londonderry.
13 Aug.	The decision to put armed members of the USC on riot duty in Dungannon without an experienced police officer to take command.
14 Aug.	A similar decision in Armagh City.
14-15 Aug.	The use of Browning machine-guns in Belfast.
14-15-16 Aug.	Failure to prevent Protestant mobs burning down Catholic houses in Belfast: Conway Street, (14-15) and Brookfield Street, (15-16).
15 Aug.	Failure to take effective action to restrain or disperse mobs or to protect lives and property in the riot areas during the hours of daylight and before the arrival of the army.

The burden of the Scarman criticism of the RUC was that its senior officers acted as though the strength of the force was sufficient to maintain the public peace. This meant, the tribunal held, that the army had not been called in until the Inspector-General of the RUC was confronted with the physical exhaustion of the police in Londonderry on 14 Aug. 1969 and in Belfast the following day. And it found that the force had struggled manfully to do its duty in a situation which it could not control, and that its courage, as long hours of stress and strain took their toll, was beyond praise. James Callaghan, who, as Home Secretary, was responsible for police matters in Great Britain, and who had been a former spokesman in parliament for the Police Federation, took an exceptional interest in changing the RUC image. His first move was to arrange for Sir Arthur Young, of the City of London Police, to take over as the new head of the force. And in consequence of the Hunt recommendations, the RUC lost much of its paramilitary character which it had inherited from the old Royal Irish Constabulary in 1922. Instead, it was remodelled on police forces in Great Britain, and the term, 'police service', became official jargon. Under the Stormont governments, the Ministry of Home Affairs handled broad police matters, but under the Police Act of 1970, a Police Authority, representative of the main sections of the community, was set up. It was financed from government funds, and given the responsibility to maintain an adequate and efficient police force. Operational control of the RUC was vested in the Chief Constable, and the title, 'Inspector-General' for the head of the RUC, was dropped. The general rank structure was also altered to conform with practice in Great Britain. An RUC Reserve was also established, with mostly part-time members. The size of the RUC, limited to 3,500 men and women up to 31 Mar. 1970, had to be quickly reassessed in the light of the security demands. The establishment was increased to 4,940 in 1970; to 6,500 in 1974; to 7,500 in 1979; and to 8,000 in 1982. In December, 1982, there were 7,017 men, 701 women, and 84 cadets – a total of 7,802. The RUC Reserve at the same time totalled 4,840 – 4,385 men and 455 women. The full-time element of the Reserve was raised by Secretary of State James Prior in 1982 by 300 to 2,500, and he also announced that the RUC would have the backing of 336 civilians recruited for support jobs. The cost of the 1982 expansion would be £37.5m over three years. The aim of Government policy has been to achieve the 'primacy of the police'; that is, a situation in which the RUC is in charge of the peace-keeping effort everywhere in the province. The Police Authority chairman, Sir Myles Humphreys, claimed at the end of 1982 that the policy of primacy had been fully implemented. Certainly, the 'Ulsterisation' of the security effort has led to the army taking a largely background role for most of the time. At one period, there were problems in army-police relations, and this was one reason for the appointment in 1979 of the late Sir Maurice Oldfield (former head of MI6) as Chief Security Co-ordinator – a post dropped in early 1982. The RUC has been specially equipped and many of its members specially trained in anti-terrorist operations. Computer-based intelligence has strengthened the vastly increased surveillance of terrorist suspects. RUC spokesmen have claimed that the RUC has become much more acceptable in Catholic areas, and that this has been evidenced by the steady flow of information through the confidential telephone. However, Nationalist politicians have continued to question the impartiality of the service, and some events have worked against all-round acceptability. Allegations of maltreatment of suspects by RUC detectives were common in the late 1970s. In 1977, the Police Complaints Board was strengthened by the introduction of an independent element. Nonetheless, in 1977 an independent judicial inquiry was set up to look at RUC interrogation practices after a report by Amnesty International (see Bennett Report p. 42). The Amnesty International team of investigators said it had found evidence of maltreatment of suspects, mainly at the Castlereagh interrogation centre in Belfast. The RUC insisted that there were detailed checks on interrogation and that conditions were good at Castlereagh, but a variety of safeguards suggested by the Bennett Committee were adopted, including closed-circuit TV monitoring. (In 1982, Sir Myles Humphreys commented that the small number of complaints over interrogation did not warrant criticism on the scale to which the police had been subjected.) The Police Authority noted at the end of 1982 that there had been a failure to attract sufficient recruits to the RUC from the Catholic community, despite the efforts of the Authority and the RUC itself. Undoubtedly the severe tension raised by the 1981 H-Block hunger strike helped to frustrate such official moves. The street violence arising from the H-Block protest also put a severe strain on the RUC. Twenty-one members of the force and its reserve were killed during 1981 – that is, the highest annual total for any year of the troubles except 1976. Chief Constable Sir John Hermon reported that there were 1,200 public demonstrations during the seven-month H-Block campaign as well as loyalist counter-demonstrations. Of the 101 deaths arising from violence, 68 were attributed to Republican terrorism and 12 to loyalists. Sir John argued that the RUC would have been legally and morally justified in resorting to the use of firearms, since riot and disorder had involved the use of explosives, rockets, firearms and petrol bombs. The Chief Constable no doubt had in mind the outcry raised in the Nationalist community at deaths from the use of plastic bullets by the security forces. (See below for anti-riot weapons.) In 1982, Nationalists and Catholic clergy were critical of several incidents in Co. Armagh in which terrorist suspects were shot dead by the RUC. But RUC chiefs have also had to face in the early 1980s some loyalist criticism that they were not cracking down sufficiently hard on the IRA and INLA. The DUP-sponsored 'Third Force' offered itself as an auxiliary, but the Government and the RUC rejected any idea of 'private armies'. In 1982, the RUC made large-scale arrests of alleged members of the PIRA, INLA and the UVF on the evidence of people who claimed to have been members of these organisations. The hundreds of terrorist charges which followed on the arrests made 1982 'the year of the supergrass.' In all, about 24 major informers appeared during the year and left senior RUC officers satisfied that even if a proportion of the charges did not stick, the operation would have yielded a massive amount of intelligence about the internal workings of the main paramilitary groups. Critics of the RUC accused the authorities of using blackmail, intimidation and offers of large sums of money to produce the 'supergrasses.' This was denied by the RUC, although several of the key informers were offered immunity from prosecution, police protection, and the means to set themselves up in new locations outside NI. Since 1979, there has been close co-operation between the RUC and the Garda in the Republic. This is believed to have prompted some of the major seizures by the Garda of arms and explosives in the Republic's border counties in 1981 and 1982. But the RUC continued to regard permission to question terrorist suspects inside the Republic as the key to using the reciprocal courts procedure. There were no signs at the end of 1982 that this would be permitted, although a recent decision by the Republic's Supreme Court had raised the possibility of extradition being extended in the Republic in a way which would make it much more difficult for terrorists to find a haven south of the border. The issuing of a special RUC Service Medal was authorised in 1982 – the 60th anniversary of the setting up of the force.

It was to be issued to those who had served since 1971 – the year PIRA decided to make police officers a special target.

THE ARMY

One of the most agonised decisions of the NI government was to call for the assistance of the army to maintain order. It was taken on 14 Aug. 1969, after RUC officers accepted that their men were too exhausted to maintain their effort on the edge of Derry's Bogside and in Belfast. James Callaghan, for the British government, endorsed the request and at 5 p.m. on 14 Aug. a company of the Prince of Wales Own Regiment went on duty in the centre of Derry. Next day 600 men of the 3rd Battalion, Light Infantry, entered W. Belfast with fixed bayonets to provide a buffer between Protestant and Catholic crowds on what later became known as the 'Peace Line'. In many Catholic areas of Belfast, the soldiers got a warm welcome since they were treated as an insurance against Loyalist incursions. This situation did not persist, though, since the rise of PIRA led most Republicans to renew their natural resentment towards British forces. The Falls Road curfew in July 1970 also tended to harden Catholic attitudes against the army. The army also displayed some extra toughness in face of attacks. The army commander, General Freeland, warned in April 1970 that anyone throwing a petrol bomb after he had been warned risked being shot. The Army GOC was acting as Director of Operations. Stormont could not have any control of the army constitutionally, and it had been agreed to put the RUC under the army commander in relation to anti-terrorist operations. The army in such a situation found itself caught up in the local politics. Unionists in 1969 resented what they regarded as toleration by the army of no-go areas in W. Belfast and in the Bogside and Creggan areas of Derry. But incidents involving the army had on occasion far-reaching political consequences. It was the shooting by the army in Derry of two men in July 1971 which led to the withdrawal of the SDLP from Stormont. The SDLP was acting in pursuance of an ultimatum that it would leave parliament if a public inquiry into the shooting was refused. The shooting dead by the army of thirteen men in Derry in Jan. 1972 was crucial in persuading the British government to suspend Stormont (see 'Bloody Sunday' p. 45). The Heath government wanted the NI government to surrender to Westminster all law-and-order powers, and when Brian Faulkner and his colleagues refused to do so, they were left with only the option of resignation. Heath was able to act firmly because he was aware of full support from the opposition leader, Harold Wilson, who had been doubtful since 1969 about allowing Stormont any real security powers. On this point, Lord O'Neill of the Maine, former NI Premier, claimed in 1978 that Stormont had been deprived of any power of decision in security matters after the entry of the army in support of the civil power. Undoubtedly, the NI campaign proved more costly in terms of manpower than the government originally expected. There were seven major units (around 7,000 men) involved in 1970. In

1971, this had risen to nine units (and this was a smaller commitment than the NI Government were demanding); while at the time of 'Operation Motorman' (see separate entry) in 1972, there were some 19 units, or 21,000 troops, in the province. By 1975 there were 15 units, in 1979, 13 and in 1982, nine. Since unit strengths vary, the numbers of troops are a more accurate guide. By 1980, the figure was 11,500; in November, 1981, 10,763; and at the end of 1982, 10,500. In addition, one spearhead unit stationed in GB has been available at all times to be moved swiftly to the province. Originally most army units came from Germany on four-month tours of duty. Up to 1978, nine major units had completed six tours, and six major units had seven tours. But in 1977, Roy Mason, as Secretary of State, announced that there would be more long-stay units, starting with one extra in the autumn of 1978. By 1982, all but 2,000 troops (or three units) were on two-year tours of duty. The army in NI has been temporarily reinforced to deal with two loyalist strikes – in 1974 and 1977 – and during the 1981 hunger strike. In 1974, the attitude of the army chiefs to the loyalist bid to bring down the power-sharing Executive stirred controversy. The power-sharing parties were deeply disappointed that the army could not provide the expertise to run the power stations and they believed more should have been done by troops to counter the erection of barricades and road blocks by supporters of the stoppage. The army, though, was obviously reluctant to put itself in a position of all-out confrontation with the loyalists once it was clear that the strike had considerable Protestant support. This approach was summed up by one senior army officer in the words, 'The game isn't worth the candle'. So, inevitably, the collapse of the Executive gave rise to some angry recriminations, some of them directed against the army. The PIRA ceasefire in 1975 raised very different problems for the army. The British government had gone to the extent of co-operating with Provisional Sinn Fein in setting up a system for monitoring the cease-fire, and it was obviously gambling on PIRA deciding at last to abandon its shooting war. So Ministers were keen to avoid a situation in which the army gave PIRA an excuse to resume its campaign. The army itself described its stance as lowering its profile, but not lowering its guard. But to some Conservative MPs and to most Unionists, it seemed that the army was going very easy on the Provisionals and that PIRA men on the wanted list were being allowed to move freely. The authorities denied, however, that people wanted for specific crimes were being ignored, and in the event the ceasefire petered out rapidly, with PIRA resuming its activities seriously in the second half of 1975. The feature of 1976 was the introduction of the under-cover Special Air Service to fight the PIRA in South Armagh, after serious violence there. Probably fewer than 100 SAS men were involved initially, but the move achieved a real reduction in PIRA assaults in this key border area. Later, the SAS (and undercover men from other units) were permitted to operate anywhere in NI, largely due to the growth of sectarian assassinations in the 'murder triangle', embracing parts of Tyrone and Armagh and in areas like N. Belfast. In 1977, the Loyalist Action Council strike in May led to the deployment of an extra three infantry battalions, but the limited nature of the stoppage did not put any serious strain on army resources. (See Economy for reference to cost of army in NI.)

Shields and Saracens

The army has been specially equipped to deal with the great variety of situations stemming from community conflict and guerilla warfare. For the handling of street disturbances, they have been issued with plastic visors fitted to their steel helmets which protect the face against bricks, stones or other missiles. On occasions, plastic shields have also been carried, and some units have leg-guards. Flak jackets, giving protection against low-velocity weapons and some resistance to nail-bombs, are normally worn. The main offensive weapons in riot conditions have been the rubber (or plastic) bullet and CS gas. (See anti-riot tactics in this section.) Two-foot-long riot batons have also been issued. The major army weapons are the 7.6mm self-loading rifle, the Sterling 9mm sub-machine gun, and the general purpose machine gun, which is held in reserve, and which is unsuitable, in any event, for use in urban conditions. Special rifle night-sights have been developed to counter snipers operating in darkness. On average two army technical officers engaged in bomb disposal work were killed each year in the early years of violence. Robot devices serve to reduce the risk of examining suspect objects. From the beginning of 1970 to the end of 1981, nearly 3,400 bombs were defused. Four vehicles have been employed in the NI campaign. The landrover, usually protected with steel sheeting and sometimes with asbestos, has been the workhorse of the mobile patrol. The Saracen armoured personnel carrier, capable of carrying ten soldiers and their equipment, has been used generally in the cities. The Ferret scout car has been a popular escort vehicle, used sometimes for patrols. The Saladin armoured car, with a 75mm gun and two Brownings, has been largely confined to border patrols. Although in the armed forces the army has provided the bulk of the manpower in support of the police, the Royal Marines have also served in an infantry role, and together with the Royal Navy, they have mounted coastal and lough patrols to prevent the smuggling of arms into the province. The RAF has been involved in transport and in reconnaissance, and the RAF regiment has guarded the airfield at Aldergrove and the radar facilities at Bishop's Court. The build-up of the RUC and UDR has gradually eased the burden of the army, although it is still seen as important in border areas and in what are termed 'hard Republican' districts. The RUC Chief Constable said the army had been 'indispensable' in the hunger strike situation in 1981. The army's losses in recent years were greatly inflated by two incidents – the deaths of 18 soldiers at Warrenpoint in August, 1979, when they were caught by two PIRA explosions; and the bombing by INLA of the pub disco at Ballykelly in December, 1982, when eleven soldiers died. (See statistics at the end of this section for detailed casualty figures.)

Ulster Defence Regiment

The Ulster Defence Regiment, a locally raised and mainly part-time force, sprang from the recommendations of the Hunt Committee. It was intended to provide a replacement for the USC, but not be open to the objection levelled against the 'B' Specials of being an exclusively Protestant force. Some Catholic politicians initially associated themselves with it, and at one point it had about 18 per cent Catholic membership. By 1978, the Catholic element had dropped to about three per cent, and it was down to around two per cent when the regiment celebrated its 10th anniversary in 1980. When it first became operational on 1 April, 1970, many prominent Unionists urged members of the disbanded USC to join the regiment, which is an integral part of the army although its role is limited to NI. Later, some Unionists complained that the vetting procedures were keeping out too many trained ex-USC men. On the other hand, some Catholic spokesmen suggested that the new force had absorbed too high a proportion of the 'Specials' and that it was becoming loyalist-orientated. UDR chiefs claimed that they were only concerned with maintaining high standards, and that there was no question of religious discrimination. Officers of the regiment have praised the few Catholic members who defy the PIRA and INLA campaign of assassination of UDR soldiers. They are obviously aware that if the tiny Catholic element were to disappear altogether it would give extra force to the PIRA claim that it is simply a revival of the 'Specials'. It is clearly Whitehall's view, however – that the UDR has been operating without bias. The 1978 Defence White Paper commented that the actions of the UDR during the 1977 loyalist strike, in response to a general call-up, 'not only contributed materially to the maintenance of law and order during the strike, but also enhanced the UDR's reputation for impartiality and effectiveness.' The White Paper mentioned that in two call-ups in 1977, the regiment's turn-out had been well over 90 per cent. The UDR had seven battalions in 1971, ten in 1972, and achieved its target of eleven battalions in 1973, which it had maintained up to 1982. In 1977, the Government decided to aim at 2,500 full-time members, and in 1981 there were about 2,100. At the end of 1982, total strength was 7,250 including some 700 women members popularly known as 'greenfinches,' after their original radio code-name. It is thus both the youngest and the biggest regiment in the British army and is believed to have been operational for a longer period than any other regiment since the Napoleonic wars. In 1981, it was heavily involved during the H-Block hunger strike, by which time it was the back-up for the RUC over about two-thirds of the province. But there was still some sensitivity about its use in Republican areas.

Internment Without Trial

The introduction of internment without trial by the NI government on 9 Aug. 1971, proved to be one of the most controversial moves of the authorities to combat violence. This was partly because it was followed by an escalation of violence, and partly because it led to the serious alienation of the Catholic community from the Stormont system. The swoop in republican areas to arrest IRA suspects came at 4 a.m. on 9 Aug., four days after the NI government had decided to use the Special Powers Act for this purpose and after talks with the British Conservative government. The action of Brian Faulkner's government was approved by the Home Secretary, Reginald Maudling, who said later that he had feared a Protestant backlash had internment not been used. The operation, code-named 'Demetrius', came after weeks of probing activity by the army and police to finalise the list of suspects. In the event, there were 452 names of people thought to be members of the IRA, or associated with it, but some of them had fled in anticipation of internment, and the actual arrests totalled 350. Of these, 104 were released within forty-eight hours. Those held in the initial raids included James O'Kane, a Belfast councillor; Michael Farrell of the PD, and Ivan Barr, chairman of the NICRA Executive. Brian Faulkner, in announcing the introduction of internment, said the main aim was to smash the IRA, but they would not hesitate to take similar action against any individual or organisation which might pose a similar threat in the future. The decision to intern was backed by most Unionists, although the Rev. Ian Paisley was against it on the ground that it was also likely to be employed against loyalists. The swoop was followed quickly by serious rioting and shooting in Belfast and many other places. Twenty-three people died on 9 and 10 Aug., and a massive civil disobedience campaign, involving the withholding of rent and rates, was launched in the Catholic community, with the backing of opposition MPs and NICRA. The Nationalist and SDLP MPs had already withdrawn from Stormont, and the SDLP now said that they would not take part in dialogue with either a British or NI government until internment was ended. Internees were held in a new camp at Long Kesh, near Lisburn (later to be known as the Maze Prison), Magilligan army camp in Co. Derry, and the ship *Maidstone* in Belfast harbour. A small number of those arrested were subjected to 'interrogation in depth', which eventually gave rise to a finding in 1978 by the European Court of Human Rights that they had been subjected to inhuman and degrading treatment, but not to torture. A month after the start of internment, a three-man advisory committee, headed by Judge James Brown QC, was set up to advise the government on individual internees. Where they recommended a release, they required the individual to take the following oath: 'I swear that for the remainder of my life, I will not join or assist any illegal organisation or engage in any violence or counsel or encourage others to do so.' In the wake of intense violence and reports of intimidation, the Republic's government set up five camps to accommodate refugees and dependants of internees. Between internment and the end of 1971, 146 people were killed, including forty-seven members of the security forces, and ninety-nine civilians, and there were 729 explosions and 1,437 shooting incidents. And immediately before direct rule was imposed in Mar. 1972, the number of detainees and internees reached a peak of 924. When William Whitelaw took over as Secretary of State, he declared his intention to review personally the cases of all internees. On 7 April 1972, he announced the release of forty-seven internees, and said they had not been asked to give any assurance about future behaviour. He also stated that no further use would be made of the prison ship *Maidstone*. In May 1972, a new advisory committee was set up under the chairmanship of Judge Leonard, from Oxfordshire, which was empowered to consider only applications for release from internees. By mid-August, the number of men held under the Special Powers Act had been cut to 243. Whitelaw was engaged in a drive to phase out internment, and looking for a response from the IRA in terms of reduced violence, and possibly some switch to political activity. But in this he was disappointed, and after the re-entry of security forces to the no-go areas in the summer of 1972, there was a further slow build-up in the total of those detained. Under the Detention of Terrorists Order, the government introduced a new system of internment in Nov. 1972. This involved an initial 'interim custody' order, and after twenty-eight days the person must be either released or referred to a commissioner, who would decide whether he should be detained. At this point, the term 'internee' was replaced by 'detainee' in official language. Meantime, the Diplock committee reported in favour of some form of continued detention without trial. Between Nov. 1972 and Sept. 1973, the Commissioners made 453 detention orders and directed release in 126 cases. In answer to the suggestion that ex-internees frequently became involved again in violence, a government spokesman said in Mar. 1973 that of the more than 800 persons released from internment or detention since direct rule, only ten had been subsequently charged with offences. With rising loyalist violence, two loyalists were served with interim custody orders on 5 Feb. 1973, the first to be so treated. Two months later, the number of loyalists held had gone up to twenty-two. In Aug. 1973 the Emergency Provisions Act replaced the Special Powers Act and the Detention of Terrorists Order as the legal basis of detention, but it kept the arrangements for interim custody and commissioners hearings, but brought in a new power to hold suspects for seventy-two hours for questioning. Between 1 Feb. 1973 and 30 Oct. 1974, interim custody orders were served on 626 Catholics and ninety-nine Protestants. Shortly before Christmas 1973, sixty-three Catholics and two loyalists were released. In Jan. 1975, the Gardiner committee said that detention without trial could only be tolerated in a democratic society in the most extreme circumstances. 'We would like to be able to recommend that the time has come to abolish detention, but the present level of violence, the risks of increased violence, and the difficulty of predicting events even a few months ahead, make it impossible for us to put forward a precise recommendation on timing. We think that this grave decision can only be made by the government.' In Aug. 1975, the Secretary of State (under the Emergency Provisions Amendment Act) took back the power to make detention orders, and ended the commissioner system. The Secretary of State would, however, consider reports on detainees from legally-qualified advisers. But the then Secretary of State, Merlyn Rees, was committed to ending internment quickly, and on 5 Dec. 1975 he signed orders for the release of the last seventy-five detainees. The power to detain without trial remained on the Statute Book, most recently through clause 12 of the Emergency Provisions Act 1979. The Standing Commission on Human Rights suggested in 1979 that the power to intern without trial should be abandoned, but Secretary of State Humphrey Atkins argued that it would be premature to drop it. But he did decide to repeal it in 1980.

Anti-Riot Tactics

Deaths in riot situations have provoked some of the angriest controversy in the NI situation. In the early days of the violence the army was permitted to shoot petrol bombers, but political considerations forced the authorities to look for weapons which fitted in with the 'minimum force' commitment. Water cannon were frequently deployed in the 1969 riots, but the main weapons have been the rubber bullet, followed by the plastic bullet and CS gas. This gas, or smoke as it was sometimes known, was used extensively, both in cartridge and grenade form in the early 1970s. It caused serious, if temporary, discomfort, and its use was abandoned because it was thought to be too indiscriminate. It often affected people not actually involved in rioting, and even members of the security forces. The main concern of the authorities has been to break up crowds engaged in stoning or petrol bombing, and the rubber bullet was widely used in this role between 1972 and 1975, when it finally gave way to the plastic bullet, which was first used in 1973. The rubber bullet, five and a half inches long and one and a half inches in diameter, weighed five ounces. It was designed to bounce off the ground, and strike at about knee level. In practice, it proved to be highly unpredictable and there were three deaths from rubber bullets and many severe injuries. The plastic bullet was introduced, according to the Defence Ministry, because it would be more effective and accurate. But the new baton round – as both rubber and plastic bullets are officially termed – was developed, according to *Jane's Infantry Weapons* (1976) because the disability and serious injury rates of the rubber bullet were not acceptable. The plastic bullet is made of pvc, and is four inches long and one and a half inches in diameter, and weighs about five ounces. Unlike the rubber bullet, it is fired directly at its target. In the 1981 H-Block hunger strike disturbances, many thousands of plastic bullets were fired by both the police and army, and four deaths resulted in two months. By the end of 1982, the plastic bullet had caused eleven deaths, and many of its critics argued that it was proving even more dangerous than the rubber bullet. Those critics have included many Nationalist spokesmen and all six NI Catholic bishops (July 83). The European Parliament has voted for a ban on plastic bullets throughout the EEC, and the British Labour Party conference in 1982 called for their prohibition throughout the UK, despite the reservations of their main NI spokesman, Don Concannon. The Government and the security forces have insisted that soldiers and policemen cannot face rioters who are themselves prepared to cause death and injury without some effective retort. In December, 1981,

Secretary of State James Prior rejected suggestions that instructions in the use of plastic bullets had been disregarded by the security forces during the hunger strike disturbances. And in May, 1982, he defended the plastic bullet as being best suited to the serious rioting experienced in NI. He added: 'We are looking with an open mind at any new ideas for the control of rioting, but the currently available options such as water cannon and CS smoke are seldom appropriate in the conditions of disorder that we face in Northern Ireland. Less effective measures would be likely to result in increased casualties both to the security forces and rioters, since the security forces might well be obliged to have recourse to conventional bullet-firing weapons.'

Emergency Powers

The Emergency Provisions Act 1978 consolidated many of the other emergency powers. These may be briefly summarised as follows:

Clause 2. Bail in cases of scheduled terrorist offences may be granted only by Supreme Court or trial judge.

Clause 6. A trial on indictment of a scheduled offence shall be held only at the Belfast City Commission. A county court judge may sit at the Commission at the request of the Lord Chief Justice.

Clause 7. A trial on indictment of a scheduled offence shall be conducted without a jury (*see* Diplock Report p. 79).

Clause 8. A court shall have power to exclude a statement made by an accused person if it is satisfied that the statement was obtained by torture or by inhuman or degrading treatment.

Clause 9. Where explosives, firearms or ammunition are found on premises, or in any vehicle, vessel or aircraft, the onus will be on an occupier to show that he did not know of its presence or if he did know that he had no control over it.

Clause 10. In the case of children or young persons convicted of scheduled offences, courts shall impose reduced sentences. Where an adult would be liable to fourteen years' imprisonment, a child or young person would be liable to five years. One month would be substituted for six months.

Clause 11. Empowers any constable to arrest without warrant any person whom he suspects of being a terrorist. A person arrested may be held without charge for up to seventy-two hours.

Clause 12. Gives power to detain without trial. (repealed 1980)

Clause 14. A member of H.M. Forces on duty may arrest without warrant, and detain for not more than four hours, a person whom he suspects of committing, having committed, or being about to commit any offence.

Clause 15. Gives power to search premises for munitions or radio transmitters.

Clause 17. Empowers a constable or member of H.M. Forces to search premises where a person is believed to be unlawfully detained.

Clause 18. Allows any constable or member of H.M. Forces on duty to stop and question any person for the purpose of ascertaining that person's identity and movements, and his knowledge of any terrorist incident. (Maximum penalties: six months' imprisonment or £400 fine or both.)

Clause 22. Makes it unlawful to collect without authorisation any information likely to be useful to terrorists. (Maximum penalties: ten years' imprisonment or £400 fine, or both.)

Clause 23. Provides that the giving of illegal training in the use of firearms or explosives shall be punishable by up to ten years' imprisonment, or £400 fine, or both.

Clause 24. Empowers any commissioned officer of H.M. Forces or officer of the RUC not below Chief Inspector to order the dispersal of any assembly of three or more persons. (Maximum penalties: six months' imprisonment or £400 fine, or both.)

Clause 25. Makes it an offence to dress or behave in a public place in such a way as to arouse reasonable apprehension that one is a member of a proscribed organisation. (Maximum penalties: six months' imprisonment or £400 fine, or both.)

Clause 26. Makes it an offence to wear a hood or mask in a public place. (Maximum penalties: six months' imprisonment or £400 fine, or both.)

Clause 28. Allows for compensation for the occupation or destruction of private property under the Act.

Clause 29. Says that only the Director of Public Prosecutions may authorise a prosecution under the Act.

Schedule 2. Lists the proscribed organisations: IRA, Cumann na mBan, Fianna na hEireann, Red Hand Commandos, Saor Eire, Ulster Freedom Fighters, Ulster Volunteer Force and Irish National Liberation Army.

Schedule 3. Gives police power to fix the route of a funeral or require those taking part to travel in vehicles. Gives Secretary of State power to close pubs or licensed premises for specified periods, or indefinitely, and also to control railways or road traffic.

Schedule 4. Lists the scheduled offences to which the Act applies. These include murder, manslaughter, kidnapping, riot, false imprisonment, assault occasioning actual bodily harm; interference with railways; offences under the following Acts: Offences Against the Person Act, 1861 (including conspiracy to murder or threat to kill); the Explosive Substances Act, 1883; Prisons Act, 1953; Firearms Act, 1969; Protection of the Persons and Property Act, 1969 (including intimidation and petrol bomb offences); Prevention of Terrorism Act, 1976 (breach of exclusion orders, etc.); Hijacking Act, 1971 (aircraft); and Criminal Damage Order, 1977 (arson, etc.). The Schedule also covers extra territorial offences under the Criminal Jurisdiction Act, 1975. This is the legislation which, together with reciprocal legislation in the Republic, permits a terrorist to be tried on whichever side of the border he is arrested.

In 1983 Secretary of State James Prior announced a review of the Emergency Provisions Act to be conducted by ex-judge Sir George Baker, and which would take into account Lord Jellicoe's report on the Prevention of Terrorism Act.

Birmingham Connection

The 1974 Prevention of Terrorism Act, introduced after the Birmingham pub bombings, which resulted in nineteen deaths, applied to NI, except for Part 1 dealing with proscribed organisations, which is covered by the NI Emergency Provisions Act. This Act empowered the Home Secretary to exclude to the Republic or NI persons involved in terrorism. It also authorised the NI Secretary to send persons to GB or the Republic. The police were also enabled to arrest suspected terrorists and detain them for 48 hours on their own authority, while either Secretary of State could extend the period of detention for up to seven days. The 1974 Act was replaced in March 1976, by a new Prevention of Terrorism Act, which also made it an offence to contribute to or solicit contributions towards acts of terrorism or to withhold information relating to acts of terrorism or persons committing them. Home Secretary William Whitelaw used the Act to prevent three PSF Assembly members – Gerry Adams, Danny Morrison and Martin McGuinness – travelling to London in December, 1982, to speak to Labour MPs and councillors on the invitation of GLC leader Ken Livingstone. Up to 30 June 1983, the NI Secretary had made 26 exclusion orders as follows:

1975	1	1979	4
1976	1	1980	3
1977	—	1981	11
1978	2	1982	2
1983	2	(to 30 June)	

About half of those detained under the Prevention of Terrorism legislation have been charged with offences. This is shown by the statistics relating to the period from 29 November, 1974, when the first Act became law, to 30 June 1982. In this period, 1,857 persons were detained, and 1,512 had their detention orders extended beyond the 48-hour period. Of these, 750 were subsequently charged – 206 with murder; 113 with attempted murder, 219 with firearms offences, 201 with membership of illegal organisations, and 156 with explosives offences. As in the case of exclusion orders, the impact of the hunger strike can be seen in the increased number of detentions in 1981 – 495, or well over a quarter of the total since 1974. Surprisingly, however, detentions reached a record total of 828 in the whole of 1982, and an even higher rate of 593, January–June, 1983. Up to 31 March 1982, there had been 68 specific charges under the 1976 Prevention of Terrorism Act – fifty-four for withholding information about terrorism, seven for contributions to acts of terrorism, and seven for failing to comply with an exclusion order. All exclusion orders are subject to review after three years, under a decision announced by the Government in 1979. In March, 1982, Lord Jellicoe was appointed by Home Secretary William Whitelaw to carry out a review of the Prevention of Terrorism legislation both in GB and NI. His report suggested a new anti-terrorism measure which would be subject to annual renewal, but have a lifespan of five years. The report also warned against complacency over terrorism, particularly in the light of the Ballykelly bombing (see separate entry). Mr Whitelaw argued that special measures of this kind were needed, although he accepted that they made 'sad inroads' into their cherished traditions of civil liberties. But the Labour Opposition opposed renewal of the powers in 1983, with Roy Hattersley, Shadow Home Secretary, insisting that a case had not been made out for continuance of the powers. Labour's 1983 election manifesto also came out against the Prevention of Terrorism Act. In July, 1983, Home Secretary Leon Brittan brought forward new legislation, embracing substantially the 1976 Act, but taking into account some of the main points in the Jellicoe report. The legislation would have a life of five years, and exclusion orders would expire after three years, although they could be replaced by fresh orders.

SECURITY STATISTICS 1968–83

Deaths since August 1969

	RUC	RUC Res.	Army	UDR	Civilians	Total	Killed in explosions	Sectarian and inter-factional
1969 (totals)	1	–	–	–	12	13	–	NA
1970 (totals)	2	–	–	–	3	25	3	NA
1971 before internment, 9 August	2	–	11	–	17	30	57	NA
After internment	9	–	32	5	97	143		NA
1971 (totals)	11	–	43	5	114	173	57	NA
1972 up to Direct Rule, 24 March	7	1	12	7	53	80	29	NA
D.R. to 26 June (start of IRA ceasefire)	1	–	32	4	66	103	31	NA
Ceasefire to 9 July (end of ceasefire)	–	–	1	–	17	18	–	NA
From 9 July to Motorman, 31 July	1	1	16	2	50	70	24	NA
After Motorman	5	1	42	12	136	196	59	NA
1972 (totals)	14	3	103	25	322	467	143	122
1973 (totals)	10	3	58	8	171	250	69	87
1974 (totals)	12	3	28	7	166	216	57	95
1975 to IRA ceasefire, 10 Feb.	1	–	2	–	11	14	5	NA
10 Feb. to end 1975	6	4	12	5	206	233	71	NA
1975 (totals)	7	4	14	5	217	247	76	144
1976 (totals)	13	10	14	15	245(3)	297	71	121
1977 (totals)	8	6	15	14	69(3)	112	13	42
1978 (totals)	4	6	14	7	50(2)	81	25	14
1979 (totals)	9	5	38	10	51	113	43	NA

	RUC	RUC Res.	Army	UDR	Civilians	Total	Killed in explosions	Sectarian and inter-factional
1980 (totals)	3	6	8	9	50	76	17	NA
1981 (totals)	13	8	10	13	57	101	14	NA
1982 (totals)	8	4	21	7	57(1)	97	35	NA
1983 (to 31 July)	4	5	3	6	19	37	9	NA

Note: Figures in parentheses after civilian deaths indicate number of prison officers included.

All deaths – monthly record

	1972	1973	1974	1975	1976	1977	1978
Jan.	26	17	19	8	48	13	2
Feb.	22	37	15	19	27	13	21
Mar.	39	30	26	13	17	14	7
Apr.	22	16	14	36	20	17	4
May	40	30	25	11	26	13	2
June	35	30	14	21	37	9	13
July	95	17	12	15	28	10	5
Aug.	55	21	14	29	20	7	6
Sept.	40	10	12	23	12	3	7
Oct.	39	8	19	31	28	6	4
Nov.	20	20	35	24	23	4	5
Dec.	34	14	11	17	11	3	5
Total	467	250	216	247	297	112	81

	1979	1980	1981	1982	1983
Jan.	2	15	7	8	6
Feb.	6	8	5	1	5
Mar.	2	4	4	8	5
Apr.	16	9	9	11	5
May	7	4	22	4	5
June	11	4	5	4	3
July	7	4	11	2	8
Aug.	25	11	5	3	
Sept.	6	3	11	9	
Oct.	11	3	8	12	
Nov.	9	5	14	13	
Dec.	11	6	–	22	
Total	113	76	101	97	

Record of violence

	Shooting incidents	Explosions	Bombs defused	Malicious fires	Armed robberies	Amounts stolen
1969	NA	8	NA	NA	NA	NA
1970	213	153	17	NA	NA	NA
1971	1,756	1,022	493	NA	437	£303,787
1972	10,628	1,382	471	NA	1,931	£790,687
1973	5,018	978	542	587	1,215	£612,015
1974	3,206	685	428	636	1,231	£572,951
1975	1,803	399	236	248	1,201	£572,105
1976	1,908	766	426	453	813	£545,340
1977	1,181	366	169	432	591	£446,898
1978	755	455	178	269	439	£230,750
1979	728	422	142	315	434	£568,359
1980	642	280	120	275	412	£496,829
1981	815	398	132	536*	587	£894,929
1982	382	219	113	499	580	£1,392,202

*No figures available for April-June, 1981.

Injuries since 1968

	RUC/ RUC Res.	Army/ UDR	Civilians	Tarred and feathered	Knee-cappings
1968	379	–	NA	–	NA
1969	711	22	NA	–	NA
1970	191	620	NA	–	NA
1971	315	390	1,838	27	NA
1972	485	578	3,813	28	NA
1973	291	548	1,812	6	74
1974	235	483	1,680	16	127
1975	263	167	2,044	22	189
1976	303	264	2,162	18	98
1977	183	187	1,027	21	126
1978	302	135	548	6	67
1979	155	135	548	4	76
1980	194	77	530	2	77
1981	332	149	877	2	82
1982	99	99	328	1	90

Houses searched and arms finds

	Number of houses	Firearms found	Explosives found (lbs)	Ammunition found (rounds)
1970	3,107	324	798	43,095
1971	17,262	717	2,748	157,944
1972	36,617	1,264	41,488	183,410
1973	74,556	1,595	38,418	187,399
1974	74,914	1,260	26,120	147,202
1975	30,002	825	11,565	73,604
1976	34,919	837	21,714	70,306
1977	20,724	590	3,819	52,091
1978	15,462	400	2,108	43,512
1979	6,452	301	1,996.25	46,280
1980	4,106	203	1,810	28,078
1981	4,104	398	7,536	47,070
1982	4,045	321	5,066	41,453

NOTE: The arms finds are those made generally, not simply in houses.

Persons charged with terrorist-type offences

	Murder	Att. Murder	Firearms	Explosives	Theft	Other
(July-Dec.)						
1972	13	16	242	86	111	63
1973	71	85	631	236	186	205
1974	75	75	544	161	232	275
1975	138	88	460	100	314	97
1976	120	211	353	215	188	279
1977	131	135	301	146	203	392
1978	60	79	225	79	151	249
1979	45	39	177	40	152	210
1980	63	59	112	39	128	149
1981	48	72	155	39	158	446
1982	51	96	173	41	130	196

Note: Consolidated figures for earlier years not available.